T0320015

Demography and the Economy

**A National Bureau of
Economic Research
Conference Report**

Demography and the Economy

Edited by   **John B. Shoven**

The University of Chicago Press

Chicago and London

JOHN B. SHOVEN is the Charles R. Schwab Professor of Economics at Stanford University, the Wallace R. Hawley Director of the Stanford Institute for Economic Policy Research (SIEPR), and a research associate of the National Bureau of Economic Research.

The University of Chicago Press, Chicago 60637
The University of Chicago Press, Ltd., London
© 2011 by the National Bureau of Economic Research
All rights reserved. Published 2011
Printed in the United States of America

20 19 18 17 16 15 14 13 12 11   1 2 3 4 5
ISBN-13: 978-0-226-75472-7 (cloth)
ISBN-10: 0-226-75472-3 (cloth)

Library of Congress Cataloging-in-Publication Data

Demography and the economy / edited by John B. Shoven.
    p. cm.
    Includes bibliographical references and index.
    ISBN-13: 978-0-226-75472-7 (cloth : alk. paper)
    ISBN-10: 0-226-75472-3 (cloth : alk. paper)   1. Demography—
Economic aspects. 2. Fertility, Human—Economic aspects.
I. Shoven, John B.
HB849.41.D456 2011
330—dc22

                                            2010007681

♾ The paper used in this publication meets the minimum requirements of the American National Standard for Information Sciences— Permanence of Paper for Printed Library Materials, ANSI Z39.48-1992.

National Bureau of Economic Research

Officers

John S. Clarkeson, *chairman*
Kathleen B. Cooper, *vice-chairman*
James M. Poterba, *president and chief executive officer*
Robert Mednick, *treasurer*

Kelly Horak, *controller and assistant corporate secretary*
Alterra Milone, *corporate secretary*
Gerardine Johnson, *assistant corporate secretary*

Directors at Large

Peter C. Aldrich
Elizabeth E. Bailey
Richard B. Berner
John H. Biggs
John S. Clarkeson
Don R. Conlan
Kathleen B. Cooper
Charles H. Dallara
George C. Eads

Jessica P. Einhorn
Mohamed El-Erian
Jacob A. Frenkel
Judith M. Gueron
Robert S. Hamada
Karen N. Horn
John Lipsky
Laurence H. Meyer
Michael H. Moskow

Alicia H. Munnell
Rudolph A. Oswald
Robert T. Parry
James M. Poterba
John S. Reed
Marina v. N. Whitman
Martin B. Zimmerman

Directors by University Appointment

George Akerlof, *California, Berkeley*
Jagdish Bhagwati, *Columbia*
Glen G. Cain, *Wisconsin*
Ray C. Fair, *Yale*
Franklin Fisher, *Massachusetts Institute of Technology*
Mark Grinblatt, *California, Los Angeles*
Saul H. Hymans, *Michigan*
Marjorie B. McElroy, *Duke*

Joel Mokyr, *Northwestern*
Andrew Postlewaite, *Pennsylvania*
Uwe E. Reinhardt, *Princeton*
Nathan Rosenberg, *Stanford*
Craig Swan, *Minnesota*
David B. Yoffie, *Harvard*
Arnold Zellner (Director Emeritus), *Chicago*

Directors by Appointment of Other Organizations

Jean-Paul Chavas, *Agricultural and Applied Economics Association*
Martin Gruber, *American Finance Association*
Timothy W. Guinnane, *Economic History Association*
Arthur B. Kennickell, *American Statistical Association*
Thea Lee, *American Federation of Labor and Congress of Industrial Organizations*

William W. Lewis, *Committee for Economic Development*
Robert Mednick, *American Institute of Certified Public Accountants*
Angelo Melino, *Canadian Economics Association*
Harvey Rosenblum, *National Association for Business Economics*
John J. Siegfried, *American Economic Association*

Directors Emeriti

Andrew Brimmer
Carl F. Christ
George Hatsopoulos

Lawrence R. Klein
Franklin A. Lindsay
Paul W. McCracken

Peter G. Peterson
Eli Shapiro
Arnold Zellner

Relation of the Directors to the Work and Publications of the National Bureau of Economic Research

1. The object of the NBER is to ascertain and present to the economics profession, and to the public more generally, important economic facts and their interpretation in a scientific manner without policy recommendations. The Board of Directors is charged with the responsibility of ensuring that the work of the NBER is carried on in strict conformity with this object.

2. The President shall establish an internal review process to ensure that book manuscripts proposed for publication DO NOT contain policy recommendations. This shall apply both to the proceedings of conferences and to manuscripts by a single author or by one or more co-authors but shall not apply to authors of comments at NBER conferences who are not NBER affiliates.

3. No book manuscript reporting research shall be published by the NBER until the President has sent to each member of the Board a notice that a manuscript is recommended for publication and that in the President's opinion it is suitable for publication in accordance with the above principles of the NBER. Such notification will include a table of contents and an abstract or summary of the manuscript's content, a list of contributors if applicable, and a response form for use by Directors who desire a copy of the manuscript for review. Each manuscript shall contain a summary drawing attention to the nature and treatment of the problem studied and the main conclusions reached.

4. No volume shall be published until forty-five days have elapsed from the above notification of intention to publish it. During this period a copy shall be sent to any Director requesting it, and if any Director objects to publication on the grounds that the manuscript contains policy recommendations, the objection will be presented to the author(s) or editor(s). In case of dispute, all members of the Board shall be notified, and the President shall appoint an ad hoc committee of the Board to decide the matter; thirty days additional shall be granted for this purpose.

5. The President shall present annually to the Board a report describing the internal manuscript review process, any objections made by Directors before publication or by anyone after publication, any disputes about such matters, and how they were handled.

6. Publications of the NBER issued for informational purposes concerning the work of the Bureau, or issued to inform the public of the activities at the Bureau, including but not limited to the NBER Digest and Reporter, shall be consistent with the object stated in paragraph 1. They shall contain a specific disclaimer noting that they have not passed through the review procedures required in this resolution. The Executive Committee of the Board is charged with the review of all such publications from time to time.

7. NBER working papers and manuscripts distributed on the Bureau's web site are not deemed to be publications for the purpose of this resolution, but they shall be consistent with the object stated in paragraph 1. Working papers shall contain a specific disclaimer noting that they have not passed through the review procedures required in this resolution. The NBER's web site shall contain a similar disclaimer. The President shall establish an internal review process to ensure that the working papers and the web site do not contain policy recommendations, and shall report annually to the Board on this process and any concerns raised in connection with it.

8. Unless otherwise determined by the Board or exempted by the terms of paragraphs 6 and 7, a copy of this resolution shall be printed in each NBER publication as described in paragraph 2 above.

Contents

Acknowledgments

This volume consists of papers presented at a conference held in Yountville, California, in April 2008. Most of the research was conducted as part of the program on the Economics of Aging at the National Bureau of Economic Research and was sponsored by the U.S. Department of Health and Human Services, through National Institute on Aging grant P01-AG005842. Any other funding sources are noted in the individual papers.

Any opinions expressed in this volume are those of the respective authors and do not necessarily reflect the views of the National Bureau of Economic Research or the sponsoring organizations.

Introduction

John B. Shoven

The dictionary definition of demography is "the study of population size, growth, and age structure (fertility, mortality, and immigration) that lead to population change" (American Heritage Dictionary 2006, 483). Of course, by referring to a dictionary, I have already identified myself as not belonging to one of the younger cohorts of Americans, whose members would have looked it up online. The topic of this volume is the interface between demography and the economy. For our purposes, demography includes not only fertility, mortality, and immigration, but also the racial and gender composition of the population, living arrangements, marriage, divorce, the timing of the entry and exit from the workforce, and age-, gender-, and race-specific health and disability. Economic demography is a giant topic and the chapters in this volume, as good as they are, only scratch the surface of the important connections between the two fields.

Attention to the demography-economics boundary is nothing new. Political economist Thomas Malthus is famous for predicting that human societies would inevitably return to subsistence-level conditions due to exponential population growth outpacing the growth in agricultural output. His 1798 *Principle of Population* made this point and led to his conclusion that "the power of population is indefinitely greater than the power in the earth to produce subsistence for man. Population, when unchecked, increases in a geometrical ratio" (13). Malthus was clearly an important economic demographer. His prediction, that societies cannot long remain above subsistence standards of living, has not stood the test of time. While

John B. Shoven is the Charles R. Schwab Professor of Economics at Stanford University, the Wallace R. Hawley Director of the Stanford Institute for Economic Policy Research (SIEPR), and a research associate of the National Bureau of Economic Research.

there still are perhaps one billion people living at subsistence levels, it is hard to reconcile his model with the fact that roughly five-sixths of the world's population enjoys a much higher standard of living. In the intervening 210 years, output, even agricultural output, has grown faster than population. Malthus can be forgiven for not foreseeing the amazing breakthroughs of electricity, wireless communication, antibiotics, and computers, not to mention chemical fertilizers, engineered seeds, and the whole green revolution. He was right, however, about the important interaction between economics and demography.

Many important economic institutions are based on Malthus' being correct—that fertility would be such that successive cohorts would be more populous. In the United States and many parts of the world, social security was partly based on that premise. The pay-as-you-go systems were based on workers supporting retirees, with workers significantly outnumbering those in retirement. Early in the history of U.S. Social Security, there were approximately nine workers for every retiree. This ratio is now roughly three and by all forecasts, headed to two within the next twenty-five years. Much of this decline is due to the low fertility rates of the past forty years, coupled with dramatically improved age-specific mortality rates. In some European countries and Japan, the ratio of workers to retirees is already two and forecast to approach one. The falling ratio of workers to retirees is placing great strain on both social security and national health insurance systems, including Medicare and Medicaid in the United States. Pay-as-you-go programs that work reasonably well when there are three or four workers per retiree cannot function at all well when the ratio is two or one. Demographics not only affects these income transfer systems, it affects such things as personal and national saving rates, life insurance and annuity markets, the demand for schools, long-term care facilities, the design of houses, and the need for public transportation. Demographics remains a central shaper of economic forces in society.

The two biggest drivers of population growth and population age structure are fertility and mortality. In fact, from a global perspective, they are the only two drivers since immigration has to net to zero. We now recognize that fertility and mortality are not simply statistical or biological constants, but rather they are determined by choices and past investments. The first two chapters of this volume deal with fertility and the orientation of the chapters would be hard for Malthus to get his mind around. In chapter 1, Samuel H. Preston and Caroline Sten Hartnett write about the future of American fertility. Roughly speaking, American fertility, the average number of children that a woman has over her childbearing lifetime, has hovered at or slightly below the zero-population growth level of 2.1 for the past forty years. Malthus would have been surprised that one of the world's richest countries would have a birth rate so low. He would be even more surprised when he learned that the American fertility rate is the one of the highest among developed economies. All of the advanced economies of Asia and Europe have birth rates well below zero-population growth rates, some amazingly so. For example, Italy, Spain, Germany, Russia, Japan, and South Korea all have fertility rates of less than 1.5. With such fertility rates, their population will shrink by 25 percent or more per generation absent net immigration. The rate of global population growth is now slowing and the world's population is expected to peak sometime in the first half of this century. Malthus would be perplexed.

Preston and Hartnett review the history of American fertility, the connection between fertility and marriage, religion, education, female labor force participation, ethnicity, the relative earnings of women and men, birth control technology, and even the composition of the Supreme Court. They look at differences in fertility across states and find that even the lowest fertility state in the United States (Rhode Island) would rank among the highest fertility countries of Europe. They address the question of whether U.S. fertility might approach the low European levels. They find that the rapid growth in the Hispanic population in the United States will tend to push our fertility rate up slightly, while the continuing trend of more years of education, particularly for women, will tend to push it downwards by a comparable amount. My reading of their chapter is that de Tocqueville's (1839) observation of "American exceptionalism" is likely to continue and that we are likely to remain a relatively high fertility country, even if we are a low fertility country by absolute historical standards.

The second chapter in the volume was written by Larry E. Jones, Alice Schoonbroodt, and Michèle Tertilt. It tries to explain the observed negative relationship between income and fertility within a standard utility maximizing economic model. The observation that richer populations have lower fertility has been repeatedly made, whether the evidence is across countries or within countries. Richer people buy more houses, cars, clothes, and gadgets—why not children? Are children literally an "inferior good?" The authors examine the leading economic models that attempt to explain the negative relationship between income and fertility and they find that the models are fragile and less than convincing. For instance, one idea is that high income people have a higher opportunity cost of time and children take lots of time, therefore they are more expensive and they choose to have fewer of them. The problem with this approach is that richer parents can purchase more and higher quality child care services. Once the possibility of purchased services such as nannies is introduced, the model no longer predicts that those with higher wages would want fewer children. The authors look at models that trade off the quality of children (the amount of time that is invested in children by parents) and the quantity of children, to see whether these models can be made consistent with the observed cross-section results. Several additional models are summarized and a new one is formulated, but I think that it is fair to say that building models that are consistent with the cross-sectional evidence and that have sensible dynamic specifications is extremely difficult. The authors highlight these difficulties and lay out an agenda for further work on this topic.

The third chapter in this volume was written by Adam Isen and Betsey Stevenson. They examine the trends in marriage, divorce, and fertility among American women. They show that over the past sixty years, marriage rates have fallen, divorce rates have risen, and fertility has fallen, and argue that the fundamental nature of marriage has changed. In his 1981 book, *Treatise on the Family,* Gary Becker proposed an economic theory of families based on "production externalities." The idea was that in a marriage there were gains from trade between the spouses, one specializing in market work and one specializing in work in the home. Clearly, this model of marriage captured the essence of the majority of American marriages for the first sixty years of the twentieth century. This production specialization model of marriage was consistent with the fact that marriage rates were lower for highly educated women (who had more valued market skills) than for less highly educated women. Isen and Stevenson contend that household technology such as dishwashers, automated laundry machines, and microwave ovens is one factor that has led to marriages being more frequently based on "consumption externalities" in recent decades. If marriages are based more on collective consumption of leisure than specialization in production, there is a stronger incentive to marry someone with comparable education and participation in the market. Isen and Stevenson show that this gradual switch in the predominant economic gain from marriage from production to consumption is consistent with the observed marriage trends. For instance, in recent years, the marriage rate for college-educated women has been roughly as high as for those who did not go to college. In addition to marriage and divorce, the authors look at changes in the pattern of remarriage and changes in the timing of childbirth.

The fourth chapter in the volume was written by Gopi Shah Goda and myself. We propose that people of any given age, say seventy, at different times, say 1940 and 2008, are not really the same age. For example, the mortality (the chance of dying within twelve months) of seventy-year-olds in 2008 was about half the mortality of seventy-year-olds in 1940. In fact, the mortality of seventy-year-olds in 2008 was approximately the same as the mortality of sixty-year-olds in 1940. We suggest that years since birth is a flawed way of measuring age and suggest four different ways of moving from nominal age (years since birth) to real age. We draw a parallel to the way that economic statistics and economic policies are often indexed for inflation and stated in terms of real dollars. The four alternative ways that we propose to adjust nominal ages to arrive at real ages are based on (a) remaining life expectancy, (b) mortality risk, (c) percent of life expectancy at birth completed, and (d) percent of life expectancy at age twenty completed.

We look at several key ages in important legislation and show how those ages would have changed if they had been stated in terms of real ages rather than nominal figures. For example, we show that the equivalent age to sixty-five in 1965 (when sixty-five was made the age of eligibility for Medicare) would have grown to seventy-two, using mortality risk as the method of age indexing. The equivalent of sixty-five in 1935 (when that was set as the age of Social Security retirement) is seventy-four in 2004. What this reflects is that the average seventy-four-year-old American has the same mortality risk in 2004 as did the average sixty-five-year-old in 1935. If men and women were indexed separately, the 2004 equivalent of sixty-five in 1935 would be seventy-five for men and seventy-three for women. The alternative methods of age indexing give somewhat different answers, but all show that there has been very serious age inflation over recent decades. The chapter also looks at how age indexation would differentially affect African Americans and Caucasians. The general result is that mortality improvement has been quite comparable for whites and blacks and therefore the appropriate age adjustments are about the same.

Chapter 5 in this volume, written by Axel Börsch-Supan and Alexander Ludwig, looks at the macroeconomic implications of population aging in Europe. Europe is worth studying—because fertility rates are lower in Europe than in America, mortality rates are slightly lower, and therefore the European age structure is similar to the future American demographic composition. Börsch-Supan and Ludwig model Italy, France, and Germany in particular. The question that they ask is whether the high standard of living in Europe can be maintained with the aging population. This question and the closely related one of whether an aging society can be a high growth economy is relevant to many other countries, ultimately including China and the United States. Börsch-Supan and Ludwig look at a number of European labor and pension market reforms that have the potential to mitigate much of the negative implications of population aging. The authors examine a number of possible reforms and the likely behavioral responses to them. Examples of behavioral responses are that married men may work less if child care is provided to encourage the labor force participation of mothers. Another example is that the demand for part-time work may increase as mandatory retirement ages are raised. The authors look at the impact of labor and pension reforms using a multicountry overlapping generations general equilibrium model of the Auerbach and Kotlikoff (1987) type. The results of the simulation model indicate that the behavioral responses to pension and labor market reforms dampen their ability to keep per capita living standards on a steady growth path despite the aging of these societies. Still, the authors find that the reforms, if correctly designed and coordinated, can have a very significant impact on future living standards in these three European countries.

Chapter 6 in the volume was written by Shripad Tuljapurkar of Stanford University. It examines what the author calls "the final inequality"—the variance in the age at death. While it is well-known that life expectancy at birth and life expectancy conditional on age ten or age twenty has increased in almost every country of the world, what is less well-known is what has happened to the inequality of the age of death. Tuljapurkar initially studies what happened in Sweden between 1950 and 2000. Over this fifty-year period, life expectancy at birth grew by 12 percent and remaining life expectancy, conditional on reaching age sixty-five, grew by 33 percent. What the author emphasizes, however, is the standard deviation in age of death, conditional on reaching age ten (he also calculates the spread in the age of death conditional on age twenty). The reader will discover two facts: first, the standard deviation in the age of death is quite high, roughly 13.4 years in 1950; and second, death inequality fell in Sweden over this period with the standard deviation in the age of death conditional on reaching age ten falling to about 12.2 by the year 2000. Still, the difference between being one standard deviation lucky and one standard deviation unlucky was approximately twenty-five years of life. He then examines death inequality in a variety of large developed countries (Canada, Denmark, France, United Kingdom, Japan, Sweden, and the United States) and finds that, once again, the United States stands out as exceptional. The United States has the highest level of inequality of the age of death of all of these countries (the standard deviation of the age of death conditional on age ten is between fifteen and fifteen-and-a-half years). Further, the level of inequality in the United States has not fallen over the past forty or fifty years, as it did in Sweden and most of the other countries. The country whose pattern was most like the United States was France. The chapter also includes a brief analysis of life expectancy and inequality for Americans with different levels of education and income. The most notable result is that less educated Americans (those with less than high school graduation) not only have significantly lower life expectancies (by 5.1 years), but also have significantly greater mortality inequality.

Chapter 7 in the volume was written by James M. Poterba, Steven F. Venti, and David A. Wise. It concerns one of the largest asset categories for present and future retirees, namely the equity in their homes. For most people, the big three asset categories in retirement are social security wealth, pension accumulations, and home equity. Poterba, Venti, and Wise have written a number of articles projecting future pension accumulations, particularly 401(k) balances. This chapter does similar cohort analyses for home equity. The authors find that the likelihood of home ownership by age changed very little over the past twenty-five years for married couples, single women, and single men. Roughly 80 percent of couples and 60 percent of singles own their home by the time of retirement. It is well-known that most retirees stay in their home and retain their home equity until late in retirement, when shocks such as the death of a spouse or entry into a nursing home may cause the home to be sold. In a way, the house serves as a "rainy day fund" for potential life changes or expensive developments later in life. This raises the natural question about whether home equity is a safe store of wealth for the rainy day fund. Even without all of the recent data about the 2006 to 2009 decline in house values, the authors estimate a nontrivial probability of between 10 and 14 percent that the value of the family's home will decline in real value between age fifty-nine and age seventy-nine. The authors caution that their estimate of the riskiness of home equity as a store of value is probably understated. This is because their model uses average home values by state, whereas people own specific individual houses subject to local market risks.

Chapter 8 in the volume was written by Sylvester Schieber, former Chairman of the Social Security Advisory Board. He examines the demographic evolution of several advanced countries and predicts a noticeable slowdown in the growth of per capita gross domestic product (GDP). Pension policies can be viewed as alternative methods for allocating the disappointing output due to the aging of the populations. Schieber's work suggests that switching from pay-as-you-go funding for national Social Security systems to funded systems may not do much in terms of alleviating the disappointing levels of output growth. He reviews the evidence that the United States move to partially prefunding Social Security, which began in 1983 and has resulted in a $2 trillion Social Security trust fund, has not increased national saving rates and has therefore not increased the productive capacity of the United States. Schieber simulates the evolution of retiree dependency ratios for the United States, India, and Italy and shows that the number of people over the age of sixty-five relative to those in their working years rises significantly in all three countries. However, the case of Italy is quite extreme. Their retiree dependency ratio in 2010 is roughly at the level projected for the United States in 2050. The Italian retiree dependency ratio in 2050 is completely unsustainable since it leads to the conclusion that the necessary payroll tax would be approximately 65 percent. Simulations such as these are forcing painful adjustments in retirement ages and the design of national pension systems. Schieber also reviews the literature on the issue of whether demographics alone can lead to a dramatic decline in national saving rates and possibly a decline in asset values.

Chapter 9 of the volume deals with the long-term financing of Medicare in the United States and was written by Orazio Attanasio, Sagiri Kitao, and Giovanni L. Violante. The authors develop an overlapping generations general equilibrium model and contrast the U.S. economy in 2005 with the model's projections for 2080. The model has a changing demographic structure and exogenous increases in health costs. Individuals face risk in terms of their own health status and health determines household productivity, mortality rates, and health expenditure. Their model features employer-provided health insurance, Medicare for the elderly, and Social Security. It is calibrated to match key statistics for the U.S. economy. It has both taxes on capital income and labor income. The baseline forecast of the model is that the labor tax rate will need to increase from 23 percent to 36 percent by 2080 and that two-thirds of that increase is caused by Medicare. This baseline forecast is for a closed economy where the exogenous price of health care is increasing by 0.63 percent per year over general inflation. The authors look at an alternative specification where the relative price of health care is increasing faster, closer to the Social Security Administration (SSA) projection. In that case, the average labor tax rate that is needed to balance the budget is 39 percent. Probably the best way to think of these tax rate forecasts is that labor taxes will have to be between 57 and 70 percent higher in 2080 than in 2005 and most of the increase is necessitated by Medicare. The authors look at other specifications, including one that models the United States as a small (relative to the world economy) open economy by 2080. While the necessary labor tax rate increase is smaller in the open economy case, it still is very sizable. The authors look at three possible policy reforms and their impact on 2080 tax rates: increases in Medicare premiums, changes in Medicare coverage, and changes in retirement age. Each of them has the potential to lower future labor tax rates, but the demographics and increases in health costs still result in a future of higher taxes.

The final chapter, chapter 10, has the title "Italians are Late: Does it Matter?" and is written by Francesco C. Billari and Guido Tabellini, both of Bocconi University. Italians are a case study in economic demography. Their fertility rate, currently about 1.3, is among the lowest in the world. Italian men study longer, or at least complete college later, they enter the labor force later, and they leave the parental home later than men in any other developed country in the world. It is not unusual for Italian men to live with their parents late into their twenties and sometimes into their thirties. Billari and Tabellini summarize the situation by characterizing Italian men as entering adulthood later than men in other countries. They state, "Italians are late. Not just a little, but a lot. They start all adult activities at a much later age than is common in other countries at comparable levels for development, from working, to living alone, to marrying, to having children." The question they address is, does it matter? They look at whether this lateness reduces the lifetime economic opportunities of individuals or not. They examine survey data for Italians in their mid-thirties. Their key finding is that the age of leaving the parental home is quite important in terms of earnings several years later. Those who leave home later earn considerably less both per year and throughout their career. The age of leaving the parents' home is more important, for instance, than the age at which one begins employment. The authors look at policies that might help with the "lateness problem." These include the possibilities of shortening the duration of higher education and policies that increase the available supply of housing to young men and women. Policies that improve job opportunities for young Italian men would likely increase the probability that they would leave their parents' home and commence the period of adult independence. The basic answer to

Billari and Tabellini's research question is that the lateness of Italians does matter and it depresses their lifetime earnings.

These ten chapters are only a sampling of important topics in economic demography. Here I will attempt to mention just a few of the additional subjects that deserve attention in further work. The size of the populations of India and China, their rapid economic development, and the consequences for the global economy and the global environment are at least partially issues of economic demography. The economic demography of Africa deserves a book by itself. More than any other continent, Malthus would find support for his theory there, with the unfortunate combination of high fertility rates, high mortality rates, and sizable subsistence populations in many countries. Immigration is another important topic that we did not cover in this volume. One question is whether the depopulation of Europe, due to its extremely low fertility rates, will be offset by immigration from elsewhere in the world, perhaps from the Middle East. Then there is the forecasting of future trends in mortality and the economic consequences of very long lifetimes. Can the pace of mortality progress of the twentieth century continue long into the twenty-first? Will the biotech revolution allow the pace of progress to accelerate or will further progress in health and mortality prove slower and more difficult? Many of these issues were tackled in the 2004 Brookings volume, *Coping with Methuselah* (Aaron and Schwartz 2004). The editors of that volume think that there is a good chance that the developed countries of the world will see further substantial increases in life expectancies.

Economic demography issues were important in the twentieth century and they will be equally important in the twenty-first. For instance, all of the extra adult lifetime for men was taken as extra retirement rather than as extra work life. At least in the United States, retirement was essentially a twentieth-century invention. In 1900, men worked until they no longer could work. On average, men died two years after they stopped working. By 2000, the average length of retirement for men was almost twenty years. This allocation of all of the extra lifetime to retirement certainly cannot be maintained in this century. If it were, the length of retirement would begin to approach the length of the work life. The simple saving and pension mathematics will not work for thirty- to thirty-five-year retirements with thirty-year careers. Of course, this is just one of the many adjustments that will be caused by the aging of all major countries and the likely transition from growing populations to stable or even shrinking populations. This transition appears to be already under way in Europe and that is why two of the chapters in this volume concentrated on European countries. Don't get me wrong—improved life expectancies, lower fertility rates, and some indication that the world's population may peak and fall slightly are positive developments worth celebrating, at least in my opinion. The point of many of the chapters in the book, however, is that economic institutions need to adjust to the new demographic realities.

Scientific progress is often most dramatic at the boundary of intellectual disciplines. It is my belief that the boundary between demography and economics is one of the most promising. My hope is that the chapters in this volume will stimulate further research on these topics and on the important topics that we could not cover in one volume.

References

Aaron, H. J., and W. B. Schwartz. 2004. *Coping with Methuselah*. Washington, DC: Brookings Institution Press.

American Heritage Dictionary of the English Language, 4th ed. 2006. New York: Houghton Mifflin Company.

Auerbach, A. J., and L. J. Kotlikoff. 1987. *Dynamic fiscal policy*. Cambridge: Cambridge University Press.

Becker, G. 1981. *Treatise on the family*. Cambridge, MA: Harvard University Press.

de Tocqueville, A. 1839. *Democracy in America,* 3rd ed. Trans. H. Reeves, Esq., New York: George Adlard and Company.

Malthus, T. R. 1798. *An essay on the principle of population*. London: J. Johnson. (Oxford's World's Classics Reprint).

1

The Future of American Fertility

Samuel H. Preston and Caroline Sten Hartnett

The level of fertility in a population is the principal determinant of the shape of its age structure, which in turn is a critical factor in the terms of trade within a pay-as-you-go system of public pensions. Simulations done by the Social Security Administration (SSA) show that the seventy-five-year actuarial balance of the social security system would be higher by $2.6 trillion in present value if fertility were high (2.3 children/woman) rather than low (1.7) (compiled from Trustees [2007]). Partly because of their age structural consequences, national fertility levels are considered "too low" by a majority of governments in developed countries (Kohler, Billari, and Ortega 2006).

This chapter reviews the major factors that appear to be affecting fertility levels in the United States, with an eye toward making defensible statements about future directions of fertility. The subject covers a vast disciplinary range including demography, economics, sociology, public health, reproductive biology, evolutionary biology, political science, and psychology. There is no single, widely accepted framework for analyzing the determinants of fertility at the level of a population. In its place, we will pursue an eclectic,

Samuel H. Preston is the Fredrick J. Warren Professor of Demography and professor of sociology at the University of Pennsylvania, and a research associate of the National Bureau of Economic Research. Caroline Sten Hartnett is a PhD candidate in the Graduate Group in Demography and Sociology program at the University of Pennsylvania.

This is a revised version of a paper presented at the National Bureau of Economic Research Conference on Demography and the Economy, Yountville Napa Valley, CA, April 11 and 12, 2008. This research was supported by a grant from the U.S. Social Security Administration (SSA) administered by NBER. The findings and conclusions expressed are solely those of the authors and do not represent the views of the SSA. We are grateful to Hans-Peter Kohler for detailed comments and suggestions, and to Frank Furstenberg, Gopi Shah Goda, Rob Mare, Philip Morgan, Kristen Harknett, and participants at the NBER conference for their comments on the paper.

inductive approach, surveying the landscape of fertility variation in search of clues about its principal drivers. Our search considers variation over time and space and across individuals.

1.1 Why Do People Have Children in the Twenty-First Century?

It is useful to begin with this provocative question posed by Morgan and King (2001). If there were no compelling answer to the question, we would have to confront the possibility that levels of fertility will approach zero. Clearly, the answer to the question does not lie in the domain of finance, since children are very costly and probably always have been. Early suggestions that children were a net economic asset in hunter-gatherer or subsistence economies appear to have been inaccurate, although children's greater contribution to the family economy in such circumstance reduced their net costs relative to children in the present (Kaplan 1994).

Sociologists have usefully distinguished between childbearing aimed at satisfying social expectations and childbearing aimed at self-fulfillment. Thornton and Young-DeMarco's (2001) review of trends in attitudes about one's own childbearing and that of others shows a huge reduction during the 1960s and 1970s in the degree of "oughtness" regarding fertility. While the desire to satisfy social expectations has not disappeared, people began to perceive less social pressure to bear children and to have less rigid expectations of others' performance. Increasingly, people justified childbearing in terms of its impact on their personal well-being, satisfaction, and happiness. One of the instrumental features of children that several sociologists have stressed is their value in forming social networks (Schoen et al. 1997).

In view of the imperatives of reproduction for the survival of a species, it would be surprising if the rewards from childbearing and child-rearing did not have a deep evolutionary basis imprinted in human biology (Foster 2000). Recent investigations in psychology help to clarify the nature of these rewards. Bartels and Zeki (2004) use fMRI imaging to measure brain activity in mothers when they viewed pictures of their own children and those of acquainted children and adults.[1] Pictures of their own children, but not of others, activated regions of the brain rich in oxytocin and vasopressin receptors—neurohormones associated with pair-bonding—while deactivating regions associated with negative emotions and social judgment. Animal studies confirm the central role of oxytocin and vasopressin in attachment and bonding (Carter et al. 2005).

Mothers are aware of the intense emotions evoked by their children. "The Motherhood Study," a nationally representative telephone survey of 2,009 mothers, found that 93 percent agreed with the statement that "I have an overwhelming love for my children unlike anything I feel for anyone else." Eighty-one percent said that they were very satisfied with their life as a

---

1. To date, there have been no equivalent studies of fathers.

mother and an equal percentage agreed that "being a mother is the most important thing that I do" (Erickson and Aird 2005). The potential rewards of parenthood—presumably social as well as emotional—are acknowledged by high school seniors, three quarters of whom believe that motherhood and fatherhood will be fulfilling. Between 1976 and 1977 and 1997 and 1998, the percentage so reporting rose by eleven points for women and seven points for men (Thornton and Young-DeMarco 2001). The increase was greatest for females and males whose fathers had attended college (Sayer, Wright, and Edin 2003).

It is possible that the rewards and costs of childbearing are not fully appreciated until one has a child. One ethnographic study reports that mothers, in fact, did not anticipate how completely they would fall in love with their offspring (McMahon 1995), which raises the possibility that the motivations for having the first child are systematically different from those of subsequent children. A study in Bulgaria (Buhler 2006) concluded that the principal attitudes predictive of having a first child were beliefs that it would strengthen relations with partner and parents, whereas the principal attitude predictive of a second child for both men and women was the perception that it would bring "increased joy and satisfaction in life." Companionship for the first child is also often cited as a motivation for having a second child (Fawcett 1983). In a careful study of reported happiness among monozygotic twins in Denmark, having one child was found to increase the happiness of young women, but there was no increment in happiness from additional children (Kohler, Behrman, and Skytthe 2005). Once partnership status was controlled, a man's happiness was unaffected by the number of children he had, including the first.

1.2   Recent Trends in American Fertility

The most common measure of fertility is the period total fertility rate (TFR), which indicates how many children would be born to a woman who survived to the end of her reproductive years and experienced at each age the observed age-specific fertility rate of a particular period. The level of the total fertility rate that allows each generation to replace itself exactly is approximately 2.08 children per woman. Figure 1.1 shows the value of the TFR in the United States since 1928. With virtually no interruption except the post–World War II baby boom, the TFR fell continuously from 1820 to 1975 (not shown). Since 1989 it has remained in the narrow range of 1.98 to 2.10. Figure 1.1 also shows the average number of children ever born to cohorts who completed their childbearing and were aged twenty-six during the year shown on the x-axis.[2] Clearly, there has been less volatility in the

---

2. The completed family size of a cohort would be identical to the TFR of the cohort if there were no differences in fertility at a particular age between migrants and nonmigrants, or between those who survive to age forty-five and those who die before reaching that age.

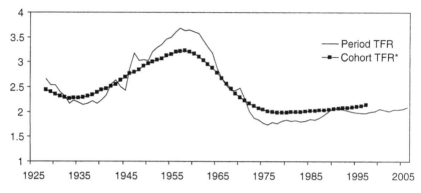

Fig. 1.1   Period and cohort total fertility rates, United States 1928 to 2005
Sources: Schoen (2004), U.S. National Center for Health Statistics (2005a, 2006b).
Notes: Last data points for CTFR used imputed data. Asterisk (*) for cohort born $t - 26$.

completed family sizes of actual cohorts than in the period measures based on synthetic cohorts. This relation is also evident in Europe (Bongaarts 2002).

The period TFR is usefully considered to consist of a volume component, measuring the completed family sizes of cohorts then bearing children, and a timing component, indicating when in the course of their lives the cohorts will bear their children. During a period when ages at childbearing are growing older, the period TFR will be systematically lower than the TFR of relevant cohorts because of a "thinning out" of lifetime cohort births.[3] Based upon age-specific rates of childbearing provided by the National Center for Health Statistics, the mean age at childbirth in the United States has risen fairly steadily from 26.00 in 1980 to 27.90 in 2005. Using an adjustment formula developed by Ryder, we find that this delay has reduced period total fertility rates in the United States during this period by about 0.15 children per woman. A more elaborate procedure developed by Bongaarts and Feeney produces a similar reduction averaging 0.14 children per woman over the period 1980 to 1997 (Schoen 2004). Faster delays in Europe have had a slightly bigger impact on period fertility levels there, averaging 0.26 in eighteen countries over the period 1990 to 1997 (Bongaarts 2002). So, the volume components of European and American fertility levels are somewhat more similar than would appear from period TFR measures.

The decline in American fertility is reflected in changes in the distribution of parities (the number of children a woman has borne) among women who have completed childbearing. Figure 1.2 shows that parity two has become

3. In the extreme, imagine that the cohort born in 1970 had all of its births at age 29.0 and the cohort born in 1971 had all of its births at age 30.0. In 2000, there would be no births at all. This deficit in period rates would not be offset by a subsequent surplus unless ages at childbearing eventually became younger again.

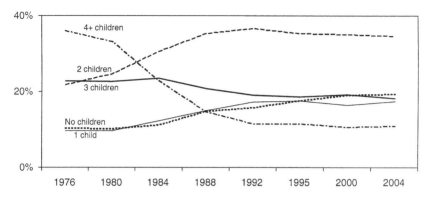

Fig. 1.2   Distribution of women 40 to 44 by number of children ever born
Source: U.S. Census Bureau (2005a).

the most common destination for women, while parities zero and one have grown steadily in frequency; families of three have become somewhat less common, and families of four or more children have fallen precipitously from being the most common in 1976 (i.e., among mothers of the baby boom) to the least frequent in 2002.

Bearing children is subject to disturbances that can raise or lower the number of births relative to intentions or expectations. Morgan (2003) finds that only 38 percent of women aged twenty-two in the National Longitudinal Study of Youth in 1982 had realized their stated intended parity by age forty. A common form of interference is poor contraception, either through method failure or failure to use any contraception when no conception is wanted. By European standards, Americans have an unusually high incidence of unwanted or mistimed births. Of births during the period 1997 to 2002, 14 percent were retrospectively classified as "unwanted" (i.e., not wanted at any time in the future) at the time of conception by their mother and 21 percent were mistimed (U.S. National Center for Health Statistics 2005b). While a mistimed birth will not necessarily increase a woman's parity above her intentions, an unwanted birth will. Of births to twenty-two to forty-four-year-old women who had not completed high school, 44 percent were classified as unwanted or mistimed, compared to only 15 percent among women who had completed college. The high incidence of unwanted and mistimed births is somewhat surprising in view of the legality of abortion. However, abortion may not be readily available, may be expensive, or may violate personal moral codes. Well-educated women are less likely to have an unwanted or mistimed birth in part because a higher proportion of their unintended conceptions result in an induced abortion.

One factor that can cause fertility to fall short of intentions is subfecundity. Of married women aged fifteen to forty-four in 2002, 7.4 percent were classified as infertile—not practicing contraception and not becoming pregnant for at least one year (U.S. National Center for Health Statistics 2005b). Separation from a partner may also cause women to fall short of childbearing expectations (Quesnel-Vallee and Morgan 2003). The balance of positive and negative forces resulted in slightly fewer births than expected by respondents in the National Longitudinal Survey of Youth; not surprisingly, women who began childbearing late were particularly likely to fall short of targets expressed at an earlier age. Falling somewhat short is the typical, but not universal, cohort pattern (U.S. Census Bureau 2000b; Hagewen and Morgan 2005).

1.3   Women, Men, Partnerships, and Children

By long-standing practices supported by powerful social norms, childbearing and child-rearing in Western countries occurred within marriage. The connection between marriage and childbearing has become more tenuous in the United States:

- Of births in 2005, 37 percent were out of wedlock, compared to 5 percent in 1960 and 18 percent in 1980 (U.S. National Center for Health Statistics 2006b; U.S. Bureau of the Census 1979).
- Fewer than half of American children aged fifteen live with both natural parents (Kiernan 2004).
- Of first births conceived before marriage in 1960 to 1964, 60 percent were "resolved" by marriage, compared to 23 percent in 1990 to 1994 (Ventura and Bachrach 2000).
- Two-thirds of adults now disagree with the statement that children are the main rationale for marriage (Thornton and Young-DeMarco 2001).

In short, marriage has become less important as a sanctioning device for childbearing and child-rearing, as well as for sexual expression and cohabitation (Thornton and Young-DeMarco 2001). And marriage itself is changing as husbands and wives are becoming more similar in their household and market activities. Married women are spending less time doing housework while their husbands are spending more time (Bianchi 2000). Of married women aged twenty-five to thirty-four, 68.5 percent participated in the labor force in 2003, compared to 38.8 percent in 1970 (U.S. Census Bureau 2005b). Signaling greater independence of decisions within the family, a married woman's labor force participation has become less responsive to her husband's wage (Blau and Kahn 2005). It has also become less responsive to the presence and ages of her children. The labor force participation rate of women with a child under age one rose from 31 percent in 1976 to 55 percent in 2004 (U.S. Census Bureau 2005a).

It is plausible to argue that the decline in marriage as a social institution and the changes that are occurring within marriage during the last four decades have the same basic sources: greater economic opportunities for women, and vastly improved means of contraception (Chiappori and Oreffice 2008; Lundberg and Pollak 2007; Preston 1987). Both have given women more power in their lives and in their relationships. The advent of the pill and the intrauterine device (IUD) in the early 1960s provided methods that were highly effective in preventing pregnancy, in part because they were independent of any particular act of intercourse and thus required less cooperation from a partner. Marriage became less essential as a precondition for sexual expression. Furthermore, women could invest in their education and in their careers with less threat of disruption from an unwanted pregnancy whether inside a marriage or out (Goldin and Katz 2002). Such investment was also encouraged by the rise in divorce.

If the rise in women's labor force participation had originated exclusively from a supply shift—resulting, for example, from fertility declines induced by contraceptive improvements—it is likely that women's wages would have declined relative to men's. Instead, the median earnings of women working full-time year-round rose from 61 percent of men's in 1960 to 77 percent in 2005 (U.S. Census Bureau 2007b). An important factor in the increase in women's participation and relative wages is probably the rise of service industries in which productivity is not associated with physical strength. Changing norms relating to equity and inequality were probably important as well. The increase in women's labor force participation would not have been as great had they not been able to find acceptable care for their children, and had they not believed that their children were not endangered by such care (Rindfuss, Guzzo, and Morgan 2003).

As Gary Becker (1981) foresaw, the "gains from trade" in the conventional breadwinner/homemaker marriage eroded as women's opportunities outside the home became more similar to those of men. The reduction in gains was likely abetted by improvements in technology for performing standard household tasks (Greenwood, Seshadri, and Vandenbroucke 2005; see also Isen and Stevenson, chapter three, this volume). What was less foreseeable was that fertility would level off and even rise modestly as the institution of marriage was fundamentally changing. Had bearing children not been a powerful goal of most American women, they would have found ample reason to avoid them by virtue of their increasingly tentative relationships and the growing attractions of work outside the home. Instead, they took advantage of their new powers to maintain a fertility level that is the envy of most other developed countries.

1.4   Individual-Level Characteristics Associated with Fertility in the United States

In this section, we examine fertility variation according to major personal characteristics in order to seek some guidance about future fertility levels.

Table 1.1   **Mean number of children ever born by women's educational attainment, women 40–44**

	1973	1988	2002
Less than high school	3.86	2.92	2.75
High school graduate/GED	2.96	2.17	2.19
Some college	3.02	2.12	2.00
Bachelor's degree or higher	2.86	1.58	1.73
Total	3.26	2.15	2.11

Source: National Surveys of Family Growth.
Note: Educational attainment based on number of years of school completed.

We focus on two variables whose distributions are expected to change in predictable ways and, therefore, might shed light on the future of fertility.

One of these variables is women's educational attainment, which has been shown to be negatively associated with fertility in many societies, including historically in the United States (Yu 2006; Billari and Philipov 2004; Jones and Tertilt 2006). Prominent interpretations of this negative relationship are that better educated women have a higher opportunity cost of time and are better contraceptors. Table 1.1 presents the (virtually) completed family sizes of women aged forty to forty-four in National Surveys of Family Growth (NSFG) from 1973 to 2004.[4] Fertility has fallen by approximately one child per woman in three of the four educational classes, and by 0.8 children among high school graduates.

More contemporary evidence can be generated by including younger women and their expected additional births. Table 1.2 is based upon women aged thirty to forty-four in these same NSFGs. It presents the coefficients relating years of completed schooling to children ever born; to additional births expected; and to the sum of these two, which we term "total births expected." We use ordinary least squares (OLS) regression, which has the convenient property that coefficients in the first two regressions add up to that in the third. We control a woman's age using a second-degree polynomial. For total births expected, the coefficient of a woman's years of schooling declined from –0.153 to –0.126 to –0.097 over this period. Schooling became less closely associated with fertility despite the fact that educational differentials in women's earnings became much steeper (Blau 1998; Goldin and Katz 2007). The reduction in the coefficient is entirely attributable to the number of additional births expected. The effect of educational attainment on the number of births that had already occurred to women remained

4. The 1973 NSFG was applied only to ever-married women. Approximately 5.7 percent of the cohort was never-married at age forty to forty-four (U.S. Bureau of the Census 1972, 104). This percentage varies from 4.5 percent for high school graduates to 11.2 percent for college graduates. Conclusions would not be materially altered if these women and their relatively low levels of fertility could be included.

Table 1.2   Coefficient of years of schooling completed among respondents aged
               30–44, National Survey of Family Growth 1973, 1988, 2002

Survey year, sex	Dependent variable		
	Total births expected	Current parity	Additional births expected
1973 Women	−0.153*	−0.157*	0.004
1988 Women	−0.126*	−0.163*	0.037*
2002 Women	−0.097*	−0.150*	0.053*
2002 Men	−0.053*	−0.101*	0.048*

Note: Age is controlled via a second-degree polynomial.
*Significant at 0.001 level.

very stable at −0.150 to −0.163. In other words, better educated women have
consistently borne fewer children than more poorly educated women by
their thirties and early forties, but they increasingly expect to catch up before
childbearing ends.

In 2002, for the first time, the NSFG was administered to men. Using the
same format employed for women, table 1.2 shows that the male coefficient
of "total births expected" on education is only −0.053 in 2002, about half
of that for women. An obvious interpretation of the sex difference is that
men do not bear as much of the time costs of children as women do. Thus,
the trade-off between parenting and earnings, which rise with education, is
less acute for men (Schultz 1994). According to table 1.2, the sex difference
is manifest not in additional births expected, but in achieved fertility, which
is substantially less influenced by educational attainment for men than it is
for women.

The regressions do not include any adjustment for marital status. We
have argued that the increasing independence and power of women has
made marital status less relevant to childbearing. Nevertheless, the large
majority of births continue to occur within marriage, and the ability of
women and men to find suitable marriage partners is doubtless a factor in
fertility levels. It is noteworthy in this context that the 2002 coefficients on
education are scarcely changed when current marital status is introduced:
−0.097 for women remains −0.097, and −0.053 for men becomes −0.059.[5] It
is not essential to introduce marital status factors in order to study the relation between educational attainment and fertility, a finding also reported in
Australia (Yu 2006).

A second major characteristic associated with variation in American fertility is ethnicity. High levels of immigration in recent years have left their
mark on the fertility of a population already distinguished by long-standing

5. The categories are never married/not cohabiting, married, cohabiting, and widowed/
separated/divorced.

Table 1.3   Total fertility rates among major ethnic groups, United States

	Total	Non-Hispanic whites	Non-Hispanic blacks	Hispanics All	Mexicans
1989	2.014	1.770	2.424	2.904	2.916
1996	1.976	1.781	2.140	2.772	3.052
2004	2.046	1.847	2.020	2.824	3.021

Source: U.S. National Center for Health Statistics (2006a).

black/white divisions. Table 1.3 presents the total fertility rates of major ethnic groups in the recent past.[6] The table shows that the fertility of non-Hispanic whites has been stable or has risen slightly during the past sixteen years. The TFR of non-Hispanic whites in the United States would rank in a tie for second highest among developed countries, behind France (see following). So, it is not correct to attribute the relatively high level of U.S. fertility exclusively to high fertility among ethnic minorities—and many European countries themselves have sizeable high-fertility ethnic minorities. In fact, the fertility of blacks has fallen sharply and is now below the national average. Hispanic fertility has been roughly level over this period.

The individual-level data files from NSFG enable us to investigate several additional questions about the relationship between ethnicity and fertility. Table 1.4 presents ethnic differentials in fertility among women aged thirty to forty-four, controlling age and years of school completed, over the period 1973 to 2002. It is clear that ethnic differentials in fertility persist when education is controlled. Over the twenty-nine-year period, the differential between blacks and whites contracted sharply while the differential between Hispanics and non-Hispanic whites expanded. In both cases, the trend in the differential is primarily attributable to changes in the number of births that have already occurred rather than to those that are expected in the future.

6. Numerators are derived from birth certificates and denominators from census estimates. The ethnic classification is not strictly comparable in the two sources and the U.S. National Center for Health Statistics (2006a) has attempted to bridge the divide. Furthermore, it is likely that the reporting of births is more complete for Hispanics than the estimates of populations. A substantial proportion of Hispanics are illegal immigrants and would not want to be reported to census authorities, whereas they have an incentive to have their births reported. Thus, the figures in table 1.3 may be overestimated for Hispanics. Weak support for this suggestion comes from the 2004 Current Population Survey (CPS), wherein Hispanic women aged forty to forty-four reported only 2.30 births, on average (U.S. Census Bureau 2005a). On the other hand, the number of births reported in the CPS are clearly deficient and especially so for out-of-wedlock births to Hispanics (www.census.gov/population/socdemo/fertility/ofw-childtx). A third source of data is the National Survey of Family Growth. Hispanic, women aged forty to forty-four in the 2002 NSFG averaged 2.49 children, about 0.2 children higher than in the CPS. Hispanic women aged thirty to thirty-four expected to bear 2.77 children in NSFG, implying rising fertility and giving some credibility to the still higher figure of NCHS.

Table 1.4   Coefficients of ethnicity among women aged 30–44, National Surveys of
                   Family Growth 1973, 1988, 2002

Survey year, race	Dependent variable		
	Total births expected	Current parity	Additional births expected
Non-Hispanic blacks			
1973	0.688*	0.634*	0.054*
1988	0.236*	0.204*	0.032
2002	0.233*	0.215*	0.018
Hispanics			
1973	0.211	0.062	0.150*
1988	0.352*	0.210	0.142*
2002	0.426*	0.336*	0.096*

Note: Age, age squared, and years of schooling completed are controlled.
*Significant at 0.01 level.

The increasing fertility differences between Hispanics and non-Hispanics are primarily a result of the changing composition of the Hispanic population itself. Cubans and Puerto Ricans, who made up a larger share of the Hispanic population in the past, have relatively low fertility levels (TFRs of 1.733 and 2.057, respectively, in 2004). In contrast, Mexican American women had a TFR of 3.021 (U.S. National Center for Health Statistics 2006a). Mexican Americans contributed 61 percent of Hispanics births in 1989 and 72 percent in 2004. The Mexican/non-Mexican differences reflect fertility differences in country of origin, as well as in length of time spent in the United States. It is unlikely that a widening of Hispanic/non-Hispanic fertility differences will continue. Mexican Americans are already a high percentage of the Hispanic population and their fertility is declining across generations in the United States (Parrado and Morgan 2008). It is worth remembering that Italian and Polish immigrants to the United States had TFRs of 6.94 and 6.97 in 1905 to 1909 when the U.S. value was 3.56 (Morgan, Watkins, and Ewbank 1994).

1.5   Spatial Differences in U.S. Fertility

Geographic differences in U.S. fertility have been used in several ways. One is to examine the impact of interstate differences in laws, programs, and regulations that may be related to fertility. Moffit's (1998) review of research on the relationship between welfare payments and fertility, most of which is based on interstate data, concludes that there are modest positive effects of benefit levels on fertility, although there are some contrary findings including a subsequent article on the "family cap" (Kearney 2004). As noted later, Klerman (1999) finds modest effects on fertility of interstate differences in access to abortion and of Medicaid payment schedules for abortion.

A second effort to use areal data focuses on identifying what may be thought to be cultural differences in attitudes, values, and practices related to childbearing. Areal differences in fertility are substantial. States in New England—Massachusetts, New Hampshire, and Rhode Island—have 2004 TFRs in the lowest range of 1.7 to 1.8. States with high Mormon concentrations, Utah and Idaho, have TFRs in the highest range of 2.3 to 2.5. Lesthaeghe and Niedert (2006) perform a factor analysis and find that a state's fertility level is closely related to its frequency of late marriage and of abortions per live birth. Since these are, in a sense, components of fertility, the results are not especially surprising.

More surprising is the high correlation that they find, –0.87, between the factor representing this demographic cluster and the percentage of a state that voted for George W. Bush in 2004. This correlation suggests to the authors that there may be important variation in the underlying structure of values and orientations that manifests itself in both family and political domains. They do not identify the main features of that structure.

A third approach to studying areal variation uses metropolitan areas rather than states as the units of analysis. Metropolitan areas form more cohesive labor markets than states, and are better suited to testing ideas about the impact of labor market conditions on fertility. We have supplemented the 2002 NSFG individual-level data on fertility histories and personal characteristics with data on characteristics of the metropolitan areas in which individuals reside. We consider four aggregate-level economic indicators: the median earnings of female full-time, full-year workers; the median earnings of male full-time, full-year workers; the unemployment rate in the area; and the median value of owner-occupied houses. All data are taken from the U.S. Census of 2000. We expect, following Becker (1981), that the level of women's earnings in an area, an indicator of economic opportunities, will have a negative effect on fertility and that men's earnings will have a positive effect. Jones, Schoonbroodt, and Tertilt (chapter two, this volume) provide a broad review of the assumptions that are required in order to generate such predictions. We expect that the median value of houses, an indicator of the housing price structure, will be negatively related to fertility because children are space intensive. We also expect fertility to be negatively related to an area's level of unemployment.

The model that we estimate includes individual-level variables whose values were established in childhood: mother's educational attainment (that is, the mother of the woman interviewed in NSFG); the religion in which a woman was raised, if any; and whether or not her parents' marriage was intact when she was aged eighteen. Coefficients of the OLS regression are presented in Appendix table 1A.1. Standard errors are not adjusted for clustering. Areal variables were available for the 280 largest metropolitan areas. Of weighted respondents, 82 percent resided in one of these areas (seventy-seven cities total) and were included in the analysis.

Coefficients of female and male earnings levels in a metropolitan area are in the expected direction, large, and statistically significant. Table 1.5 summarizes the coefficients in relevant equations. As before, the coefficients of births achieved and additional births expected sum to the coefficient of total births expected. Both achieved fertility and the additional number of children expected are significantly affected by female and male earnings. The coefficient of female earnings on total births expected of –2.7 implies that a 10 percent increase in relative women's earnings would provoke a reduction of 0.27 children. This very large effect is highly reflective of the fertility expectations—rather than achievements—of younger women. If estimation is confined to women aged thirty to forty-four, where expected family sizes have for the most part already been achieved, the female earnings coefficient for total births expected declines in absolute value to –1.421 and the male declines to 1.638.

As in the case of a woman's educational attainment, a woman's marital and partnership status is not material to interpreting the coefficients in table 1.5. When marital and cohabiting status is controlled, the values of coefficients on female and male earnings change by less than 10 percent.

The female and male earnings coefficients are roughly equal in value and opposite in sign, so that the ratio of female-to-male earnings in an area is a good predictor of fertility. Among large cities, the highest ratios of female-

Table 1.5	Coefficients of median female and male earnings in various fertility regressions		
Dependent variable		Coefficient of ln F^a	Coefficient of ln M^b
Total births expected		–2.726**	2.077**
		(.387)	(.353)
Total births achieved		–1.654**	1.265**
		(.321)	(.265)
Total additional births expected		–1.072**	0.811*
		(.329)	(.261)
Total births expected, controlling marital status[c]		–2.492**	1.955**
		(.375)	(.354)
Total births expected, women aged 15–29		–3.591**	2.219**
		(.516)	(.419)
Total births expected, women aged 30–44		–1.421*	1.638*
		(.529)	(.535)

Note: Control variables listed in Appendix table 1.A1.

[a]F = Median annual earnings of full-time, full-year female workers in a metropolitan area.

[b]M = Median annual earnings of full-time, full-year male workers in a metropolitan area.

[c]Marital status categories are never married/noncohabiting; currently married; currently cohabiting; and widowed/divorced/separated.

*Significant at .01.

**Significant at .001.

to-male earnings (range of 0.76 to 0.81) are found in San Diego, Miami, Los Angeles, Tampa, Washington DC, and New York City. The lowest ratios (0.62 to 0.70) are found in the interior rust-belt cities of Detroit, St. Louis, Pittsburgh, Cleveland, and Chicago. Among smaller metropolitan areas, the range goes from 0.57 to 0.91.

For purposes of prediction we would like to be able to treat relative earnings levels as exogenous, but there is no question that selective migration is affecting results. Women with high tastes for work or low tastes for childbearing would be more likely to move to, or remain in, an area of relatively high women's earnings. Likewise, women with high tastes for childbearing and low tastes for work might be more likely to move to, or remain in, an area of relatively high male earnings. It would be a mistake to use the coefficients that we have estimated to make predictions about the future of fertility since those coefficients include the effects of selective migration. A second upward bias in the coefficient may result from the effect of fertility patterns in an area on women's earnings; for example, nonmarket factors inducing low fertility in an area may cause women to accumulate more labor market experience, and hence raise their earnings. No equivalent bias is expected on the coefficient of male earnings.

The relationship between women's earnings in an area and fertility could be expected to be stronger for well-educated women than for poorly educated women because areal variation in the opportunity cost of children, as well as in the gains from work-related migration, should be greater for those with higher potential earnings. To test this hypothesis, we created an interactive variable equal to a woman's completed years of schooling times the mean earnings for women in her metropolitan area. When added to the regression model for women aged fifteen to forty-four shown in Appendix table 1A.1, the coefficient of the interactive variable is positive and significant ($p < .0005$). The largest (negative) coefficients are for births achieved, rather than future births expected. So, it does appear that the fertility of better educated women is more responsive to the level of earnings in a metropolitan area, although the role of selective migration adds complexity to the interpretation.

The coefficient of an area's unemployment level is not significant. The median price of owner-occupied houses in an area has a significant positive coefficient, an unanticipated result that may reflect a wealth effect.

1.6   International Differences

An international perspective permits the examination of the effects of a broader range of institutional and cultural settings than is available within any single country. Table 1.6 shows that U.S. fertility is higher than that in any other developed country with 5 million or more inhabitants. Even the lowest-fertility U.S. state, Rhode Island, with a TFR of 1.71 in 2004, would rank well above the median of 1.35. As noted previously, the period TFR

Table 1.6   **Total fertility rates in selected developed countries[a]**

Country	TFR (year)	Country	TFR (year)
United States	2.10 (2006)	Hungary	1.35 (2006)
France	1.98 (2006)	Spain	1.34 (2005)
Sweden	1.85 (2006)	Germany	1.34 (2005)
Denmark	1.85 (2006)	Greece	1.34 (2005)
Australia	1.81 (2005)	Czech Republic	1.33 (2006)
Finland	1.81 (2006)	Ukraine	1.32 (2006)
United Kingdom	1.79 (2005)	Russia	1.31 (2006)
Belgium	1.72 (2005)	Romania	1.31 (2006)
Netherlands	1.68 (2006)	Poland	1.28 (2006)
Canada	1.52 (2005)	Slovakia	1.25 (2005)
Switzerland	1.43 (2006)	Japan	1.25 (2005)
Portugal	1.41 (2005)	South Korea	1.13 (2006)
Bulgaria	1.38 (2006)	Taiwan	1.12 (2005)
Austria	1.38 (2006)	Hong Kong	0.99 (2006)
Italy	1.35 (2006)		

Source: Population Reference Bureau http://www.prb.org/pdf07/TFRTable.pdf.
[a]Countries with populations above 5 million.

underestimates cohort fertility when ages of childbearing are rising. Few cohorts who have recently completed childbearing in Europe have TFRs less than 1.7 (Frejka and Sardon 2004). In terms of parity distributions, the major difference between Europe and the United States is not in the prevalence of childless women, but rather of women with 3+ children (Caldwell and Schindlmayr 2003). The mean "ideal family size" in Europe remains at two or above except in Germany and Austria. In low-fertility Italy, it is 2.1 (Goldstein, Lutz, and Testa 2003).

One prominent explanation of declining fertility in Europe is called "the second demographic transition," according to which the emergence of individualism and its emphasis on self-fulfillment have undercut familistic norms (e.g., Lesthaeghe and Neidert 2006; van de Kaa 1996). However, this explanation does a poor job of accounting for cross-national variation. The northern European countries where ideational changes have been among the most far-reaching have the highest fertility levels in Europe (McDonald 2002), whereas many southern and eastern European countries with low fertility have retained relatively high levels of familism in value surveys and in many other behaviors such as cohabitation and divorce (Coleman 2004; Kertzer et al. 2006).

Perhaps the most important observation about cross-national variation in fertility is that the international correlation between the TFR and women's labor force participation in western Europe has become strongly positive at +0.81 (Billari and Kohler 2004). In 1975, the correlation for these same countries was −0.61. This demonstration has been replicated by several other analysts using slightly different groupings of Organization for Economic Cooperation and Development (OECD) countries (e.g., Morgan 2003). So, countries in which the largest proportion of women work are now countries with the highest fertility. This relation is also apparent regionally in Italy (Kertzer et al. 2006).

It is very likely that, because of industrial and occupational changes, the relative wages for women have risen in virtually all developed countries. Some countries appear to have been able to adapt to this change in ways that better accommodate the combination of women's work with childbearing. These countries—for example, the United States, Sweden, and Norway— exhibit both high fertility and high female labor force participation. Some of the accommodations have been in the form of government programs. Hoem (2005) cites a battery of public policies in Sweden that he believes to be responsible for its relatively high fertility, including parental leave for thir- teen months at 80 percent of salary and state-run day care centers. Reviews of the effectiveness of family-friendly policies on fertility in Europe conclude that there have been several relatively modest successes (McDonald 2002, 2006; Kohler, Billari, and Ortega 2006).

According to independent accounts of close observers in Italy (Kertzer et al. 2006) and Japan (Retherford and Ogawa 2006), a major obstacle to higher fertility levels and greater participation of women in the labor force in these countries is the persistent strength of norms that idealize the tra- ditional breadwinner/homemaker family. These norms discourage mothers from working and discourage unmarried women from becoming mothers. Mothers are thought to be the best guardians of their children, and men participate relatively little in child-rearing. Policy initiatives may have little impact under these circumstances. Japan has made very costly efforts to raise its fertility levels. The programs include generous child allowances, heavily subsidized state child care facilities, changes in educational standards to reduce the costs of child tutoring, and laws designed to encourage men's greater participation in child-rearing. But the Japanese TFR remains in the neighborhood of 1.3.

The institution of marriage appears to be more important in sanctioning childbearing and sexual behavior in these countries. In Japan, only 2 percent of births are out of wedlock and in Italy, 10 percent (Kiernan 2004). To state the obvious: discouraging out-of-wedlock childbearing discourages childbearing. If the United States were to eliminate all out-of-wedlock births and not replace them with marital births, its TFR would have been only 1.31 in 2004. Countries with higher proportions of births out of wedlock have higher TFRs: the correlation is +0.65 across thirty-seven European coun- tries in 1999. In 1975, when marriage was a stronger institution, it had been −0.35 (Billari and Kohler 2004). Ironically, the maintenance of traditional family values, especially in the form of rigid norms about appropriate sex roles within the family and the sanctity of marriage as a child-rearing institution, may be responsible for very low levels of fertility in many places (see also McDonald [2000]; Caldwell and Shindlmayr [2003]).

Strong norms supportive of traditional family relations were also very prominent in the United States but they have substantially eroded. For example, the General Social Survey asked whether respondents agreed or disagreed with the statement that "It is more important for a wife to help her husband's career than to have one herself." Only 36 percent of women disagreed with the statement in 1977 to 1978, while 80 percent disagreed in 1996 to 1998 (Thornton and Young-DeMarco 2001). Perhaps the incentives to abandon the breadwinner/homemaker model were higher in the United States or perhaps, as de Tocqueville (1945) argued 170 years ago, American society is more flexible and adaptive than European.

Whatever adaptations occurred in the United States were not primarily a product of public policy (Morgan 2003). The U.S. tax code is not unusually friendly to families with children (d'Addio and d'Ercole 2005), and welfare benefits per child are low relative to child allowances in many European countries (Blau 1998). Government plays a relatively small role in day care for children in the United States in terms of both finance and management. The adaptations permitting more mothers to work in the United States were primarily a result of private negotiations between women and various child care providers, including their partners. They were facilitated by institutional adaptations such as longer store hours, which provided both opportunities for shopping by people who worked during the day and jobs at an hour when a spouse may be available for child care (Kohler, Billari, and Ortega 2006). The labor market in the United States may also be more accommodating to young workers than are European labor markets, which are more rigid on many quantitative indicators (Nickell 1997). American businesses, less encumbered by industrial policies, may have been able to provide more flexible hours and days. The declining coefficient relating fertility to women's educational attainment is another indication that the tensions between childbearing and work are easing in the United States.

Another major theme of de Tocqueville's is that Americans are unusually prone to form and gather in private associations. One institution that they join in far greater numbers than Europeans is the church. Of American women, 50 percent report that religion is very important to them, compared to 16 percent of European women. Of American women aged eighteen to forty-four, 50 percent attend church at least once a month, compared to 26 percent of European women (European Values Survey data cited in Frejka and Westoff [2006]). The frequency of church attendance is highly positively correlated with actual and expected fertility both in the United States and in Europe (Frejka and Westoff [2006]; Philipov and Berghammer 2007). For young parents, a church often provides opportunities for interaction with other young families, child care services, and moral support for the difficult endeavors of parenthood (Wuthnow 2005). These features may lift fertility levels among members. Taking literally the empirical relation between religiosity and fertility, Frejka and Westoff (2006) estimate that the fertility of American women aged thirty-five to forty-four would be 6 percent lower if Americans attended church as infrequently as Europeans, and 18 percent lower if they perceived the same importance of religion as Europeans.

These estimates represent upper bounds because there is undoubtedly self-selection of family-oriented people into the community of church-goers, a tendency that would spuriously elevate the correlation between fertility and religious behavior. Nor does their analysis control other variables, such as educational attainment, that are correlated with both fertility and church attendance. To partially overcome these problems, we have used the 2002 NSFG to estimate the relationship between fertility and the religion of one's upbringing in controlling a woman's years of schooling and ethnicity. The results are shown in table 1.7. Fertility differs substantially—by half a child or more—between those raised with no religion (about 6 percent of all women) and those raised with any religion. The additional variance explained by introducing the religious variables is significant at .001.

Thus, religious differences in fertility are not readily explained by mechanisms of selection or contamination by third variables. The greater religiosity of the American population may, in fact, be contributing to U.S./European differences in fertility. The fertility differences by religious affiliation hold out the possibility that fertility will rise as high-fertility groups have more children who inherit the religion of their parents and maintain their high fertility levels. This possibility is not entirely theoretical. The growth of fundamentalist Protestant groups in the past century is attributable primarily to their unusually high fertility combined with a 70 to 80 percent intergenerational retention rate (Hout, Greeley, and Wilde 2001). The example illustrates a more general point: there is upward pressure on fertility each generation by virtue of the fact that each generation is born disproportionately to the high-fertility members of the previous generation. The upward bias should be particularly strong when the high fertility example of one's own parents is reinforced by pronatalist norms and associations such as those typically found in churches.

Why are Americans more likely to attend church and espouse religious beliefs than Europeans? One prominent explanation is that American reli-

Table 1.7   Coefficients relating the expected number of births to religious affiliation at age 16, women aged 30–44, National Survey of Family Growth 2002

No religion	−0.444
Mainline Protestant	0.000
Fundamentalist Protestant	0.194
Catholic	0.127
Other non-Christian religion	0.264

Note: Age, age squared, years of schooling completed, and race/ethnicity are controlled.

gious institutions are more flexible and entrepreneurial than are European (Finke and Stark 2005). Whereas European countries often face a virtual monopoly of religious institutions, staffed by clerics determined to maintain the monopoly, American religious institutions vigorously compete for adherents and use attendance and participation as principal gauges of success. Churches represent another instance in which institutional adaptability may help account for high fertility in the United States relative to Europe.

1.7   Implications

What have we learned that bears upon the future of American fertility? Several variables robustly associated with fertility are changing in predictable ways, as summarized in table 1.8. One of these is ethnicity. The U.S. Census Bureau projects the size and ethnic composition of the U.S. population using data on fertility achievements and expectations and anticipated immigration. Its latest projections suggest that the Hispanic population will grow from 12.6 percent of the population in 2000 to 20.1 percent in 2030 (U.S. Census Bureau 2004b). Combined with the large Hispanic/non-Hispanic fertility differentials shown in table 1.3, and assuming that fertility levels remain constant within ethnic categories, this increase in Hispanic representation would increase the TFR from 2.046 to 2.113, an increase of .07 children. If Hispanic/non-Hispanic differentials contract, as has happened with other immigrant groups, the effect would be reduced.

A second variable related to fertility and moving in predictable directions is educational attainment. The U.S. Census Bureau (2000a) projects educational attainment distributions to 2028. For adult women, their projections imply a gain of approximately 0.7 years of school completed between 2003 and 2028.[7] Combined with the fertility coefficient on years of schooling of $-.097$, such changes would produce a reduction in fertility of .07 children. The effect is not large, and it should be recalled that the coefficient of women's education has been declining.

So, the two most predictable changes in population composition, educational attainment and ethnicity, are expected to induce relatively small changes in fertility by 2028 to 2030, and these changes essentially offset one another. In a multivariate framework, the combined changes in distributions of education and ethnicity would produce a decline in fertility of 0.02 children.[8]

We anticipate that the ratio of female-to-male earnings will continue to increase as industrial structures change and as equity norms become more

---

7. This is the mean gain for the high and low projections, weighted by ethnicity distributions in 2000 and assigning ten years of schooling to those who did not complete high school, twelve to those who did, fourteen to those who started but did not finish college, and seventeen to those who finished college.

8. The coefficient of educational attainment in a regression controlling age and ethnicity is $-.083$.

Table 1.8   Summary of positive and negative pressures on TFR

	Effect on TFR	Projection year
Increases in proportion Hispanic	+0.07	2030
Increases in women's education	−0.07	2028
Increases in F/M earnings ratio (upper bound)	−0.24	2030
Possible restrictions on abortion access	+0.10	
Stabilization in mean age of childbearing	+0.15	

universal. As noted earlier, our coefficients on female and male earnings represent an upper bound on the sensitivity of fertility to exogenous variation in these variables. To illustrate the potential impact of changes in the earnings ratio, we use the fertility equation for thirty- to forty-four-year-old women. The ratio of median female-to-male earnings of full-time, full-year workers grew from 0.738 in 1995 to 0.788 in 2005 (U.S. Census Bureau 2008). If the same rate of annual increase occurred between 2005 and 2030, the effect on fertility would be approximately −1.5 {0.163} = −0.24 children, where −1.5 is the approximate coefficient of the earnings ratio (from table 1.5) and 0.163 is the projected change in the natural log of the earnings ratio over a twenty-five-year period. Thus, a continuing growth of women's earnings relative to men's may put significant downward pressure on fertility. But we reiterate that ours is an upper bound estimate because of possible upward biases in the coefficient resulting from selective migration and reverse causation. Moreover, a more egalitarian distribution of child-raising responsibilities would be expected to reduce the sensitivity of fertility to the sex ratio of earnings.

Other factors that may play a role:

- Improvements in contraceptive technology should put mild downward pressure on fertility. Contraceptive improvements have been very slow since the 1960s, especially in the area of male contraception, and any improvements may be significantly offset by improvements in proceptive technologies for subfecund individuals. Barring advances in technology, improvements in contraceptive use could be expected to accompany improvements in educational attainment and to be captured by the estimated effects thereof.
- A more conservative Supreme Court may result in greater restrictions in access to abortion. Based on studies of interstate differences in access to abortion and in Medicaid funding thereof, the estimated effects on fertility would not be large. Klerman (1999) estimates that eliminating public funding altogether would increase the TFR by 2 percent, and that making all abortions illegal would increase it by an additional 3 percent.
- Eventually, the rise in ages at childbearing must come to an end. This process has reduced the period TFR by approximately 0.15 children per

woman. When it stops, period rates (but not necessarily cohort rates) will be pushed upwards. At the rate at which the mean age at childbearing has been rising in the United States, approximately 0.08 years per year, it would take twenty years before the mean age in the United States reached the level of 29.5 years already observed in Sweden (and longer to reach the mean age currently observed in France, the Netherlands, Ireland, and Spain; compiled from U.S. Census Bureau [2004a]). So, the timing-induced depression in U.S. period rates could last a long time.

It is clear that modeling fertility timing is an important element in fertility projections. As figure 1.1 demonstrated, the sharp changes in American fertility over the past eighty years have been powerfully influenced by timing factors. The baby boom and baby bust could not be predicted or accounted for by the marginalist approach taken here. It seems likely that elements of social contagion have operated in the past to add volatility to period measures of fertility. There is no reason to believe that they cannot reappear in the future.

Fertility in the United States is relatively high, even for its lowest-fertility groups. Compared to most countries in Europe and East Asia (but not northwestern Europe), fertility is high even for white non-Hispanics, for states with the lowest fertility, and for college graduates. One possible explanation of American "exceptionalism" is an unusually flexible and adaptive society, one in which women were able to react quickly to the rise in their work opportunities and find ways to combine motherhood and work while many other societies stayed wedded to more traditional family forms. If American women have simply been quicker to find ways to do things that women elsewhere also want to do—have at least two children even when they have attractive earnings prospects outside of the home—then fertility elsewhere should rise to American levels as women and men adapt to new circumstances and abandon older cultural forms.

A second, related explanation of American exceptionalism is the unusually high degree of religious belief and participation among Americans. Projecting religiosity into the future is risky, in part because recent trends are not entirely consistent. The proportion of American adults identifying their religious affiliation as "no religion" in the General Social Survey rose from 7 percent to 14 percent between 1991 and 2000 (Hout and Fischer 2002); the rise was especially sharp among young adults. On the other hand, the proportion of adults who identify as conservative Christians continues to grow, fueled by differential fertility and high rates of intergenerational retention. The proportion of American children attending church and participating in youth groups rose sharply between 1997 and 2003 (Hofferth 2008). The possibility that American fertility has strong religious underpinnings does not suggest a clear-cut direction for future fertility trends, but it does add uncertainty to them.

Appendix

Table 1.A1   **Coefficients of regressions of fertility on individual and areal variables, National Survey of Family Growth 2002**

	Women 15–44			Women 30–44
	Total births expected	Current parity	Additional births expected	Total births expected
Age	0.131	0.318	–0.187	0.071
	(0.000)	(0.000)	(0.000)	(0.548)
Age²	–0.002	–0.004	0.002	–0.001
	(0.000)	(0.000)	(0.000)	(0.433)
Religion				
Mainline Protestant (ref)				
No religion	–0.414	–0.162	–0.251	–0.438
	(0.000)	(0.002)	(0.000)	(0.000)
Catholic	0.055	0.057	–0.002	0.134
	(0.324)	(0.236)	(0.96)	(0.08)
Fundamentalist Protestant	0.101	0.143	–0.042	0.153
	(0.193)	(0.056)	(0.48)	(0.173)
Non-Christian	0.151	0.205	–0.051	0.414
	(0.175)	(0.025)	(0.526)	(0.013)
Mother's education				
Less than high school	0.193	0.157	0.036	0.284
	(0.003)	(0.007)	(0.335)	(0.001)
High school (Ref)				
Some college	0.079	–0.006	0.085	0.075
	(0.141)	(0.895)	(0.047)	(0.317)
Bachelor's degree or higher	0.165	0.037	0.129	0.237
	(0.005)	(0.432)	(0.008)	(0.004)
Family intact at age 18	0.112	–0.056	0.168	0.010
	(0.016)	(0.166)	(0.000)	(0.89)
Race/Ethnicity				
White, Non-Hispanic (Ref)				
Hispanic	0.237	0.214	0.023	0.326
	(0.000)	(0.000)	(0.601)	(0.001)
Black	0.143	0.258	–0.114	0.247
	(0.009)	(0.000)	(0.002)	(0.003)
Other race	0.276	–0.037	0.312	0.007
	(0.024)	(0.653)	(0.007)	(0.953)
Highest grade of school completed	–0.064	–0.153	0.088	–0.078
	(0.000)	(0.000)	(0.000)	(0.000)
Percent unemployed in	0.027	0.009	0.018	0.049
metropolitan area	(0.092)	(0.574)	(0.062)	(0.061)
Log of male income in	2.077	1.265	0.811	1.638
metropolitan area	(0.000)	(0.000)	(0.002)	(0.002)
Log of female income in	–2.726	–1.654	–1.072	–1.421
metropolitan area	(0.000)	(0.000)	(0.001)	(0.007)
Value of owner-occupied housing in	0.204	0.008	0.196	0.004
metropolitan area (per $100,000)	(0.000)	(0.853)	(0.000)	(0.957)

Note: Values in parentheses are *p*-values.

References

Bartels, A., and S. Zeki. 2004. The neural correlates of maternal and romantic love. *NeuroImage* 21 (3): 1155–66.

Becker, G. 1981. *A treatise on the family.* Cambridge, MA: Harvard University Press.

Bianchi, S. 2000. Maternal employment and time with children: Dramatic change or surprising continuity? *Demography* 37 (4): 401–14.

Billari, F. C., and H.-P. Kohler. 2004. Patterns of low and lowest-low fertility in Europe. *Population Studies* 58 (2): 161–76.

Billari, F. C., and D. Philipov. 2004. Education and the transition to motherhood: A comparative analysis of western Europe. *European Demographic Research Papers no. 3.* Vienna: Vienna Institute of Demography.

Blau, F. D. 1998. Trends in the well-being of American women, 1970–1995. *Journal of Economic Literature* 36:112–65.

Blau, F. D., and L. M. Kahn. 2005. Changes in the labor supply behavior of married women: 1980–2000. NBER Working Paper no. 11230. Cambridge, MA: National Bureau of Economic Research, March.

Bongaarts, J. 2002. The end of the fertility transition in the developed world. *Population and Development Review* 28 (3): 419–43.

Buhler, C. 2006. On the structural value of children and its implication on intended fertility in Bulgaria. In MPIDR Working Papers no. 2006-003. Rostock, Germany: Max Planck Institute for Demographic Research.

Caldwell, J. C., and T. Schindlmayr. 2003. Explanations of the fertility crisis in modern societies: A search for commonalities. *Population Studies* 57 (3): 241–63.

Carter, C. S., L. Ahnert, K. E. Grossmann, S. B. Hrdy, M. E. Lamb, S. W. Porges, and N. Sachser. 2005. *Attachment and bonding: A new synthesis.* Cambridge, MA: MIT Press in cooperation with Dahlem University Press.

Chiappori, P., and S. Oreffice. 2008. Birth control and female empowerment: An equilibrium analysis. *Journal of Political Economy* 116 (1): 113–40.

Coleman, D. 2004. Why we don't have to believe without doubting in the "Second Demographic Transition"—some agnostic comments. In *Vienna yearbook of population research,* ed. F. C. Billari and A. Liefbroer, 11–22. Vienna: Austrian Academy of Sciences.

D'Addio, A., and M. M. d'Ercole. 2005. Trends and determinants of fertility rates in OECD countries: The role of policies. OECD Social, Employment, and Migration Working Paper no. 27. Paris: Organization for Economic Cooperation and Development.

De Tocqueville, A. 1945. *Democracy in America, volume 1.* New York: Vintage Books.

Erickson, M. F., and E. G. Aird. 2005. *The motherhood study: Fresh insights on mothers' attitudes and concerns.* New York: Institute for American Values.

Fawcett, J. T. 1983. Perceptions of the value of children: Satisfactions and costs. In *Determinants of fertility in developing countries: Supply and demand for children,* ed. R. A. Bulatao and R. D. Lee, 429–57. New York: Academic Press.

Finke, R., and R. Stark. 2005. *The churching of America, 1776–2005: Winners and losers in our religious economy.* New Brunswick, NJ: Rutgers University Press.

Foster, C. 2000. The limits to low fertility: A biosocial approach. *Population and Development Review* 26 (2): 209–34.

Frejka, T., and J. Sardon. 2004. *Childbearing trends and prospects in low-fertility countries: A cohort analysis.* Dordrecht, The Netherlands: Kluwer Academic Publishers.

Frejka, T., and C. F. Westoff. 2006. Religion, religiousness, and fertility in the U.S.

and Europe. MPIDR Working Paper no. 2006-013. Rostock, Germany: Max Planck Institute for Demographic Research.

Goldin, C., and L. F. Katz. 2002. The power of the pill: Oral contraceptives and women's career and marriage decisions. *Journal of Political Economy* 110 (4): 730–70.

———. 2007. Long-run changes in the U.S. wage structure: Narrowing, widening, polarizing. NBER Working Paper no. 13568. Cambridge, MA: National Bureau of Economic Research, November.

Goldstein, J., W. Lutz, and M. R. Testa. 2003. The emergence of sub-replacement family size ideals in Europe. *European Demographic Research Papers no. 2.* Vienna: Vienna Institute of Demography.

Greenwood, J., A. Seshadri, and G. Vandenbroucke. 2005. The baby boom and baby bust. *American Economic Review* 44 (3): 183–207.

Hagewen, K. J., and S. P. Morgan. 2005. Intended and ideal family size in the United States, 1970–2002. *Population and Development Review* 31 (3): 507–27.

Hoem, J. M. 2005. Why does Sweden have such high fertility? MPIDR Working Paper no. 2005-009. Rostock, Germany: Max Planck Institute for Demographic Research.

Hofferth, S. 2008. Changes in preadolescent and early adolescent children's time, 1997 to 2003. University of Maryland, Population Research Center. Working Paper.

Hout, M., and C. S. Fischer. 2002. Why more Americans have no religious preference: Politics and generations. *American Sociological Review* 67:165–90.

Hout, M., A. Greeley, and M. Wilde. 2001. The demographic imperative in religious change in the United States. *American Journal of Sociology* 107 (2): 468–500.

Jones, L. E., and M. Tertilt. 2006. An economic history of fertility in the U.S.: 1826–1960. NBER Working Paper no. 12796. Cambridge, MA: National Bureau of Economic Research, December.

Kaplan, H. 1994. Evolutionary and wealth flows theories of fertility: Empirical tests and new models. *Population and Development Review* 20 (4): 753–91.

Kearney, M. S. 2004. Is there an effect of incremental welfare benefits on fertility behavior? A look at the family cap. *Journal of Human Resources* 39 (2): 295–325.

Kertzer, D., M. White, L. Bernardi, and G. Gabrielli. 2006. Italy's path to very low fertility: The adequacy of economic and second demographic transition theories. MPIDR Working Paper no. 2006-049. Rostock, Germany: Max Planck Institute for Demographic Research.

Kiernan, K. 2004. Unmarried cohabitation and parenthood: Here to stay? European perspectives. In *The future of the family,* ed. D. P. Moynihan, T. M. Smeeding, and L. Rainwater, 66–95. New York: Russell Sage Foundation.

Klerman, J. A. 1999. U.S. abortion policy and fertility. *American Economic Review* 89 (2): 261–64.

Kohler, H.-P., J. R. Behrman, and A. Skytthe. 2005. Partner + children = happiness? The effects of partnerships and fertility on well-being. *Population and Development Review* 31 (3): 407–45.

Kohler, H.-P., F. C. Billari, and J. A. Ortega. 2006. Low fertility in Europe: Causes, implications, and policy options. In *The baby bust: Who will do the work? Who will pay the taxes?,* ed. F. R. Harris, 48–109. Lanham, MD: Rowman.

Lesthaeghe, R. J., and L. Neidert. 2006. The second demographic transition in the United States: Exception or textbook example? *Population and Development Review* 32 (4): 669–98.

Lundberg, S., and R. A. Pollak. 2007. The American family and family economics. NBER Working Paper no. 12908. Cambridge, MA: National Bureau of Economic Research, February.

McDonald, P. 2000. Gender equity in theories of fertility transition. *Population and Development Review* 26 (3): 427–39.

———. 2002. Sustaining fertility through public policy: The range of options. *Population-E* 57 (3): 417–46.

———. 2006. Low fertility and the state: The efficacy of policy. *Population and Development Review* 32 (3): 485–510.

McMahon, M. 1995. *Engendering motherhood.* New York: Guilford Press.

Moffit, R. 1998. The effects of welfare on marriage and fertility. In *Welfare, the family, and reproductive behavior,* ed. R. Moffit, 50–97. Washington, DC: National Academies Press.

Morgan, S. P. 2003. Is low fertility a twenty-first-century demographic crisis? *Demography* 40 (4): 589–603.

Morgan, S. P., and R. B. King. 2001. Why have children in the 21st century? Biological predisposition, social coercion, rational choice. *European Journal of Population* 17 (1): 3–20.

Morgan, S. P., S. C. Watkins, and D. Ewbank. 1994. Generating Americans: Ethnic differences in fertility. In *After Ellis island: Newcomers and natives in the 1910 census,* ed. S. C. Watkins, 83–124. New York: Russell Sage Foundation.

Nickell, S. 1997. Unemployment and labor market rigidities: Europe versus North America. *Journal of Economic Perspectives* 11 (3): 55–74.

Parrado, E. A., and P. Morgan. 2008. Intergenerational fertility among Hispanic women: New evidence of immigrant assimilation. *Demography* 45 (3): 651–73.

Philipov, D., and C. Berghammer. 2007. Religion and fertility ideals, intentions and behaviour: A comparative study of European countries. *Vienna Yearbook of Population Research* 2007:271–305.

Preston, S. H. 1987. Changing values and falling birth rates. In *Below replacement fertility in industrial societies,* ed. K. Davis, M. S. Bernstam, and R. Ricardo-Campbell, 176–95. Cambridge: Cambridge University Press.

Quesnel-Vallee, A., and S. P. Morgan. 2003. Missing the target? Correspondence of fertility intentions and behavior in the U.S. *Population Research and Policy Review* 22 (5-6): 497–525.

Retherford, R. D., and N. Ogawa. 2006. Japan's baby bust: Causes, implications, and policy responses. In *The baby bust: Who will do the work? Who will pay the taxes?,* ed. F. R. Harris, 5–47. Lanham, MD: Rowman & Littlefield.

Rindfuss, R. R., K. B. Guzzo, and S. P. Morgan. 2003. The changing institutional context of low fertility. *Population Research and Policy Review* 22 (5): 411–38.

Sayer, L., N. Wright, and K. Edin. 2003. Differences in family attitudes by education. Presented at the annual meetings of the Population Association of America. Minneapolis, MN.

Schoen, R. 2004. Timing effects and the interpretation of period fertility. *Demography* 41 (4): 801–19.

Schoen, R., Y. Kim, C. Nathanson, J. Fields, and N. M. Astone. 1997. Why do Americans want children? *Population and Development Review* 23 (2): 333–58.

Schultz, T. P. 1994. Marital status and fertility in the United States: Welfare and labor market effects. *Journal of Human Resources* 29 (2): 637–69.

Thornton, A., and L. Young-DeMarco. 2001. Four decades of trends in attitudes toward family issues in the United States: The 1960s through the 1990s. *Journal of Marriage and Family* 63:1009–37.

Trustees, Federal Old-Age and Survivors Insurance and Federal Disability Insurance Trust Funds. 2007. *2007 Annual report.* Washington, DC: GPO.

U.S. Bureau of the Census. 1972. *Census of population: 1970.* Marital status. Final Report PC (2)-4C. Washington, DC: GPO.

————. 1979. *Statistical abstract of the United States, 1979*. Washington, DC: U.S. Bureau of the Census.

U.S. Census Bureau. 2000a. Have we reached the top? Educational attainment projections of the U.S. Population. Population Division Working Paper no. 43. Available at: http://www.census.gov.

————. 2000b. Methodology and assumptions for the population projections of the U.S. 1999 to 2100. Population Division Working Paper no. 38. Washington, DC: U.S. Census Bureau.

————. 2004a. International data base. International Program Center. Available at: http://www.census.gov.

————. 2004b. U.S. interim population projections by age, sex, race, and Hispanic origin. Available at: http://www.census.gov.

————. 2005a. Fertility of American women: June 2004. Current Population Report no. P20-555. Washington, DC: U.S. Census Bureau.

————. 2005b. *Statistical abstract of the United States: 2004–2005*. Washington, DC: U.S. Department of Commerce, U.S. Census Bureau.

————. 2007b. Historical income tables. P38. Available at: http://www.census.gov.

————. 2008. Historical income tables. Available at: http://www.census.gov/hhes/www/income/histinc/incpertoc.html.

U.S. National Center for Health Statistics. 2005a. *Births: Final data for 2003*. Vital and Health Statistics Series 54 (2). Hyattsville, MD: U.S. Department of Health and Human Services.

————. 2005b. *Fertility, family planning, and reproductive health of U.S. women: Data from the 2002 national survey of family growth*. Vital and Health Statistics Series 23 no. 25. Hyattsville, MD: U.S. Department of Health and Human Services.

————. 2006a. *Births: Final data for 2004*. National Vital Statistics Reports. 55 (1). Hyattsville, MD: National Center for Health Statistics.

————. 2006b. *Births: Preliminary data for 2005*. National Vital Statistics Reports 55 (11). Hyattsville, MD: National Center for Health Statistics.

Van de Kaa, D. J. 1996. Anchored narratives: The story and findings of half a century of research into the determinants of fertility. *Population Studies* 50 (3): 389–432.

Ventura, S. and C. Bachrach. 2000. *Non-marital childbearing in the United States, 1940–99*. National Vital Statistics Reports 48 (16). Hyattsville, MD: National Center for Health Statistics.

Wuthnow, R. 2005. The family as contested terrain. In *Family transformed: Religion, values, and society in American life,* ed. S. Tipton and J. Wittee, 71–93. Washington, DC: Georgetown University Press.

Yu, P. 2006. Higher education, the bane of fertility? An investigation with the HILDA Survey. Centre for Economic Policy Research. Discussion Paper no. 512. Canberra: The Australian National University.

Comment   Gopi Shah Goda

The chapter by Preston and Hartnett takes on a formidable task: that of forecasting the future of American fertility. Predicting future responses in

Gopi Shah Goda is Postdoctoral Fellow Program Coordinator and Research Scholar at the Stanford Institute for Economic Policy Research, Stanford University.

human behavior is never easy, and given the large swings in fertility behavior over the last century, fertility rates seem to often be the result of factors that are unobservable to researchers. However, the authors make progress in increasing our understanding of fertility responses to a set of demographic and economic factors, such as the role of ethnicity, educational attainment, and relative wages between men and women.

Figure 1C.1 shows actual period total fertility rates that have been experienced since 1917, as well as predicted future period fertility rates under three alternate scenarios for projecting Social Security finances based on the 2004 Trustees Report. The figure shows that while fertility rates have been stable over the last few decades, previous fluctuations in fertility rates were much higher than the range of projected fertility rates under the three alternate scenarios. However, the impact of even these historically modest fluctuations in terms of Social Security-projected finances is enormous: the difference between the seventy-five-year actuarial deficit varying only the assumption on fertility from the high fertility (low cost) assumption to the low fertility (high cost) assumption is 0.70 percent of taxable payroll, or a present value of almost $2 trillion. This amount represents approximately half of the current shortfall in projected Social Security benefits over this window. This fact highlights both the important role that fertility plays in pay-as-you-go programs such as Social Security, and the difficulty in predicting with any level of certainty what fertility rates will look like in the future.

The authors begin by cataloging several factors that have been thought

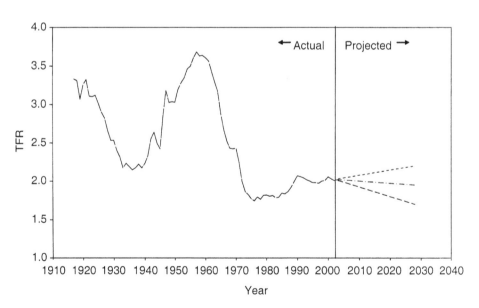

Fig. 1C.1   Actual and projected period total fertility rates, Social Security Administration cost scenarios

to influence fertility. Sociological determinants include the role of social expectations and norms related to the number of children a woman decides to have and the role of out-of-wedlock births, social rewards of parenting, and the ethnicity of the mother, which may play a role in forming cultural attitudes toward children and values and practices related to childbearing. Technological determinants include factors that may reduce fertility levels, such as the advent of the birth control pill and abortion, and factors that may increase fertility levels, such as advances in medical treatments for adults who suffer from infertility. Lastly, economic factors that may influence fertility include educational attainment and earnings of both men and women, unemployment rates, and the value of owner-occupied housing.

There are two aspects of fertility that are important—timing and volume. Volume, in the context of period fertility rates, refers to the change in age-specific fertility rates that add up to the total fertility rate. A shift in the timing of births, by contrast, could have no effect on the total fertility rate. Figure 1C.2 highlights the change in the mean age of mothers at childbirth over the same period as figure 1C.1. During years of high fertility rates, the mean age of mothers tends to be higher, but in recent years, there has been a trend of higher ages of childbearing without corresponding movements in underlying fertility rates. It is also interesting to note that while all three cost scenarios by Social Security predict a slight increase in the mean age of mothers, the three scenarios do not differ from one another in this regard.

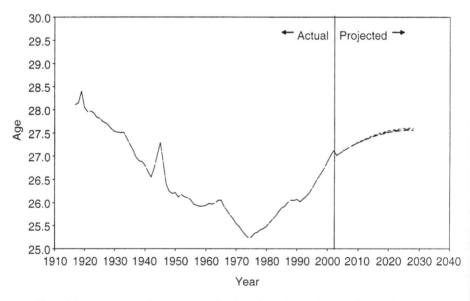

Fig. 1C.2   Mean age of mother at childbirth, Social Security Administration cost scenarios

The authors discuss several empirical facts about fertility in the United States and how it relates to international fertility levels. A large factor in the reduction in the total fertility rates after 1976 is the shift from families with four or more children to families with two children, while the increase in families with zero or one child was small. More than a third of births in 2005 were out of wedlock, representing a large shift compared to 1960 and deemphasizing the role of marriage in explaining fertility outcomes. While it is commonly argued that high levels of Hispanic immigration account for the United States relatively high fertility rates, the total fertility rate of non-Hispanic whites in the United States is still high by international standards. Social norms likely play a role in explaining differences in international fertility levels, such as traditional mind-sets that discourage mothers from working and unmarried women from having children. Americans are more religious than Europeans, and within the United States, church attendance is positively correlated with fertility (though the effects may be at least partially attributable to self-selection).

The main results of the Preston and Hartnett chapter relate to the association of three particular factors with fertility rates, and the predicted influences of these three factors on future fertility. The three factors examined are: the correlation between female education and fertility, fertility levels by ethnicity, and the association of female and male earnings with fertility levels. The authors use variation over time and geographic area to estimate the responses and find that the magnitude of the correlation between fertility and female education has declined, the differential between Hispanic and non-Hispanic white fertility has widened, and higher female earnings are associated with lower fertility, while the opposite is true for male earnings.

To predict what will happen in the future, the authors forecast how these three components will change and use their results to predict what fertility will look like. Higher predicted female education levels are predicted to lead to slightly lower fertility, changes in ethnicity are predicted to have the opposite effect, and increases in relative female earnings are predicted to have a potentially large negative effect on fertility.

The authors acknowledge several caveats in interpreting these as causal determinants of fertility. Perhaps the largest confounding factor in regressions that use geographic variation as a source of identification is selective migration. Unobservable factors such as tastes for work and childbearing may influence where a woman chooses to locate. In addition, reverse causation is also a concern. Geographic characteristics that may depress fertility rates (for instance, high costs of housing) may cause women to make larger investments in human capital, thus raising their earnings. Exogenous shifts in earnings levels are difficult to isolate. One place to look in future studies of female earnings and fertility levels may be variation in after-tax earnings over time, across states, and across households.

Another issue in interpreting the authors' results as a causal effect of earnings on fertility is a mismatch between the timing of the fertility decision and the value of the covariates. If there was a large change in relative female earnings from the time women made their fertility decisions and the time of the survey, the results of this analysis will be biased. A similar point could be made about other covariates that may change within a geographic area over time, such as unemployment, housing prices, and male income.

In their analysis, the authors use median earnings of full-time, full-year female workers as a proxy for market opportunities for women. However, it is possible that two geographic areas with the same level of median earnings among full-time and full-year workers may differ in the underlying reservation wage of the female population in that area if they have very different levels of female labor force participation. It is unclear whether omitting the female labor force participation rate would dramatically affect their results, and including this covariate would introduce similar identification problems—as discussed previously—such as simultaneous causation and mismatch of timing.

The authors estimate the effects of female education, ethnicity, and earnings separately, but it is possible that there is an interaction effect of these three factors. Do highly educated individuals respond more to relative wages than women with low levels of education? Do ethnic groups respond differently to relative wages? The answers to these questions would provide a larger picture of how these three factors relate to fertility behavior.

As the authors state, the association between education and fertility behavior has changed from decade to decade. This fact highlights the difficulty of using their estimates to predict future fertility levels if this association may change in the future. Similarly, there is reason to believe that future generations of Hispanic immigrants will not share the same high fertility rates as their ancestors.

The evidence presented in the chapter is inconclusive about the effects of housing prices on fertility. The authors find that a higher median price of owner-occupied houses is associated with higher fertility, against their intuition that higher housing prices should increase the cost of having additional children due to larger space requirements. This result is puzzling, but the authors state that this may be due to a wealth effect: wealthier individuals can afford to live in more expensive houses and have more children. Further investigation into this question would be an interesting area for future research, particularly with recent fluctuations in home prices over time, which may serve as an additional source of identification.

The authors mainly focus on volume rather than the timing of births. However, each has different implications for programs like Social Security. Because Social Security financing largely depends on the ratio of young workers to retirees, changes in timing of births have a transitional effect, but no long-run effect on the old-age dependency ratio (once the first delayed generation grows to be in the old age category). By contrast, as mentioned

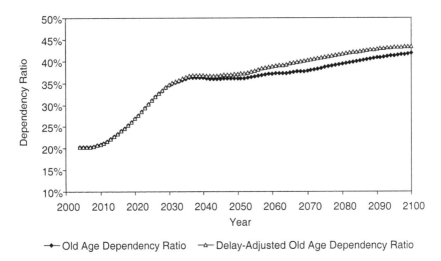

—•— Old Age Dependency Ratio   —△— Delay-Adjusted Old Age Dependency Ratio

Fig. 1C.3   Projected old-age dependency ratios

earlier, changes in volume can have large effects on Social Security financing. Figure 1C.3 simulates the old-age dependency ratio under two scenarios: one is simply the intermediate scenario as defined by Social Security, and the other has the same underlying total fertility rate, but adjusts the timing of births to change according to past changes in timing. The old-age dependency ratio is defined as the ratio of the number of people aged sixty-five and older to the number of people aged twenty to sixty-four. Note the delay-adjusted old-age dependency ratio is higher than the old-age dependency ratio, but that the difference between the two ratios decreases once the population has matured.

Overall, the Preston and Hartnett chapter provides an interesting look at many factors that influence fertility. The analysis highlights the difficulties in predicting characteristics of future fertility, and outlines several problems with isolating exogenous factors that influence fertility behavior.

2

Fertility Theories
Can They Explain the Negative Fertility-Income Relationship?

Larry E. Jones, Alice Schoonbroodt, and Michèle Tertilt

2.1 Introduction

Empirical studies find a clear negative relationship between income, or wages, and fertility. This finding has been confirmed across time and for different countries. For example, Jones and Tertilt (2008) document a negative cross-sectional relationship between income and fertility in the United States and find that the relationship has been surprisingly stable over time. In particular, the paper shows a negative relationship for thirty birth cohorts between 1830 and 1960, with the income elasticity of fertility remaining roughly constant at about –0.30.[1]

Why do richer people have fewer children, and what explains the relatively time-invariant nature of the relationship? The negative correlation is particularly puzzling if one thinks about children as a consumption good, unless one believes that children are an inferior good. An early discussion of

Larry E. Jones is chair and professor of economics at the University of Minnesota, a visiting scholar at the Federal Reserve Bank of Minneapolis, and a research associate of the National Bureau of Economic Research. Alice Schoonbroodt is a lecturer in economics at the University of Southampton. Michèle Tertilt is an assistant professor of economics at Stanford University, a research affiliate of the Center for Economic and Policy Research, and a faculty research fellow of the National Bureau of Economic Research.

We thank Todd Schoellman, John Knowles, and the participants at the NBER preconference in Boston, the Stanford Junior Faculty Bag Lunch, and the Economics and Demography conference in Napa California for helpful suggestions. We thank Amalia Miller in particular for a thoughtful discussion. Financial support by the NSF (grants SES-0519324 and SES-0452473) and the Stanford Institute for Economic Policy Research (SIEPR) is greatly appreciated. William G. Woolston provided excellent research assistance. Part of this research was completed while Michèle Tertilt was a National Fellow at the Hoover Institution at Stanford.

1. We discuss the empirical evidence in more detail in section 2.2.

this fact appears in the seminal article on fertility choice by Becker (1960). Indeed, this puzzling correlation was the main impetus behind Becker's early work.[2] The ensuing literature can be roughly divided into two strands. One attacks the question from a theoretical point of view and finds that, properly interpreted or with the appropriate additions in choice variables, economic theory says that fertility *should* be negatively related to income. The basic idea is that the price of children is largely time, and because of this, children are more expensive for parents with higher wages. Another argument is that higher-wage people have a higher demand for child quality, making quantity more costly, and hence those parents want fewer children. The other strand of literature attacks the question from an empirical point of view, arguing that the negative relationship is mainly a statistical fluke—due to a missing variables problem. This literature focuses on identifying those crucial missing variables, such as female earnings potential. Once those missing variables are controlled for, fertility and income—so the argument goes—are actually positively related.[3]

In this chapter, we revisit these theories of the cross-sectional relationship between income and fertility. They are largely based on ability or wage heterogeneity. We also formalize a new theory, based on heterogeneity in the taste for children, in which wages are also endogenous. For each of the theories, we catalogue whether they basically never work (i.e., never produce the negative income-fertility relation), whether they work only with specific additional assumptions, or whether they are relatively robust to changes in assumptions. We also often compare the results to the conditional correlations found in the statistical strand of the literature. For those theories that work sometimes, we try to be as explicit as possible about what kinds of conditions are needed (e.g., curvature and/or functional form restrictions) to generate a negative relationship between income and fertility. We also show what goes wrong by giving examples about how they fail. Finally, of the theories that work and appear robust, we ask for more. Can the theory also match the time series properties of fertility? If so, what exactly does it take? If not, why not? Finally, we want to know whether such a theory is consistent with a recursive formulation of dynastic altruism.

Our main findings can be summarized as follows:

---

2. Quoting from Becker (1960, 217): "Having set out the formal analysis and framework suggested by economic theory, we now investigate its usefulness in the study of fertility patterns. It suggests that a rise in income would increase both the quality and quantity of children desired; the increase in quality being large and the increase in quantity small. The difficulties in separating expenditures on children from general family expenditures notwithstanding, it is evident that wealthier families and countries spend much more per child than do poorer families and countries. The implication with respect to quantity is not so readily confirmed by the raw data. Indeed, most data tend to show a negative relationship between income and fertility." See also the discussion in Hotz, Klerman, and Willis (1993).

3. See Hotz, Klerman, and Willis (1993) for a survey. An early literature review on fertility choice is Bagozzi and Van Loo (1978).

1. (Almost) all theories depend on the assumption that raising children takes time and that this time must be incurred by the parents.

2. Theories based on exogenous wage heterogeneity crucially depend on the assumption of a high elasticity of substitution between consumption and children.

3. Adding a quality choice by itself does not generate a negative fertility-income relationship. The quantity-quality trade-off works only in conjunction with assumptions similar to those needed in list entry (2).

4. Theories based on heterogeneity in tastes for children are able to generate a negative fertility-income relationship without requiring a high elasticity of substitution between consumption and children.

5. Theories that explicitly distinguish between fathers and mothers are very similar to one-parent theories. However, to get fertility to be decreasing in men's income, one needs to assume that there is positive assortative matching of spouses.

6. Several of the theories that match the cross-sectional patterns of fertility also match, at least loosely, some of the broad time series trends in fertility. Theories based on wage heterogeneity produce this relationship more naturally.

7. Extending the models that are successful at matching the cross-sectional properties of fertility choice to fully dynamic models based on parental altruism is very challenging. Basic theories with wage heterogeneity do not appear to be robust to this extension. Theories based on heterogeneity in tastes are more promising, but leave many open questions.

Our findings may be relevant in several different contexts. First, there has been a recent increase in research relating the demographic transition and economic development among macroeconomists.[4] Similarly, several recent contributions try to understand why fertility is higher in poor countries than in rich ones.[5] Further, there is a recent literature that uses dynamic macro-style models to analyze the interplay between fertility, labor force participation, marriage, and inequality[6]—including studies of gender wage gap[7] and the baby boom following World War II.[8] Often dynamic macro-style models are used to analyze the impacts of various policy changes—for example, parental leave policies, the impact of tax reform, welfare reform, and social

---

4. See, for example, Becker, Murphy, and Tamura (1990); Galor and Weil (1996, 1999, 2000), Greenwood and Seshadri (2002); Hansen and Prescott (2002); Boldrin and Jones (2002); Doepke (2004, 2005); Greenwood, Seshadri, and Vandenbroucke (2005); Moav (2005); Tertilt (2005); Jones and Schoonbroodt (Forthcoming), Murtin (2007); and Bar and Leukhina (Forthcoming). See Galor (2005a, 2005b) for an extensive analysis and a critical survey of theories of the demographic transition.

5. See Manuelli and Seshadri (2009).

6. See Alvarez (1999); Caucutt, Guner, and Knowles (2002); and Falcão and Soares (2008).

7. See Erosa, Fuster, and Restuccia (2005).

8. See Greenwood, Seshadri, and Vandenbroucke (2005); Doepke, Hazan, and Maoz (2007); and Jones and Schoonbroodt (2007).

security.[9] Typically, they use an "off-the-shelf" fertility model as one of their building blocks, and need to make a careful decision about which one to use. What may help guide this choice is an informed understanding of the implications of the models for the fertility-income relationship in the cross section. Because of this, it is natural to use successful models of the cross sectional properties of fertility as a way to inform that choice.

This is easier said than done, however. Economists have been developing and testing theories of fertility ever since Gary Becker's seminal paper, but still there is no full consensus on the motivations behind fertility choices. Here, we provide a systematic comparison of the properties of various fertility theories. We hope that this catalogue may be a useful step toward finding a consensus.

This chapter is organized as follows. In the next section, we summarize the empirical evidence on the fertility-income relationship. Section 2.3 describes a basic model with wage heterogeneity. Section 2.4 develops a new theory based on preference heterogeneity in the desire to have children, which generates endogenous wage heterogeneity. Section 2.5 adds quality to the basic model. In section 2.6 we depart from the simplest framework and analyze more realistic theories with two parents. We investigate whether theories are robust to allowing parents to hire nannies in section 2.7. Section 2.8 pushes several of the working theories to also address the secular decline in fertility, while section 2.9 concludes. The appendix analyzes the extent to which our results apply to a dynastic formulation of fertility.

2.2   Data on Fertility and Income

A robust fact about fertility is that it is decreasing in income. This fact has been documented from a time-series point of view, across countries, and across individuals. Quoting from Becker (1960, 217): "Indeed, most data tend to show a negative relationship between income and fertility. This is true of the Census data for 1910, 1940 and 1950, where income is represented by father's occupation, mother's education or monthly rental; the data from the Indianapolis survey, the data for nineteenth century Providence families, and several other studies as well."[10]

In a recent study, Jones and Tertilt (2008) use U.S. Census Data on lifetime fertility and occupations to document this negative cross-sectional relationship in the United States.[11] They find a robust negative cross-sectional rela-

9. Recent contributions include Aiyagari, Greenwood, and Guner (2000); Erosa, Fuster, and Restuccia (Forthcoming), Fernandez, Guner, and Knowles (2005); Greenwood, Guner, and Knowles (2003); Sylvester (2007); and Zhao (2008).
10. The studies Becker is referring to are U.S. Census (1945, 1955); Whelpton and Kiser (1951); and Jaffe (1940).
11. Income is based on the median annual income for a given occupation in 1950 and adjusted for TFP growth. A measure of income based on occupation is a better measure of

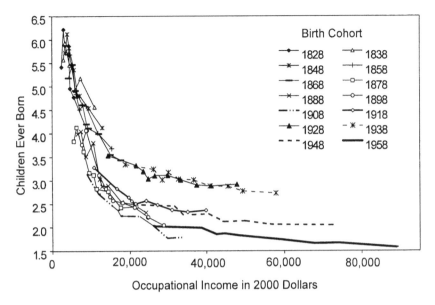

Fig. 2.1   Fertility by occupational income in 2000 dollars
Source: Jones and Tertilt (2008).

tionship between husband's income[12] and fertility for all cohorts for which data is available; that is, for women born between 1826 and 1960.[13] Not only are the correlations always negative, but also they are surprisingly similar in magnitude over time. Figure 2.1, reproduced from their paper, shows this very clearly. While the relationship is not perfect, it seems that most of the fertility decline over time can be "explained" by rising incomes alone, at least in a statistical sense.

To give a sense of the magnitudes, table 2.1 reproduces some of the most relevant numbers from Jones and Tertilt (2008). For a selected number of

lifetime income than income in any particular year. See Ruggles et al. (2004) for a description of how occupational income scores (OIS) are constructed as well as its robustness as a proxy for income. See Jones and Tertilt (2008) for a description of how the OIS was converted into 2000 dollars.

12. The focus on husband's income allows a consistent analysis over time. In particular, it allows the analysis of periods for which data on wife's income is practically nonexistent.

13. Fertility is measured as children ever born (CEB) to the current wife. Of course, this measure could differ from male completed fertility if men had children with different women. Unfortunately not much data on male completed fertility are available. We are aware of two exceptions. First, the 2002 National Survey of Family Growth asked men and women independently about their fertility. Preston and Sten (2008) use this data to construct a measure of the elasticity of male fertility to male education and also find a negative coefficient. Given that divorce was rare for most of the period under consideration, we believe that the wife's fertility is a good proxy. Second, Shiue (2008) compiled Chinese data from 1300 to 1850. She finds a weak positive relationship between male fertility and social status, but since richer men also had more women on average, fertility per wife is actually decreasing.

Table 2.1   Fertility-income relationship for 14 U.S. cross sections

Birth cohort	Income elasticity	Top/bottom fertility gap	Fertility	Annual income in 2000 dollars	Number of observations
1826–1830	–0.33	0.95	5.59	4,154	452
1836–1840	–0.20	0.74	5.49	5,064	1,960
1846–1850	–0.32	1.26	5.36	6,173	4,520
1856–1860	–0.35	1.24	4.90	7,525	7,241
1866–1870	–0.34	1.27	4.50	9,173	7,347
1876–1880	–0.42	1.06	3.25	11,182	3,203
1886–1890	–0.45	1.05	3.15	13,631	6,644
1896–1900	–0.50	0.93	2.82	16,616	8,462
1906–1910	–0.42	0.57	2.30	20,255	11,812
1916–1920	–0.25	0.34	2.59	24,690	46,908
1926–1930	–0.17	0.27	3.11	30,097	97,143
1936–1940	–0.19	0.31	3.01	36,688	44,428
1946–1950	–0.20	0.26	2.22	44,723	62,210
1956–1960	–0.22	0.23	1.80	54,517	71,517

Source: Jones and Tertilt (2008).

birth cohorts, the table displays average husband's income and average fertility.[14] To quantify the fertility-income relationship, two different empirical measures were constructed: the income elasticity of fertility, and the fertility gap between the top and bottom 50 percent of the income distribution. The income elasticity roughly hovers around minus one-third, meaning that for a family with an income that is 10 percent higher than another family, the number of children is about 3 percent lower. This is a large difference. For example, for women born during the nineteenth century, those in the bottom half of the income distribution had easily one child more on average than those in the top half. Today, the difference is much smaller in absolute numbers, with a fertility gap of roughly a quarter of a child. But since fertility is significantly lower for all women, the income elasticity has declined only very mildly over time, to about –0.20 for the most recent cohorts.

Note that the income measure used in figure 2.1 and table 2.1 is based on occupations, and can also be viewed as a proxy for wages. Therefore, the findings can be interpreted as showing a negative fertility-wage relationship.

Many other studies have documented this kind of relationship, typically for a specific geographic area at a particular point in time. For example, Borg (1989) finds a negative relationship using panel data from South Korea in 1976, and Docquier (2004) documents a similar relationship for the United States using data from the Panel Study of Income Dynamics (PSID) in 1994.

14. The definitions of fertility and income in the table are identical to those used in figure 2.1.

Westoff (1954) finds a negative relationship between fertility and occupational status for the years 1900 to 1952 using U.S. Census data.

Part of the literature argues that a negative income-fertility relationship is primarily a statistical fluke—that is, it is due to a problem of missing variables. The idea is that once enough variables are controlled for, one would actually find a positive income-fertility relation. Indeed, this was Becker's original view on the topic. He went into great detail focusing on knowledge of the proper use of contraceptives as the important missing variable.[15] Similarly, many authors have argued that a distinction between male and female income is crucial and that the relationship between male income and fertility is indeed (weakly) positive once one correctly controls for female income.[16] Authors of studies that find a positive relationship after controlling for women's wages often interpret such finding as having resolved the "puzzle." This is, however, not necessarily the case. The reason is that even though the finding reconciles the conditional correlations in the data with the simplest model of fertility, the question remains of what kind of theories would explain the unconditional negative correlation of men's wages and fertility. At the very least it requires some assumptions about matching.[17] In this chapter we take a somewhat different approach: rather than controlling for important factors (such as wives' wages) in the data, we try to add such important factors into the model and then ask whether the augmented model delivers the same qualitative facts as the data does.

It is sometimes argued that early on in the development process, a positive relationship between income and fertility existed.[18] Most of the studies that document such a positive relationship are set in agrarian economies, and often income is proxied by farm size. Examples include Simon (1977, chapter 16), who documents a positive relationship between farm size in hectares and the average numbers of children born for rural areas in Poland in 1948, and Clark and Hamilton (2006), who document a positive relationship between occupational status and the number of surviving children in England in the late sixteenth and early seventeenth century (see also Clark

15. He showed that, in his sample, in those households that were actively engaged in family planning, fertility and income were positively related, while the opposite was true for families not engaged in family planning. Other early papers along this line are cited by Becker in his original piece. They include Edin and Hutchinson (1935) and Banks (1955).

16. Empirical studies distinguishing explicitly between husbands and wives include Cho (1968); Fleischer and Rhodes (1979); Freedman and Thorton (1982); Schultz (1986); Heckman and Walker (1990); Merrigan and Pierre (1998); Blau and van der Klaauw (2007); and Jones and Tertilt (2008). The findings are mixed.

17. We discuss this in detail in section 2.6.

18. A more recent version of such a positive relationship is that U.S. fertility is higher than most other countries in the Organization for Economic Cooperation and Development (OECD) even though U.S. income is higher. This does not hold for a larger set of countries, however. See Ahn and Mira (2002) and Manuelli and Seshadri (2009) for a discussion of related points. Bongaarts (2003) finds a slight U-shaped fertility-education relationship in Portugal and Greece using three education levels of women. The other eight countries concur with previous findings of a strictly negative relationship.

[2005] and Clark [2007]). Weir (1995) finds a weakly positive relationship between economic status and fertility in eighteenth century France, while Wrigley (1961) and Haines (1976) document higher fertility in the coal mining areas of France and Prussia than in surrounding agricultural areas during the end of the nineteenth century. Also, Lee (1987) documents a similar finding using data from the United States and Canada.[19] This body of work suggests that the fundamental forces determining the demand for children might be different in areas where agriculture is the primary economic activity.

Of course, there is no reason why the fertility-income relationship should not change over time or vary in different cross sections. It may be that in some subgroups of the population, fertility increases in income once all other relevant correlates are controlled for, while in other subgroups the primary change across the income distribution is in the price of a child and, because of this, that fertility is lower at higher income levels. And in fact, it is plausible that fertility and wealth were indeed positively related in early agrarian economies, but that this relationship was reversed after industrialization.[20]

To sum up, the fact that people with higher lifetime earnings have fewer children seems very robust, at least during the last century and a half in the United States. Other countries and other episodes display a similar relationship. Inspired by these facts, this chapter analyzes which theories of fertility are consistent with this relationship.

2.3   Basic Framework and Results

In this section we introduce notation and explore some basic models of fertility choice. The basic examples that we discuss here focus on the roles played by the nature of the cost of children, the sources of family income, and the formulation of preferences. We find that the simplest versions of these ideas do not generate a negative relationship between fertility and income. Special assumptions on the nature of costs of children, the utility function, the sources of income, and/or the child quality production function are needed. This is not to say that these theories are wrong. Rather, by making explicit the assumptions behind the ideas we hope to facilitate the testing of the theories and, ultimately, to improve our understanding of fertility decision-making.

---

19. See also the papers cited in Lee (1987).

20. For example, Skirbekk (2008) (using a large data set including various world regions over time) finds that as fertility declines, there is a general shift from a positive to a negative or neutral status-fertility relation. Those with high income/wealth or high occupation/social class switch from having relatively many to fewer or the same number of children as others. Education, however, depresses fertility for as long as this relation is observed (early twentieth century).

To keep the analysis tractable, we focus on a static, monoparental setup. This approach allows for closed form solutions and lets us focus on the basic mechanics behind the results. Obviously, there are many dynamic elements in real world fertility decision-making; for example, choices about the timing of births, and so forth. We see our basic examples as a way to gain insights into modeling ingredients of more complex dynamic models. Clearly, many important features are left out in the simplest example we start with. Some of these features are particularly important and we come back to those in later sections of this chapter. One such element is that any child necessarily has a father and a mother. In fact, many authors have emphasized that it may be female time rather than male time that is important to generate the negative relationship between fertility and income. We get back to this in section 2.6. In later sections of the chapter we extend the model to include more dynamic elements, including limited forms of human capital/child quality (sections 2.4 and 2.5) and parental altruism (appendix).

Two more caveats are in order. First, throughout the chapter we analyze only rational theories of fertility.[21] Behavioral concerns might be relevant, especially for teenage childbearing, but are not considered here. Second, we focus on theories in which children provide direct utility benefits; that is, children are a consumption good. Note that children are sometimes also viewed as an investment, providing old-age security.[22] While the investment motive may have important implications for the fertility-income relationship, this analysis is beyond the scope of this chapter and is left for future research.

2.3.1 The Basic Model

The general static model of fertility choice that we consider is as follows. People maximize utility subject to a budget constraint, a time constraint, and a child quality production function. People (potentially) derive utility from four different goods: consumption, c, number of children, n, the average quality of children, q, and leisure, ℓ. Producing children takes b_0 units of goods and b_1 units of time (per child). We let l_w denote the time spent working and normalize the total time endowment to one. The wage per unit of time is denoted by w. In addition to labor income, we also allow for nonlabor income, y. Finally, child quality is a function of educational child inputs, s (we abstract from direct parental time inputs into child quality). Thus, the choice problem is as follows:

21. We also abstract from costs and technologies to prevent births or to inseminate artificially. Several authors have given these issues more thought, and we refer the reader to them (see, e.g., Hotz and Miller (1988); Goldin and Katz (2002); Bailey (2006); and Greenwood and Guner, (Forthcoming)).

22. Examples include Ehrlich and Lui (1991); Boldrin and Jones (2002); and Boldrin, De Nardi, and Jones (2005). Zhao (2008) uses the Boldrin-Jones framework to jointly address the fertility decline and the narrowing of fertility differentials by income in response to changes in social security.

(1) $\max\limits_{c,n,q,e,l_w}$ $U(c, n, q, \ell)$

                              s. t. $l_w + b_1 n + \ell \leq 1$

                                        $c + (b_0 + s)n \leq y + wl_w$

                                        $q = f(s)$.

In order to highlight the crucial ingredients to generate a negative income (or wage) to fertility relationship, we distinguish between various combinations of utility specifications, concept of wealth/income/earnings used, costs of children, and quality production functions. We now briefly discuss each of these components.

Utility: We focus on separable utilities. That is:

$$U(c, n, q, \ell) = u_c(c) + u_n(n) + u_q(q) + u_\ell(\ell).$$

We consider the CES utility case, $u_x(x) = \alpha_x(x^{1-\sigma_x} - 1)/(1 - \sigma_x)$ for values of $\sigma_x > 0$. We will often distinguish three cases: (a) $\sigma_x > 1$ (high curvature, low elasticity of substitution); (b) $\sigma_x < 1$ (low curvature, high elasticity of substitution); and (c) $\sigma_x = 1$ corresponding to log utility.[23]

Income/Wealth: We use the following (standard) language: w is the wage, $W = w + y$ is total wealth, and $I = wl_w$ is earned income (often also called labor earnings). In most of our examples, there are only two uses of time (working and child-rearing), in which case earned income is equal to $w(1 - b_1 n)$. An interesting special case is where all income is labor income, $y = 0$ and $W = w$. In several examples, we focus on the fertility-earnings (rather than wage) relationship. In these examples, there is no wage heterogeneity. However, the logic underlying those examples can easily be generalized to (endogenous) wage heterogeneity. We do so in section 2.4. In this context, the wage will be equal to human capital, H, and human capital is a function of schooling inputs. For simplicity, we will omit H and say that the wage w is a function of schooling inputs.

Costs of Children: We allow for both goods and time costs, denoted by b_0 and b_1, respectively. To get starker results, we sometimes shut down one of the two types of costs. It turns out that a time cost appears to be essential to almost all the theories and examples we present here. To see this, note that with separable utility, no time cost ($b_1 = 0$) and no quality in utility ($\alpha_q = 0$), n is a normal good, and hence, it follows that n is increasing in both

---

23. This utility function has the added advantage that, in some cases, it can be interpreted as the problem in Bellman's equation for a Barro-Becker style dynasty with parental altruism. There, the term $u_n(n)$ is the value function for continuations. This interpretation is only valid for certain choices of the α_n's however. See appendix for details.

y and w.[24] Thus, we will typically require that $b_1 > 0$. While it seems fairly obvious that it takes time to raise a child, it is less clear whether the time spent must be the parent's time rather than a nanny or a day care center. We analyze the implications of allowing for nannies in section 2.7.[25]

Quality Production Function: One important feature for the quantity-quality trade-off to generate the desired relationship is the specification of the quality production function, $f(\cdot)$. We experiment with various specifications. Note that making special assumptions on $f(\cdot)$ is technically equivalent to making special assumptions on $u_q(\cdot)$. That is, let $v_q(\cdot) = u_q(f(\cdot))$ and make assumptions about this function. The interpretation, however, can be quite different. With homothetic preferences to start with, unless $f(s)$ is of the form $f(s) = s^\kappa$, this introduces nonhomotheticity into the overall problem (1). We will analyze quality production functions in some detail in section 2.5.

Leisure: For some of the examples in sections 2.6 and 2.7, we need leisure as an alternative use of time in order to reproduce the negative fertility-income relationship. For most examples, this is not necessary, and hence we will typically assume that $\alpha_\ell = 0$.

2.3.2   The Price of Time Theory

To highlight the necessary ingredients, we start by discussing a simple example that does not generate the desired negative relationship between fertility and income. We then show what special assumptions are needed to obtain the desired result.

Starting from the general formulation (1), we assume log utility ($u_x(x) = \alpha_x \log(x)$), no utility from child quality ($\alpha_q = 0$) or leisure ($\alpha_\ell = 0$), and no nonlabor income ($y = 0$). Then the problem reduces to

$$(2) \qquad \max_{c,n} \quad \alpha_c \log(c) + \alpha_n \log(n)$$

$$\text{s. t.} \quad c + b_0 n \le w(1 - b_1 n).$$

The solution for fertility is:

$$n^* = \frac{\alpha_n w}{(\alpha_c + \alpha_n)(b_0 + wb_1)}.$$

24. When $\alpha_q > 0$, the constraint becomes nonlinear, which complicates matters. In certain cases, the problem can be written in aggregate quality $Q = nq$. In this case, if $b_1 = 0$, both n and Q are normal goods and hence increase in both y and w.

25. We restrict attention to linear child costs. Analyzing the robustness of our results to other child cost specifications would be of interest. There seems to be little consensus in the empirical literature on the shape of the child cost function, however. Empirical papers that estimate the costs of children and economies of scale in the household include Hotz and Miller (1988), Bernal (2008), Lazear and Michael (1980), and Espenshade (1984). Taking maternal health and maternal mortality risk into account, one might also want to argue that a convex cost function is the most reasonable formulation (e.g., Tertilt 2005).

As is apparent from this example, as long as the goods cost of children is positive ($b_0 > 0$) higher-wage households (higher w) will have strictly *more* children in this setup. This is the *opposite* prediction from what we observe in the data. Setting the goods cost to zero with just a time cost results in fertility choice being independent of w—still, not a negative relationship. Adding leisure or child quality (say, with $q = f(e) = e$) will not reverse this result (see section 2.5).

To give the price of time theory a chance, it seems fairly obvious that a deviation from log utility is needed; that is, a specification where income and substitution effects do not cancel out. Thus, we turn now to general Constant Elasticity of Substitution (CES) utility functions. Also, since a time cost is essential here and a goods cost does not really add anything, we set $b_0 = 0$ and assume $b_1 > 0$, but reintroduce nonlabor income, $y \geq 0$. Thus, our next example takes the form

$$(3) \qquad \max_{c,n} \quad \alpha_c \frac{c^{1-\sigma} - 1}{1 - \sigma} + \alpha_n \frac{n^{1-\sigma} - 1}{1 - \sigma}$$

$$\text{s. t.} \qquad c \leq y + w(1 - b_1 n).$$

It is easy to solve for a closed form solution of this specification. Optimal fertility is given by:

$$n^* = \frac{y/w + 1}{(\alpha_c b_1 / \alpha_n)^{1/\sigma} w^{(1-\sigma)/\sigma} + b_1}.$$

Elasticity of substitution: In problem (3) wage heterogeneity leads indeed to a negative wage-fertility relationship if the right amount of curvature is assumed in the utility function. To see this, assume first that $y = 0$. If the only way in which individuals differ is in their wages, we can see that when $\sigma \geq 1$, fertility is either independent of or increasing in w. However, when $\sigma < 1$, it follows that $n^*(w)$ is decreasing.

The intuition here is simple: when the only cost of children is time, and that time must be the parents' own time, higher wage families face a higher price of children. This induces the usual wealth and substitution effects familiar from demand theory. Certainly it implies that compensated demand for children is decreasing. This is not sufficient, however, to automatically imply that the demand for children is decreasing in income, since those families that face higher prices also have more wealth. Thus, it depends on which of the two forces is stronger. If the elasticity of substitution between children and consumption is high enough (low σ), the substitution effect dominates and $n^*(w)$ is decreasing, as in the data.

Moreover, it can be seen that this relationship is approximately isoelastic when y is small and w is large relative to b_1. In this example, the income elasticity of demand for children is $(\sigma - 1)/\sigma$.

In sum, this theory works, but not without extra restrictions on preferences. An additional requirement could be that the formulation be consistent with dynamic maximization in a setting with parental altruism à la Barro and Becker (1989) (i.e., parents care about number and utility of children multiplicatively). In the first section of the appendix we discuss the relationship between this static problem and a reinterpretation of it as the Bellman equation of a dynamic problem. The difficulty with the dynamic reinterpretation of the current example is that α_n is no longer a parameter but represents children's average level of utility. It therefore becomes a function of the wage. It turns out that once this is taken into account properly, fertility is independent of the wage independently of σ. Moreover, Jones and Schoonbroodt (Forthcoming) show that in this kind of model, $\sigma > 1$ is needed to generate the decreases in fertility observed over the past 200 years in response to increased productivity growth and decreased mortality. Hence, it seems that this dynamic interpretation of the static model presented here is at an impasse to get both the cross-sectional and trend features of fertility at the same time. In the first section of the appendix, we show that with preference heterogeneity, both the cross section as well as the trend observations can be generated.

Nonlabor Income: An alternative specification that also works is to assume log utility but positive nonlabor income. Assume $\sigma \to 1$ and $y > 0$, then the solution to (3) becomes

$$n^* = \frac{\alpha_n(y/w + 1)}{(\alpha_c + \alpha_n)b_1}.$$

Note that for $y > 0$, fertility is indeed decreasing in the wage.[26] Note that the slope of the relationship depends on the size of the nonlabor income. That is, for small amounts of nonlabor income fertility is decreasing in the wage only very mildly, and in the limit, when nonlabor income is zero, fertility does not depend on the wage at all.

Note, however, that the only income that would really qualify as nonlabor income here are gifts, lottery income, bequests, and the like.[27] Since most families have no or very little such nonlabor income, it is questionable whether this should be the main mechanism by which fertility and income are connected. Yet variations of this formulation are used a lot in the literature. For example, the refinement that it is *female* time that determines the opportunity cost falls into this category. In particular, sometimes y is interpreted as the husband's income and w as the wife's wage. Then fertility

---

26. Adding nonlabor income effectively changes the curvature of the utility function, and hence the technical reason that makes this example succeed is similar to the $\sigma < 1$ case shown previously. The interpretation, of course, is very different.

27. Any interest income from assets that are accumulated labor earnings would be proportional to labor income, and hence would not generate the result outlined here.

is decreasing in the latter. We will turn our attention to two-parent fertility models in section 2.6.

Nonhomothetic preferences: Another way to generate the desired relationship is to move away from homothetic utility.[28] Assume, for example, that $\sigma_c = 0$. Then the problem to solve is

(4)
$$\max_{c,n} \quad \alpha_c c + \alpha_n \frac{n^{1-\sigma} - 1}{1 - \sigma}$$

$$\text{s.t.} \quad c \leq (1 - b_1 n)w.$$

And the solution is:

$$n^* = \left[\frac{\alpha_n}{\alpha_c b_1} \right]^{1/\sigma} w^{-1/\sigma},$$

which is clearly decreasing in w for any value of σ.[29] We are not emphasizing nonhomothetic utilities any further, because one broader aim of the proposed research agenda here is to develop a theory that encompasses cross-sectional, trend, and cyclical features of fertility choice. Embedding this example into a fully dynamic growth model has the unfortunate property that income shares to consumption tend to one. Because of this these models would be of limited use.

2.4   Endogenous Wage Differences

In the previous section we focused on theories of the cross-sectional relationship between fertility and wages in which the fundamental difference was exogenous variation in ability (wages). In this section, we explore an alternative view with an alternative causation. Suppose that the basic source of heterogeneity is in tastes for children versus material goods—some people want large families and others want to travel the world, go to fancy restaurants, and drive a sports car. This basic difference in taste for either "lifestyle" affects the investment in human capital and hence, wages. That is, parents who want large families will allocate less time to developing market-based skills in anticipation of having many children, and will therefore have lower wages and lower earned income.

Rather than assuming people differ in their taste for children, one could simply assume that people differ exogenously in fertility and choose human capital investments accordingly. This kind of model also gets the basic relationship right, and is useful for understanding the basic mechanism. We

---

28. See, for example, Greenwood, Guner, and Knowles (2003).
29. This specification (with $\sigma \to 1$) is used in Fernandez, Guner, and Knowles (2005); Erosa, Fuster, and Restuccia (Forthcoming); and Erosa, Fuster, and Restuccia (2005). Note that the income elasticity of demand for children here is $-1/\sigma$, which is close to the data for $\sigma = 3.0$.

start with this simple version, even though the interpretation of exogenous fertility is not straightforward. We then move to a more general case that has a more plausible interpretation: deterministic heterogeneity in the taste for children versus consumption goods. Here schooling is chosen in anticipation of fertility decisions.

Finally, as long as raising children takes time, a simpler mechanism can be considered. Again assuming taste heterogeneity, parents who choose large families will have less time available to work and hence will have lower earned income, even if wages are exogenous. This simplification will be helpful in subsequent sections. Note that whenever the simple mechanism works and one can generate a negative fertility-*income* relationship, it is straightforward to also generate a negative fertility-*wage* relationship by adding endogenous human capital investments to the model.

2.4.1   Exogenous Fertility and Endogenous Wages

The simplest version illustrating the mechanism we want to focus on is one where fertility is exogenously different across people. Let $\bar{n}_i$ be the number of children that are attached to adult i. Each child requires b_1 units of parental time. The parent solves one lifetime maximization problem by choosing how much time (net of child-rearing time) to allocate to schooling versus earning wages. Even though we write this as a one-period problem, the decisions are best interpreted in a sequential fashion: time is first spent on schooling, l_s, which determines future human capital al_s. Normalizing the wage per unit of human capital to one, al_s is also the wage, so that total lifetime income simply becomes $wl_w = al_s l_w$. The problem then is:

(5)
$$\max_{c,l_w,l_s} \quad \alpha_c \frac{c^{1-\sigma}}{1-\sigma} + \alpha_n \frac{\bar{n}_i^{1-\sigma}}{1-\sigma}$$

$$\text{s. t.} \quad l_s + l_w \le 1 - b_1 \bar{n}_i$$

$$w = al_s$$

$$c \le wl_w.$$

The solution is

$$l_s^i = l_w^i = \frac{1 - b_1 \bar{n}_i}{2}.$$

It follows immediately that the wage is decreasing in fertility.

$$w_i = al_s^i = \frac{a}{2}(1 - b_1 \bar{n}_i).$$

Note that the derived negative relationship is quite robust; that is, it does not depend on specific functional forms or parameter restrictions. The only crucial assumption is that it takes time to raise children.

One interpretation of this example is that people are ex ante identical, but are exposed to stochastic fertility shocks (e.g., birth control failures). Then, ex post, people will have different fertility realizations, which leads them to optimally invest different amounts into human capital. However, for such shocks to be the main driving force behind the negative fertility-income relationship, it would need to be the case that most people know their fertility realizations *before* they make their human capital accumulation decisions. While this seems implausible for schooling decisions, it is more plausible for human capital that is accumulated on the job through experience. Exogenous fertility shocks may also be important for some margins, such as drop-out decisions for girls who become pregnant in high school.

2.4.2   Endogenous Fertility and Endogenous Wages

Next, we extend the basic intuition given before to allow for both the choice of fertility and the endogenous determination of wages. Assume now that parents differ in their preferences for children; that is, some people value children more than others. To do this, we add a fertility choice to problem (5) and allow for preference heterogeneity. We also generalize the model along two other dimensions, which will turn out to be useful later on. First, following Ben-Porath (1976) and Heckman (1976), we allow for decreasing returns in the human capital accumulation process: $w = al_s^{v_s}$, $v_s \in (0, 1]$. Second, we allow for decreasing returns when working. That is, an individual working l_w units (hours/weeks/years) will earn a total income of $wl_w^{v_w}$, $v_w \in (0, 1]$. While this formulation is nonstandard (i.e., most of the literature assumes that income is linear in hours worked), we find it quite plausible since many jobs pay a premium for full-time work. Note also that setting $v_w = 1$ gives the standard model in which income is the product of an hourly wage and hours worked. The modified problem then is

$$(6) \qquad \max_{c,n,l_w,l_s} \quad \alpha_c \frac{c^{1-\sigma}}{1-\sigma} + \alpha_n \frac{n^{1-\sigma}}{1-\sigma}$$

$$\text{s. t.} \qquad l_s + l_w \le 1 - b_1 n$$

$$w = al_s^{v_s}$$

$$c \le wl_w^{v_w}.$$

The first-order conditions are:

$$l_s: \qquad \alpha c(al_s^{v_s}l_w^{v_w})^{-\sigma}av_s l_s^{v_s-1}l_w^{v_w} = \alpha_n \left(\frac{1-l_s-l_w}{b_1}\right)^{-\sigma}\frac{1}{b_1}$$

$$l_w: \qquad \alpha c(al_s^{v_s}l_w^{v_w})^{-\sigma}av_w l_s^{v_s}l_w^{v_w-1} = \alpha_n \left(\frac{1-l_s-l_w}{b_1}\right)^{-\sigma}\frac{1}{b_1}.$$

It follows immediately that $l_s = (v_s/v_w)l_w$. Using this, the optimal amount of work solves the following equation

$$\alpha_c a^{1-\sigma} v_s \left(\frac{v_s}{v_w}\right)^{v_s-1-v_s\sigma} l_w^{-(v_s+v_w)\sigma+v_s+v_w-1} = \alpha_n \left(\frac{1}{b_1}\right)^{1-\sigma} \left(1 - \frac{v_s+v_w}{v_w} l_w\right)^{-\sigma}.$$

It is easy to derive closed form solutions for two special cases: (a) constant returns to scale ($v_w + v_s = 1$) and a general σ; and (b) general production function, but assuming log utility $\sigma = 1$.[30] The solution for case (b) is

$$l_w^* = \frac{\alpha_c v_w}{\alpha_n + (v_s + v_w)\alpha_c}$$

$$l_s^* = \frac{\alpha_c v_s}{\alpha_n + (v_s + v_w)\alpha_c}$$

$$n^* = \frac{1}{b_1}\left(\frac{\alpha_n}{\alpha_n + (v_s + v_w)\alpha_c}\right).$$

Note that the wage rate is

$$w^* = a(l_s^*)^{v_s},$$

which increases monotonically in time spent at school. Taking derivatives with respect to the child preference parameters, α_n, gives

$$\frac{\partial n^*}{\partial \alpha_n} = \frac{(v_s + v_w)\alpha_c}{b_1[\alpha_n + (v_s + v_w)\alpha_c]^2} > 0$$

$$\frac{\partial l_s^*}{\partial \alpha_n} = \frac{-\alpha_c v_s}{[\alpha_n + (v_s + v_w)\alpha_c]^2} < 0.$$

Thus, clearly, people who have a higher preference for children will have both—more children and a lower wage.

As can be seen from these expressions, fertility is independent of the raw learning ability, a. That is, without differences in preferences, parents will all have the same fertility.[31]

There are a couple of special cases where the implicit relationship between fertility and wages can be solved for explicitly.

In addition to $\sigma = 1$, now assume that $v_w = v_s = 1$: human capital is linear in years of schooling, and total income is simply the wage multiplied time spent working. For this case, we can substitute out all preference parameters to derive an equilibrium relationship between wage and fertility that will hold across all consumers (i.e., independent of their individual α_n and α_c):

$$n^* = \frac{1}{b_1}\left(1 - \frac{2}{a}w^*\right).$$

In this case, it follows that fertility is linearly decreasing in wages.

---

30. We analyze case (a) with dynastic altruism in the second section of the appendix.
31. Of course, if in addition one assumes that $\sigma < 1$, then fertility decreases in a for the same reasons as in section 2.3.2.

A second case that admits a straightforward closed form solution is when $v_s = v_w$. Then, the relationship can be written as:

$$n^* = \frac{1}{b_1}\left(1 - 2\left(\frac{w^*}{a}\right)^{1/v_s}\right).$$

In this case the relationship between the wage and fertility is nonlinear, with its curvature determined by the parameter v_s.

In sum, this direction of causation generates the negative income-fertility and wage-fertility relationships under fairly general assumptions. In the second section of the appendix, we add parental altruism to this model. Similar results go through.

2.4.3   An Aside on Wages vs. Income

Here we have focused on the cross-sectional relationship between wages and fertility when the basic heterogeneity is differences, across people, in preferences for children vis-à-vis consumption goods. To do this we need a model in which wages themselves are endogenous. An alternative, weaker version of a similar property can be derived without explicitly including human capital formation in the model. This involves the relationship between fertility and income. For simplicity, assume that all households have the same w. Recall the solution to problem (3).

$$n^* = \frac{(y/w) + 1}{(\alpha_c b_1/\alpha_n)^{1/\sigma}w^{(1-\sigma)/\sigma} + b_1},$$

and consider two families that differ only in their values of α_n and/or α_c. As we can see, the family with the higher α_n will have more children for any value of σ and y. It also follows that this family will have lower earned income, $I = [1 - b_1 n^*(\alpha_n, \alpha_c)]w$, simply because it will spend more time raising children and less time working. Thus, preference heterogeneity of this type will also generate a negative correlation between fertility and earned income, without further assumptions on elasticities, or the formation of human capital, as long as children take parental time.

2.4.4   Empirical Evidence and Related Work

Empirical papers have confirmed the mechanism emerging from section 2.4.1 in the data, though most research (with the exception of Angrist and Evans [1998]) focuses on its importance for female wages, or income, and has little to say about the relationship between male income and fertility as shown in figure 2.1.[32] Similarly, the structural microeconomics literature, as well as some authors in the macroeconomics literature, also primarily focuses

---

32. Nor do they say much about most of the time period we are discussing, in which few women were earning market wages. In addition, good data for IV estimation (on twins, for example) has only become available recently.

on female wages. These papers address the mechanism emerging from section 2.4.2, though not in isolation. We review these results following.

Empirical Evidence

There is a large statistical literature that tries to assess the effect of (exogenous) fertility variation on labor supply, experience accumulation, and wages and/or earned income (see Browning [1992] for an early review). Mincer and Polachek (1974) find that work interruptions for childbearing have led to large human capital depreciations. Mincer and Ofek (1982) find that longer interruptions cause larger human capital losses. While there is a large and rapid increase in wages upon reentry, full earnings potential is not regained after interruption and reentry. These findings suggest that children have a lasting effect on income through forgone experience, which is a specific type of human capital accumulation.[33]

These papers view the number of children as exogenous. More recent research has focused on identifying valid instruments for fertility, such as miscarriages and unwanted pregnancies. For example, Miller (Forthcoming) finds that an exogenous *delay* in childbirth leads to a substantial increase in earnings, wage rates, and hours worked. She finds evidence for both fixed wage penalties and lower returns to experience for mothers. Since delay in fertility is typically associated with lower completed fertility, this result suggests that the number of children may have a strong effect on human capital accumulation of various types.

While all the papers mentioned so far focus on female earnings and leave father's and family income aside, Angrist and Evans (1998) use instrumental variable (IV) estimation to look at both parents' labor supply and labor income as well as family income. They look at families with two children and use the gender composition of the existing children as an instrument for the desire to have a third child. The authors find that families with a stronger desire for a third child work less and earn less. This is true for wives alone, husbands alone, and family income.[34] Unfortunately, nothing is said about hourly wages. Note that income is measured *before* the family actually has the third child. The fact that income is already lower prior to childbirth is in line with the aforementioned theory: people who want to have more children (i.e., higher α_n) anticipate working less in the future, and thus have a weaker incentive to accumulate human capital through experience.

33. Mincer and Polachek (1974) go on to answer the question: "Do family size and number of children currently present affect the accumulation of earning power beyond the effect on work experience? The answer is largely negative: when numbers of children and some measures of their age are added to work histories in the [regression] equations, the children variables are negative but usually not significant statistically" (S 95).

34. Their instrument is based on the following observation. Families with two children of the same sex are more likely to have a third child because sex mix is presumably preferred. Since gender of children is exogenous, the willingness to bear a third child—in the hope for the opposite sex—is also largely exogenous.

Related Theory

As for the mechanism in section 2.4.2 with endogenous fertility, the structural microeconomics literature on joint fertility and female labor supply choices also use preference heterogeneity to generate a distribution of fertility and wages as observed in the data. Again, the focus is on *female* labor supply, experience, schooling, and wages or earnings, while our mechanism is meant to address men (see figure 2.1) as well as women (see section 2.6 for details). Furthermore, permanent taste is typically not the only source of heterogeneity in these papers. Fixed and stochastic ability heterogeneity, as well as preference shocks over the life cycle, are additional necessary ingredients to fit the data. Francesconi (2002) estimates such a combined model with part-time and full-time employment. In a similar framework, Del Boca and Sauer (2009) analyze the effects of institutions on fertility, timing, and labor supply decisions. Finally, Keane and Wolpin (2006) add schooling and marriage decisions to estimate the effects of welfare programs on fertility and female labor supply.[35] All these papers use some version of the mechanism described here, though not in isolation. Our aim is to contrast pure taste and pure ability heterogeneity. In reality, of course, both may be relevant.

Finally, this mechanism is also sometimes used in the macroeconomics literature. For example, Erosa, Fuster, and Restuccia (Forthcoming) have stochastic fertility opportunities and stochastic values of children, together with learning-by-doing on the job, so that higher fertility translates into lower wages.[36] Again, male investment decisions are assumed not to be affected by fertility preferences and realizations. A similar mechanism is also at work in Erosa, Fuster, and Restuccia (2005) and Knowles (2007).[37]

2.4.5   Outlook

While the empirical evidence seems to support the idea that heterogeneity in tastes for children is to some extent responsible for the observed negative fertility-income relationship, this mechanism has received far less attention in the theoretical literature. Rather, most research starts with the assumption that exogenous differences in income (or ability) cause fertility to vary systematically across the income distribution. We therefore address

35. This literature is based on a combination of two basic models: Eckstein and Wolpin (1989), who analyze female labor force participation and experience accumulation with exogenous fertility heterogeneity, and Hotz and Miller (1988), who analyze contraceptive effort with taste heterogeneity, thereby endogenizing fertility but abstracting from labor supply and human capital accumulation of any kind.

36. Although, this is not the only channel through which fertility and income are related in their model.

37. Attanasio, Low, and Sanchez-Marcos (2008) analyze a similar model to Eckstein and Wolpin (1989) with exogenous fertility and endogenous experience to account for the increase in female labor force participation across cohorts.

the preference channel in all subsequent sections. Recall from section 2.4.3 that a simpler version of the mechanism can be used to derive a negative fertility-income relationship. For tractability, we use this shortcut when we analyze preference heterogeneity in sections 2.5 and 2.6. However, in all cases, the model can easily be extended to human capital accumulation and wages. We reintroduce endogenous wages in section 2.7, where we present an example in which parental time is not essential and in the appendix, where we build the dynastic analog of problem (6).

2.5 Quantity-Quality Theory

In this section, we revisit the idea that the demand for child quality naturally leads richer parents to want more quality and thus less quantity, what is often called the quantity-quality hypothesis.[38] This idea turns out not to be a very robust theory of the negative fertility-income hypothesis.

In his seminal work, Becker (1960) argued that there is a trade-off between quantity and quality of children. Originally, however, Becker did not propose the quantity-quality trade-off as an explanation for why fertility and income were negatively correlated. Indeed, in the 1960 paper Becker argues, by analogy with other durable goods, that economic theory suggests that fertility and income should be positively related, but perhaps only weakly so, while quality of children and income should be strongly positively correlated. The intuition for Becker's argument is simple. While richer parents do spend more on their children (better schools, better clothes, higher bequests, etc.), richer people spend more on everything. They have higher quality houses and cars as well, yet no one would argue that we should expect rich people to have fewer houses than poor people. As a first cut, the same logic should apply to children: richer people would want more quality, but probably not less quantity, the same way they also would not want better but fewer cars.

So what makes children different? Hotz, Klerman, and Willis (1993),

38. Empirical evidence about the quantity-quality trade-off is mixed (see Schultz [2005] for a useful summary). While the negative relationship between family size and various measures of child quality—in terms of investments or outcomes—is clearly negative, it is controversial whether this is a causal relationship. In particular, when using twin births as exogenous fertility variations, researchers have not always found a negative effect on these quality investments or outcomes of children. One regularity seems to carry through most studies, however: the negative relationship between number and quality of children is more strongly negative in developing countries (e.g., Rosenzweig and Wolpin (1980) for India; Li, Zhang, and Zhu (2008) for rural China) than it is in more advanced societies (e.g., Angrist, Lavy, and Schlosser (forthcoming) for Israel; Black, Devereux, and Salvanes (2005) for Norway). Yet Cáceres-Delpiano (2006) finds that a twin on a later birth reduces the likelihood that older children attend private school in U.S. Census data from 1980. One reason for the discrepancies between rich and poor countries might be the availability of high quality public schools in developed countries. For example, De la Croix and Doepke (2009) find that the effect of income on household choices, in terms of fertility and private schooling, diminishes as the quality of public schooling goes up.

reviewing Becker's arguments, seem to emphasize that what might be the case is that not children per se are normal goods, but that expenditures on children are: "If children are normal goods in the sense that total expenditures on children are an increasing function of income, then the sum of the income elasticities of the number and quality of children must be positive [. . .], but it is still possible that the income elasticity of demand for the number of children is negative [. . .] if the income elasticity of quality is large enough" (295). This is not our reading of the paper. Our reading is that, by analogy, quantity should be slightly increasing in income and quality should be greatly increasing in income. Becker's argument is, then, that the observation of a negative relationship is a missing variables problem, namely knowledge about contraceptives. Becker and Lewis (1973) and Becker and Tomes (1976) were important follow-ups on Becker (1960). Becker and Lewis (1973) argue that, once income is measured correctly, the true fertility-income elasticity is positive, even if the observed one is negative. Becker and Tomes (1976) argue that the quality production function has an endowment component that generates a negative correlation between fertility and income.

Following, we derive conditions under which simple examples including child quality can generate this negative correlation without making children inferior goods. We start with the simplest specification of the example in section 2.3 with log utility and a linear quality production function. In this example, it becomes apparent that even with quality choice and ability heterogeneity, we need a positive time cost and zero goods costs for fertility to be nonincreasing in income. Next, we derive the requirements on the quality production function for fertility to be strictly decreasing in wages—under both wage and taste heterogeneity. One example that generates the desired relation is an affine production function with a positive constant, as in Becker and Tomes (1976), together with the assumption that children take time while child quality requires purchased inputs as in Moav (2005). Various interpretations of this specification can be used to accommodate the cross section of fertility with respect to income and the trend in fertility over time. Finally, under preference heterogeneity, none of these requirements on the quality production function are needed.

2.5.1   A Simple Example

First, we show by example that including a quality choice in and of itself does not necessarily lead to a negative relationship between fertility and income. That is, including quality does *not* necessarily lead richer people to want fewer children. They might want more quality and accordingly, a smaller increase in number of children—as argued in Becker (1960)—but the relationship between fertility and income is still positive.

Suppose $U(c, n, q) = \alpha_c \log c + \alpha_n \log n + \alpha_q \log q$, $\alpha_q > 0$, $q = f(s) = s$ and $y = 0$. Then the problem from section 2.3 is:

$$\max_{c,n,q,s,l_w} \quad \alpha_c \log c + \alpha_n \log n + \alpha_q \log q$$

$$\text{s. t.} \quad l_w + b_1 n \leq 1$$

$$c + (b_0 + s)n \leq wl_w$$

$$q \leq s.$$

This is a version of the problem considered in Becker and Lewis (1973), while Becker (1960) assumed $b_0 = b_1 = 0$. The constraint set in this problem is not convex because of the term ns. We therefore rewrite the problem in terms of total quality, $Q = qn$.[39] We also know that the constraints hold with equality. Using this, the problem becomes:

$$\max_{c,n,Q} \quad \alpha_c \log c + (\alpha_n - \alpha_q) \log n + \alpha_q \log Q$$

$$\text{s. t.} \quad c + b_0 n + Q \leq w(1 - b_1 n).$$

This is now a standard problem under the assumption that $\alpha_n > \alpha_q$. The solution is given by:

$$n^* = \frac{\alpha_n - \alpha_q}{(\alpha_c + \alpha_n)(b_0 + b_1 w)} w$$

$$q^* = \frac{\alpha_q(b_0 + b_1 w)}{\alpha_n - \alpha_q}$$

$$c^* = \frac{\alpha_c}{\alpha_c + \alpha_n} w.$$

Similar to what we found in the example in section 2.3.2, as long as the goods cost is positive ($b_0 > 0$), fertility is strictly increasing in the wage, w.[40] On the other hand, if $b_0 = 0$, fertility is independent of w, while earned income is $I = w(1 - b_1 n^*)$. Again, this does not give a negative relationship between income and fertility since there is no heterogeneity in fertility choice. Instead, we get an extreme version of Becker's original argument. That is, if there is only a time cost of children, $b_0 = 0$, then we have high income elasticity of quality per child (q is strictly increasing in w and hence I) and low income elasticity of number of children (n is independent of w or I).[41]

---

39. Rosenzweig and Wolpin (1980) write a model with $b_1 = 0$, but a children-independent price of quality. If this price is strictly positive, our formulation cannot be used.

40. Whether earned income, $I = (1 - b_1 n)w$, increases or decreases depends on the size of the increase in n in response to an increase in w. In the present example, we have:

$$\frac{dI}{dw} = (1 - b_1 n) - b_1 w \frac{dn}{dw} = \frac{(\alpha_c + \alpha_q)(b_0 + b_1 w)^2 + (\alpha_n - \alpha_q)b_0^2}{(\alpha_c + \alpha_n)(b_0 + b_1 w)^2} > 0.$$

Thus, in this case, income and fertility are positively related.

41. It is useful to note that the time intensity in the cost of children matters (the relative size of b_0 and b_1) for the size of these effects. Also, similarly to the cost of time theory, one could vary the elasticity of substitution in the utility function. We leave this part to the reader.

There are at least two ways in which this "negative result" can be overturned. First, keeping wage heterogeneity, the quality production function can be generalized. Second, one can consider preference heterogeneity instead of ability heterogeneity in this simple example. We consider these two avenues in turn following.[42]

2.5.2   The Quality Production Function

The next example is based on the analysis in Moav (2005), who argued that producing children takes time, while educating each child requires goods costs. This assumption makes quality relatively cheaper for higher wage people and one might expect a quantity-quality trade-off to result. However, the comparative advantage alone does not imply that higher wage people have fewer children, as we have seen before. The properties of the human capital production function are also a crucial ingredient, as noted in Moav (2005).

We make the same assumptions as before, except that we let $q = f(s)$ be unspecified for now. The maximization problem is given by:

(7)
$$\max_{c,n,q,s} \quad \alpha_c \log c + \alpha_n \log n + \alpha_q \log q$$

$$\text{s. t.} \quad c + b_0 n + sn \le w(1 - b_1 n)$$

$$q = f(s).$$

The first order conditions give

(8)
$$\frac{sf'(s)}{f(s)} = \frac{\alpha_n}{\alpha_q} \left(\frac{s/w}{b_0/w + b_1 + s/w} \right)$$

(9)
$$n^* = \left(\frac{\alpha_n}{\alpha_c + \alpha_n} \right) \frac{1}{b_0/w + b_1 + s^*/w}.$$

Let the elasticity on the left-hand side of equation (8) be $\eta(s) \equiv sf'(s)/f(s)$.[43]

---

42. We have also explored a third channel—nonseparable preferences—to a limited degree (cf. Jones and Schoonbroodt, Forthcoming). For example, assume $q = s$ and solve:

$$\max_{\{c,n,q\}} \quad \alpha_c \log c + \log [[(\alpha_n - \alpha_q)n^\rho + \alpha_q(nq)^\rho]^{1/\rho}]$$

$$\text{s. t.} \quad c + (b_0 + b_1 w)n + nq \le w.$$

In this case, if $\rho \in (0, 1)$ then n and $Q = nq$ are substitutes in utility and fertility is decreasing in w, while the opposite is true if $\rho < 0$. In the text, we are implicitly assuming the case where $\rho \to 0$. The substitutes case works because number of children is time intensive and hence more costly to high wage parents while the price of quality is the same across people. Another way of generating a negative income-fertility relationship through a quantity-quality trade-off is to assume that the educational choice is indivisible: the choice is between skilled and unskilled children. This mechanism was used in Doepke (2004). In this case, low ability people would choose (some) unskilled children and have more of them than high ability people who have skilled children. Among the latter group, however, fertility will be increasing in ability again.

43. Note that unless $f(s) = s^\lambda$ for some $\lambda > 0$, this formulation is very similar to the nonhomothetic preference example given in section 2.3 since we can rewrite the utility function as $\alpha_c \log c + \alpha_n \log n + \alpha_q \log f(s)$.

Ability Heterogeneity

Suppose that households differ in their abilities, w. In the case where $b_0 = 0$, we can see from equation (9) that for n^* to be a decreasing function in w, s^*/w needs to be increasing in w. But the right-hand side of (8) is increasing in this ratio. Thus, the left-hand side has to be increasing as well. Hence, we need that $\eta'(s) > 0$, which is purely a property of $f(s)$. An example of a human capital production function that satisfies this property was first introduced by Becker and Tomes (1976):[44]

$$f(s) = d_0 + d_1 s, \qquad d_0 > 0, d_1 > 0.$$

In this case, the solution is:

$$s^* = \frac{(\alpha_q/\alpha_n)b_1 w - d_0/d_1}{(1 - \alpha_q/\alpha_n)},$$

which is well-defined as long as $\alpha_q < \alpha_n$ and d_0 is small enough; that is, $d_0 < d_1(\alpha_q/\alpha_n)b_1 w$.[45] Solving for n^* gives

$$n^* = \frac{(\alpha_n - \alpha_q)/(\alpha_c + \alpha_n)}{b_1 - d_0/wd_1}.$$

From this it is clear that $\partial n^*/\partial w < 0$.

Finally, notice that this example still requires a time cost. In fact, in the case with $b_0 > 0$, the solution is given by:

$$s^* = \frac{(\alpha_q/\alpha_n)(b_0 + b_1 w) - d_0/d_1}{(1 - \alpha_q/\alpha_n)},$$

which is well-defined as long as

(10) $\qquad \alpha_q < \alpha_n \qquad$ and $\qquad \dfrac{\alpha_q}{\alpha_n}(b_0 + b_1 w) > \dfrac{d_0}{d_1}.$

Solving for n^* gives

$$n^* = \frac{(\alpha_n - \alpha_q)/(\alpha_c + \alpha_n)}{b_1 + b_0/w - d_0/wd_1}.$$

Hence, fertility is decreasing in w if and only if

(11) $\qquad \dfrac{d_0}{d_1} > b_0.$

In the case where $b_1 = 0$, conditions (10) and (11) are mutually exclusive.

44. De la Croix and Doepke (2003, 2004) use a more complex production function that allows quality to depend on parental human capital, but overall has similar properties: $f(s, w) = d_1(d_0 + s)^\gamma w^\tau$, where $\gamma, \tau \in (0, 1)$ are parameters. Examples of production functions that do *not* satisfy the condition include $f(s) = s^a$ and $f(s) = as$, which lead to a constant s^*/w, and $f(s) = \log(s)$ and $f(s) = \exp(as)$, which lead to decreasing s^*/w.
45. Otherwise $s = 0$ is the solution.

Interpretation and Further Predictions of the Model

Becker and Tomes (1976) interpret d_0 as an endowment of child quality, or "innate ability." In this interpretation, one might want to take intergenerational persistence in ability into account. If the child's quality endowment and parent's ability, w, are positively correlated in the sense that $E(d_0) = w$, then fertility is, again, independent of w while quality is still increasing in w. An alternative would be that in those families in which parents have higher market wages, the marginal value of education is higher—d_1 is perfectly positively correlated with w. For example, assume that $d_1 = \kappa w$. Then even if innate ability, d_0, is perfectly correlated with w, fertility is still decreasing while education is increasing in w. This educational investment does not require time per se. Instead, for a given amount of goods, the high ability parent produces more quality.

An alternative interpretation of d_0 is publicly-provided schooling. Since this has increased over time, we see that the predicted response is that fertility will increase, at least holding w fixed. In contrast, holding d_0 fixed, an increase in income over time would cause fertility to decrease. Hence, under this interpretation the example suggests that the increase in income was more important than the increase in publicly-provided schooling.[46]

Preference Heterogeneity

Next, assume that w is the same for all households, but suppose that people differ in their preference for the consumption good, α_c. In all the previous examples, the more people like the consumption good, the fewer children they will have and, as long as $b_1 > 0$, the more income they will earn. However, the quality choice, q, is independent of α_c and hence income, I.

If, on the other hand, we consider heterogeneity in the preference for children, α_n, we see that the more people like children, n (relative to both consumption, c, and quality, q), the more they will have, the less income they will earn, and the less quality investments they make per child. Thus, in this case, fertility and income are still negatively related, while quality per child will be positively related with income.

Note that this does not depend on any particular assumption about goods costs or the quality production function. As usual, however, a positive time cost is required so that earned income, I, is decreasing in number of children, n, which generates the negative correlation.[47]

---

46. See the conclusion for suggestive simulations of such changes over time.
47. Pushing the idea of preference heterogeneity one step further, Galor and Moav (2002) argue that the forces of natural selection selected individual preferences that are culturally or genetically predisposed toward investment in child quality, bringing about a demographic transition.

2.6   Married Couples and the Female Time Allocation Hypothesis

A refinement of the price of time theory of fertility is to view the decision-making unit as a married couple and to explicitly distinguish between the time of the wife and the husband. In this version, since it is typically the case that most child care responsibility rests with the woman, it is the time of the wife that is critical to the fertility decision.[48] In its simplest form, the idea is that the price of children is higher for high productivity couples, even if only the husband works.[49]

The aim of this section is threefold. First, we test how robust the results derived in previous sections are to introducing women explicitly. In particular, we ask whether the same restrictions on parameters are necessary to generate a negative fertility-relationship when the division of labor within couples is taken into account. Second, we move to more general formulations that model home production explicitly, examining the restrictions needed on the home production technology under log utility (in the spirit of Willis [1973]). Third, we show that specific patterns of assortative mating are needed to match the data. A richer model also necessitates a more nuanced look at the data. The findings in the empirical literature can be summarized as the following three findings:

1. The correlation between fertility and wife's wage (or productivity). Evidence suggests that this correlation is strongly negative whether controlling for the husband's wage or not.

2. The conditional correlation between fertility and husband's wage, holding the wife's wage constant. Evidence here is very mixed (e.g., Blau and van der Klaauw [2007] find it is strongly positive, Jones and Tertilt [2008] find it is negative, and Schultz [1986] finds that it depends on the exact subgroup of the population one considers; see following).

3. The unconditional correlation between fertility and husband's wage. Evidence suggests that this correlation is strongly negative in the data.

---

48. A related idea was first formalized in Willis (1973), who studied the time allocation problem for a couple in which the time of both the husband and wife are used in raising children while consumption is produced using the time of the wife and market-purchased goods.

49. In the words of Hotz, Klerman, and Willis (1993): "A second major reason for a negative relationship between income and fertility, in addition to quality-quantity interaction, is the hypothesis that higher income is associated with a higher cost of female time, either because of increased female wage rates or because higher household income raises the value of female time in nonmarket activities. Given the assumption that childrearing is a relatively time intensive activity, especially for mothers, the opportunity cost of children tends to increase relative to other sources of satisfaction not related to children, leading to a substitution effect against children. As noted earlier, the cost of time hypothesis was first advanced by Mincer (1963) and, following Becker's (1965) development of the household production model, the relationship between fertility and female labor supply has become a standard feature of models of household behavior" (298–99).

We show that simple examples imply that fertility should be decreasing in the productivity or wage of the wife (1) and (weakly) increasing in the wage of the husband (2). Because of this theoretical result, much of the empirical literature has taken the stand that the negative estimated correlation between income of the husband and fertility (3) is contaminated by a missing variables problem—the productivity of the wife. Since productivities or wages within couples are typically positively correlated, a downward bias (perhaps enough to change the sign) is induced on the true effect of husband's income on fertility. One might think that this effect is large enough, in theory, that any restrictions on the form of preferences, and so forth, are no longer necessary. This is not what we find in the following examples. Rather, we find that specific assumptions on elasticity, the home production function, and assortative mating (either in terms of productivities or preferences) are still required to generate facts (1) and (3).[50] We summarize those combinations of assumptions that successfully generate facts (1) and (3) in table 2A.1 in the appendix.

2.6.1   Empirical Findings

Testing predictions (1) and (2) in the data is complicated because of the difficulty in obtaining direct measures of the value of the wife's time. Until recently many wives did not work and even now, those that do are a "selected" sample. Hence, other proxies must be used, such as inferred productivities based on a Mincer regression or education. The evidence on (1) and (3) are quite robust while evidence on (2) is mixed. Following is a summary of the findings of three recent studies.

Schultz (1986) estimates a reduced-form fertility equation based on his household demand framework:[51]

$$n_i = \beta_0 + \beta_1 \ln w_{fi} + \beta_2 w_{mi} + \beta y_i + \varepsilon_i,$$

where n is the number of children, w_f and w_m are female and male wages, respectively, y is asset income, and ε is an error term. This equation is estimated separately for different age and race groups. The data are from the 1967 Survey of Economic Opportunities, an augmented version of the Current Population Survey. He finds that

[I]n every age and race regression the wife's wage is negatively associated with fertility. The coefficient on the husband's predicted wages changes sign over the life cycle, adding to the number of children ever born for

---

50. Given the mixed evidence on fact (2), we do not focus too much on the model prediction for fact (2).

51. Schultz (1986, 91) also says: "Empirical studies of fertility that have sought to estimate the distinctive effects of the wage opportunities for men and women generally find β_1 to be negative, while β_2 tends to be negative in high-income urban populations and frequently positive in low-income agricultural populations (Schultz (1981))."

younger wives [. . .] but contributing to lower fertility among older wives. [. . .] For white wives over age 35 and for black wives aged 35–54, a higher predicted husband's wage is significantly associated with lower completed fertility. The elasticities of fertility with respect to the wage rates of wives and husbands are of similar magnitude for blacks and whites, although for blacks the level of fertility is higher and wage levels are lower. [. . .] These estimates give credence to the hypothesis that children are time-intensive. In all age and race regressions the sum of the coefficients on the wife's and husband's wage rates is negative and increases generally for older age groups. [. . .] The hypothesis that children are more female than male time-intensive is also consistent with these estimates. (Table 1, 93)

Using National Longitudinal Survey of Youth (NLSY) longitudinal data for women born between 1957 and 1964, Blau and van der Klaauw (2007) find that

[A] one standard deviation increase in the male wage rate is estimated to have some fairly large effects on white women, but none of the underlying coefficient estimates are significantly different from zero. Several of the black and Hispanic interactions are statistically significant, however, and the simulated effects are in some cases quite large. A higher male wage rate increases the number of children ever born to black women by 0.169. . . . For Hispanic women, a higher male wage rate [also] increases fertility. . . . [A] higher female wage rate generally has effects that are of the opposite sign from those of the male wage rate. As with the male wage rate, the effects are not significantly different from zero for whites, but for blacks and Hispanics a higher female wage rate has negative effects on fertility that are significantly different from zero. Children ever born decline by about 0.1 for blacks and Hispanics. (29–30)

Jones and Tertilt (2008) also experiment with this hypothesis. Since very few women worked in the early cohorts, education is chosen as a measure of potential income. They find that children ever born (CEB) is declining in both the education level of the wife and the husband, and significantly so. Moreover, the coefficients on husband's and wife's education are similar in size (the wife's being slightly larger) and there is no systematic time trend.

2.6.2 Theory

It is convenient to break this variant of the story into two separate parts: one in which the woman does not work in the market, and one in which she can and does. Roughly, we can think of the first version as corresponding to a time in history when very few married women participated in the formal labor market. The second corresponds to more recent history. It is clear that the critical features necessary to reproduce the observations must be different in the two cases. We summarize all models that are consistent with the facts in table 2A.1 in the appendix.

Full Specialization in the Household

In this example, the husband works in the market, l_m, earning wage, w_m, or enjoys leisure, ℓ_m, while the wife works only in the home, l_{hf}, so that her trade-off is between how much time to allocate to producing home goods versus raising children, $b_1 n$, or enjoying leisure, ℓ_f. Her productivity in home production is denoted w_f. This setup may be more relevant to the early period in the data when (married) women's labor force participation was roughly zero.

The gender-specific utility function is given by

$$U_g = \alpha_{cg} \log(c_g) + \alpha_{ng} \log(n) + \alpha_{\ell g} \log(\ell_g) + \alpha_{hg} \log(c_{hg}),$$

where $g = f, m$ indicates gender, c_g is market consumption, n is the number of children, ℓ is leisure, and c_{hg} is the home good. Note that only the husband's leisure is needed for some of the following results. That is, $\alpha_{\ell f}$ could be zero, while the husband needs an alternative use of time to generate any endogenous wage/income heterogeneity for the husband. Given our previous results, we assume that children cost only time (i.e., $b_0 = 0$).

We assume that there is unitary decision making in the household. The family solves the problem:

(12)
$$\max_{\{c_m, c_f, c_{hm}, c_{hf}, n, \ell_m, \ell_f, l_m, l_{hf}\}} \lambda_f U_f + \lambda_m U_m$$

$$\text{s. t.} \quad c_f + c_m \leq w_m l_m$$

$$l_m + \ell_m \leq 1$$

$$c_{hf} + c_{hm} \leq w_f l_{hf}$$

$$l_{hf} + \ell_f + b_1 n \leq 1.$$

Here ℓ_f and ℓ_m are leisure of the female and male respectively, w_m is the wage of the man, w_f is the productivity of the woman in home production, and c_{hf} and c_{hm} are consumption of home goods by the woman and the man, respectively. Note that it is assumed that the wife spends b_1 hours for each child being raised (and the husband spends none). To keep it simple, assume perfect agreement of couples: assume $\alpha_{xf} = \alpha_{xm} = \alpha_x$ for $x = c, h, n, \ell$. Further, without loss of generality, assume $\lambda_f + \lambda_m = 1$ and $\alpha_c + \alpha_n + \alpha_\ell + \alpha_h = 1$.

This problem separates into two maximization problems, one concerning the allocation of the man's time and one concerning the allocation of the woman's time. The one for the man is straightforward and does not involve fertility. Notice however, that male earnings are increasing in α_c since leisure becomes less desirable relative to consumption. The problem for the woman's time allocation is:

$$\max_{\{c_{hm}, c_{hf}, n, \ell_f\}} \lambda_f \alpha_\ell \log(\ell_f) + \lambda_f \alpha_h \log(c_{hf}) + \lambda_m \alpha_h \log(c_{hm}) + (\lambda_f + \lambda_m)\alpha_n \log(n)$$

$$\text{s. t.} \quad b_1 w_f n + c_{hf} + c_{hm} + \ell_f \leq w_f.$$

The solution is:

(13) $$n^* = \frac{\alpha_n}{\lambda_f \alpha_\ell + \alpha_h + \alpha_n} \frac{1}{b_1}.$$

Ability Heterogeneity, Elasticity, and the Home Production Function   Suppose households differ in their productivities, (w_f, w_m). We see that n^* is independent of woman's productivity in the home. If education is a good proxy for female home productivity, then the evidence in Jones and Tertilt (2008) contradicts this model implication. That is, this model is not consistent with fact (1).[52] Fertility is also independent of w_m, holding w_f fixed. Finally, even if the productivity of the husband and wife are positively correlated (or independent), fertility is independent of both productivities. Thus, fact (3) is not predicted here either.[53] Clearly, something is missing in the theory.

As can be seen from the previous, since the couple's problem splits into two separate maximization problems, and the one for the wife's time looks just like those discussed in section 2.3 (additional goods permitting), the natural next step is to analyze a more general version in which utility is given by:

$$U_g = \alpha_c \frac{c_g^{1-\sigma}}{1-\sigma} + \alpha_n \frac{n^{1-\sigma}}{1-\sigma} + \alpha_\ell \frac{\ell_g^{1-\sigma}}{1-\sigma} + \alpha_h \frac{c_{hg}^{1-\sigma}}{1-\sigma}.$$

With $\sigma < 1$, it follows that n^* will be decreasing in the productivity at home of the wife, w_f, fact (1). Holding the wife's productivity fixed, fertility is still independent of the husband's wage—fact (2). Thus, if w_f and w_m are positively correlated, and $\sigma < 1$, the partial correlation between n^* and w_m is negative as well—fact (3). This example is summarized in the first row of table 2A.1.

A second variation that also reproduces the negative correlation in the cross section can be obtained by making the home production technology slightly more complex. Assume that utility is given by

$$U_g = \alpha_n \log(n) + \alpha_h \log(c_{hg}),$$

where the home good, c_{hg}, is produced using market goods, c, and time of the wife, l_{hf}, with productivity w_f; that is, $c_{hf} + c_{hm} = F(c, w_f l_{hf})$. To simplify

---

52. One should note that though fact (1) is based on evidence from the twentieth century, so a model where fertility is constant across women, conditional on husband's income, could still be a good description of the nineteenth century.

53. It can also be shown that if children have a nonmarket goods cost, $b_0 > 0$, n^* is increasing in w_f. It follows that if w_f is positively correlated with w_m (which is what we might expect), n^* and w_m will also be positively correlated.

the analysis, we now assume that leisure is not valued, $\alpha_{\ell g} = 0$. Thus the problem is:

$$\max_{\{c_m, c_f, c_{hm}, c_{hf}, n, \ell_m, l_{hf}\}} \quad \lambda_f U_f + \lambda_m U_m$$

$$\text{s. t.} \quad c \leq w_m$$

$$b_1 n + l_{hf} \leq 1$$

$$c_{hf} + c_{hm} \leq F(c, w_f l_{hf}).$$

The first-order conditions can be reduced to one equation involving the amount of time the wife spends making home goods, which directly relates to fertility:

$$(1 - l_{hf}) = \frac{\alpha_n}{\alpha_h} \frac{1}{w_f} \frac{F(w_m, w_f l_{hf})}{F_2(w_m, w_f l_{hf})}$$

$$n^* = \frac{1 - l_{hf}}{b_1}.$$

That is, time spent in child-rearing $(1 - l_{hf})$ is positively related to the relative desirability of children to consumption, α_n/α_h, and negatively related to the productivity of the wife, w_f, all else equal. Thus, so is fertility, n^*. When F is assumed to be CES, $F(c, w_f l_{hf}) = [\delta c^\rho + (1 - \delta)(w_f l_{hf})^\rho]^{1/\rho}$, this becomes:

$$(14) \quad n^* = \frac{1 - l_{hf}}{b_1} = \frac{\alpha_n}{\alpha_h}(b_1(1 - \delta))^{-1}\left[\delta\left[\frac{w_m}{w_f}\right]^\rho l_{hf}^{1-\rho} + (1 - \delta)l_{hf}\right].$$

We can see from the second equality that in the Cobb-Douglas case $(\rho \to 0)$, $(1 - l_{hf})$ is independent of both w_m and w_f, but does depend on α_n/α_h. Thus, the same must be true of n^* (first equality).

We can also see that for any value of ρ, if w_f and w_m are proportional $(w_f = \phi w_m)$, then l_{hf} is independent of w_m and w_f and hence the same is true for fertility. That is, under perfect assortative mating, fertility and the wage of the husband and the productivity of the wife are independent.

When this correlation is imperfect and $\rho \neq 0$, the analysis is more complicated. We will assume another extreme, that w_m and w_f are independent, in what follows. When $\rho > 0$, market goods and female time are substitutes in the production of consumption. An increase in w_m holding w_f fixed causes l_{hf} to fall. Hence, n^* rises in this case. That is, fertility is an increasing function of husband's wage if w_m and w_f are independent.

On the other hand, when $\rho < 0$, market goods and female time are complements in the production of consumption. An increase in w_m holding w_f fixed causes l_{hf} to rise. Hence, n^* falls in this case. That is, fertility is a decreasing function of husband's wage if time and goods are complements and wages of husbands and wives are independent.

Thus, assuming enough complementarity between time and goods in production, F, and enough independence between productivities of husbands and wives, also gives a model that can reproduce the negative correlation between husbands income and fertility—fact (3). From equation (14) it is also obvious that female and male productivities enter in the opposite ways. Thus, if $\rho < 0$, it follows immediately that a higher female home productivity leads to lower optimal fertility. Of course, home productivity is difficult to measure, and hence, it is not obvious that this implication is counterfactual. Alternatively, assume $w_f = \bar{w}$, that is, women are homogenous in their home productivity (e.g., perhaps because more schooling does not increase productivity in cooking, cleaning, etc.). Then, we still generate fact (3), while the model has nothing to say about women. But again, given that home productivity is difficult to assess empirically, this may well be in line with the facts. This result is summarized as row 2 in table 2A.1.

In sum then, we see that fertility and wages/home productivities are uncorrelated without the same kinds of assumptions over utility function curvature that we have identified in earlier sections. As a substitute, we can generate the observed curvature, even with unitary elasticity in preferences, if we move away from unitary elasticity in the home production technology. But this requires the right correlation between husband's wages and wife's productivity in the home.

Preference Heterogeneity   Now assume there is heterogeneity in tastes rather than productivities; that is, households differ in how much they like children, α_n, consumption, α_c, and/or the home good, α_h. Going back to problem (12), the comparative statics of fertility with respect to preference parameters can immediately be derived from equation (13). Similarly, one can solve for labor earnings. Note that since the woman does not work in the market in this version, total household earnings are equal to male earnings and are given by:

$$I_m = w_m(1 - \ell_m^*) = w_m\left(1 - \frac{\alpha_\ell}{\alpha_c[\lambda_f/\lambda_m + 1] + \alpha_\ell}\right).$$

The results are as follows:[54]

1. With heterogeneity in α_c alone, while (male) earnings are increasing in α_c, fertility is the same for all households.

2. With heterogeneity in α_n or α_h alone, (male) earnings are the same for all households while fertility is decreasing in α_h and increasing in α_n.

3. With simultaneous heterogeneity in α_c and α_h and a positive correlation of these preferences within households, fertility will be negatively correlated with husband's earnings, fact (3). This finding hinges on the husband having

---

54. Using a model along the lines of section 2.4, these findings can be generalized to apply to male wages instead of labor earnings.

an alternative use of time to market work—leisure, in this case. This case is row 3 in table 2A.1.

In sum, only the third case (heterogeneity in tastes for all consumption goods, and positive correlation of these tastes within couples) can generate the negative income-fertility relationship observed for men. Similar results can be derived in the examples with general elasticities or home production functions.

Partial Specialization

To capture better the realities of the twentieth century, we now allow for more gender symmetry. Women and men both work in the market and there is no home production. We still assume that only women can raise children. Also, as before, we add leisure, ℓ_g. Then, husbands have to allocate their time between work and leisure, while women's time is allocated between three activities: working, enjoying leisure, and child-rearing. This example might be more relevant for the more recent experience, when women's labor force participation has been relatively large.

The gender-specific utility function is given by:

$$U_g = \alpha_{cg} \log(c_g) + \alpha_{ng} \log(n) + \alpha_{\ell g} \log(\ell_g),$$

and the couple solves the problem:

$$\max_{\{c_m, c_f, n, \ell_m, \ell_f\}} \lambda_f U_f + \lambda_m U_m$$

$$\text{s. t.} \quad c_f + c_m \leq w_m(1 - \ell_m) + w_f(1 - \ell_f - b_1 n),$$

where ℓ_f and ℓ_m are leisure of the female and male, respectively, and w_f and w_m are the respective wages. Each child takes b_1 units of female time. Without loss of generality, assume that $\lambda_f + \lambda_m = 1$ and $\alpha_c + \alpha_n + \alpha_\ell = 1$. Define $W = w_f + w_m$ as total wealth.

Given the assumption of logarithmic utility, we obtain the standard result that expenditure on each good is a constant fraction of wealth, given by preferences:

$$c_f = \lambda_f \alpha_c W;$$

$$c_m = \lambda_m \alpha_c W;$$

$$w_f \ell_f = \lambda_f \alpha_\ell W;$$

$$w_m \ell_m = \lambda_m \alpha_\ell W;$$

$$b_1 w_f n = (\lambda_m + \lambda_f) \alpha_n W.$$

This immediately implies that:

(15) $$n^* = \frac{(\lambda_m + \lambda_f)\alpha_n}{b_1} \left[1 + \frac{w_m}{w_f} \right].$$

Comparing equation (15) to the full specialization analogue (13), one can see that the main difference is that the male wage and the husband's weight affect optimal fertility in the partial specialization versions, but not when full specialization is assumed. With partial specialization, the time allocation of husband and wife is more interdependent since they can, to some extent, substitute tasks between them. This is technologically infeasible in the full specialization model and hence, male wages are irrelevant for fertility choices.

Ability Heterogeneity   Suppose households differ in their market wages, w_f and w_m. We see that fertility, n^*, is decreasing in the wife's wage, w_f, if the husband's wage, w_m, is held constant. Further, fertility, n^*, is increasing in the husband's wage, w_m, if the wife's wage, w_f, is held constant.

Thus, this model is consistent with fact (1) and in line with some authors' findings on fact (2) (e.g., Blau and van der Klaauw 2007). What remains to be seen are conditions under which fact (3)—that is, the negative correlation between male wages and fertility—can be accommodated as well. From equation (15), we also see that:

$$E\left[n|w_m\right] = \frac{(\lambda_m + \lambda_f)\alpha_n}{b_1}\left[1 + w_m E\left[\frac{1}{w_f}\middle|w_m\right]\right].$$

Thus, the partial correlation between fertility and husband's income depends on $E[1/w_f|w_m]$. That is, it depends on the correlation between husband's and wife's market wages. Depending on the matching pattern, we can distinguish three cases:

1. Perfectly (positively) correlated wages within couples:
    (a) If $w_f = \phi w_m$, then $E[1/w_f|w_m] = 1/\phi w_m$, and so n^* is independent of w_m.
    (b) Similarly, if $w_f = \phi w_m^v$, then $w_m E[1/w_f|w_m]$ is increasing (decreasing) in w_m if $v < 1$ ($v > 1$). That is, n^* is increasing in w_m for $v < 1$ and decreasing in w_m for $v > 1$. Note that $v > 1$ means that a 1 percent increase in the husband's wage is associated with a more than 1 percent increase in the productivity of his wife.
    (c) More generally, assuming matching can be characterized by a deterministic function $w_f(w_m)$, then n^* is decreasing in w_m if and only if $[w_f'(w_m)]/(w_f/w_m) > 1$. In words, the elasticity of female wages with respect to male wages must be larger than one. This seems unlikely. This case is summarized in row 4 in table 2A.1.
2. Independent wages within couples:
    Then $E[1/w_f|w_m] = E[1/w_f]$, and so n^* is increasing as a function of w_m.
3. Negatively correlated wages within couples:
    Suppose that $w_f = D - v w_m$ (where $D > 0$ so that $w_f > 0$). In this case $w_m E[1/w_f|w_m] = w_m/(D - v w_m) = 1/(D/w_m - v)$. Again this is increasing in w_m.

Thus, this version of the theory is consistent with fact (1)—that the regression coefficient on wife's wage is positive—and with the "debated fact (2)" that the regression coefficient on husband's income is positive (as in Blau and van der Klaauw [2007]). But this version is not consistent with a negative partial correlation between husband's income and fertility (unless the correlation is positive with $v > 1$, which seems unlikely). Thus, simply considering couples does not remove the need for special assumptions about the curvature on utility as in the previous simpler examples.

Preference Heterogeneity   From equation (15), we can also see the relationship between income and fertility when the basic source of heterogeneity is in preferences. For example, if couples differ in their values of α_c and assuming both α_ℓ and α_n are lower so that $\alpha_c + \alpha_\ell + \alpha_n = 1$ for all households, those with higher desire for consumption choose lower leisure (both ℓ_f and ℓ_m), and also lower fertility, n^*. Because of this, those couples with higher α_c will have both higher incomes, since they work more, and lower fertility (row 5, table 2A.1). Note that we have assumed that couples are matched perfectly in terms of their preferences.

2.7   Nannies

So far, the assumption that children take time has been an essential ingredient for deriving a negative wage-fertility relationship. It is easy to see that with goods costs only, none of the previous examples work. That is, with $b_0 > 0$ and $b_1 = 0$, the negative wage-fertility relationship gets reversed in any of the (working) examples of sections 2.3, 2.4, 2.5, and 2.6.

While it is fairly obvious that children are time-intensive, it is less clear that it is specifically the parent's time that is needed. In fact, outsourcing child care is quite common, and has been throughout history. Examples include nannies, au pairs, relatives, wet nurses, and even orphanages.[55] In short, these kind of arrangements mean that even though children take time to raise, this time, in principle, can be hired. Hence, it is not clear why the price of children should be higher for high wage people.

In this section we first show how, when buying nanny-time is an option, higher wage parents will choose to have *more* children in simple models. We then ask what assumptions would restore the negative wage-fertility relationship, *even when* hiring nannies is possible. We give one example where a specific type of preference heterogeneity gives the desired result.

---

55. In the nineteenth century, many poor children were sent to orphanages, even when the parents were still alive, but too poor to feed the children. In 1853, Charles Loring Brace founded the Children's Aid Society, which rescued more than 150,000 abandoned, abused, and orphaned children from the streets of New York City and took them by train to start new lives with families on farms across the country between 1853 and 1929.

2.7.1   An Example with Ability Heterogeneity

To see that the assumption of *parental* time is a critical one, consider the following simple example:

$$\max_{c,n,\gamma} \quad \alpha_c u(c) + \alpha_n u(n)$$

$$\text{s.t.} \quad c + w_n(1 - \gamma)b_1 n \leq w(1 - \gamma b_1 n),$$

where $b_1 n$ is the total time requirement for raising n children, as before, but the time cost of children can now be split into parental time, $\gamma b_1 n$, or nanny time, $(1 - \gamma)b_1 n$, where $\gamma \in [0, 1]$. We denote the cost of a nanny by w_n per unit of time.

The optimal use of nannies in this example depends on the relative market wage of nannies versus parents. As long as $w < w_n$, it is never optimal to hire a nanny ($\gamma^* = 1$), and hence, this case is analog to our previous analysis of examples in which children require parental time. On the other hand, when $w > w_n$, parents prefer to hire a nanny, so that $\gamma^* = 0$. This case is equivalent to examples where children are a goods cost only, and there we have seen that $dn^*/dw \geq 0$. So while in this example $dn^*/dw < 0$ is possible, it occurs only in the region where nannies are irrelevant.

Thus, if some people have market wages that are lower than wages of nannies and others have higher wages, this model implies a v-shaped wage-fertility relationship. That is, fertility is downward sloping in wages for people with wages below the nanny wage and upward sloping thereafter. Recall from figure 2.1 however, that the data do not display such a v-shaped relationship.[56]

Going one step further, one may ask: what determines the nannies' wage? Notice that in this model, everyone is equally productive at child care. One unit of time produces $(1/b)$ children. Since this is the case, everyone with a market ability, w, below the nannies' wage would be better off becoming a nanny and raising $(1/b)$ children since leisure is not valued. Everyone with ability above the nannies' wage would hire a nanny. The nannies' wage is then determined through demand and supply and w_n should be the lowest wage observed in the data. That is, we would observe an increasing relationship between wages and fertility throughout the income ladder.

One might rephrase the question as follows: why is fertility decreasing in wages even for those people whose (after-tax) wages are higher than the hourly cost of day care or nannies?

---

56. Some authors have argued that at the very top of the income distribution, the fertility-income relation might be positive. Due to top coding and small samples at the top of the income distributions, these estimates are often statistically insignificant. Also, if this theory were applied to such a v-shape, it would mean that nannies are so expensive (either due to high wages or high tax wedges) that only the top income group finds it worthwhile hiring nannies. This seems to be at odds with the evidence as well.

There are, of course, several plausible answers to this question, such as the moral hazard problem involved in child care. Even though, in principle, nannies can be hired, if there is some effort involved in raising a high quality child, then the incentives for a nanny might be different from those of a parent. If monitoring is costly, parents might optimally choose to do the child-rearing themselves. In this case, the opportunity cost of a child again is increasing in income. Alternatively, perhaps parents *enjoy spending time* with their children over and above the pure utility effect of having children. If people derive pleasure from, say, spending the weekend with their children, then nannies are a poor substitute for own child-rearing. To the best of our knowledge, these ideas have not been formalized seriously, yet.[57] Also, not everyone is equally productive in raising children; in particular, if nannies are also teachers. While we believe these are interesting and potentially promising channels, they are well beyond the scope of this chapter, and are left for future research. In the next subsection, we pursue yet another possibility, based on preference heterogeneity and endogenous wages along the lines of section 2.4.

2.7.2   A Working Example with Preference Heterogeneity

The idea is that people differ in how much they like "material goods" goods vis-à-vis nonmaterial goods such as children and leisure. That is, some people like a "market-consumption lifestyle" while others like a "family-leisure lifestyle." Because of these different preferences, the former invest more in human capital and therefore have a higher wage, while the latter know they will enjoy leisure, which makes human capital investments less profitable. These are also the people who like large families. As we will see in the next example, one can recover the negative wage-fertility relationship in this setup, even allowing for nannies. However, the result rests on a particular form of preference heterogeneity across households. Therefore, rather than seeing this example as a definite answer to the question raised at the beginning of this section, we view it as a starting point for discussion and further research.

The starting point here is the example of section 2.4, where parents make schooling choices for themselves, which in turn determine their wage. To keep it simple, assume $v_s = v_w = 1$. We add one additional good to the utility function: leisure, ℓ. As before, each child requires a time input, b_1. Again, this can be a nanny's time, $(1 - \gamma)b_1 n$, or the parent's time, $\gamma b_1 n$, (where $\gamma \in [0, 1]$). In this choice, the parent takes the nanny's wage, w_n, as given.

The choice problem is:

57. Erosa, Fuster, and Restuccia (Forthcoming) have an indirect way of modeling the idea that parents like to spend time with children. That is, the value of staying at home can only be enjoyed if the mother gave birth in the past but has not returned to work since.

$$\max_{c,n,\ell,l_s,l_w,\gamma} \quad \alpha_c \log(c) + \alpha_n \log(n) + \alpha_\ell \log(\ell)$$

$$\text{s.t.} \quad l_s + l_w + \ell + \gamma b_1 n \leq 1$$

$$w = a l_s$$

$$c + w_n(1 - \gamma) b_1 n \leq w l_w.$$

It is easy to see that $l_s^* = l_w^*$. That is, given the child care choice, γ, and the leisure choice, ℓ, this maximizes market income. In terms of the nanny choice, one can show that an interior choice is never optimal. We therefore solve the problem for $\gamma = 1$ and $\gamma = 0$ and show that, assuming people differ in preferences, fertility and wages are negatively related for both $\gamma = 1$ and $\gamma = 0$.[58] Finally, we compare utilities across the two choices and derive the condition on parameters for which parents optimally hire a nanny.

Suppose the parent cares for the child, $\gamma = 1$. Then the solution is given by:

$$l_s^* = \frac{\alpha_c}{\alpha_\ell + \alpha_n + 2\alpha_c}$$

$$n^* = \frac{\alpha_n}{(\alpha_\ell + \alpha_n + 2\alpha_c)b_1}$$

$$\ell^* = \frac{\alpha_\ell}{\alpha_\ell + \alpha_n + 2\alpha_c}.$$

This is very similar to the solution in section 2.4, except that leisure is an additional choice variable. All the results go through. In particular, if parents take care of their children themselves, those who like the consumption good more; that is, higher α_c relative to α_n and α_l, will invest more in human capital, l_s, and hence have higher wages, $w = al_s$. They will also choose fewer children and less leisure.

In the case where parents choose to outsource child care, $\gamma = 0$, the solution is given by:

$$l_s^* = \frac{\alpha_c + \alpha_n}{\alpha_\ell + 2(\alpha_n + \alpha_c)}$$

$$n^* = \frac{\alpha_n(\alpha_c + \alpha_n)}{[\alpha_\ell + 2(\alpha_c + \alpha_n)]^2} \frac{a}{w_n b_1}$$

$$\ell^* = \frac{\alpha_\ell}{\alpha_\ell + 2(\alpha_c + \alpha_n)}.$$

Again, suppose that people differ in their preference for the consumption good α_c. Then, time in school, and hence wages, are strictly increasing in α_c

---

58. Formally, when $\gamma = 0$, the problem reduces to a pure goods cost example with $b_0 \equiv w_n b_1$.

and fertility is strictly decreasing in α_c as long as leisure is not too important (the exact condition is: $2(\alpha_c + \alpha_n) > \alpha_\ell$). Hence, we obtain the negative fertility-wage relationship even if nannies are hired.

Finally, the condition for using a nanny is given by:

$$U|_{\gamma=0} > U|_{\gamma=1}$$

iff

$$\frac{a}{w_n} > \left[\frac{\alpha_c^{\alpha_c}(\alpha_\ell + 2(\alpha_n + \alpha_c))^{(\alpha_\ell + 2(\alpha_n + \alpha_c))}}{(\alpha_\ell + \alpha_n + 2\alpha_c)^{(\alpha_\ell + \alpha_n + 2\alpha_c)}(\alpha_n + \alpha_c)^{(\alpha_n + \alpha_c)}} \right]^{1/\alpha_n}.$$

The higher one's ability, a, relative to nanny wages, w_n, the more likely it is that the parent will hire a nanny. This is similar to the logic in the previous example with the v-shaped (or increasing) fertility-wage relationship. What is different here is that, assuming households differ in α_c, fertility and wages will be negatively related even among those parents who do use nannies; that is, those who choose a goods cost rather than a time cost.

Figure 2.2 illustrates the model graphically. In this example, all households have the same ability, a, but differ in their preferences, α_c. The figure then plots optimal choices as a function of α_c, both conditional on using a nanny

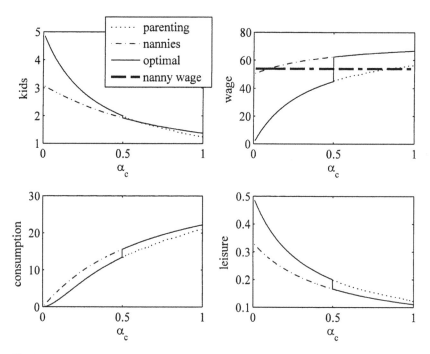

Fig. 2.2   Example with nanny choice

or parenting one's own child. The solid line depicts the solution under the optimal nanny choice. The figure shows clearly how fertility decreases and wages increase in the desire to consume (α_c). Once consumption becomes important enough, people optimally will use a nanny. At this point, the wage jumps up discretely: the decision to use a nanny frees up time, which will be used partly for schooling, which directly translates into the wage. At this point, consumption jumps up and leisure jumps down. Fertility falls somewhat, but note that for high α_c types, parents who use nannies have higher fertility than they would have had if nannies did not exist.

The mechanism behind this example is essentially the same as in section 2.4. People who put a higher weight on consumption goods will invest more in schooling, and hence have higher wages. At the same time, they care less about children and hence have fewer. Note that having leisure in this example is crucial, because once nannies become an option, parents allocate their time only between investing in (own) human capital and working. Given our functional forms, without leisure ($\alpha_\ell = 0$), the optimal allocation would be $l_s^* = l_w^* = 0.5$. But then wages would no longer differ across people, since independent of the preference parameters, everyone would make the same schooling choice. Adding leisure allows for an alternative use of time so that optimal schooling, and hence wages, actually differ across people with different preferences.[59] People who value consumption goods more choose more schooling and less leisure, and therefore have higher wages. These same people also have fewer children. This logic holds even when child care time can be outsourced to nannies, since it is ultimately the relative dislike of children that drives the low fertility of high wage people, and not the high time cost of children. Because of this logic, heterogeneity in *preferences*, rather than in exogenous ability, is essential for this result. Starting from exogenous ability heterogeneity would lead to very different conclusions, as is obvious from the previous solution (and recalling $w = al_s^*$): higher a people have both higher wages *and* more children.

Of course, the mechanism in this example is probably not the only (or even the main) reason for why higher wage people choose lower fertility, even when nannies are an option. Our goal here is to raise an important question and propose a first attempt to answer it. One limitation of the present example is that nanny quality is not a choice. When nanny quality is an input into child quality, specific functional form assumptions are needed to preserve the desired result. This relates back to the quantity-quality trade-off analyzed in section 2.5.

---

59. This is similar to the preference heterogeneity examples in the couples section, in which the leisure of the husband generated the desired correlation even if his time was not needed to raise children.

2.8   Time Series Implications

Throughout most of this chapter, we have focused on what kind of theories of fertility can match the downward sloping fertility-wage relationship observed in cross-sectional data. We have seen that special assumptions are needed, such as a high elasticity of substitution between fertility and (parent's) consumption. One might want to ask more of such theories. For example, one might want to know the conditions under which such models could also match the decline in average fertility over the last century and a half. In other words, which of these theories can also get the time series facts right, or, how must they be modified to do so?[60] Our static examples are too stylized to empirically test them in any serious fashion. Yet, from section 2.2 there emerged several stylized facts and one way to tackle this question is to see which of the theories can produce a picture that looks qualitatively like figure 2.1. The stylized facts that emerge from this figure can be summarized as:

1. Fertility is very high at low wages (about 6).
2. Fertility is very low at high wages (about 2).
3. Fertility is decreasing (and convex) in wages for each cross section.
4. Fertility falls over time, as consecutive cross sections move to the right.

In terms of forcing variables, it is not obvious which exogenous changes over time to consider. One obvious change over this time period are increases in wages driven by Total Factor Productivity (TFP) growth. Another potentially important change is the development of education, both through technological change that made human capital production more efficient and changes in government policies through the (free) public provision of schooling. Sometimes it is argued that children have become more costly over time, and so we look at this change as well. The interpretation of this change, however, is not straightforward.

Next, we show four numerical examples, each based on a different theory analyzed in the text. Each graph displays four cross-sectional relationships between income and fertility. Depending on the example, the difference between people within a cross section (i.e., on one line) is either wages or preferences, while the difference between different cross sections (i.e., between the four different lines) is either wages, schooling technology, and/or child-rearing costs.

The first two figures are based on two different examples from section 2.3. Figure 2.3 is based on problem (3) while figure 2.4 is based on problem (4),

---

60. One could also ask the opposite question: which of the existing theories of the demographic transition can generate the cross-sectional fertility facts? Such an analysis is beyond the scope of this chapter.

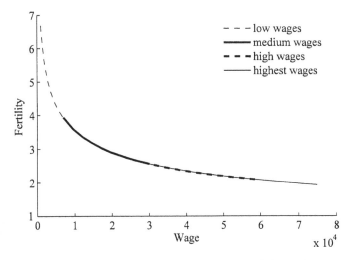

Fig. 2.3   Time series based on price of time example, $\sigma \subset 1$, increasing wages

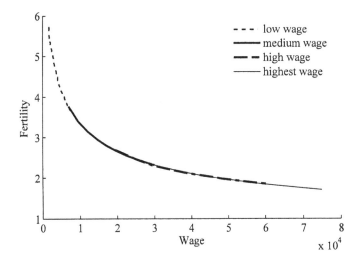

Fig. 2.4   Time series in example with nonhomothetic utility, increasing wages

both variants of the simplest "price of time theory."[61] In each case, the only difference across people (both in the cross section and over time) is wages. Both examples match the stylized facts described before fairly well. Thus, as long as one is willing to assume a high elasticity of substitution between parent's consumption and fertility, the basic theory seems to work well—at

61. The main qualitative difference between the two examples is that the income elasticity is constant in figure 2.4, while it is increasing in absolute value in figure 2.3. Recall also that the empirical elasticity appears to slightly decrease over this time horizon (as shown in table 2.1).

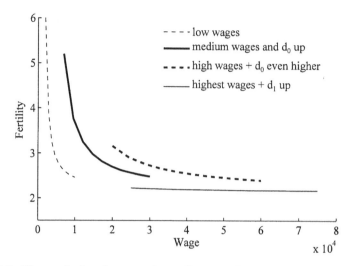

Fig. 2.5   Time series based on quantity-quality example

least in this simple formulation. Once one moves to a truly dynamic formulation, where parents have preferences over their children's utility, the same logic no longer holds, as we discuss in the first section of the appendix. The intuition is simple: when wages go up, both parents' and children's wages are affected. Thus, while the opportunity cost of having a child is higher for richer parents, the benefit of having a child also increases (because the wage of a child of a rich parent is also high). Thus, even though these results seem like strong successes for the theory at first glance, there are other reasonable, but more stringent, requirements for which their success is more limited.

Figure 2.5 considers the quantity-quality trade-off example from problem (7) with $f(s) = d_0 + d_1 s$. Note that to distinguish this example from the first two pictures, this assumes log-utility, and all curvature comes in through the child quality production function only. In this example, fertility is essentially hyperbolic in wages, and hence the shape of the curve does not match figure 2.1 very well.[62] However, this example lends itself to think about potential changes in the education sector. In addition to increasing wages, consecutive cross sections in figure 2.5 face different quality production functions. In particular, the second cross section has a higher d_0, which one could interpret as the introduction of elementary public education. The third cross section has an even higher d_0, which might represent a further expansion of the public education system. The last cross section has a higher d_1, which is a parameter that determines the returns to parental education inputs. This could be interpreted as improvements in education technology. Alterna-

---

62. One way of stating the qualitative difference between figure 2.5 and the data is that the income elasticity of fertility in the example converges to zero very fast as wages increase, while in the data, the elasticity is roughly constant.

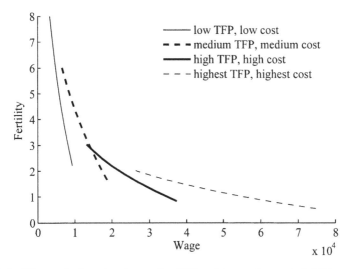

Fig. 2.6   **Time series based on increasing TFP and increasing cost of children, cross section due to preference heterogeneity**

tively, without this last change in the child quality production function, the last cross section would simply be a continuation of the third cross section, converging to 2.14 children (in this example) as wages go to infinity. So while this picture matches figure 2.1 qualitatively, more work on the underlying changes in education technology (i.e., their historical analogues) would be required before one could call this theory a success.

Finally, figure 2.6 is based on the preference heterogeneity example from section 2.4. In this figure the cross section and time series both slope downward, but the mechanisms behind the two are different. The cross section is based on preference heterogeneity. That is, people who like children invest less in market-specific human capital and therefore have lower wages, while those who put a higher weight on consumption goods do the opposite and therefore have higher wages. Over time, as in the previous examples, we assume that average productivity, a, goes up. However, in this example, increases in productivity do not affect fertility decisions. Hence, without more bells and whistles (e.g., changing the curvature to the utility function), this example will not lead to falling fertility for consecutive cross sections. Thus, we have added a second channel to the time series in the figure: increases in child costs—that is, the units of time required per child increase exogenously over time. This picture looks roughly like the data, but its interpretation is not clear; that is, what is the real-world analogue of an increase in child-rearing costs (measured in units of time)?[63]

---

63. One rationale for this change may be the progressive introduction of child labor laws. That is, while the time cost remained the same, the time that children contribute to the household's income decreased. Hence, this would be equivalent to a net increase in the time cost.

These simple examples are only meant to spur thinking about the possibilities of the models examined in this chapter. Much more work in carefully calibrating/estimating the relevant parameters and documenting the needed changes in the forcing variables, is necessary before any final conclusions can be drawn. In the end, we cannot offer a clear answer to our own question, but we hope that the ideas here will stimulate further research, leading to a better understanding of fertility decision-making.

2.9   Conclusion

We have investigated the ability of fertility theories to match the cross-sectional relationship between fertility and income. The main focus has been on comparing two sets of theories, one in which ability heterogeneity causes fertility differences and another in which heterogeneity in the taste for children causes income differences. Several interesting findings emerge and are summarized in table 2.2. In particular, we find that low incomes *cause* high fertility only if the elasticity of substitution between consumption and the number of children is high. Empirical research estimating this elasticity would be desirable.

Theories based on taste heterogeneity, on the other hand, do not require any elasticity assumptions. The mechanism causing the negative income-fertility relationship is a very different one, and does not depend on the relative sizes of income and substitution effects. Thus, one may conclude that taste-based theories are more robust. Another advance of taste-based theories is that the assumption of parental time as a critical input into child production is not necessarily needed.

One may also require theories to generate simultaneously a negative income and child quality relationship. While this follows immediately from ability-driven stories, the result is somewhat harder to generate within the class of taste-driven stories. Whether two-parent versions of these theories can generate male wages to be negatively correlated with fertility depends on the details of the models. Generally speaking, with additional assumptions, both classes of theories can do so. However, these both require specific assumptions about how spouses are matched, or about how male and female inputs are combined in family production. In particular, taste-based stories require assortative matching along *preference* lines, while ability-driven stories require assortative matching (or complementarities in production) in *abilities*. Finally, one may ask whether the same driving force that explains the cross-section can also generate the time trend. This is a relatively easy task to accomplish for ability-based stories, because literally the same force that causes richer people to have fewer children in the cross-section also operates as incomes go up for everyone, and thereby mechanically causes a demographic transition. It seems clear that the same mechanism will *not* be able to generate a demographic transition in taste-based theories, unless one believes that tastes for children declined systematically over time.

Table 2.2   Comparison

Assumptions and robustness	Ability heterogeneity	Taste heterogeneity
Elasticity (c,n)	Elasticity < 1	Elasticity irrelevant
Parental time	Crucial	Not necessary
Can also get child quality to increase in income?	Yes, plus may help relax elasticity assumption	Depends on details of preference heterogeneity
Can get fertility to decrease in male income, when women do child-rearing?	Need positive assortative matching in ability or complementarities in home production	Need matching along preference lines
Can model also match time series?	Yes	No

In some ways, the analysis in this chapter raises more questions than it answers. It points to several directions for further research, both theoretical as well as empirical. On the empirical side, estimates of the elasticity of substitution between own consumption and children (and child quality versus quantity) would be useful. More generally, clever ways of empirically estimating the contribution of taste-based versus ability-based theories in explaining the negative fertility-income correlation would be valuable. One such attempt is provided in Amialchuk (2006), who uses PSID data and finds that in response to income shocks (specifically, job displacements), couples do not change their lifetime fertility in a significant way. Angrist and Evans (1998), on the other hand, estimate the impact of exogenous variation in fertility (due to twins) on parents' labor supply and find little effect. To the extent that human capital is accumulated on the job, this finding can be interpreted as showing a negligible causal effect from fertility shocks to income. It does not, however, invalidate theories based on preference heterogeneity for consumption goods vis-à-vis children. Clearly, further empirical research to test the various theories is needed.

In addition, a better empirical understanding of the spousal matching process would be helpful. While assortative mating in education has long been documented in the data (e.g., Pencavel 1998), assortative mating in preferences has received less attention. Recent research estimating preferences for marriage markets (e.g., Ariely, Hitsch, and Hortacscu 2006; Lee 2008) may prove useful for understanding better why higher income men have fewer children even though, typically, their wives do most of the child-rearing. Is it because high ability men tend to marry high ability women? Or is it because men with a preference for consumption goods tend to marry women with similar preferences, leading them to spend most of their income on material goods and less on children accordingly?

New research should also develop models of fertility that allow parents to outsource child care. All successful theories of fertility rely on the assumption that it takes the parents' time to raise children. Alternative child care options exist, yet as soon as child care can be bought in the market, the time cost becomes a goods cost for the parents. However, models with only goods cost cannot generate a negative income fertility relationship (with one very specific exception). More theoretical research would be of interest here. For example, modeling explicitly that nannies require monitoring, which in itself may be time-intensive, could be a promising avenue to pursue.

Finally, we found that expanding the successful models to full dynamic versions based on parental altruism is very challenging. Dynamic models are very important for understanding the connection between cross-sectional fertility differences and the demographic transition. More research in this area is needed.

Appendix
Adding Parental Altruism

So far, our focus has been on examining simple models of fertility choice that give rise to the observed pattern in the cross section with respect to income. As we have seen, there are several examples that are capable of this, though they differ in their details. One property that is missing from all of the examples in the main text, however, is altruism of parents toward their children. That is, parents are made happy by things that increase the utility of their children. Altruism introduces an additional dynamic aspect to the fertility choice automatically: when choosing their own fertility levels, parents must forecast the utility levels of their own children. Following this logic, the utility of the children will depend on the utility levels of their own children—that is, the grandchildren—and so forth. Thus, the utility of the current period decision maker depends on the entire future evolution of the path of consumption and fertility, not just the levels chosen this period.

Although this task sounds complex, models of fertility choice based on parental altruism of this form have been worked out in detail in Becker and Barro (1988) and Barro and Becker (1989). Here we develop a simple version of the Barro-Becker model (B-B henceforth) and discuss its relationship with the examples developed in the main text. We show that the simple example discussed in section 2.3 can be interpreted as the problem solved by the typical parent under a setting with dynastic altruism, but that this requires some extra assumptions and has some additional implications. In particular, the simple, static problem with homothetic preferences can be interpreted as the problem from the Bellman's equation for the fully dynamic model where the term relating to fertility choice corresponds to the value function for continuation payoffs. However, this interpretation has the additional implication that the value function also depends on the wage, and because of this, has the property that families with different base wage rates all make the same fertility choices. Thus, although the high elasticity homothetic example has the correct cross-sectional property in the static example, this property does not extend to the fully dynamic version of the model.

In the simplest version of the B-B model, the time t parent solves:

$$\max_{c_t, n_t} \quad u(c_t) + \beta g(n_t) U_{t+1},$$

$$\text{subject to:} \quad c_t + \theta_t n_t \leq w_t,$$

where c_t is current period consumption, n_t is the fertility choice, and U_{t+1} is the utility level of the typical child. Assuming that $g(n) = n^\eta$, $u(c) = c^{1-\sigma}/(1 - \sigma)$, successively substituting and changing to aggregate variables for all of the descendants of a given time 0 household, the equilibrium sequence of choices can be represented as the solution to the following time 0 maximization problem:

$$\max_{\{C_t, N_t\}} \quad \sum_{t=0}^{\infty} \frac{\beta^t N_t^{\eta + \sigma - 1} C_t^{1-\sigma}}{1 - \sigma}.$$

Subject to:

$$C_t + \theta_t N_{t+1} \leq w_t N_t,$$

$$N_0 \text{ given,}$$

where C_t is aggregate consumption in period t, N_t is the number of adults in period t, θ_t is the cost of producing a child, and w_t is the wage rate. Implicit in this formulation is the assumption that each adult has the same level of consumption $C_t/N_t = c_t$ in any period.

For this problem to satisfy the typical monotonicity and concavity restrictions, some restrictions on σ and η must be satisfied. There are two sets of parameter choices that satisfy these requirements. The first is the original assumption in Becker and Barro (1988) and Barro and Becker (1989): $0 \leq \eta + \sigma - 1 < 1, 0 < 1 - \sigma < 1$ and $0 < \eta = \eta + \sigma - 1 + 1 - \sigma < 1$. In this case, $U > 0$ for all $(N, C) \in R_+^2$. The second possibility is one that allows for intertemporal elasticities of substitution in line with the standard growth and business cycle literature: $\sigma > 1, \eta + \sigma - 1 \leq 0$. In this case, utility is negative and $\eta < 0$. When $\eta = 1 - \sigma$ (allowed under both configurations), utility becomes a function of aggregate consumption only.[64]

There are two types of situations under which this maximization problem becomes a stationary dynamic program (where the state variable is N).

---

64. This formulation for the dynasty utility flow gives rise to some very useful simplifications that we will exploit later. One disadvantage of it, however, is that it is not equivalent to logarithmic utility when $\sigma = 1$. However, when $\eta = 1 - \sigma$ and $\sigma \to 1$, the preferences will converge to those given by the utility function $\Sigma \beta^t \log(C_t)$. See Bar and Leukhina (forthcoming) for an explicit derivation of Barro-Becker preferences with an intertemporal elasticity of substitution (IES) equal to one.

Both cases require constant growth in wages: $w_t = \gamma_w^t w_0$. The first is when the cost of children is in terms of goods, and this cost grows at the same rate as wages: $\theta_t = a\gamma_w^t$. The second case is when the cost of having a child is in terms of time only, $\theta_t = b_{1t}w_t$, where b_{1t} is the amount of time it takes to raise one surviving child.

In either of these cases, the problem of the dynasty overall has a homogeneous of degree one constraint set and an objective function that is homogeneous of degree η. Because of this structure, it follows that the solution to the sequence problem has several useful properties that we will exploit later.

Following the discussion in section 2.3, it follows that only the time cost case is capable of matching the facts from the cross section and hence, we will limit our attention to this case.

Under the special case that $\eta = 1 - \sigma$, it follows that the value function for this problem, $V(N)$, is homogeneous of degree $1 - \sigma$ in N – $V(N) = V(1)N^{1-\sigma}$. Because of this fact, it follows that, after detrending, Bellman's equation for this problem can be written as:

$$V(N) = \sup_{\{C,N'\}} \frac{c^{1-\sigma}}{(1-\sigma)} + \hat{\beta}V(1)N'^{(1-\sigma)}$$

$$\text{s.t.} \quad C + \theta N' \le wN,$$

where $\hat{\beta} = \beta\gamma_w^\eta$. Variable $V(1)$ can be found explicitly. It is given by:

$$V(1) = \frac{(w + \theta(\pi - \gamma_N))^{1-\sigma}}{(1-\sigma)(1 - \beta\gamma_N^\eta\gamma^{1-\sigma})}.$$

It follows that the solution to the dynastic problem has a representation in which each date t adult chooses his own consumption and fertility level so as to solve:

$$\max_{\{c,n\}} \frac{c_t^{1-\sigma}}{1-\sigma}\hat{\beta}V(1)n_t^{1-\sigma}$$

$$\text{s.t.} \quad c_t + \theta_t n_t \le w_t.$$

Note that this problem is similar to the CES utility function problem laid out in section 2.3.2. However, there is one important difference. The coefficient on fertility cannot be chosen freely. In particular, it is easy to see that $V(1)$ depends on the wage. Indeed, it follows directly that it is increasing in the wage. Because of this, it follows that the results from the comparative statics concerning the dependence of fertility on the wage are not necessarily valid. In the dynamic version of the problem both the objective function (i.e., Bellman's Equation) and the constraints depend on the wage.

In fact, it can be shown that the equilibrium choice of fertility is given by:

$$\text{(A1)} \quad n_t = \frac{N_{t+1}}{N_t} = \gamma_N = \left(\beta\gamma_w^{1-\sigma}\left[\frac{w_0}{\theta_0} + \pi\right]\right)^{1/\sigma} = \left(\beta\gamma_w^{1-\sigma}\left[\frac{1}{b_1} + \pi\right]\right)^{1/\sigma},$$

where the last equality follows from assuming that all costs of children are in terms of time, $\theta_0 = b_1 w_0$.

It follows that fertility choices are independent of the level of wages of the family. Thus, although it seems as if the time cost case can reproduce the cross-sectional properties of fertility choice (when $\sigma < 1$ is assumed), this is not true once one restricts attention to static problems that have a dynamic rationalization.[65]

We can also use this framework to get some idea about the implications for differences in fertility across families when preferences for children are the basic source of heterogeneity. For example, we can see that if families differ in their levels of patience, β, differences in the cross section are preserved in the time series. Thus, for example, if for two families, i and i', we have that $\beta_i > \beta_{i'}$, it follows that $n_{it} > n_{i't}$ for all t. Thus, the cross-sectional variation in fertility choice is preserved in the time series.[66] It should be noted however, that this will also have the implication that families with higher fertility also have higher savings rates. This probably does not hold in the cross section.

A Dynamic Version of the Endogenous Wage Example

Next, we develop a version of the endogenous wage model in section 2.4 that is consistent with parental altruism, as in the B-B model.

Assume that the resource constraints are given by those of problem (6), but assume that $v_s + v_w = 1$. (To simplify notation, write $v_s = v$ and $v_w = 1 - v$.) Using capital letters to denote aggregate quantities (i.e., defining $L_t \equiv N_t l_t$, etc.), the planner's problem can be rewritten as:

(A2)
$$\max \quad \sum_{t=0}^{\infty} \frac{\beta^t N_t^{\eta+\sigma-1} C_t^{1-\sigma}}{1-\sigma}$$

$$\text{s.t.} \quad L_{st} + L_{wt} + L_{nt} \leq N_t$$

$$C_t \leq a L_{st}^v L_{wt}^{1-v}$$

$$b N_{t+1} \leq L_{nt}.$$

As just shown, the constraint correspondence is homogeneous of degree 1 and the utility function is homogeneous of degree η in initial condition N_0.

<hr/>

65. Here we have assumed that wage differences across families are permanent—that is, if i and i' represent two distinct families then we are assuming that $w_{it+1}/w_{i't+1} = w_{it}/w_{i't} = \gamma w$. An interesting question is whether this result will be overtuned when one moves away from this assumption. Jones and Schoonbroodt (forthcoming) find that a high growth rate lowers fertility if $\sigma > 1$ and vice-versa (see also equation [16]). This suggests that with intergenerational mean reversion in income, poor households expect a high income growth rate and would have more children than rich ones as long as $\sigma < 1$. In this context, Zhao (2008) uses a model with filial altruism as in Boldrin and Jones (2002), where mean reversion is crucial, both in the cross section and over time (when social security crowds out fertility). We leave the analysis of intermediate cases (i.e., partially correlated dynastic incomes) to future research.

66. As mentioned before, this assumes that the differences across families is permanent: $\beta_{it} > \beta_{i't}$ for all t.

Assuming that $\eta = 1 - \sigma$ as just shown, the value function is of the form $V(N) = V(1)N^{1-\sigma}$. It follows that the Bellman Equation is:

$$V(N) = \sup_{C,N'} \frac{C^{1-\sigma}}{1-\sigma} + \beta V(1)N'^{(1-\sigma)}$$

$$\text{s.t.} \quad L_s + L_w + bN' \leq N$$

$$C \leq aL_s^\nu L_w^{1-\nu}.$$

So for the appropriate choice of α_n and α_c, the solution to problem (6) can be interpreted as the solution to the dynamic problem (A2) with $N_0 = 1$ in some cases. Here, normalizing $\alpha_c = 1$, it follows that $\alpha_n = \beta V(1)$.

It is not clear in this framework exactly which comparative statics exercise corresponds to the one in section 2.4, where α_n is increased. In principle, it could correspond either to an increase in β, or to any increase that makes $V(1)$ larger. In what follows, we consider only the implications of increases, across dynasties, of increases in β's.

Using the first order conditions to the problem in sequence form and simplifying, we obtain a characterization of the balanced growth path dynamics. The system is determined by the division of time between schooling and working and the intertemporal choice of family size involving fertility. It is given by:

$$\frac{L_{wt}}{L_{st}} = \frac{1-\nu}{\nu}, \text{ and}$$

$$n_t^\sigma = \gamma_N^\sigma = \frac{\beta}{b_1}.$$

That is, fertility is increasing in β. Because of this fact, it follows that both L_{st}/N_t and L_{wt}/N_t are decreasing in β, and hence, fertility and income (or wages) are negatively related as desired.

Thus, for the endogenous wage example, an explicit dynastic form can be provided that is still consistent with the cross-sectional facts. There are still some issues here, however. Foremost, when discount factors differ across agents, strong forces for borrowing and lending are typically present. The analysis here ignores these considerations. It is not certain that the results will be robust to this extension.[67]

Summary of Findings for Couples' Models

In table 2A.1 we summarize the sets of assumptions that are able to generate both a negative correlation between husband's as well as wife's income and fertility.

---

67. Another issue not considered here is variants of intergenerational persistence in preferences.

Table 2A.1   Couples: Model versions that work

Specialization in production	Exogenous heterogeneity	Curvature in utility	Spousal matching	Other	< 0 (1) $\delta n/\delta w_f$	Mixed (2) $(\delta n/\delta w_f)|w_f$	< 0 (3) $\delta n/\delta w_m$
1 Full[c]	Ability	$\sigma < 1$	$\mathrm{corr}(w_f, w_m) > 0$		< 0	$= 0$	< 0
2 Full[c]	Ability	$\sigma = 1$	$w_f = w$	$\rho < 0$[d]	n.a.[b]	< 0	< 0
3 Full[c]	Taste	Any σ	Prefs matching	Leisure	< 0[a]	n.a.[e]	< 0[a]
4 Partial	Ability	$\sigma = 1$	$w'_f(w_m)\dfrac{w_m}{w_f} > 1$		< 0	> 0	< 0
5 Partial	Taste	Any σ	Prefs matching	Leisure	< 0[a]	n.a.[e]	< 0[a]

Note: n.a. = not applicable.

[a] The correlation here is for earnings not wages, but including schooling, as in section 2.4, will extend the results to wages.

[b] All women have the same productivity in this example, hence the correlation $\delta n/\delta w_f$ is not well-defined.

[c] In the full specialization version, w_f refers to female productivity at home and cannot be compared directly to data on female wages.

[d] Market goods and female time are complements in home production.

[e] The conditional correlation will depend on the details of the matching process. With perfectly aligned preferences, there is no residual variation in the husband's wage/earnings, conditional on the wife's wage/earnings. Hence the conditional correlation is not well-defined in the model analyzed in the chapter.

References

Ahn, N., and P. Mira. 2002. A note on the changing relationship between fertility and female employment rates in developed countries. *Journal of Population Economics* 15 (4): 667–82.

Aiyagari, S. R., J. Greenwood, and N. Guner. 2000. On the state of the union. *Journal of Political Economy* 108 (2): 213–44.

Alvarez, F. E. 1999. Social mobility: The Barro-Becker children meet the Laitner-Loury dynasties. *Review of Economic Dynamics* 2 (1): 65–103.

Amialchuk, A. 2006. The effect of husband's earnings shocks on the timing of fertility. University of Houston. Unpublished manuscript.

Angrist, J., and W. N. Evans. 1998. Children and their parents' labor supply: Evidence from exogenous variation in family size. *The American Economic Review* 88 (3): 450–77.

Angrist, J. D., V. Lavy, and A. Schlosser. Forthcoming. New evidence on the causal link between the quantity and quality of children. *The Journal of Labor Economics*. Cambridge, MA: National Bureau of Economic Research, December.

Ariely, D., G. Hitsch, and A. Hortacscu. 2006. What makes you click? An empirical analysis of online dating. University of Chicago. Unpublished Manuscript.

Attanasio, O., H. Low, and V. Sanchez-Marcos. 2008. Explaining changes in female labour supply in a life-cycle model. *The American Economic Review* 98 (4): 1517–52.

Bagozzi, R. P., and M. F. Van Loo. 1978. Fertility as consumption: Theories from the behavioral sciences. *The Journal of Consumer Research* 4 (4): 199–228.

Bailey, M. J. 2006. More power to the pill: The impact of contraceptive freedom on women's lifecycle labor supply. *Quarterly Journal of Economics* 121 (1): 289–320.

Banks, W. H. 1955. Differential fertility in Madison Country, New York, 1965. *Milbank Memorial Fund Quarterly* 33:161–86.

Bar, M., and O. Leukhina. Forthcoming. Demographic transition and industrial revolution: A macroeconomic investigation. *Review of Economic Dynamics*.

Barro, R., and G. Becker. 1989. Fertility choice in a model of economic growth. *Econometrica* 57 (2): 481–501.

Becker, G. S. 1960. An economic analysis of fertility. In *Demographic and economic change in developed countries,* no. 11 in Universities—National Bureau Conference Series, ed. Universities National Bureau Committee for Economic Research, 225–56. Princeton, NJ: Princeton University Press.

———. 1965. A theory of the allocation of time. *The Economic Journal* 75 (299): 493–517.

Becker, G., and R. Barro. 1988. A reformulation of the theory of fertility. *Quarterly Journal of Economics* 103 (1): 1–25.

Becker, G. S., and H. G. Lewis. 1973. On the interaction between the quantity and quality of children. *Journal of Political Economy* 81 (2): S279–88.

Becker, G., K. Murphy, and R. Tamura. 1990. Human capital, fertility, and economic growth. *Journal of Political Economy* 98:812–37.

Becker, G. S., and N. Tomes. 1976. Child endowments and the quantity and quality of children. *Journal of Political Economy* 84 (4): S143–62.

Ben-Porath, Y. 1976. Fertility response to child mortality: Micro data from Israel. *Journal of Political Economy* 84 (4): S163–78.

Bernal, R. 2008. The effect of maternal employment and child care on children's cognitive development. *International Economic Review* 49 (4): 1173–1209.

Black, S. E., P. J. Devereux, and K. G. Salvanes. 2005. The more the merrier? The effect of family size and birth order on children's education. *The Quarterly Journal of Economics* 120 (2): 669–700.

Blau, D., and W. van der Klaauw. 2007. The impact of social and economic policy on the family structure experiences of children in the United States. Department of Economics and Carolina Population Center, University of North Carolina. Unpublished Manuscript.

Boldrin, M., M. De Nardi, and L. E. Jones. 2005. Fertility and social security. NBER Working Paper no. 11146. Cambridge, MA: National Bureau of Economic Research, February.

Boldrin, M., and L. E. Jones. 2002. Mortality, fertility and saving in a Malthusian economy. *Review of Economic Dynamics* 5:775–814.

Bongaarts, J. 2003. Completing the fertility transition in the developing world: The role of educational differences and fertility preferences. *Population Studies* 57 (3): 321–35.

Borg, M. O. 1989. The income–fertility relationship: Effect of the net price of a child. *Demography* 26 (2): 301–10.

Browning, M. 1992. Children and household economic behavior. *Journal of Economic Literature* 30 (3): 1434–75.

Cáceres-Delpiano, J. 2006. The impacts of family size on investment in child quality. *Journal of Human Resources* 41 (4): 738–54.

Caucutt, E., N. Guner, and J. Knowles. 2002. Why do women wait? Matching, wage inequality, and the incentives for fertility delay. *Review of Economic Dynamics* 5 (4): 815–55.

Cho, L.-J. 1968. Income and differentials in current fertility. *Demography* 5 (1): 198–211.

Clark, G. 2005. Human capital, fertility, and the industrial revolution. *Journal of the European Economic Association* 3 (2-3): 505–15.

———. 2007. *Farewell to alms: A brief economic history of the world.* Princeton, NJ: Princeton University Press.

Clark, G., and G. Hamilton. 2006. Survival of the richest: The Malthusian mechanism in pre-industrial England. *Journal of Economic History* 66 (3): 707–36.

De la Croix, D., and M. Doepke. 2003. Inequality and growth: Why differential fertility matters. *The American Economic Review* 93 (4): 1091–1113.

———. 2004. Public versus private education when differential fertility matters. *Journal of Development Economics* 73 (2): 607–29.

———. 2009. To segregate or to integrate: Education politics and democracy. *Review of Economic Studies* 76:597–628.

Del Boca, D., and R. M. Sauer. 2009. Life cycle employment and fertility across institutional environments. *European Economic Review* 55 (3): 274–92.

Docquier, F. 2004. Income distribution, non-convexities and the fertility-income relationship. *Economica* 71 (282): 261–73.

Doepke, M. 2004. Accounting for fertility decline during the transition to growth. *Journal of Economic Growth* 9 (3): 347–83.

———. 2005. Child mortality and fertility decline: Does the Barro-Becker model fit the facts? *Journal of Population Economics* 18 (2): 337–66.

Doepke, M., M. Hazan, and Y. Maoz. 2007. The baby boom and World War II: A Macroeconomic analysis. NBER Working Paper no. 13707. Cambridge, MA: National Bureau of Economic Research, December.

Eckstein, Z., and K. I. Wolpin. 1989. Dynamic labour force participation of married women and endogenous work experience. *The Review of Economic Studies* 56 (3): 375–90.

Edin, K. A., and E. P. Hutchinson. 1935. *Studies of differential fertility.* London: P.S. King and Son.

Ehrlich, I., and F. T. Lui. 1991. Intergenerational trade, longevity, and economic growth. *Journal of Political Economy* 99 (5): 1029–59.

Erosa, A., L. Fuster, and D. Restuccia. Forthcoming. A general equilibrium analysis of parental leave policies. *Review of Economic Dynamics.*

———. 2005. A quantitative theory of the gender gap in wages. Working Papers tecipa-199, University of Toronto, Department of Economics.

Espenshade, T. J. 1984. *Investing in children: New estimates of parental expenditures.* Washington, DC: Urban Institute Press.

Falcão, B. L. S., and R. R. Soares. 2008. The demographic transition and the sexual division of labor. *Journal of Political Economy* 116 (6): 1058–1104.

Fernandez, R., N. Guner, and J. Knowles. 2005. Love and money: A theoretical and empirical analysis of household sorting and inequality. *The Quarterly Journal of Economics* 120 (1): 273–344.

Fleischer, B. M., and G. Rhodes. 1979. Fertility, women's wage rates, and labor supply. *The American Economic Review* 69 (1): 14–24.

Francesconi, M. 2002. A joint dynamic model of fertility and work of married women. *Journal of Labor Economics* 20 (2): 336–80.

Freedman, D. S., and A. Thorton. 1982. Income and fertility: The elusive relationship. *Demography* 19 (1): 65–78.

Galor, O. 2005a. From stagnation to growth: Unified growth theory. In *Handbook of economic growth,* vol. 1, ed. P. Aghion and S. Durlauf, 171–293. North Holland: Elsevier.

———. 2005b. The demographic transition and the emergence of sustained economic growth. *Journal of the European Economic Association* 3 (2–3): 494–504.

Galor, O., and O. Moav. 2002. Natural selection and the origin of economic growth. *The Quarterly Journal of Economics* 117 (4): 1133–91.

Galor, O., and D. N. Weil. 1996. The gender gap, fertility and growth. *The American Economic Review* 86 (3): 374–87.

———. 1999. From Malthusian stagnation to modern growth. *The American Economic Review, Papers and Proceedings* 89 (2): 150–54.

———. 2000. Population, technology, and growth: From Malthusian stagnation to the demographic transition and beyond. *The American Economic Review* 90 (4): 806–28.

Goldin, C., and L. F. Katz. 2002. The power of the pill: Oral contraceptives and women's career and marriage decisions. *Journal of Political Economy* 110 (4): 730–70.

Greenwood, J., and N. Guner. Forthcoming. Social change: The sexual revolution. *International Economic Review.*

Greenwood, J., N. Guner, and J. A. Knowles. 2003. More on marriage, fertility, and the distribution of income. *International Economic Review* 44 (3): 827–62.

Greenwood, J., and A. Seshadri. 2002. The U.S. demographic transition. *The American Economic Review, Papers and Proceedings* 92 (2): 153–59.

Greenwood, J., A. Seshadri, and G. Vandenbroucke. 2005. The baby boom and baby bust. *The American Economic Review* 95 (1): 183–207.

Haines, M. R. 1976. Population and economic change in nineteenth century eastern Europe: Prussian upper Silesia, 1840–1913. *The Journal of Economic History* 36 (2): 334–58.

Hansen, G. D., and E. C. Prescott. 2002. Malthus to Solow. *The American Economic Review* 92 (4): 1205–17.

Heckman, J. J. 1976. A life cycle model of earnings, learning, and consumption. *Journal of Political Economy* 84 (4): S11–S44.

Heckman, J. J., and J. R. Walker. 1990. The relationship between wages and the timing and spacing of births: Evidence from Swedish longitudinal data. *Econometrica* 58 (6): 1411–41.

Hotz, V. J., J. A. Klerman, and R. J. Willis. 1993. The economics of fertility in developed countries. In *Handbook of population and family economics,* vol. 1, ed. M. Rosenzweig and O. Stark, 275–347. North Holland: Elsevier.

Hotz, J. V., and R. A. Miller. 1988. An empirical analysis of life cycle fertility and female labor supply. *Econometrica* 56 (1): 91–118.

Jaffe, A. J. 1940. Differential fertility in the white population in early America. *Journal of Heredity* 31:407–11.

Jones, L. E., and A. Schoonbroodt. 2007. Baby busts and baby booms: The fertility response to shocks in dynastic models. Discussion Papers in Economics and Econometrics, no. 0706, University of Southampton.

———. Forthcoming. Complements versus substitutes and trends in fertility choice in dynastic models. *International Economic Review.*

Jones, L. E., and M. Tertilt. 2008. An economic history of fertility in the U.S.: 1826–1960. In *Frontiers of family economics,* vol. 1, ed. P. Rupert, 165–230. Bingley, UK: Emerald Press.

Keane, M. P., and K. I. Wolpin. 2006. The role of labor and marriage markets, preference heterogeneity and the welfare system in the life cycle decisions of black, hispanic and white women. PIER Working Paper Archive no. 06-004, Penn Institute for Economic Research, Department of Economics, University of Pennsylvania.

Knowles, J. 2007. Why are married men working so much? The macroeconomics of bargaining between spouses. IZA Discussion Papers no. 2909, Institute for the Study of Labor.

Lazear, E. P., and R. T. Michael. 1980. Family size and the distribution of real per capita income. *The American Economic Review* 70 (1): 91–107.

Lee, R. 1987. Population dynamics of humans and other animals. *Demography* 24 (4): 443–66 (Presidential Address to the Population Association of America).

Lee, S. 2008. Preferences and choice constraints in marital sorting: Evidence from Korea. Stanford University. Unpublished Manuscript.

Li, H., J. Zhang, and Y. Zhu. 2008. The quantity-quality tradeoff of children in a developing country: Identification using Chinese twins. *Demography* 45:223–43.

Manuelli, R. E., and A. Seshadri. 2009. Explaining international fertility differences. *Quarterly Journal of Economics* 124 (2): 771–807.

Merrigan, P., and Y. S. Pierre. 1998. An econometric and neoclassical analysis of the timing and spacing of births in Canada from 1950–1990. *Journal of Population Economics* 11 (1): 29–51.

Miller, A. Forthcoming. The effects of motherhood timing on career path. *Journal of Population Economics.*

Mincer, J. 1963. Market prices, opportunity costs, and income effects. In *Measurement in economics: Studies in mathematical economics and econometrics in honor of Yehuda Grunfeld,* ed. C. F. Christ, L. A. Goodman, and D. Patinkin, 67–82. Stanford, CA: Stanford University Press.

Mincer, J., and H. Ofek. 1982. Interrupted work careers: Depreciation and restoration of human capital. *The Journal of Human Resources* 17 (1): 3–24.

Mincer, J., and S. Polachek. 1974. Family investments in human capital: Earnings of women. *The Journal of Political Economy* 82 (2): S76–S108.

Moav, O. 2005. Cheap children and the persistence of poverty. *Economic Journal* 115 (500): 88–110.

Murtin, F. 2007. American economic development or the virtues of education. Stanford Center for the Study of Poverty and Inequality. Unpublished Manuscript.

Pencavel, J. 1998. Assortative mating by schooling and the work behavior of wives and husbands. *The American Economic Review* 88 (2): 326–29.

Preston, S., and C. Sten. 2008. The future of American fertility. University of Pennsylvania, Discussion Paper. Manuscript prepared for NBER Conference on Demography and Economics. April, Napa, California.

Rosenzweig, M. R., and K. I. Wolpin. 1980. Testing the quantity-quality fertility model: The use of twins as a natural experiment. *Econometrica* 48 (1): 227–40.

Ruggles, S., M. Sobek, T. Alexander, C. A. Fitch, R. Goeken, P. K. Hall, M. King, and C. Ronnander. 2004. Integrated public use microdata series: Version 3.0. Minneapolis: Minnesota Population Center.

Schultz, T. 1981. *Economics of population.* Reading, MA: Addison Wesley.

———. 1986. The value and allocation of time in high-income countries: Implications for fertility. *Population and Development Review* 12:87–108.

———. 2005. Effects of fertility decline on family well being: Opportunities for evaluating population programs. Yale University. Working Paper.

Shiue, C. H. 2008. Human capital and fertility in Chinese clans, 1300–1850. University of Colorado at Boulder. Unpublished Manuscript.

Simon, J. L. 1977. *The economics of population growth.* Princeton, NJ: Princeton University Press.

Skirbekk, V. 2008. Fertility trends by social status. *Demographic Research* 18 (5): 145–80.

Sylvester, M. S. 2007. The career and family choices of women: A dynamic analysis of labor force participation, schooling, marriage and fertility decisions. *Review of Economic Dynamics* 10 (3): 367–99.

Tertilt, M. 2005. Polygyny, fertility, and savings. *Journal of Political Economy* 113 (6): 1341–71.

U.S. Census. 1945. Differential fertility 1910 and 1940. U.S. Bureau of the Census, Census of Population. Washington, DC: GPO.

———. 1955. Fertility. U.S. Bureau of the Census, Census of Population. Washington, DC: GPO.

Weir, D. R. 1995. Family income, mortality, and fertility on the eve of the demographic transition: A case study of Rosny-Sous-Bois. *The Journal of Economic History* 55 (1): 1–26.

Westoff, C. F. 1954. Differential fertility in the United States: 1900 to 1952. *American Sociological Review* 19 (5): 549–61.

Whelpton, P., and C. Kiser, eds. 1951. *Social and psychological factors affecting fertility.* Milbank Memorial Fund.

Willis, R. J. 1973. A new approach to the economic theory of fertility behavior. *Journal of Political Economy* 81 (2): S14–S64.

Wrigley, E. A. 1961. *Industrial growth and population change.* Cambridge: Cambridge University Press.

Zhao, K. 2008. Social Security, differential fertility, and the dynamics of the earnings distribution. University of Western Ontario. Unpublished Manuscript.

Comment   Amalia R. Miller

The chapter begins with an empirical regularity: the negative association between household income and completed fertility, as measured by the number of children ever born to a woman. The authors provide compelling evidence of a robust relationship that is present in comparisons both within and between birth year cohorts. Figure 2.1 in the chapter (reproduced from Jones and Tertilt [2008]) shows the surprising consistency of the relationship over the past century-and-a-half in the United States, and table 2.1 shows that the measured elasticity has been remarkably stable over time.

Having established their main stylized fact, the authors proceed to carefully explore the types of theoretical models that can generate the negative relationship observed in the data. The approach in the chapter is to use a series of simple cases to exemplify the models, which they classify into two main types, based on their underlying primitive source of heterogeneity across agents. The major division is between models that start with income heterogeneity and produce fertility differences and those that start with fertility differences (or differences in preferences for children) and endogenously generate income differences. The models represent the two potential directions for an immediate causal relationship between income and fertility. Indirect sources for the relationship based on outside factors are not considered.

The main contribution of the chapter is that it lays out a broad yet coherent framework for exploring the fertility-income relationship. The second contribution is the identification of the fundamental modeling choices and assumptions, such as functional form or parameter requirements for utility or production functions, necessary for each model to produce the key relationship. These assumptions are not equally plausible, and may provide testable implications for future empirical work. The authors argue that the exercise is useful for macroeconomic theorists who want to incorporate fertility in their models in a reasonable way. In addition, the chapter can provide a useful framework for empirical researchers studying demographic and labor economics.

The first type of model, characterized by the price theory of time, starts with exogenous wealth or wage heterogeneity, and endogenously produces fertility differences. If children are inferior goods, clearly the relationship between income and fertility is negative. Without that assumption, this first type of model requires a high elasticity of substitution between children and consumption, a source of nonlabor income, or nonhomothetic preferences to reproduce the key stylized fact. The authors demonstrate the sensitivity

Amalia R. Miller is assistant professor of economics at the University of Virginia.

of these models in generating even the cross-sectional relationship. They also provide a useful discussion of how the well-known "quantity-quality" trade-off is insufficient to produce a negative correlation between fertility and income. Models of the first type with quality require restrictive assumptions regarding preferences or the quality production function.

The second type of model treats wages as endogenous, and reverses the direction of causality in the key correlation from number of children to earned income. Agents exogenously differ in one of two ways: in their tastes for children or their realized fertility. The model is introduced in section 2.4 as the less conventional approach, and is considered in later sections in combination with quantity-quality and the theory of female time allocation. One channel through which children reduce household income is a reduction in market work hours. In a stronger form of the model, not only does income decline with fertility, but wage rates do as well. The channel for the latter effect is through lower human capital investment in formal education or on-the-job training and experience.

The chapter's emphasis on the second model type is appropriate. These models have been generally overlooked by macroeconomic theorists, despite their ability to generate the main stylized relationship under less restrictive assumptions than the first model type. A potential drawback of the approach is that the primitive source of variation is in preferences, and economic models have traditionally had less to say about preference formation than about income distribution.

Another advantage of the second approach is that its casual mechanism is consistent with empirical evidence from labor economics and economics of the family. Researchers have identified a gap in pay between mothers and similar nonmothers, termed the family gap (Waldfogel 1998), and motherhood remains a key source of income inequality between the sexes (Fuchs 1988).

In a recent paper (Miller 2006), I find that early childbearing harms women's career outcomes. Biological shocks to fertility timing from miscarriage, failed contraception, and extended time to conception are used as instrumental variables to estimate the effects of a year of motherhood delay: a 10 percent increase in income, 5 percent increase in total hours worked, and 3 percent increase in wage rates. The paper also estimates the effect of motherhood itself on wages using the same instrumental variables on panel data. There is evidence that mothers experience both a fixed penalty in the form of permanently lower wages as well as a flattening of the wage-age profile, reflecting lower returns to experience or a "mommy track." The underlying source of the family gap may be changes in labor supply or investment behavior of women after motherhood. It may be that employers offer mothers fewer opportunities for advancement and promotion. In fact, the two are likely interconnected. Although this evidence is consistent with the models of the second type presented in the paper, it is important to note that the estimates constitute only a portion of the endogenous wage channel. The empirical results in Miller (2006) are conditioned on educational attainment, test scores, and in some cases, accumulated work experience. Without these conditioning factors, the total relationship is even larger.

An important feature of the second type of models is that they depend on the assumption that a mother's time is an essential input in child development. In section 2.7, the authors consider the theoretical implications of relaxing that assumption and allowing mothers to substitute their own time with purchased child care. The motherhood penalty in wages would be eliminated, but the authors are able to generate an example with the basic negative correlation between fertility and income when they include leisure in the model. The empirical evidence that women experience career penalties for childbearing suggests, however, that the time costs of children remain important and are borne in large part by mothers. The authors speculate as to the possible reasons that nannies have not completely replaced working mothers at home; the barriers are substantial. Among them are unequal tax treatment of family and hired inputs into child care (leisure and home production, including child care, are untaxed, but income spent on hired care is taxable), and asymmetric information about quality and effort (leading to potential adverse selection and moral hazard problem: hence demand for services from agencies and monitoring devices). Finally, if the utility from children flows from time spent with them, paid care will always be an imperfect substitute for parental time.

After exploring a range of static models that generate the cross-sectional relationship, the authors return to their empirical inspiration in figure 2.1 and put their models to a more ambitious test: can they be extended to explain the time-series variation as well? For the models with preference heterogeneity, one approach would be to have preferences for children change exogenously over time and themselves generate changes in gross domestic product (GDP) within the model. Rather than relying on changing fertility to explain economic growth, the authors instead develop a model in the appendix with additional exogenous variation from technological change in the productivity of the economy and in the costs of children. With the right choice of parameters, the authors can produce a figure that resembles the pattern in the data. A question that warrants future exploration is how the distribution of tastes would evolve endogenously in such a model. For example, if children inherit tastes (even imperfectly) from their parents, and those with greater desire for children choose higher fertility, do average preferences in society tend to increase, or are there mitigating forces?

An interesting area for future work is to consider models that produce the negative correlation between female wages and fertility, but depend on channels not explored in the chapter. One possibility is marital disagreement over desired fertility. The models in the chapter are all unitary, in that either one adult creates one child or the partners agree on their desired number of children. What would happen if they did not agree? The direction of causality is open: children may reduce woman's power within a relationship and earned income, or women with more power from higher wages may bargain for fewer children. More effective birth control can also shift the "balance of power" toward women (Chiappori and Oreffice 2008).

The National Longitudinal Survey of Youth 1979 provides some anecdotal evidence that men and women disagree about desired fertility, or at least that women report such disagreements with their partners and spouses. Starting with the 1982 wave of the survey, women were asked, following each live birth: "Prior to becoming pregnant, did you want to become pregnant?" The 1982 responses for first child born (women aged seventeen to twenty-five reveal a high rate of undesired pregnancies, based on the self-reported preferences of the mother. The distribution of responses was: 192 women said "yes"; 69 said "didn't matter"; 1,058 said "no, not at that time"; and 340 said "no, none at all." Only 11.6 percent report having wanted to conceive. If we include first births to older women, using data through 2004, the rate increases, but only to 13.5 percent. The same women were also asked if their husband or partner wanted the pregnancy. The 1982 responses were as follows: 1,103 said "yes"; 130 said "didn't matter"; 718 said "no, not at that time"; and 420 said "no, none at all." Although fewer than one in eight women reported wanting her own pregnancy, nearly half of the women reported the belief that their husband or partner wanted it.

Another way to fruitfully extend the models would be to incorporate imperfect control over fertility. The survey responses just mentioned suggest that random shocks play an important role in human reproduction. Limiting fertility has a cost, either practicing abstinence or using contraception. The supply of contraceptives and knowledge about fertility control varies over time and in the cross-section. Expanding the models to include contraceptive choices would also provide a natural way to introduce other "extra-economic" factors such as culture and religion, which are clearly related to fertility.

To summarize, through a series of simple examples and cases, the chapter provides an overview of the modeling options available to researchers who want to generate a negative cross-sectional correlation between fertility and income, consistent with the documented demographic pattern. The authors demonstrate that a wide range of economic models produce predictions consistent with the facts, but that the necessary assumptions are less restrictive if one begins with preference heterogeneity rather than income heterogeneity. The chapter contains useful insights that will inform economists and demographers in their thinking about variation in completed fertility, its sources, and its consequences.

References

Chiappori, P. A., and S. Oreffice. 2008. Birth control and female empowerment: An equilibrium analysis. *Journal of Political Economy* 116:113–40.

Fuchs, V. 1988. *Women's quest for economic equality.* Cambridge, MA: Harvard University Press.

Jones, L. E., and M. Tertilt. 2008. An economic history of fertility in the U.S.: 1826–1960. In *Frontiers of family economics,* vol. 1, ed. P. Rupert, 165–230. Bingley, UK: Emerald Press.

Miller, A. 2006. The effects of motherhood timing on career path. University of Virginia. Unpublished Manuscript.

Waldfogel, J. 1998. Understanding the "family gap" in pay for women with children. *Journal of Economic Perspectives* 12:137–56.

Women's Education and Family Behavior
Trends in Marriage, Divorce, and Fertility

Adam Isen and Betsey Stevenson

3.1 Introduction

The family is a constantly changing institution. In the last half century, marriage and fertility rates have fallen, divorce rates have risen (and subsequently fallen), and the character of marriage has changed. These developments have occurred in the wake of widespread social, legal, and technological changes that have impacted the incentives for individuals to form and invest in marriages and children. These changes have not impacted all families equally, and in this article, we investigate how family behavior has changed for men and women of different educational backgrounds.

To understand how these changes have impacted the incentives for people to form families, it is useful to start by understanding the gains from forming a family. Gary Becker's 1981 *Treatise on the Family* proposed an economic theory of families based on "production complementarities," in which husband and wife specialize in the market and domestic spheres, respectively, and hence, are more productive together than apart. Becker emphasized

Adam Isen is a doctoral candidate in applied economics at the Wharton School, University of Pennsylvania. Betsey Stevenson is assistant professor of business and public policy at the Wharton School, University of Pennsylvania, a research fellow of CESifo, and a faculty research fellow of the National Bureau of Economic Research.

The authors would like to thank Stephanie Coontz, Paula England, Jerry Jacobs, Enrico Moretti, Sam Preston, Robert Pollak, Michele Tertilt, and Justin Wolfers for useful discussions and seminar participants at Washington University, St. Louis, and NBER's Topics in Demography and the Economy conference. Betsey Stevenson would like to thank Sloan for support through a Work-Family Early Career Development Grant and the National Institutes of Health-National Institute on Aging (grant P30 AG12836), the Boettner Center for Pensions and Retirement Security at the University of Pennsylvania, and National Institutes of Health–National Institute of Child Health and Human Development Population Research Infrastructure Program (grant R24 HD-044964) at the University of Pennsylvania for funding.

that families are production units that produce both goods in the house (like clean laundry and well-cared for children) and in the marketplace. By having one person specialize in domestic responsibilities (most often a wife as homemaker), while the other supports the spouse and children financially (typically a husband as breadwinner), couples are more efficient than singles.

This view of the family as a source of production efficiencies has become less relevant over time. The twentieth century brought the development of labor- and skill-saving technological progress in the home.[1] This technological change simplified clothes washing and drying, cooking (through the development of preprocessed foods and microwaves), dishwashing, and housecleaning. Technological progress also encouraged the shift from home production to purchasing items in the market through the development of cheaper mass-produced items like ready-made clothes. These changes have impacted home production through three channels: by making home production more efficient; by reducing the returns to specialized domestic skills as these technologies substitute capital for skilled labor; and by making market-produced goods a closer substitute for home-produced goods, which in turn makes market work a closer substitute for domestic work. While some of the effect of these changes was likely an increase in the amount and/or quality of home-produced goods and services (such as investing more in the care of children), overall time spent in home production fell. Moreover, there was a shift in home production away from specialists toward nonspecialists. Between 1965 and 2003, home production by women fell by twelve hours a week on average, while home production by men rose by four-and-a-half hours (Aguiar and Hurst 2007). In the wake of these changes, the production efficiencies realized by families have been eroded.

During this period, the costs of having such a specialist also rose. Women's increased control over fertility (allowing them to better time and plan pregnancies), their improved access to education, and a decline in labor market discrimination all led to higher market wages for women (Goldin and Katz 2002; Blau and Kahn 1997, 2000). These higher wages represent a greater opportunity cost for a couple contemplating a stay-at-home spouse. Further, changes in divorce law have made specialization in the home riskier (Stevenson 2007).

The declining value of production efficiencies from marriage decreases the value of marriage and, if this is the only relevant margin along which the value of family life is changing, it should lead to a decline in marriage rates overall. Indeed, Greenwood and Guner (2009) develop a model in which technological change in household production is used to explain the fall in marriage rates since World War II. However, the recent technological changes should not impact all women equally. The Beckerian model

---

1. For an overview of the research on these changes see Stevenson and Wolfers (2007).

of the family suggests that those best positioned to benefit from household specialization will gain the most from marriage and, therefore, be the most likely to marry. When many of the benefits of marriage arise from the greater efficiency achieved through household specialization, women who are uninterested in, or not well-suited for, specializing in home production will have fewer gains from marriage. Thus, these women will be less likely to find it in their interest to marry. This prediction is consistent with an empirical fact: college-educated women have historically been the least likely group of women to marry. The declining value of household specialization affects these women less, as they were less likely to enjoy the benefits in the past.

While the past several decades have witnessed a decline in marriage rates, it has been small relative to the large decline in specialized homemakers. In 1970, among women with children under the age of five, the majority, 70 percent, were out of the labor force—presumably full-time homemakers. In the ensuing decades, labor market participation became the norm for mothers with young children and only 36 percent were out of the labor force in 2007. In contrast, the decline in marriage was less dramatic: in 1970 94 percent of women had married by age forty, declining to 84 percent by 2007.[2]

One explanation for why marriage rates have not fallen further is that other dimensions of family life have become relatively more important and have also changed in absolute terms. Families have experienced an increase in leisure and consumption that has likely increased the benefits of shared public goods (Aguiar and Hurst 2007). Housing and health insurance costs, both important family public goods, have increased (Newhouse 1992; Glaeser, Gyourko, and Saks 2005). Moreover, there may be consumption and leisure complementarities that become more valuable as the time and money available to pursue consumption and leisure has risen. These changes in family life offer increased benefits from marriage, partly offsetting some of the decrease in the returns to specialization. Such changes in the returns to married life—from production efficiencies to consumption complementarities—should impact not only the probability that matches form, but the type of matches that form.

A shift from production-based marriage to consumption-based marriage should make marriage more appealing to those with more disposable income relative to those with less. Since personal and household income within a marriage is a bargained outcome reflecting the skills of each spouse and the preferences for home production and leisure, one would prefer to measure potential earnings, rather than actual earnings (Pollak 2005). A reasonable proxy for potential earnings is education and, as such, one would similarly

---

2. Sharper decreases in marriage rates are seen when one looks at younger women due to the rising age of first marriage. In 1970, 84 percent of twenty-five-year-olds had married, compared to 42 percent of twenty-five-year-olds in 2007.

predict that marriage should become more appealing to those with more education relative to those with less education among both men and women. In addition, there is an important gender shift occurring. While woman with more education are less likely to find the old specialization model of marriage useful, a modern marriage based on consumption complementarities is likely more enticing for educated women as the new model of marriage thrives when households have the time and resources to enjoy their lives. In contrast, less educated women have less to gain through household specialization in marriage today than in the past.

In addition to differences in the probability of ever marrying, there are differences by education in the optimal timing of first marriage. As Becker (1981) argued, those who plan to be specialist homemakers have an incentive to enter marriage early to begin to invest in their skills as a homemaker and reap the returns to specialization. Among women who do not plan to be household specialists, this incentive is not present. Indeed, it is likely that these women face an opposite incentive, to invest in their career before finding a spouse and children.

The hypothesis that the benefits of marriage are shifting from production efficiencies to consumption complementarities has a number of testable implications. The first implication is that marriage should become more common among those with more disposable income and/or more leisure time, relative to those with less. The second is that in a consumption-based model of marriage people will be more likely to marry someone with similar preferences, which will likely manifest itself as an increase in positive assortative mating along dimensions such as age, educational background, and occupation, as well as consumption and leisure preferences. The third is that, among couples without kids, their hours of work should become increasingly similar, as the value of an hour of leisure is greater when it is coordinated with one's spouse. Child care makes this coordination more complicated for those with children. Finally, similar (albeit oppositely signed) patterns should be seen for divorce, with divorce being less common among those who work similar hours, have more shared interests, and more disposable income (with which to enjoy consumption complementarities).

This chapter focuses on two of these implications by carefully documenting the changes over recent decades in family formation, dissolution, and expansion by education.[3] We show that while college-educated women used to be the least likely to marry, today they are about as likely as those without a college degree to marry. There are large racial differences in this trend: college-educated white women remain less likely to marry than those with

---

3. With regards to the second implication, see Schwartz and Mare (2005), who find an increase in educational assortative mating since 1960. See also Sweeney and Cancian (2004), who document an increase in earnings homogamy.

less education, while college-educated nonwhite women are the most likely to marry among nonwhites. This difference is due to the larger shift away from marriage among blacks, particularly among those with less education. College-educated whites and blacks have also become less likely to marry in recent decades; however, the downward shift has been less than that experienced by women with less education. Women of all educational backgrounds have delayed marriage, although the delay has been longer among the more highly educated.

Turning to the divorce rate, we show that it initially rose for all groups but has, in recent decades, dropped off more sharply among college graduates. Remarriage rates have fallen for everyone, and while the drop has been larger for those with less education, college-educated white women are still less likely to remarry than those with less education. Lastly, while trends in the average number of children ever born have been similar across groups, the delay in fertility is concentrated almost exclusively among women who have attended college.

The rest of the chapter is organized as follows: section 3.2 examines trends from the 1950s through 2007 in the timing and propensity to enter marriage by education. The patterns of marriage and the differences by education differ significantly by race, and thus, we will examine white and black women separately and will compare the patterns for both to the experiences of men. Section 3.3 turns to marital stability, examining divorce and remarriage rates for women and men, separately by race and education, while section 3.4 focuses on changes in fertility. Section 3.5 explores subjective well-being data and finds that there are important differences in marital and family happiness by education. Section 3.6 concludes with a discussion of the interpretation of the results, noting that many of the changes over time in family behavior by women's educational attainment may simply reflect the shift of many women into higher educational categories.

3.2 Marriage Patterns

In figure 3.1 we examine the proportion of women who have ever married, by age, among those with and without a college degree. Examining the most recent large-scale data—the 2007 American Community Survey—we see in the first panel of figure 3.1 that among white women, those with a college degree are less likely to have ever married and that this holds at every age. A very different pattern is seen for black women in the second panel, for whom marriage rates are highest for those with the most education after the early twenties. While previous research (Goldstein and Kenney 2001) had forecasted a demographic shift in marriage with college-educated women more likely to marry today than noncollege graduates, the gap has not closed as fast as predicted and the higher rates of marriage for college-educated

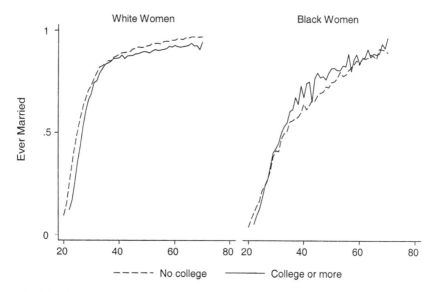

Fig. 3.1   Proportion of white and black women ever-married by age in 2007

Source: 2007 American Community Survey.

Notes: The percent who have ever married at each age are shown in the left and right panels for white and black women, respectively. Each panel shows ever-married rates separately for those with and without a college degree.

women born in 1950 to 1965 that they forecasted had not occurred by the time these women were forty years old.[4]

At the turn of the last century, women attended college at rates similar to that of men, yet few of these women ever married (Goldin, Katz, and Kuziemko 2006). Thirty percent of college-educated women born in the last twenty years of the nineteenth century remained unmarried at age fifty, a rate four times that of women without a college degree (Goldin 2004). While the marriage gap has clearly closed, the data in figure 3.1 point to the fact that for no generation of women have we witnessed a crossover in which college-educated white women are marrying at higher rates compared to white women with less education. Among forty-six- to sixty-year-old white women there is a fairly stable gap in which college-educated women are around 3 percentage points less likely to have married compared to women with less education. The stability of this gap among older women illustrates that the lower likelihood of college-educated women ever marrying persisted for some time, even as the number of women completing college was rising.

Among older women, the differences in ever-married rates are indicative

4. Martin (2004b), using more recent data also finds that the shift is taking longer than earlier forecasts had suggested but predicts that the crossover may occur for women born after 1965.

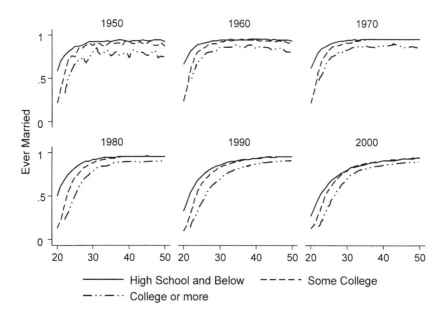

Fig. 3.2   Proportion of white women ever-married by age, 1950–2000
Source: 1950, 1960, 1970, 1980, 1990, and 2000 Censuses of Population.
Notes: Each panel shows the percent who have ever married at each age in a specific decade for those with high school or below, some college, or a college degree for white women.

of changing behavior across cohorts. Ever-married rates were falling slightly for all women in the birth cohorts from 1937 to 1961, while education was increasing rapidly.[5] Differences in the gap in marriage rates by education at younger ages reflect both changing behavior across cohorts and differences in the life cycle pattern of marriage by educational attainment.

Examining life cycle patterns of marriage by cohort reveals that the "marriage gap" between college-educated women and their less-educated counterparts has been shrinking for many generations. Figure 3.2 uses the decennial censuses of population from 1950 through to 2000 to show the evolution over time in both the marriage gap and the timing of first marriage by education for white women. For each decade, the percent of white women who have ever married is shown at each age for those with a high school degree or less and separately for those who attended some college, but did not receive a four-year college degree, and college graduates. In each decade white female college graduates are clearly less likely to ever marry compared to women with no or some college. The graphs show that between 1950 and

5. Goldin (2006) notes that the increase in women's college attendance and completion relative to men began with the birth cohorts of the late 1940s and that this is also the cohort for whom an inflection point in the growth in female enrollment in graduate programs is seen.

2000 marital behavior has changed for all groups both in terms of the timing of marriage in the life cycle and in the probability of ever marrying.

Women with a college degree increasingly delayed marriage to older ages both earlier, and to a greater extent, than women with either a high school degree or some college. The age at first marriage of female college graduates began to rise with those graduating in the late 1960s (Goldin 2004). In 1970, 74 percent of twenty-five-year-old college graduates had ever married; this compares to 53 percent, 43 percent, and 36 percent in 1980, 1990, and 2007, respectively. In contrast, the percent of twenty-five-year-old high school graduates who had ever married was 90 percent, 83 percent, 73 percent, and 52 percent in 1970, 1980, 1990, and 2007, respectively. Indeed, in the last seventeen years there has been a larger decrease in marriage among women in their early twenties with no college compared with previous decades, while the largest shift away from early marriage among college-educated women occurred between 1970 and 1980.[6] The pattern among women with some college has been similar to that of those with no college, although the shift toward later marriage happened a decade earlier for these women.

Overall, the increased delay in marriage is consistent with the changing incentives affecting individuals. Goldin and Katz (2002) demonstrate that the availability of the birth control pill enabled later marriages and greater labor force participation among college-educated women. The technological advance of the birth control pill was complemented by other technological changes that lowered the relative cost of maintaining a household as a single (Greenwood and Guner 2009) and reduced the value of specialization in the home. More recent increases in marital postponement among college-educated women likely reflect increasing returns to education and experience, both of which increase the incentives to postpone potential career disruptions. Finally, a shift toward spousal matching on consumption and leisure preferences may lead to greater heterogeneity in matching and thus an increased benefit of time spent searching.

The large gaps in marriage rates by education seen among women in their twenties dissipate by their thirties. To get a better understanding of marital outcomes it is useful to look at ever-married rates for women at older ages; as such, we turn to the end data points in figure 3.2, when the women are age fifty. For white women born in 1900, 76 percent of those who were college-educated women had ever married by age fifty.[7] In contrast, 90 percent of high school graduates in this cohort had married by age fifty.[8] Marriage rates for college-educated women grew rapidly for women born between 1900

6. Goldin (2006) finds similar movement in those years for college-educated women using the CPS Marital and Fertility Supplements.

7. This comes from the 1950 Census. By examining women at age fifty in each of the Censuses from 1950 to 2000, we are presenting ever-married rates (by age fifty) for the 1900 to 1950 birth cohorts.

8. As previously noted, women born two decades before were even less likely to marry and the gap between college-educated women and those without a college degree shrunk in the decades before the turn of the twentieth century (Goldin 1997).

and 1930 and by the 1980 Census, 91 percent of college-educated fifty-year-old women had married. During this period, marriage rates were also growing for women in this cohort with less education and ever-married rates hit 97 percent for those with a high school degree or less. Thus, between the 1950 and 1980 Censuses, the closing of the educational marriage gap for white women was driven by large increases in the marriage rates of college-educated women, much of which occurred at older ages.[9]

Since 1980, there has been little change in the likelihood that college graduates ultimately marry. Between 1980 and 2007 the percent ever-married fell by 4 and 2 percentage points among forty- and fifty-year-old college graduates, respectively. The fall in marriage among high school graduates was somewhat greater, with ever-married rates falling by 8 and 4 percentage points among forty- and fifty-year-olds, respectively. The ever-married rates of those with some college are similar to high school graduates. In sum, those with less education had larger relative declines in marriage between 1980 and 2007 and it is this relatively larger decline in marriage rates among those with less education that led to further decreases in the educational marriage gap since 1980.

Two facts seen in figure 3.2 are worth noting: among white women, while marriage rates have fallen overall in recent decades, they are still similar to that seen in the 1950s. Indeed, among those with a high school degree, by age forty, a greater percentage had entered into marriage in 2007 than had done so in 1950. A similar increase was also seen among women with some college and, as has already been noted, a large increase in marriage rates has occurred among women with a college degree. Marriage rates immediately following World War II were at a historic high, leading to historically high ever-married rates for women who were of marrying age during this period, and thus, high ever-married rates in the 1960 and 1970 Censuses (Stevenson and Wolfers 2007). The second fact is that between 1950 and 1980 the percent ever-married plateaued, and did so at a relatively early age. In contrast, between 1990 and 2007 ever-married rates continue to increase among women over the age of forty. While some of the upward age slope at older ages seen in figure 3.2 reflects the decline in marriage among more recent cohorts, marriage rates among older adults have risen in recent decades. For example, 93 percent of forty-year-old white women had married in 1990 and this had risen to 94 percent by age fifty in 2000 for this cohort. Thus, in the decade after age forty, 15 percent of those who had never married did so.

As previously discussed, the age of first marriage has risen for all white women, but markedly more for those with a college degree. In 2000, by age twenty-two, 50 percent of white women with less than a high school degree had married. In comparison, the 50 percent threshold was crossed at age twenty-three, twenty-four, and twenty-seven for those with a high school degree, some college, and a college-degree, respectively. While some

9. These facts are similar to those presented in Goldin (1997) and Goldin (2004).

education may occur later, an examination of marital history data suggests that these patterns hold even when education is measured at a later point in life.[10]

While white women with a college education are increasingly postponing marriage, as previously noted, they have also increased their likelihood of ever marrying. In contrast, women with less education are postponing marriage, albeit to a lesser extent, and, in recent decades, they have also become somewhat less likely to ever marry. What is less known is how much of this shift reflects the changes in the composition of women in each of the educational categories, a change in how educational attainment may impact the desire or value of marriage for these women, or a change in how educational attainment affects the attractiveness of women to men in the marriage market. We will return to these issues in section 3.6.

A different picture emerges when we examine marital trends among black women by education. Figure 3.3 shows the percent of black women by education who have married by each age across the decades.[11] The most striking fact is the large declines in marriage rates among black women of all educational backgrounds. While the ever-married rates of forty-year-old white female college graduates fell only 4 percentage points between 1980 and 2007, the fall among black female college graduates was 19 percentage points. Among high school graduates the ever-married rates of black women fell by 25 percentage points, compared to a fall of 8 percentage points among whites. Moreover, black women who have not married by age forty have a smaller probability of marrying in the ensuing decade compared to white women in their cohort. In 1990, 82 percent of black women had married by age forty. Ten years later, we see that 83 percent of fifty-year-old black women have married—a closure of the never-married rate of about 10 percent.

In the 1960s through to the 1980s, black women with any college education married later than those with no college. However, after accounting for differences in the age of first marriage, black female college graduates have historically been as likely to marry as black women with less education. By 1990, black women with any college education had become more likely to ever marry compared with those with no college, and this trend has continued. As with white women, the decrease in marriage rates was lower among college-educated black women. These shifts have led to a positive gap in

10. Since most people who will complete college have done so by their late twenties, we examine twenty-eight- to thirty-year-old women in the 2004 SIPP, an age group that allows the most comparability with those in the 2000 Census. For these women, the age at which 50 percent had entered a first marriage was twenty-three, twenty-three, twenty-four, and twenty-six, for women with less than high school, high school, some college, and college, respectively.

11. The panel begins in 1960 for blacks because there are too few African Americans with education beyond high school in 1950 to generate meaningful estimates. In the 1950 Census only 2 percent of eighteen- to fifty-year-old black women had any education beyond high school; by 1960, the proportion had tripled to 6 percent.

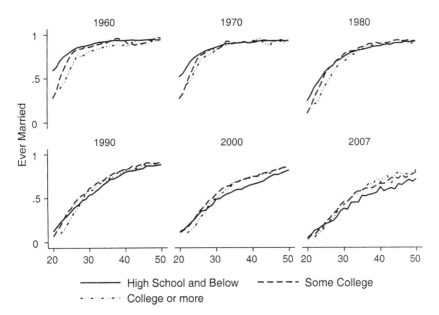

Fig. 3.3   Proportion of black women ever-married by age, 1960–2007

Source: 1960, 1970, 1980, 1990, and 2000 Censuses of Population and the 2007 American Community Survey.

Notes: Each panel shows the percent who have ever married at each age in a specific year for black women with high school or below, some college, or a college degree. Because of small sample sizes a three-year moving average centered at each age is used for 1960 and 1970.

which college-educated black women are more likely to marry compared to black women with less education.

Turning to men, we see smaller differences in marital formation behavior by educational backgrounds than is seen for women. Figures 3.4 and 3.5 show ever-married rates by age and education for white and black men, respectively, from 1960 through 2007. As with women, men with more education tend to marry at later ages and the age of first marriage has been rising for all men. Among white men, there have historically been few differences in the eventual likelihood of marrying by educational attainment. However, between 1990 and 2007, male college graduates became slightly more likely than those with less education to ever marry and, as with women, this change has arisen because of overall declines in marriage that have been sharpest for those with the least education.

A similar pattern is seen among black men, although the timing differs by several decades and, as with black women, there have been much steeper declines in marriage among blacks regardless of education. Starting in 1980, black male college graduates became more likely than black high school graduates to ever marry. This gap widened in the ensuing decades, a pattern that, as with whites, largely reflects bigger declines in marriage among those

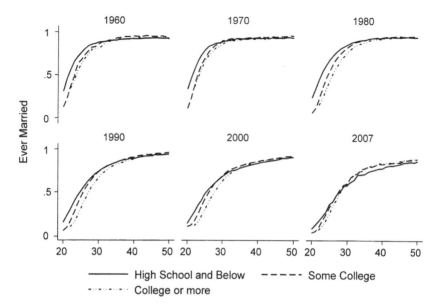

Fig. 3.4 Proportion of white men ever-married by age, 1960–2007

Source: 1960, 1970, 1980, 1990, and 2000 Censuses of Population and the 2007 American Community Survey.

Notes: Each panel shows the percent who have ever married at each age in a specific year for white men with high school or below, some college, or a college degree.

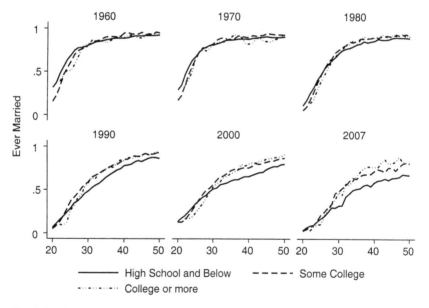

Fig. 3.5 Proportion of black men ever-married by age, 1960–2007

Source: 1960, 1970, 1980, 1990, and 2000 Censuses of Population and the 2007 American Community Survey.

Notes: Each panel shows the percent who have ever married at each age in a specific year for black men with high school or below, some college, or a college degree. Because of small sample sizes a three-year moving average centered at each age is used in 1960 and 1970.

with less education. In 2007, college-educated black men in their forties were 5 percentage points less likely to have ever married, compared with college-educated white men, yet they were more likely to have married compared to black men with less education or compared to black women of any educational background. Thus, college-educated men remain the most likely to marry among blacks.

In summary, for both men and women, marriage rates have declined since the 1980s among people of all educational backgrounds. However, these declines have been steeper among those with less education. Because college-educated white women had historically been less likely to marry, these shifts in marital behavior have led to a closing of the education gap in marriage for white women and there has been little difference by education in the likelihood of a woman marrying during her lifetime for recent generations. Among white men, a small gap has emerged in recent years in which those who attend college are more likely to marry than are those who do not.

Among blacks, the decline in the proportion marrying began in the 1950s. Between 1950 and 1980, the proportion of blacks who had married by the end of their thirties fell for all education groups, while the marriage rate rose for all whites. These different trends reversed the racial trends in marriage, opening a new gap in which whites were more likely to marry than were blacks. In the ensuing period the declines in marriage have been most stark among blacks and a wide gap has opened in marriage rates by race. Additionally, there are now large differences in marriage by education among both black men and women in which those with more education have become more likely to marry.

3.3   Marital Stability

Divorce rates rose for much of the twentieth century, reaching a peak in 1979 and falling thereafter (Stevenson and Wolfers 2007). One explanation for the high divorce rates of the 1970s may be that this period reflected a transition, with many having married the right partner for the old specialization model of marriage, only to find that pairing inadequate for the modern consumption-based marriage (Stevenson and Wolfers 2008a). As such, it is perhaps not surprising that current divorce rates are similar to those witnessed at the end of the 1960s. This fall in divorce rates is seen whether divorces are measured relative to the population or the stock of married people. Moreover, examining individual marriages, those who have married in recent years have been more likely to stay together than their parents' generation (Stevenson and Wolfers 2008b).

These patterns have not, however, occurred equally among those with more and less education. We examine the trends in divorce using the marital histories collected in the 2004 Survey of Income and Program Participation (SIPP). In general, divorce rates are lowest among those with a college degree, are the highest for those with some college, while those with a high school degree or below have divorce rates that fall in between the two groups.[12] The fact that it is those with "some college" that are the most at risk of divorce illustrates the potential role of selection in explaining why marital and divorce outcomes differ by educational attainment. Those with "some college" have either attended a two-year program or have failed to complete a four-year program.[13] As such, those with some college disproportionately represent those without the stamina or resources to complete their education. It is perhaps not surprising that this group would have similar difficulties maintaining their marriage.[14]

The inverted u-pattern of divorce rates by educational attainment is seen for both men and women and for both blacks and whites, across most decades. However, the magnitude of the differences in divorce by education has changed over time. Divorce rates rose during the 1960s and 1970s and couples who married during this time period experienced more marital dissolutions when compared to the men and women who married in the 1950s. The rise in divorce culminated in smaller differences by education in divorce rates twenty-five years post-marriage for those marrying in the 1970s. Among white men and women with a high school degree or less, 43 percent and 42 percent, respectively, of their marriages had ended within twenty-five years. For those with a college degree, 41 percent of women and 37 percent of men had divorced, and for those with some college, the percent divorcing hit the 50 percent mark for women and was just below—48 percent—for men.

These patterns can be seen in figures 3.6 and 3.7, which show the proportion of women's and men's first marriages, respectively, ending in divorce by cohort, educational attainment, and race.[15] The top row of each figure shows the divorce hazard for blacks, while the bottom row shows the divorce hazard for whites.[16] In addition, table 3.1 reports the percent of women and men who have divorced following ten and twenty years of marriage.

12. Several recent papers using different data sets have examined marital dissolution by education and also find a trend in lower divorce rates among college graduates (Raley and Bumpass 2003; Sweeney and Phillips 2004; and Martin 2006).

13. Among adults in the 2000 Census, around 78 percent of those with some college had received no degree.

14. For a similar argument, see Glick (1957).

15. Divorce is measured using retrospective marital histories from the 2004 SIPP in which individuals report the year of their first marriage and, if that marriage has ended by divorce, the year that the divorce occurred. In addition, individuals report the year of death if their marriage ended via their spouse's death (deaths that occur after a divorce are not reported). Marriages that end through the death of a spouse, and for which no divorce occurred, are included in the denominator. Excluding these marriages from the analysis has little effect on divorce rates in the first twenty years of marriage and raises divorce rates at twenty-five years post-marriage by a few percentage points. The reason for including these marriages is that excluding them mechanically raises the divorce rate as people age, since all marriages must end either through death or divorce.

16. We concentrate on first marriages so that the divorce hazards reflect the average person's experience rather than the average marital experience. The patterns are similar for second marriage, although second marriages are more likely to end in divorce.

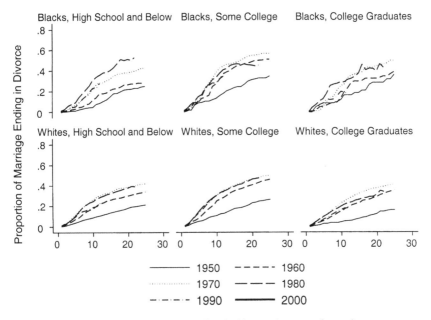

Fig. 3.6   **First marriages of women ending in divorce, by year of marriage**

Source: 2004 Survey of Income and Program Participation. Data are from marital histories in which respondents report the year a marriage began and, if it ended by divorce, the year the divorce occurred.

Notes: Each panel reports the proportion of women's first marriages ending in divorce at each year since the marriage occurred for six decadal cohorts. Cohorts are formed based on the year of marriage.

The divorce experience subsequent to the overall rise in divorce among those marrying in the 1970s has differed by education. For college graduates, the cohort marrying in the 1970s was the most likely to divorce. Subsequent cohorts of college graduates have had greater stability in their marriages. Marriages of college graduates that began in the 1980s have been less likely to end in divorce than those that began in the 1970s, and those that began in the 1990s were even less likely to do so.

Table 3.1 illustrates these trends by showing the percent divorcing within ten and twenty years of marriage. Among those marrying in the 1950s, only 12 percent of the marriages of white female college graduates and 17 percent of those of white male college graduates ended by divorce within the first twenty years of marriage. For those marrying in the 1960s, the dissolution rates had roughly doubled. They rose even further for those marrying in the 1970s, with 37 percent and 34 percent of the marriages of female and male college graduates ending within twenty years. The trend reversed after the 1970s cohort, and, among those marrying in the 1980s, the divorce rates of this marriage cohort had fallen back to rates similar to those experienced by the 1960s marriage cohort. For more recent cohorts, it is only possible to assess their marital dissolution rates earlier in marriage, but, in the first

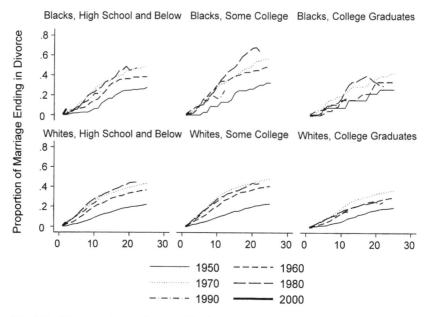

Fig. 3.7   First marriages of men ending in divorce, by year of marriage

Source: 2004 Survey of Income and Program Participation. Data are from marital histories in which respondents report the year a marriage began and, if it ended by divorce, the year the divorce occurred.

Notes: Each panel reports the proportion of men's first marriages ending in divorce at each year since the marriage occurred for six decadal cohorts. Cohorts are formed based on the year of marriage.

decade of marriage, divorce rates for those marrying in the 1990s were lower than those experienced by the previous cohort.

The experience of black college graduates is similar; however, the estimated divorce hazards for black college graduates are higher. Indeed, among all educational groups the estimated divorce rates are often higher among blacks. Yet, it is important to note that the much smaller sample size yields imprecise estimates. In nearly all cases the divorce rates of blacks are not statistically significantly different from those of whites.

Turning to those without a college degree we see that the high divorce rates experienced by those marrying in the 1970s continued for those marrying in the 1980s. Examining those marrying in the 1990s, it appears as if the divorce rates for those with less than a college degree have begun to fall with this most recent marriage cohort, particularly among those with a high school degree or less. Those with no college who married in the 1990s were about as likely to have made it to their tenth anniversary as were those who married in the 1960s. In contrast, among those with only some college, a statistically significant fall in divorce rates by the tenth anniversary occurred only among African American males.

Table 3.1 **Percent of marriages ending in divorce within ten and twenty years of marriage**

| Education | Divorced by 10 years following marriage | | | | Divorced by 20 years following marriage | | | |
| | White | | Black | | White | | Black | |
	Women (1)	Men (2)	Women (3)	Men (4)	Women (5)	Men (6)	Women (7)	Men (8)
			1950					
College	4	5	11	8	12	17	28	22
	(1.2)	(1.1)	(4.7)	(7.6)	(1.8)	(1.8)	(7.5)	(11)
Some college	11	9	13	9	23	20	31	26
	(1.1)	(1.2)	(4.0)	(5.4)	(1.6)	(1.8)	(5.4)	(7.4)
High school or less	9	9	4	6	18	19	22	25
	(.7)	(.9)	(1.2)	(2.4)	(1.0)	(1.3)	(3.1)	(4.2)
			1960					
College	15	13	13	16	29	26	32	34
	(1.4)	(1.2)	(4.4)	(6.5)	(1.7)	(1.6)	(6.4)	(9.5)
Some college	25	20	27	31	41	37	48	44
	(1.3)	(1.3)	(4.2)	(5.3)	(1.5)	(1.6)	(4.6)	(5.5)
High school or less	18	20	11	14	30	34	27	36
	(1.0)	(1.2)	(2.1)	(2.9)	(1.2)	(1.5)	(3.1)	(4.0)
			1970					
College	23	18	25	19	37	34	44	36
	(1.4)	(1.2)	(5.2)	(5.4)	(1.6)	(1.5)	(5.9)	(6.9)
Some college	30	29	38	29	46	44	54	50
	(1.2)	(1.3)	(3.4)	(4.1)	(1.3)	(1.4)	(3.5)	(4.4)
High school or less	26	25	22	26	39	39	38	45
	(1.1)	(1.1)	(2.9)	(3.5)	(1.3)	(1.4)	(3.5)	(3.9)
			1980					
College	20	15	29	17	31	25	39	33
	(1.2)	(1.1)	(5.7)	(4.9)	(2.0)	(1.9)	(8.5)	(8.5)
Some college	30	27	33	30	46	44	45	67
	(1.1)	(1.2)	(3.2)	(3.7)	(1.7)	(2.0)	(4.8)	(5.3)
High school or less	25	27	31	23	38	44	51	45
	(1.1)	(1.2)	(3.6)	(3.1)	(1.8)	(1.9)	(5.8)	(5.4)
			1990					
College	16	13	19	14				
	(1.5)	(1.4)	(5.0)	(5.6)				
Some college	31	25	28	17				
	(1.7)	(1.7)	(3.9)	(4.0)				
High school or less	19	23	23	21				
	(1.5)	(1.6)	(4.4)	(5.1)				

Source: 2004 Survey of Income and Program Participation.

Notes: Divorce rates are measured from marital history reports and include all marriages that formed during the decade under consideration. Marriages that end by the death of one spouse are included in the denominator. Standard errors are in parentheses.

While forecasting divorce rates is tricky, the data point to divorce happening earlier in marriage among more recent cohorts. Across all education groups, the divorce rate in the first five years has been little changed since the 1970s, even when the divorce rate at ten or twenty years has fallen. This pattern suggests that divorces that do happen are increasingly happening earlier in the marriage. This shift toward divorce earlier in marriage has been even more pronounced among those with a high school degree or less. Thus, differences in marital survival by education in recent decades are more extreme when looking at only the first decade of a marriage. Therefore, the early signs of further falls in divorce for those marrying in the 1990s are suggestive of greater declines in divorce rates in the coming decade for this group.

In sum, both men and women with a college degree have been consistently less likely to divorce and have also experienced a larger decline in divorce probabilities in the last few decades.

3.4   Remarriage

The high divorce rates of the 1970s and the increasing age of first marriage both contribute to thicker remarriage markets. As such, one might suspect that remarriage rates would have risen over time. What we see instead is that remarriage rates have fallen over time for all groups of women. Figures 3.8 and 3.9 show remarriage hazards among divorced white and black women, respectively.[17] The percent who have remarried is shown for each year post-divorce for women by their educational attainment.

In 1971, the majority of divorced women had remarried within five years following a divorce. Among whites, college-educated women were the least likely to remarry with only two-thirds remarried ten years post-divorce, compared with three-quarters of those with a high school degree or less. In contrast, there was little difference in remarriage rates among black women of differing educational backgrounds, with around 70 percent of all black women having remarried within ten years of a divorce. The 1980 sample shows a retreat from remarriage that is most pronounced among black women with a high school degree or less and among white women with a college degree. Ten years post-marriage, only 55 percent and 58 percent of these two groups had remarried. The percent of white women with a high school degree or less who had remarried after ten years was only 2 percentage points lower than that seen in the 1971 sample, while the percent of college-educated white women had fallen 7 percentage points.

In 1995, remarriage rates are somewhat higher among whites and are similar to those seen in 1971. Remarriage rates for all educational groups

---

17. Remarriage rates are calculated from marital histories collected in 1971, 1980, and 1995 from the Current Population Survey (CPS) and in 2004 from the SIPP.

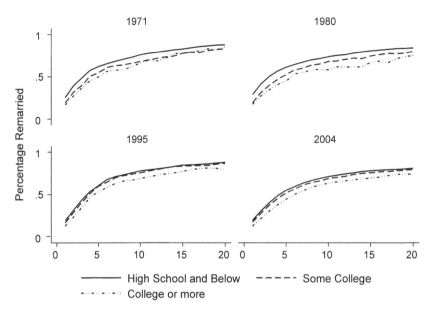

Fig. 3.8   Proportion of white women remarried by years since divorce 1971–2004
Sources: Current Population Survey (June 1971, 1980, and 1995) and Survey of Income and Program Participation (2004). Data are based on reports of marital history.
Notes: Each panel reports the proportion of white women who experienced a divorce who had remarried for each year since divorce separately by education.

of white women are, however, lower in the 2004 sample. Turning to black women, a different picture emerges. The fall in remarriage among black women has been greater and was most pronounced in the 1980 sample among those with a high school degree or below. As such, in 1980 these less educated black women were the least likely to remarry. The fall in remarriage among black women has continued in the 1995 and 2004 samples and the differences by education have largely been eroded. By the 2004 sample, it is ten years post-marriage before the majority of black women have remarried.

Figure 3.10 shows that a similar decrease in remarriage has occurred among both white and black men of all educational groups. However, remarriage is more common among men than among women and, unlike women, remarriage rates rise with education among both black and white men.[18] In 1971, 85 percent of white, and 87 percent of black, college-educated men had remarried within ten years following a divorce. In 2004, these rates had fallen to 76 percent and 61 percent, respectively. Remarriage rates for those with a high school degree or below also fell, but to a lesser extent, thereby eroding some of the remarriage gap by education.

18. See also Bumpass, Sweet, and Martin (1990), who note this phenomenon when examining the 1980 and 1985 CPS.

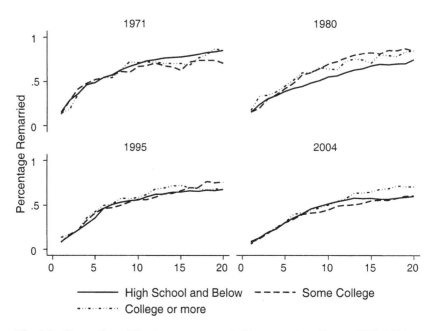

Fig. 3.9   Proportion of black women remarried by years since divorce 1971–2004

Sources: Current Population Survey (June 1971, 1980, and 1995) and Survey of Income and Program Participation (2004).

Notes: Each panel reports the proportion of white women who experienced a divorce who had remarried for each year since divorce separately by education.

Table 3.2 shows the decline over time in the likelihood of remarriage in a regression context, using alternative data sources.[19] The first column shows that remarriage rates have been lower in each survey wave we examine. In the second column we add controls for changes in first marriage behavior as measured by cohort and age of first marriage. These controls suggest that remarriage has fallen even more steeply over time. The next four columns examine the trends separately by race and sex. Since 1980, white men, the group most likely to remarry, have experienced sharper declines in remarriage compared to white women. However, the largest declines in remarriage have occurred among blacks. Both black men and women have become substantially less likely to remarry.

Some of the decline in remarriage may reflect couples cohabiting rather than remarrying. Remarriages are more likely than first marriages to be preceded by a period of cohabitation. In the 2000s, 75 percent of those entering a second or higher order marriage had cohabited prior to the marriage,

19. The regression analysis uses data from the 1970 and 1980 decennial Censuses and the 1991, 1992, 1993, and 2004 Panels of the SIPP. We turn to the SIPP beginning in 1991, as questions used to infer remarriage from the Census were discontinued after 1980.

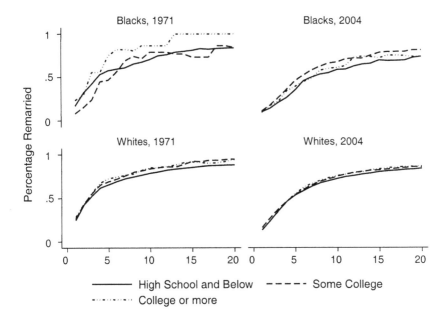

Fig. 3.10 Proportion of men remarried by years since divorce 1971–2004

Sources: Current Population Survey (June 1971) and Survey of Income and Program Participation (2004).

Notes: Each panel reports the proportion of white or black men who experienced a divorce who had remarried for each year since divorce separately by education.

Table 3.2   Trends in remarriage

Regression coefficients	Full sample		White women	Black women	White men	Black men
	(1)	(2)	(3)	(4)	(5)	(6)
1980 dummy	−.074***	−.062***	−.054***	−.139***	−.050***	−.104***
	(.001)	(.002)	(.002)	(.005)	(.002)	(.005)
1990 dummy	−.086***	−.094***	−.068***	−.220***	−.105***	−.159***
	(.004)	(.004)	(.005)	(.015)	(006)	(.021)
2004 dummy	−.105***	−.135***	−.087***	−.256***	−.167***	−.261***
	(.004)	(.004)	(.006)	(.016)	(.007)	(.021)
Age at marriage		−.012***	−.017***	−.010***	−.016***	−.009***
		(.001)	(.000)	(.001)	(.001)	(.001)
Age		.007***	.006***	.011***	.009***	.009***
		(.001)	(.001)	(.001)	(.001)	(.001)
Sample size	1,503,866	1,503,866	698,836	96,519	590,483	71,772

Sources: Census of Population 1970 and 1980. Survey of Income and Program Participation 1991, 1992, 1993, and 2004. Marginal effects reported.

Note: Probit regression dependent variable: Remarried. Robust standard errors in parentheses.

***Significant at the 1 percent level.
**Significant at the 5 percent level.
*Significant at the 10 percent level.

while 59 percent of those entering a first marriage had done so (Stevenson and Wolfers 2007). Additionally, the thicker matching market may lead to an increased duration of search by increasing the option value of continued search and/or by increasing one's utility while single (aside from the potential to meet mates, being single may be more enjoyable when there are lots of singles in one's age bracket).

While remarriage rates have fallen overall, the pattern of remarriage by education has not changed. Remarriage among white women falls with educational attainment, while there are little differences in remarriage by education among black women. Among men, remarriage rises with education. These patterns are similar to what we see when examining first marriages, with the exception that college-educated white women remain much less likely to remarry compared to those with less education. Unlike the education gap in first marriages, the remarriage gap by education has not closed in recent years.

One explanation for this may lie in the changing patterns of first marriage. Table 3.3 shows that a college degree is associated with a lower likelihood of having remarried among white women in the 2004 SIPP. However, adding controls for length of marriage and years since the divorce reduces the coefficient on the college indicator variable, and adding a control for the age at marriage attenuates the coefficient further. In recent years more highly educated women have tended to marry later and have longer duration marriages. It is these differences in the patterns of first marriage that explain much of the recent differences in remarriage rates by education among white women. However, this is not the case in earlier periods. Examining remarriage in the 1971, 1980, and 1995 Current Population Survey (CPS) marital

Table 3.3   Education and remarriage

	2004 SIPP			1995 CPS	1980 CPS	1971 CPS
Regression coefficients	(1)	(2)	(3)	(4)	(5)	(6)
College dummy	−.078***	−.032**	0.025	0.005	−0.039*	−.095***
	(0.015)**	(.015)	(0.015)	(.016)	(.023)	(.030)
Yrs. since divorce		.016***	.014***	.023***	0.016***	.013***
		(.001)	(0.001)	(.001)	(.001)	(.001)
Length of marriage		−.015***	−.016***	−.014***	−.008***	−.009***
		(.001)	(.001)	(.001)	(.002)	(.001)
Age at marriage			−.028***	−.028***	−.028***	−0.012***
			(.002)	(0.002)	(.002)	(.003)
Sample size	8,319	8,319	8,319	8,851	7,303	5,252

Notes: Probit regression dependent variable: Remarried. Robust standard errors in parentheses. Marginal effects reported. The 1971 CPS survey only asked about the first and most recent marriage. If individuals are married three or more times, their second marriage is assumed to begin halfway between the end of their first marriage and the beginning of their latest marriage.

history supplements, columns (4) through (6) show that college-educated women in the 1971 and 1980 samples were less likely to remarry even once controls are added for timing of their first marriage. In 1995, however, this difference by education was, as in 2004, explained by the patterns of first marriage. Remarriage has thus largely followed the patterns seen in first marriage, with remarriage rates falling over time and a closing over time of the education gap among white women.

3.5 Fertility

Fertility declines starkly as maternal education rises and the educational differences have not changed despite enormous increases in the educational attainment of women. Figure 3.11 shows the number of children in the household from 1950 to 2007 for white women by age and level of education. As with marriage, these graphs show both differences in fertility timing and changes in fertility across cohorts. In 1950, college graduates had the fewest number of children in the household at every point in the life cycle. However, in subsequent decades, the number of children in the homes of older women became greatest for college graduates—illustrating a shift toward later fer-

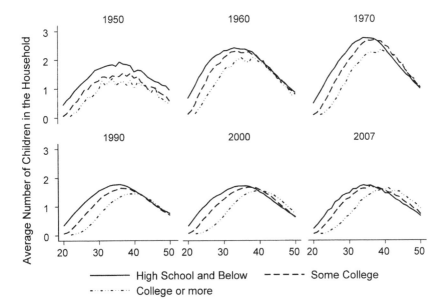

Fig. 3.11 Average number of children in the household by age (white women)
Sources: 1950, 1960, 1970, 1990, and 2000 Censuses of Population and 2007 American Community Survey.
Notes: Each panel shows the percent of white women with children in the household at each age in a specific decade for those with high school or below, some college, or a college degree for white women.

tility that has continued through to the present time.[20] In each successive Census there is a steady decrease in the probability that college-educated women have children in the home in their twenties and thirties. Since the 1970s, college graduates in their thirties have become more likely than they were in the past, and more likely than other women, to have children (Martin 2000). This rise in maternal age is also illustrated by the fact that the median age at which mothers with a college degree have an infant in the household has risen by four years over this period.

In contrast, there has been little increase in the likelihood that those with less education have children later in life and the age distribution of women with children in the home among those with a high school degree or less is little changed. This is further illustrated by the fact that there has been no change in the median age at which mothers without any college education have an infant in the household. Thus, the well-publicized delay in fertility has been occurring almost exclusively among women with more education.[21]

Figure 3.12 shows a similar pattern among black women. Ellwood and Jencks (2002) highlighted the fact that black women with less education have increasingly delayed marriage, yet have not delayed or reduced childbearing to the same extent. The result is a rise in out-of-wedlock births, which has happened for both black and white women with less education. As the ever-married rates of black women with no college fell by three times as much as the fall among white women with no college, the rise in out-of-wedlock childbirths has been greatest among black women with less education. Thus changes in marriage, not fertility, account for the rise in out-of-wedlock childbirth.

Greater access to education and higher potential wages, combined with improved control over fertility, has altered the incentives that women face. Birth control has lowered the cost of postponing pregnancy, while better human capital and market options and the rising returns to work experience have increased the opportunity cost of career disruptions, particularly in the early stages of one's career. That the delay has occurred most strongly among women at the top of the educational ladder point to the fact that these developments have most sharply affected those with more education. Although only suggestive evidence has been provided that the costs to fertility have risen over time (Loughran and Zissimopoulos 2007), Miller (2007) shows in a cross-section of women that delaying fertility increases lifetime

20. Completed fertility by birth cohort was calculated from the 1980 and 1990 Censuses. In the 1980 and 1990 Censuses children ever born peaked for forty-seven- and fifty-seven-year-old women, respectively, or those born in 1933. Among college-educated women, the peak occurred a few years earlier with the 1930 birth cohort (women who were ages fifty and sixty in the 1980 and 1990 Censuses, respectively).

21. Rindfuss, Morgan, and Offut (1996); Martin (2004a); and Yang and Morgan (2004) examine the issue through the early 1990s and similarly find a larger delay for more educated women.

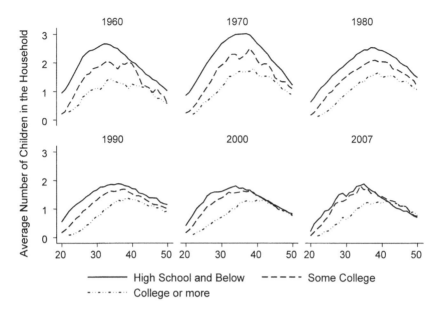

Fig. 3.12   Average number of children in the household by age (black women)

Sources: 1960, 1970, 1980, 1990, and 2000 Censuses of Population and 2007 American Community Survey.

Notes: Each panel shows the percent of black women with children in the household at each age in a specific decade for those with high school or below, some college, or a college degree for white women. Because of small sample sizes a three-year moving average centered at each age is used in 1960 and 1970.

earnings, and the gains are highest for college graduates. Further evidence comes from Goldin and Katz (2008), who examine the family and work behavior of multiple cohorts from Harvard/Radcliffe. Patterns for women from this selective institution, who tend to be more strongly tied to the labor market, indicate a much larger increase in fertility delay relative to other college graduates.

In addition to changes in the timing of fertility, total fertility has fallen steadily since the baby boom for white and black women of all educational backgrounds. Table 3.4 shows the number of children ever born to forty-five-to fifty-year-old women (a reasonable proxy for completed fertility) over the past five decades.[22] Despite changes in total fertility across the decades, the pattern of falling fertility with education is similar in all time periods for all women, and this is seen when examining the National Survey of Family Growth as well (Preston and Sten Harnett 2008)[23] College graduates have the

22. The Census stopped asking about children ever born after the 1990 Census and thus the most recent data come from the 2004 SIPP.
23. Goldin (2004) shows a similar pattern by education in the percent that never have children.

Table 3.4   Children ever born among forty-five- to fifty-year-old women

	College graduates	Some college	HS graduates	HS dropouts	All
White women					
1950	1.22	1.75	1.74	2.69	2.33
1960	1.50	1.81	1.84	2.50	2.18
1970	2.22	2.49	2.46	2.92	2.63
1980	2.40	2.90	2.92	3.39	2.99
1990	1.85	2.33	2.49	2.99	2.40
2004	1.56	1.90	1.97	2.86	1.91
Black women					
1950	1.73	1.99	2.13	2.76	2.67
1960	1.37	1.69	1.96	2.84	2.62
1970	1.80	2.32	2.64	3.49	3.19
1980	2.10	3.23	3.45	4.37	3.80
1990	1.89	2.54	2.85	3.63	2.92
2004	1.50	2.22	2.22	2.78	2.13

Sources: Census of Population (1950–1990) and Survey of Income and Program Participation (2004).

Notes: The "Children Ever Born" question was asked in 1950 and 1960 only of women who had ever married. To provide numbers that are representative of all women, the above statistics are constructed from the ever-married women of 1950 and 1960, and the never-married women aged sixty-five to seventy and fifty-five to sixty, respectively, from the 1970 Census. The number of never-married forty-five- to fifty-year-olds in 1950 and 1960 that had married by 1970 is negligible.

fewest children, followed by those with some college, then high school graduates, and finally high school dropouts have the greatest number of children. Fertility for all groups of forty-five- to fifty-year-olds rose between the 1950 and 1980 Censuses, and has decreased thereafter such that fertility rates in 2004 are similar, albeit slightly higher, to those seen in 1960 for each education group. However, total fertility has dropped throughout the period, as women's educational attainment has risen enormously with no subsequent erosion of the negative relationship between fertility and education.

3.6   Marital Happiness

Families have clearly changed their behavior in terms of formation, expansion (through children), and dissolution in a way that is correlated with education. Subjective well-being data can perhaps help us better understand more subtle differences in the family experience between people with differing educational backgrounds. Data from the General Social Survey (GSS) asks individuals how satisfied they are with their family life and how happy they are with their marriage as well as other attitudinal questions such as whether married people are happier than unmarried people. The GSS is a nationally representative sample of about 1,500 respondents each year from

1972 to 1993 (except 1992), and continues with around 3,000 respondents every second year from 1994 through to 2004, rising to 4,500 respondents in 2006. Analyzing these data, we quickly see that the perceived benefits of marriage differ by education. Nearly four times as many noncollege graduates as college graduates agree that "financial security is the main benefit of marriage," and are slightly more likely to agree that "children are the main purpose of marriage." Not surprisingly, those with a college degree are less likely to see "production complementarities" as the main benefit of marriage.

Turning to expectations of marital happiness, we see in table 3.5 that when people are asked generally whether they would agree with the statement that married people are happier than unmarried people (1988, 1994, and 2002), there is a clear trend, with fewer people agreeing over time. Consistent with the changing marital behavior patterns, college-educated women have become slightly more likely to believe that married people are happier; while women without a college degree have become substantially less likely to agree that married people are happier. Moreover, in 1988, women without a college degree were more likely than college graduates to agree that married people are happier and, by 2002, they were much less likely than college graduates to agree. A similar pattern has not occurred among men, rather both those with and without college degrees became less likely to agree over time. Despite this fall, men remain more likely than women to believe that married people are happier than unmarried people.

Turning to actual happiness in their marriage, tables 3.6 and 3.7 show that people with more education are happier in their marriages and with their family life, just as they are more likely to think that married people are

Table 3.5   Trends in expectations regarding marriage and happiness: "Married people are generally happier than unmarried people?"

	Women			Men		
	Agree	Disagree	Neither	Agree	Disagree	Neither
1988						
College graduate	47.4	11.1	41.6	62.2	5.6	32.2
Noncollege graduate	53.7	14.7	31.6	57.8	12.5	29.7
1994						
College graduate	46.6	17.8	35.6	57.8	8.0	34.2
Noncollege graduate	45.2	19.0	35.8	48.5	22.2	29.3
2002						
College graduate	50.7	19.5	29.9	47.9	18.8	33.3
Noncollege graduate	37.4	24.9	37.8	49.2	17.5	33.3

Notes: Data are from the General Social Survey in 1988, 1994, and 2002. The "Agree" category includes those that "strongly agree" and "agree," while the "Disagree" category includes those that "strongly disagree" and "disagree." The "Neither" category includes those who "can't choose" and those who "neither agree nor disagree."

happier than unmarried people. The college/noncollege differential is particularly stark for women. And as with expectations regarding the happiness of married people, the marital happiness data reveal that men are typically happier in their marriages than are women.

In table 3.6 we run ordered probits by gender on how happy respondents are with their marriage. College-educated white women have been consistently happier in their marriages, with no apparent time trend in these differences. However, the coefficient is reduced by 40 percent when we add

Table 3.6 **Trends in marital happiness**

Regression coefficients	Women		Men	
	(1)	(2)	(3)	(4)
College*white	.222***	.132***	.106***	.094***
	(.032)	(.037)	(.032)	(.035)
College*black	.004	−.105	−.015	−.034
	(.114)	(.117)	(.121)	(.121)
College*time trend	−0.004	−.001	.014***	.014***
	(.005)	(.005)	(.004)	(.004)
Time trend	−.005**	−.009***	−.009***	−.010***
	(.002)	(.003)	(.002)	(.003)
Black	−.379***	−.329***	−.364***	−.388***
	(.046)	(.048)	(.049)	(.051)
Controls		✓		✓
Percent very happy	White women	Black women	White men	Black men
College				
1970s	74	59	70	49
2000s	67	55	74	51
Noncollege				
1970s	66	46	70	55
2000s	59	55	63	54

Notes: Ordered probit regression dependent variable: "Taking things all together how would you describe your marriage?" [3] Very happy [2] Pretty happy [1] Not too happy. Sample size for women is 11,228 and for men is 10,111. Data are from the General Social Survey from 1973–2006. Robust standard errors in parentheses. "Employment status" includes indicators for full-time, part-time, temporary illness/vacation/strike, unemployed, retired, in school, keeping house, and other; "Income" is based on imputations of real family income, collapsed into indicator variables, one for each decile; "Children" includes indicator variables for the number of children ever born, up to eight; "Education" variables are coded the highest degree earned by the respondent, respondent's father, and respondent's mother, including separate variables for <high school, high school, associates/junior college, bachelor's, or graduate degrees; "Religion" includes separate indicators for Protestant, Catholic, Jewish, None, and Other; "Region" includes indicator variables for each of nine regions. Separate dummy variables are also included for missing values of each control variable. Check marks indicate that control variables are added to the regressions for columns (2) and (4).

***Significant at the 1 percent level.
**Significant at the 5 percent level.
*Significant at the 10 percent level.

controls, a reduction that is being driven by differences in the number of children, income, and parents' education. College-educated white men are also more likely to be happier in their marriage compared with noncollege-educated white men, and this difference increases over time. On the other hand, college-educated black men and women appear to be no happier in their marriages than are those without college degrees.

Table 3.7 explores how much satisfaction respondents get from their family life by education, again using ordered probits. We find that, as with marital satisfaction, college-educated white women consistently get more satisfaction from their family life, although the relationship is being driven solely by college-educated white women who were married at the time of their interview. Black college-educated women do not appear to get any more satisfaction than those with no college, and we can reject that the black-white college estimates are the same when controls are added. However, college-educated black and white men get more satisfaction at a marginally significant level without covariates, although no difference is found for men of either group when controls are added.

3.7 Discussion

This chapter has documented changes in the family experience for women and men at the bottom and top of the educational distribution by race. College-educated women born at the beginning of the last century were the women least likely to marry. As we enter the twenty-first century these women are poised to become the most likely to ever marry. This shift occurred in two stages. In the first stage, college-educated women had rapid increases in the probability of marrying. In the second stage, college-educated women had smaller falls in marriage compared to those with less education. Both of these stages have contributed to a closing of the marriage gap by education. Like women, male college graduates in the latter period had smaller falls in marriage compared to men with less education, opening a small marriage gap in which men with the most education have the greatest likelihood of marriage.

Since 1950 the percent of women earning college degrees has increased tremendously. This substantial increase in educational attainment, shown in table 3.8, might mean that compositional shifts explain the trends in family behavior by women's education. That is, it might be that the family behavior of the women who would have been in each educational group in an earlier period has not changed, but rather that recent cohorts of college graduates have expanded to include those with greater preferences for marriage. To look at the role of compositional changes we divided college graduates in 2007 into two groups. The first represents the proportion of women in 1950 who went to college—roughly 6 percent of women. This group was assigned the marriage rates of women who went to college in 1950. The second group—the remaining quarter of women who were college graduates in

Table 3.7   **Trends in family satisfaction**

Regression coefficients	Women		Men	
	(1)	(2)	(3)	(4)
College*white	.155***	−.064	.052*	−.082
	(.034)	(.058)	(.031)	(.061)
College*black	.150	.129	.221*	.227
	(.099)	(.131)	(.126)	(.166)
College*time trend	−.005	−.003	.003	−.003
	(.007)	(.007)	(.006)	(.006)
Black	−.336***	−.207***	−.258***	−.106**
	(.036)	(.040)	(.046)	(.051)
Time trend	.002	−.003	−.003	.000
	(.003)	(.004)	(.006)	(.004)
College*married*white		.258***		.073
		(.070)		(.070)
College*married*black		−.250		−.277
		(.193)		(.229)
Married		.403***		.933***
		(.030)		(.038)
Controls		✓		✓
Percent very great deal	White women	Black women	White men	Black men
College				
1970s	53	33	44	44
1990s	53	24	47	39
Noncollege				
1970s	45	32	41	32
1990s	46	28	40	31

Notes: Ordered probit regression dependent variable: "How much satisfaction do you get from your family life?" [7] A very great deal [6] A great deal [5] quite a bit [4] A fair amount [3] Some [2] A little [1] None. Sample size for women is 11,321 and for men is 8,699. Data are from the General Social Survey from 1973–1994. Robust standard errors in parentheses. "Employment status" includes indicators for full-time, part-time, temporary illness/vacation/ strike, unemployed, retired, in school, keeping house, and other; "Income" is based on imputations of real family income, collapsed into indicator variables, one for each decile; "Children" includes indicator variables for the number of children ever born, up to eight; "Education" variables are coded the highest degree earned by the respondent, respondent's father, and respondent's mother, including separate variables for <high school, high school, associates/junior college, bachelor's, or graduate degrees; "Religion" includes separate indicators for Protestant, Catholic, Jewish, None, and Other; "Region" includes indicator variables for each of nine regions. Separate dummy variables are also included for missing values of each control variable. Check marks indicate that control variables are added to the regressions for columns (2) and (4).

***Significant at the 1 percent level.
**Significant at the 5 percent level.
*Significant at the 10 percent level.

Table 3.8   Educational attainment of women ages forty-five to fifty, by decade

	College graduates	Some college	HS graduates	HS dropouts
White women				
1950	6	10	20	65
1960	7	11	27	56
1970	7	13	41	39
1980	11	16	44	29
1990	20	27	36	17
2000	30	33	28	9
2007	30	32	30	8
Black women				
1950	2	2	4	92
1960	3	4	9	84
1970	4	6	19	71
1980	8	13	29	51
1990	13	23	31	33
2000	18	33	30	20
2007	19	33	34	14

Notes: 1950–2000 data are from the Censuses of Population. The 2007 data are from the American Community Survey. Each cell represents the percent of white or black forty-five- to fifty-year-old women with that level of educational attainment.

2007—was assigned the marriage rates of women who did not go to college in 1950. For forty-five- to fifty-year-old women in 2007, this exercise replicates almost perfectly the actual percent that have ever married. A similar exercise shows that simple compositional shifts cannot, however, explain the trends in fertility.

However, Goldin (2004) notes that many of the trends in marital behavior among college-educated women can be seen when the group is limited to a particular college. For example, (Goldin and Katz 2008) find that men and women attending Harvard in the late 1960s and early 1970s experienced a divorce rate that was nearly twice that of those graduating two decades later. The divorce patterns seen among the Harvard graduates are similar to those seen when one examines college graduates in general.

The differences in marital behavior that we have documented yield very different marital experiences over the life cycle. The growing difference in the patterns of marriage entry for women of different educational backgrounds and race combined with different patterns in divorce and remarriage rates has led to stark differences in the probability of being married at specific ages. In figure 3.13, we show the percent of white and black women who are currently married by education. In 1960, college-educated women were less likely to be married at every age. Today, those without a college degree are the most likely to be married in their twenties, while those with a college degree are more likely to be married in their thirties and forties. These

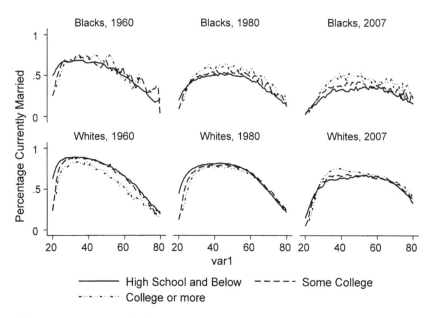

Fig. 3.13   Proportion of white and black women currently married

Sources: 1960 and 1980 Censuses of Population and 2007 American Community Survey.

Notes: Each panel shows the percent of white and black women who are currently married at each age in a specific decade for those with high school or below, some college, or a college degree for white women. Because of small sample sizes a three-year moving average centered at each age is used in 1960 for black women. The sample size for black college graduates aged seventy and older in 1960 is too small to warrant any form of inference and hence is excluded.

differences reflect the different patterns of age at marriage and the likelihood of divorce.

What is missing from our analysis is cohabitation. Unfortunately cohabitation data is relatively sparse and so does not lend itself easily to the long-run analysis that we pursue here. Yet it is likely that such an analysis would reveal that cohabitation cannot explain the entire decline in marriage and remarriage. Adults today are spending more time as singles. For college graduates those years tend to occur early in the life cycle, with most spending much of their twenties outside marriage, while those with less education are more likely to spend some of their thirties and forties outside of a marital relationship.

In 1981 Andrew Cherlin described the new typical life course as "marriage, divorce, remarriage." Today, marriage is happening later, divorce is less likely, and remarriage is less common. Moreover, the typical life pattern differs by race and education. Among college graduates the typical life pattern now involves a prolonged period of being single before entering marriage and having children. Divorce and remarriage are now experienced by a shrinking minority of the college-educated. Among those with no college, the typical life experience remains marriage, children, divorce, remarriage, but is quickly shifting toward children, marriage, divorce, and a prolonged period of being single or cohabiting before remarriage.

References

Aguiar, E., and M. Hurst. 2007. Measuring trends in leisure: The allocation of time over five decades. *Quarterly Journal of Economics:* 969–1006.

Becker, G. 1981. *A treatise on the family.* Cambridge, MA: Harvard University Press.

Blau, F., and L. Kahn. 1997. Swimming upstream: Trends in the gender wage differential in the 1980s. *Journal of Labor Economics:* 1–42.

———. 2000. Gender differences in pay. *Journal of Economic Perspectives:* 75–99.

Bumpass, L., J. Sweet, and T. C. Martin. 1990. Changing patterns of remarriage. *Journal of Marriage and the Family* 52 (3): 747–56.

Cherlin, A. 1981. *Marriage, divorce, remarriage.* Cambridge, MA: Harvard University Press.

Ellwood, D., and C. Jencks. 2002. The spread of single-parent families in the United States since 1960. Kennedy School of Government Harvard University. Unpublished Manuscript.

Glaeser, E., J. Gyourko, and R. Saks. 2005. Why have housing prices gone up? NBER Working Paper no. 11129. Cambridge, MA: National Bureau of Economic Research, February.

Glick, P. 1957. *American families.* New York: Wiley.

Goldin, C. 1997. Career and family: College women look to the past. In *Gender and family issues in the workplace,* ed. F. Blau and R. Ehrenberg, 20–58. New York: Russell Sage Foundation.

———. 2004. The long road to the fast track. *AAPSS Annals* 596 (November): 20–35.

———. 2006. The quiet revolution that transformed women's employment, education, and family. *American Economic Review Papers and Proceedings* 96 (2): 1–21.

Goldin, C., and L. Katz. 2002. The power of the pill: Oral contraceptives and women's career and marriage decisions. *Journal of Political Economy* 110 (4): 730–70.

———. 2008. Transitions: Career and family life cycles of the educational elite. *American Economic Review Papers and Proceedings* 98 (2): 363–69.

Goldin, C., L. Katz, and I. Kuziemko. 2006. The homecoming of American college women: The reversal of the college gender gap. *Journal of Economic Perspectives* 20 (4): 133–56.

Goldstein, J., and C. Kenney. 2001. Marriage delayed or marriage forgone? New cohort forecasts of first marriage for U.S. women. *American Sociological Review* 66 (4): 506–19.

Greenwood, J., and N. Guner. 2009. Marriage and divorce since World War II: Analyzing the role of technological progress on the formation of households. In *NBER macroeconomics annual 2008,* ed. D. Acemoglu, K. Rogoff, and M. Woodford, 231–76. Chicago: University of Chicago Press Journals.

Loughran, D., and J. Zissimopoulos. 2007. Why wait? The effect of marriage and childbearing on the wage growth of men and women. RAND Working Paper no. 482-1.

Martin, S. 2000. Diverging fertility among U.S. women who delay childbearing past age 30. *Demography* 37 (4): 523–33.

———. 2004a. Delayed marriage and childbearing: Implications and measurement of diverging trends in family timing. In *Social inequality,* ed. K. Neckerman, 79–119. New York: Russell Sage.

———. 2004b. Reassessing delayed and forgone marriage in the United States. University of Maryland. Unpublished Manuscript.

———. 2006. Trends in marital dissolution by women's education in the United States. *Demographic Research* 15 (20): 537–60.

Miller, A. 2007. The effects of motherhood timing on career path. University of Virginia. Unpublished Manuscript.

Newhouse, J. 1992. Medical care costs: How much welfare loss? *Journal of Economic Perspectives* 6 (3): 3–21.

Pollak, R. 2005. Bargaining power in marriage: Earnings, wage rates and household production. NBER Working Paper no. 11239. Cambridge, MA: National Bureau of Economic Research, April.

Preston, S., and C. Sten Harnett. 2008. The future of American fertility. NBER Working Paper no. 14498. Cambridge, MA: National Bureau of Economic Research, November.

Raley, R. K., and L. Bumpass. 2003. The topography of the divorce plateau: Levels and trends in union stability in the United States after 1980. *Demographic Research* 8-8:245–59.

Rindfuss, R., S. P. Morga, and K. Offutt. 1996. Education and the changing age pattern of American fertility: 1963–1989. *Demography* 33 (3): 277–90.

Schwartz, C., and R. Mare. 2005. Trends in educational assortative marriage from 1940 to 2003. *Demography* 42 (4): 621–46.

Stevenson, B. 2007. The impact of divorce laws on marriage-specific capital. *Journal of Labor Economics* 25 (1): 75–94.

Stevenson, B., and J. Wolfers. 2007. Marriage and divorce: Changes and their driving forces. *Journal of Economic Perspectives* 21 (2): 27–52.

———. 2008a. Marriage and market. *Cato Unbound,* January 8. Available at: http://www.cato-unbound.org.

———. 2008b. Trends in marital stability. University of Pennsylvania. Unpublished Manuscript.

Sweeney, M., and M. Cancian. 2004. The changing importance of economic prospects for assortative mating. *Journal of Marriage and the Family* 66:1015–28.

Sweeney, M., and J. Philips. 2004. Understanding racial differences in marital disruption: Recent trends and explanations. *Journal of Marriage and Family* 66 (3): 639–50.

Yang, Y., and S. P. Morgan. 2004. How big are educational and racial fertility differentials in the U.S.? *Social Biology* 50:167–87.

Comment   Enrico Moretti

This chapter is motivated by the observation that, over the past several decades, there has been a marked decline in the value of production efficiencies

Enrico Moretti is the Michael Peevey and Donald Vial Chair in Labor Economics and professor of economics at the University of California, Berkeley, a research fellow of the Centre for Economic Policy Research and the Institute for the Study of Labor (IZA), and a research associate of the National Bureau of Economic Research.

from marriage because of technological improvements and higher women's earnings. Higher earnings for women imply a higher opportunity cost for women who stay at home. The authors argue that this decline in the value of production efficiencies from marriage should have led to a significant decline in marriage rates, but the actual decline in marriage rates that we observe in the data is limited.

Motivated by the empirical puzzle, the chapter seeks to address three important questions:

1. What are the economic advantages of getting married?
2. Have these advantages changed over time?
3. Have these advantages changed differentially for high-income and low-income individuals?

The main contribution of this chapter is that it asks a series of ambitious and unexplored questions and provides a broad historical perspective on important demographic shifts. The thesis is that the economic benefits of marriage have changed significantly. In particular, there has been a shift away from *production-based* marriage to *consumption-based* marriage. The authors hypothesize that this shift is caused by significant increases in the benefits of shared public goods within marriage and by significant increases in consumption complementarities within marriage.

If this hypothesis is true, then there are several empirical patterns that we should observe in the data. First, marriage should become more common among those with more leisure time and more disposable income. Consistent with this hypothesis, the data indicates that while in the 1950s college-educated women had low marriage rates, today they have marriage rates near the average. Furthermore, there has been a marked shift toward late marriages and an increase in divorce rates, and these changes are larger for the college-educated.

A second implication of the shift away from *production-based* marriage to *consumption-based* marriage is that we should see measurable increases in the degree of assortative mating along education and racial lines. A third implication is that hours of work of members of the couple should become increasingly similar, in order to allow the consumption of shared public goods within marriage.

An appealing feature of the chapter is that it uses economic hypotheses to explain demographic changes. Moreover, it does not rely on ad hoc assumptions on changes in tastes to explain the demographic changes. In general, it is easy to use changes in tastes to explain virtually any demographic shift. While this approach may be valid in other contexts, it is rather unsatisfactory for this subject.

While the theoretical argument is intriguing and ambitious, some of the evidence is indirect and open to alternative interpretations. In my view, the argument proposed would benefit from more direct empirical tests. For example, the authors could exploit exogenous geographical differences in the changes over time in women's wages and labor force participation. Exogenous shifts in the relative demand for female occupations have different impact on different states depending on the historical industrial mix. These shifts can be used to identify the effect of increases in women's earnings potential outside the household. Alternatively, the authors could exploit exogenous changes in the benefits of marriage that arise from differences across states in the changes over time in the price of small housing units relative to price of large units. Finally, the increased availability of the Time Use Survey may also provide a way to directly measure increases in consumption complementarities and increase in the benefits of shared public goods.

In conclusion, the question of whether there has been a shift from *production-based* marriage to *consumption-based* marriage is important, relevant, and understudied. This chapter has the merit of raising the question, and providing an intriguing narrative and some suggestive evidence. Given the relevance of the question, I hope that future research will be able to provide additional empirical tests of this hypothesis.

4

Adjusting Government Policies for Age Inflation

John B. Shoven and Gopi Shah Goda

It is commonly agreed upon that government programs such as tax systems, welfare programs, and retirement programs must adjust for price inflation to account for the fact that a fixed amount of dollars can buy items of different values from one time period to the next. Few would argue that a $10,000 income in 1970 is the same in real terms as a $10,000 income in 2008, and most government programs explicitly take this difference into account. In fact, the year-to-year adjustments that are needed to keep systems in line with their initial intentions are often automatic. When comparing U.S. economic statistics for different time periods, economists and policy analysts state the figures in "real dollars" or "dollars of constant purchasing power" rather than using unadjusted nominal dollars. Just like a dollar in 1950 is not the same unit as a dollar in 2008, we argue that a year of age or a year since birth is not a constant unit of age. We will propose different ways of coming up with "real ages" rather than nominal years since birth and then illustrate how various ages in the law would have to be adjusted in order to maintain constant real ages.

A particular age, as conventionally measured by years since birth, has a different "value" or meaning associated with it over time. We call this effect "age inflation." The typical sixty-five-year-old in 1935, when Social Security

John B. Shoven is the Charles R. Schwab Professor of Economics at Stanford University, the Wallace R. Hawley Director of the Stanford Institute for Economic Policy Research (SIEPR), and a research associate of the National Bureau of Economic Research. Gopi Shah Goda is Postdoctoral Fellow Program Coordinator and Research Scholar at the Stanford Institute for Economic Policy Research, Stanford University.

This chapter was presented at the National Bureau of Economic Research Conference on Demography and the Economy, the Villagio Inn, Yountville, CA, April 11–12, 2008. The authors would like to thank Mary Ho and Susan Putnins for outstanding research assistance. The chapter's shortcomings are solely the responsibility of the authors.

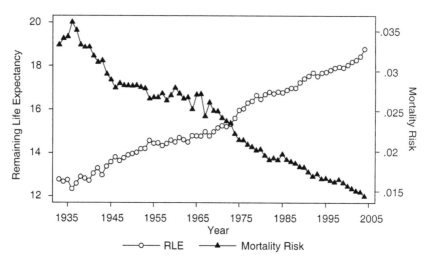

Fig. 4.1   Remaining life expectancy and mortality risk at age 65
Source: Human Mortality Database.

was enacted, had a much higher mortality risk and lower life expectancy than the typical sixty-five-year-old in 2004 (see figure 4.1). In 1935, sixty-five-year-olds could expect to live just over twelve additional years on a gender-blended basis, while a sixty-five-year-old in 2004 could expect an additional nineteen years of life. Their mortality risk, or their chance of dying within a year, was over 3 percent in 1935, but less than 1.5 percent in 2004. In addition, sixty-five represents two very different stages in the life cycle for these individuals, as measured by the percent of the life expectancy completed. Figure 4.2 shows the percent of the life expectancy completed by age sixty-five, where life expectancy is measured at birth, and at age twenty, again on a gender-blended basis. In 1935, age sixty-five was greater than the life expectancy of a newborn, and represented roughly 95 percent of the life expectancy of a twenty-year-old. By 2004, both of these percentages had fallen to approximately 85 percent. Figure 4.3 displays the percent of the population aged sixty-five and older from 1940 through 2004. In 1940, 7 percent of the population was aged sixty-five or older, so a sixty-five-year-old individual was in the ninety-third percentile of the age distribution. In 2004, a sixty-five-year-old was instead in the eighty-eighth percentile because the number of people living aged sixty-five and beyond has grown significantly relative to the younger population. The U.S. Census forecasts that a sixty-five-year old will be in the seventy-eighth or seventy-ninth percentile of the population by 2050.

Despite these large changes in what it means to be age sixty-five, there has been almost no adjustment in the Social Security program to account for these differences. If we think of individuals with a higher life expectancy and

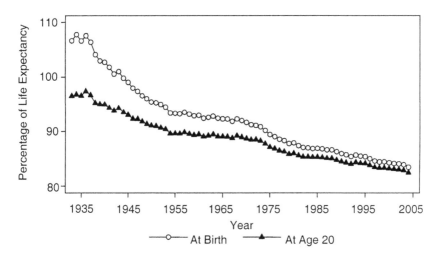

Fig. 4.2   Percent of life expectancy completed by age 65, life expectancy measured at birth and at age 20
Source: Human Mortality Database.

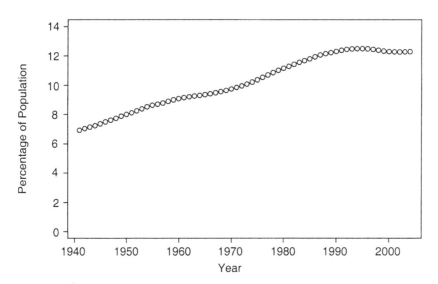

Fig. 4.3   Percent of population age 65 or older
Source: Social Security Administration.

lower mortality rate as effectively "younger," absent adjustments to Social Security rules, participants are allowed to commence a Social Security life annuity at younger and younger real ages.

In this chapter, we examine the rules governing three public programs—Social Security, Medicare, and Individual Retirement Accounts—and determine what the ages in the legislation would be today if we assume that the initial ages when the legislation was enacted defined the original intent of each program in terms of real ages. We also project the level of these legislated ages to 2050 under two different scenarios: (a) automatic age adjustments began when the law was enacted, and (b) automatic age adjustments begin now.

Four different methods are used to make adjustments for age inflation. The first method adjusts an age from year X to year Y by finding the age in Y with an equivalent remaining life expectancy. The second method is similar, but finds the age in Y that faces the same mortality risk. In the third method, the adjusted age in Y represents the same percentage point in the life expectancy as the original age in Y, where life expectancy is measured at birth. The fourth method is similar, but measures the life span as the total life expectancy given survival to age twenty. Each of these methods is applied to the whole population, as well as to different demographic groups, to examine whether there have been differential rates of mortality improvement across race and gender.

This chapter builds on earlier work in Shoven (2007) that discusses alternative ways of measuring age. Shoven shows that there has been remarkable progress in age-specific mortality, and that as measured by mortality risk, a fifty-nine-year-old man in 1970 was the same real age as a sixty-five-year-old man in 2000. The mortality improvement among women was somewhat slower over the last thirty years of the twentieth century, but still significant: a fifty-nine-year-old woman in 1970 had the same mortality risk as a sixty-three-year-old woman in 2000. He also shows that the measurement of the elderly as a percentage of the U.S. population differs based on whether conventional measures of age are used or a definition of age based on mortality risk.

Other literature that has presented similar ideas include Fuchs (1984); Cutler and Sheiner (2001); Shoven (2004); Sanderson and Scherbov (2005, 2007); Cutler, Liebman, and Smyth (2006); and Lutz, Sanderson, and Scherbov (2008). Fuchs states that remaining life expectancy may be a better measure of age and suggested that "nominal ages" could (or should) be adjusted to real ages based on mortality or remaining life expectancy. Cutler and Sheiner note that for acute care and nursing home care, demand is more a function of remaining life expectancy than it is of age. They find that the high medical costs associated with the last year of life have been occurring at older and older ages. Similarly, Shoven (2004) finds that Medicare spends roughly the same amount on men and women with the same mortality risk or remaining life expectancy. Sanderson and Scherbov (2005, 2007) and Lutz, Sanderson, and Scherbov (2008) show how forward-looking measures of age (such as remaining life expectancy) in combination with traditional backward-looking measures (years since birth) can lead to a better understanding of global population aging. Cutler, Liebman, and Smyth (2006) model the optimal Social Security retirement age in light of changes in the underlying health of the population. They summarize several measures of health status over time, such as self-reported health status, annual bed days for people with specific health conditions, and disability rates. Across these different measures, it is evident that the health status of individuals of a given age has improved significantly over time.

4.1   The Relationship between Age, Remaining Life Expectancy, and Mortality Risk

Over time, there has been significant mortality improvement that is persistent across age, gender, and race. There is a wide variety of statistics that illustrate this point, and we present some of them here. There are two other interesting empirical facts to highlight that will show up in our later analysis. The first is that while women have always experienced higher life expectancies than men of the same age and continue to do so, the mortality improvement among women over the last thirty years has been lower than that among men. In addition, holding life expectancy constant through time, individuals have a lower mortality risk today than they had decades ago.

Figures 4.4 and 4.5 display mortality risk by age in 1940, 1970, and 2004, for men and women respectively. In moving to each successive time period, the curves shift down and to the right by an amount that represents the degree of mortality improvement. Individuals at each age face a lower chance of dying within a year in 1970 and 2004 compared to 1940. If we placed figures 4.4 and 4.5 on top of each other, we would see that women at each age face lower mortality risk than men. The degree of mortality improvement

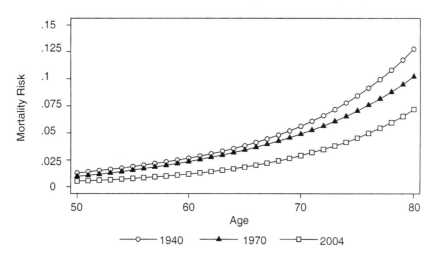

Fig. 4.4   Male mortality risk by age in 1940, 1970, and 2004
Source: Social Security Administration.

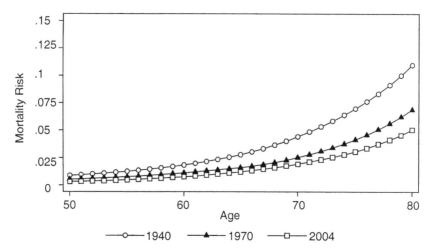

Fig. 4.5   Female mortality risk by age in 1940, 1970, and 2004
Source: Social Security Administration.

also differed by gender in the two periods. Women saw greater improvement in mortality from 1940 to 1970, while men experienced greater improvement from 1970 to 2004. The mortality risk progress over the entire sixty-four-year period is roughly the same for men and women, and nothing short of remarkable. The magnitude of the change can be illustrated by noting that the mortality risk of both seventy-year-old men and women in 2004 is very close to the mortality of sixty-year-old men and women in 1940. The saying "seventy is the new sixty" is not just a cute phrase on a birthday card. It's true!—at least in terms of mortality risk.

Remaining life expectancy and mortality risk are two alternative mortality-related measures of age. Remaining life expectancy at a given age takes into account the mortality risk in that age as well as the mortality risk in successive years, while the mortality risk measure is limited to the chance of death within one year. If a person's chance of dying was zero in one year and 100 percent the next, this individual would look very young by the mortality risk measure, but older by the remaining life expectancy measure. The data show that the relationship between these two measures over time is that individuals with a given life expectancy face a lower chance of dying in the next year now relative to what they used to. For instance, men with an eighteen-year remaining life expectancy in 1935 had a 1.9 percent mortality risk, whereas such a man in 2004 had approximately a 1.5 percent mortality risk. This suggests that even with the same remaining life expectancy, people are "healthier" in 2004 than in 1935. This phenomenon is consistent with a larger concentration of high mortality in the last years of life.

4.2   Ages Fixed in Government Policies

We focus on three public programs primarily for the elderly: Social Security retirement benefits, Medicare, and Individual Retirement Accounts (IRAs). Social Security defines the rules under which beneficiaries are eligible to receive full retirement benefits (commonly referred to as the Normal Retirement Age, or NRA), a reduced level of benefits (Early Retirement Age, or ERA), and the age at which benefits stop increasing with later retirement due to delayed retirement credits. Medicare defines the age at which beneficiaries are first eligible to receive health insurance benefits. The rules governing IRAs (and 401(k)s, 403(b)s, and 457 plans) indicate the age at which funds can be withdrawn without penalty, and the age at which a minimum distribution must be taken to avoid penalty.

Social Security began with the Social Security Act of 1935. The program originally was designed to give retirement benefits to those over the age of sixty-five, with no provision for reduced benefits at earlier ages or higher benefits for delayed retirement. In 1956, all female workers and widows were eligible for reduced benefits at age sixty-two, and in 1961, the option of reduced benefits at sixty-two was extended to men.[1] The next changes came in 1972 when delayed retirement credits were instituted for those who retired after age sixty-five, and these accrued until an individual reached age seventy-two. The 1983 amendments lowered this maximum age to seventy, and most significantly, increased the normal retirement age for the first time in the program's history gradually to age sixty-seven (SSA Title II 2007). The increase in the NRA will be completed by 2023 and was motivated by the program's financial difficulties rather than an explicit recognition that age inflation meant that sixty-five was not the same real age that it had been in 1935.

Medicare's age of eligibility has been sixty-five since the program was enacted in 1965 (SSA Title XVIII 2007). Similarly, the age limits for IRAs and other defined contribution retirement plans have not changed since they were created by Employee Retirement Income Security Act (ERISA) legislation in 1974. The earliest age at which funds can be withdrawn without penalty is fifty-nine-and-a-half, and the age where the minimum required withdrawals are imposed is seventy-and-a-half.

4.3   Data Sources

Several data sources were obtained to determine the adjustment of government program rules for age inflation. The primary source of mortality

---

1. Widows later became eligible for reduced benefits at age sixty in 1965, but here we focus on retirement benefits.

data is the set of period life tables used by the Social Security Administration (SSA) to construct the 2007 Trustees Report. These were obtained by request. The tables cover the historical period 1900 to 2004, and project future mortality rates under three different alternative scenarios. For all calculations of projected age adjustment, the intermediate scenario, Alternative II, is used. The SSA maintains projected mortality tables from 2005 to 2100. Population data from the SSA were also used to determine the percent of the population eligible for government programs under alternative measures of age.

Mortality tables for the gender-blended population were obtained for 1933 to 2004 from the Human Mortality Database, which compiles detailed mortality data for a variety of countries. In addition, mortality statistics by race through 2004 were obtained from the National Center for Health Statistics (National Vital Statistics Reports, various years).

The analysis is based on period life tables, which report age-specific mortality rates in a given year, rather than cohort life tables, which display age-specific mortality data for a group of individuals born in the same year. While cohort life tables may give more accurate descriptions of mortality statistics because they take into account improvements in mortality beyond the current period, they are necessarily largely based on projected mortality improvements. For example, the period remaining life expectancy of a sixty-five-year-old female in 2004 is based on mortality rates for 65-, 66-, . . . , 100-year-old females in 2004. These mortality rates are likely to be higher than the mortality that a sixty-five-year-old female in 2004 will actually experience because she will be sixty-six in 2005, sixty-seven in 2006, and so on. However, the cohort remaining life expectancy of a sixty-five-year-old female in 2004 computed today would have to assume rates of mortality improvement for years beyond 2004.

4.4   Adjusting Government Policies for Age Inflation

Four methods are used to adjust ages in Social Security, Medicare, and IRAs for changes in mortality:

1. *Constant RLE.* Under the Constant Remaining Life Expectancy (RLE) method, two ages are equivalent if their remaining life expectancies are equivalent.
2. *Constant Mortality Risk.* The Constant Mortality Risk method assumes that two ages are equivalent if they have the same mortality risk.
3. *Constant Percent of Life Expectancy (measured at birth).* Two ages that have the same ratio to the life expectancy of a newborn are equivalent under this method.
4. *Constant Percent of Life Expectancy (measured at age twenty).* This method is similar to the previous one (number three), except that life expec-

tancy is measured at age twenty. This method addresses the implausibility introduced by method three, when the age of interest is greater than the life expectancy at birth.

To illustrate these four methods further, suppose we would like to find the inflation-adjusted age in 2004 of a sixty-five-year-old woman in 1965. The remaining life expectancy of a sixty-five-year-old female in 1965 was 16.34. In 2004, a sixty-eight-year-old woman had a remaining life expectancy of 16.80, and a sixty-nine-year-old woman had a remaining life expectancy of 16.06. The true RLE-adjusted age in 2004 by the first method would be between sixty-eight and sixty-nine, but because we do not have mortality data by fractional years, we apply a decision rule to use the younger age so that the individual at the adjusted age would have at least the same life expectancy in 2004 relative to 1965. Therefore, this method gives sixty-eight as the answer we are looking for.

The mortality risk of a sixty-five-year-old woman in 1965 was 1.79 percent. In 2004, the mortality risk of a sixty-nine-year-old woman was 1.75 percent, and that of a seventy-year-old woman was 1.93 percent. The adjusted age under the second method would therefore be between sixty-nine and seventy, and we record the adjusted age to be sixty-nine, the age where the mortality risk is at most 1.79 percent.

A newborn girl in 1965 had an life expectancy of 73.84, and the remaining life expectancy at age twenty for a female was 56.08. These values for 2004 were 79.6 and 60.36, respectively. Age sixty-five represented $65/73.84 = 88$ percent of the life expectancy of a newborn in 1965, and the equivalent age in 2004 is $(0.88)(79.6) = 70.1$, which would be the adjusted age under the third method. If we instead use the life expectancy of a twenty-year-old, sixty-five represented $65/(56.08 + 20) = 85.4$ percent of the life expectancy, so the equivalent age in 2004 under the fourth method would be $(0.854)(60.36 + 20) = 68.7$.

These four methods of calculation were done for seven different eligibility ages in the rules governing Social Security, Medicare, and IRAs and defined contribution retirement plans to find the mortality-equivalent ages in 2004. Each adjustment was done using gender-blended mortality, as well as by using male and female mortality separately. The results are summarized in table 4.1.

Depending on the initial year of legislation and the method used, the adjustments are on the order of three to eight years. For the majority of cases, the four methods yield similar results. One exception is the adjustment of age sixty-five in 1935 to 2004, using the method that equates the percent of the life expectancy measured at birth. This occurs because the life expectancy in 1935 at birth is actually less than age sixty-five. Using instead the percent of life expectancy at age twenty yields estimates that are more in line with the other two methods, implying that some of the mortality improvement

Table 4.1   Mortality-adjusted ages in 2004

Method	Male	Female	Total
SSA—Normal retirement age in 1935 = 65			
1	73.0	71.0	73.0
2	75.0	73.0	74.0
3	83.0	81.9	81.8
4	76.1	74.8	76.0
SSA—Early retirement age in 1961 = 62			
1	67.0	67.0	66.0
2	69.0	69.0	66.0
3	68.7	69.0	67.0
4	67.0	67.1	65.6
SSA—Delayed retirement credits to 72 in 1972			
1	75.0	74.0	76.0
2	77.0	74.0	77.0
3	79.8	76.2	78.6
4	78.1	75.1	77.3
SSA—Normal retirement age in 1983 = 67			
1	69.0	67.0	69.0
2	71.0	68.0	70.0
3	70.6	68.3	69.8
4	70.0	67.9	69.3
Medicare eligibility age in 1965 = 65			
1	70.0	68.0	70.0
2	72.0	69.0	72.0
3	72.7	70.1	71.9
4	70.7	68.7	70.2
IRA minimum withdrawal age in 1974 = 60			
1	64.0	62.0	64.0
2	66.0	63.0	66.0
3	65.6	62.8	64.8
4	64.4	62.0	63.8
IRA maximum withdrawal age in 1974 = 71			
1	74.0	72.0	75.0
2	76.0	73.0	75.0
3	77.7	74.3	76.7
4	76.3	73.4	75.6

between 1935 and 2004 was in infant and childhood mortality. Mortality improvements from age twenty onward may be more relevant in adjusting policies relating to work and retirement.

Adjusting ages using mortality risk consistently produces adjustments that are larger than those calculated by the constant RLE method. This reflects the higher concentration of mortality in later ages discussed earlier. The superiority of one method over the other depends on which measure—

remaining life expectancy or mortality risk—better proxies for the factors taken into account when determining eligibility.

The ages adjusted for female mortality are lower than those adjusted for male mortality because women experienced less mortality improvement over most of the time periods examined. The lower rate of improvement among women means that the gap in life expectancy between men and women has been decreasing over this time period.

The overall results from table 4.1 show that very significant adjustments would have to be made in the ages in the laws we examine in order to restore the law to the original real age. For instance, the Normal Retirement Age for Social Security in 2004 would have to be at least seventy-one (using lowest number in the table) and more likely seventy-three or seventy-four (using the gender-blended results from methods one and two) in order to be consistent with the real age of sixty-five in 1935. Using the same logic, the age of Medicare eligibility would have needed to have been advanced by at least five years. Such adjustments would be politically difficult, but age inflation and the lack of adjusting for it has quite a bit to do with the solvency problems of Social Security and Medicare.

Next, we project the adjustments forward to 2050 using Social Security's intermediate estimates of future mortality. We produce estimates by gender separately, and use two different starting points—the year of legislation, as assumed in table 4.1, and 2004, the latest year of nonprojected mortality statistics. Assigning the year of legislation as the starting point addresses the question of what the eligibility ages we consider would be in 2050 if ages were indexed from the beginning using each of the four methods of age adjustment. Using 2004 as the starting point speculates how things would look in 2050 based on projected mortality improvement if we started indexing ages in 2004.

Table 4.2 summarizes the projected ages of eligibility in 2050. Because mortality is projected to improve throughout the 2004 to 2050 period, the adjusted ages continue to go up. Again, the four methods yield largely similar results. Adjusted ages using female mortality continue to be less than ages adjusted using male mortality, indicating that projected mortality rates also exhibit less mortality improvement among women. The mortality-equivalent ages assuming adjustment starts in 2004 are much less dramatic than those calculated from the legislation date, providing another indication of how much mortality has improved already.

The results that adjusting for age inflation would have on the number of people eligible to receive entitlement benefits are striking. Figures 4.6 and 4.7 show the percent of the population projected to meet age eligibility requirements for full retirement benefits in Social Security and Medicare health insurance benefits under three different situations—ages were adjusted beginning when the legislation was written; age adjustments began in 2004; and no age adjustment occurs. The adjustment method assumed in these

Table 4.2   Mortality-adjusted ages in 2050

	Adjustments starting in			
	Legislation year		2004	
Method	Male	Female	Male	Female
SSA—Normal retirement age in 1935 = 65				
1	75.0	75.0	68.0	67.0
2	77.0	78.0	69.0	68.0
3	87.1	85.4	69.2	67.9
4	79.1	79.0	68.7	67.5
SSA—Early retirement age in 1961 = 62				
1	70.0	68.0	65.0	64.0
2	74.0	70.0	66.0	65.0
3	73.5	70.0	66.0	64.7
4	70.9	68.2	65.6	64.4
SSA—Delayed retirement credits to 72 in 1972				
1	79.0	76.0	75.0	74.0
2	81.0	78.0	76.0	75.0
3	84.9	79.6	76.6	75.2
4	82.6	78.0	76.1	74.8
SSA—Normal retirement age in 1983 = 67				
1	73.0	70.0	70.0	69.0
2	75.0	71.0	71.0	70.0
3	75.1	71.3	71.3	70.0
4	74.0	70.5	70.9	69.6
Medicare eligibility age in 1965 = 65				
1	73.0	71.0	68.0	67.0
2	76.0	72.0	69.0	68.0
3	77.4	73.2	69.2	67.9
4	74.8	71.3	68.7	67.5
IRA minimum withdrawal age in 1974 = 60				
1	68.0	64.0	64.0	62.0
2	71.0	66.0	65.0	63.0
3	69.9	65.6	63.9	62.6
4	68.1	64.5	63.4	62.3
IRA maximum withdrawal age in 1974 = 71				
1	77.0	75.0	74.0	73.0
2	80.0	76.0	75.0	74.0
3	82.7	77.6	75.6	74.1
4	80.6	76.3	75.1	73.8

figures was the second method, which finds the equivalent age based on mortality risk, computed for men and women separately, and then averaged.

Figure 4.6 shows that without any adjustment in the age of eligibility for full retirement (including the 1983 amendments that changed the normal retirement age gradually from sixty-five to sixty-seven), the percent of the population that would be eligible would rise from just under 7 percent in

1941 to over 20 percent in 2050. If adjustments had happened automatically, only 9.35 percent of the population would be eligible in 2050. Even if adjustments start occurring today, the projections show that more than 17 percent of the population would receive full retirement benefits in 2050. The data in Figure 4.7 show a similar pattern. This indicates that because all of the substantial life expectancy improvements that have occurred thus far

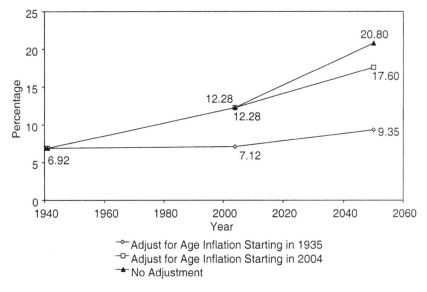

Fig. 4.6   Percent of population eligible for full Social Security benefits

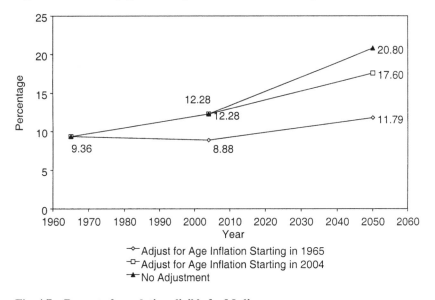

Fig. 4.7   Percent of population eligible for Medicare

have been allocated as eligible years rather than noneligible years, adjusting in the future will have less dramatic an effect.

4.5   Heterogeneity in Mortality Improvement

An important concern for a policy that indexes ages of eligibility to life expectancy improvements is that mortality improvement in most cases will not be uniform across all demographic groups. It was already shown that men and women experienced different rates of improvement in mortality historically, causing the adjusted age to be different depending on whether male- or female-based mortality statistics were used.

We explore this issue further by tabulating mortality-adjusted ages by race and gender to the extent that sufficient data are available. Data limitations allow us to only examine two racial distinctions (black and white), and to examine historical changes in mortality but not projected changes. For starting years prior to 1965, detailed data on mortality risk and remaining life expectancy is not available, but we are still able to calculate adjustments using the third and fourth methods of adjustment using life expectancy at birth and at age twenty. Our results are summarized in table 4.3. The data generally support the idea that while the level of mortality varies significantly across different racial groups, with blacks having worse mortality than whites, the amount of mortality *improvement* does not vary as dramatically. In fact, within each gender group, the implied adjustment is higher for blacks than it is for whites in a majority of cases. This phenomenon is particularly true when comparing black women to white women.

Which racial group has had more improvement also seems to depend on what definition of improvement is used. Under the first method of adjusting ages, which uses increases in remaining life expectancy as the relevant measure of mortality, the mortality-equivalent ages for whites tend to be higher than those for blacks, indicating a greater degree of mortality improvement. The measures that use percent of life expectancy as the relevant measure tend to yield higher adjusted ages for blacks relative to whites, and the results using mortality risk are more mixed. These results imply that blacks have had larger gains in mortality early in life, but that the racial gap in mortality among the elderly has persisted.

It is important to note that the current policy of a single age of eligibility applying to the entire population implicitly redistributes from individuals with short life expectancies to those with higher life expectancies. Social Security and Medicare benefits are paid as lifetime benefits and actuarial adjustments to retirement benefits are based on average mortality. Thus, while heterogeneity in mortality improvement implies that some groups would benefit more from indexing eligibility ages to age inflation, heterogeneity in mortality rates indicate that current eligibility rules also redistribute between demographic groups.

Table 4.3   Mortality-adjusted ages in 2004 by race and gender

Method	Black	White	Black male	White male	Black female	White female
			SSA—Normal retirement age in 1935 = 65[a]			
3	88.2	78.4	86.4	78.3	89.3	78.1
4	79.8	74.0	77.8	73.5	81.4	74.2
			SSA—Early retirement age in 1961 = 62[a]			
3	70.9	68.6	70.1	69.5	71.2	67.5
4	68.1	67.0	67.1	67.6	68.8	66.2
			SSA—Delayed retirement credits to 72 in 1972[b]			
1	75.0	77.0	75.0	78.0	75.0	76.0
2	79.0	78.0	78.0	79.0	79.0	76.0
3	80.2	78.3	81.4	79.8	78.6	76.6
4	78.4	77.1	79.4	78.3	77.2	75.7
			SSA—Normal retirement age in 1983 = 67			
1	70.0	70.0	70.0	71.0	69.0	69.0
2	70.0	71.0	71.0	72.0	70.0	69.0
3	70.4	69.8	71.2	70.7	69.5	68.8
4	69.8	69.3	70.6	70.2	69.0	68.4
			Medicare eligibility age in 1965 = 65[b]			
1	71.0	71.0	70.0	72.0	71.0	70.0
2	75.0	72.0	74.0	73.0	76.0	70.0
3	74.2	71.7	74.4	72.8	73.6	70.3
4	71.7	70.1	71.6	71.0	71.4	69.1
			IRA minimum withdrawal age in 1974 = 60[b]			
1	64.0	65.0	64.0	66.0	64.0	63.0
2	67.0	67.0	66.0	68.0	66.0	64.0
3	65.5	64.6	66.3	65.9	64.2	63.3
4	64.3	63.7	65.0	64.7	63.3	62.6
			IRA maximum withdrawal age in 1974 = 71[b]			
1	74.0	75.0	74.0	76.0	74.0	75.0
2	78.0	76.0	77.0	78.0	78.0	74.0
3	77.5	76.5	78.4	78.0	76.0	74.9
4	76.1	75.4	76.9	76.6	75.0	74.1

[a]Mortality statistics for 1935 and 1961 obtained from NCHS 2007 report, table 11. Years 1939–1941 used for base year 1935, and years 1959–1961 used for base year 1961.
[b]Mortality data from NCHS in 1966, 1972, and 1974 does not distinguish "Black" separately; "Nonwhite" or "All Other" used as indicated.

One way to address the issue of heterogeneous rates of mortality improvement would be to have a different age of eligibility for each race-sex cell, with each eligibility age indexed based on the mortality improvements in that cell. However, this would likely be impractical to administer. Another way would be to index to the minimum level of mortality improvement. While some groups have had more improvement than others in mortality, all of the groups examined have experienced substantial gains. This approach would not address the fact that age indexation would benefit some groups more than others, but it would decrease the possibility that one group would be significantly worse off due to another group's mortality improvements.

4.6   Disability-Free Life Expectancy

Our four methods of adjusting nominal ages to real ages are all based on mortality or life expectancy—that is, they depend on the evolution over time of survival probabilities as reflected in a time series of period life tables. In some sense, they are based on a two-state model where people are either alive or dead. What many people mean when they categorize people as elderly is people who have disabilities or reduced functionality. This raises the question of whether the increase in life expectancies and the decrease in age-specific mortality rates imply an increase in disability-free life expectancy and a decrease in the age-specific disability rates.

There is a large literature on this matter. There is some evidence that disability-free life expectancies have grown by at least as much as overall life expectancies, and that age-specific disability rates have fallen in line with mortality rates. For instance, a recent paper by Manton and Lamb (2007) shows that while life expectancy of eighty-five-year-olds increased by one year between 1965 and 1999, their "active life expectancy" increased by 1.5 years (and the expected disabled years actually fell by 0.5 years). Manton and Lamb find that the expected future years in disability for eighty-five-year-olds decreased for both men and women. Manton and Land (2000) find that 13.7 of the 15.7 years of remaining expected life for sixty-five-year-old men are disability-free, whereas for women, the corresponding numbers are 15.7 of the remaining 22.2 years. The overall findings of Manton and his coauthors is that the number of years in disability has not been growing in the past few decades.

Cutler, Liebman, and Smyth (2006) come to similar conclusions. They show that the same percentage of men aged sixty-two in the mid-1970s report themselves to be in fair or poor health as seventy-two-year-old men in the mid-1990s. They also show that impairment associated with heart disease has declined over the same period as measured by the number of days spent in bed, and that the share of the population with limitations in activities of daily living has declined. They state, "Our best guess is that people aged sixty-two in the 1960s or 1970s are in equivalent health to people aged seventy or more today" (18). All of these results conflict with previous work by Crimmins, Saito, and Ingegneri (1997), which found that healthy life expectancies grew by much less than total life expectancies between 1970 and 1990. However, the majority of the evidence suggests that health status has been improving along with mortality.

Our feeling is that while the growth in active life expectancies or healthy life expectancies would be useful for indexing nominal ages in retirement laws, the data are not yet of the same quality as the mortality data contained in the period life tables. This means that more research and information about the transitions between functional and disabled status is necessary before disability-free life expectancies are ready to be used for age inflation indexing.

4.7   Conclusion

The significant mortality improvement that has been experienced in the United States over the last century means that age, as conventionally measured by years since birth, has a different meaning today than it did in the past. Government policies that are based on age fail to adjust to the fact that a given age is associated with a higher remaining life expectancy and lower mortality risk with each passing year.

In this chapter, we evaluate eligibility ages contained in the rules governing three public programs: Social Security, Medicare, and Individual Retirement Accounts. We calculate adjustments to these eligibility ages using four different definitions of mortality-equivalence—remaining life expectancy, mortality risk, or percent of expected life expectancy at age zero and at age twenty. We first assume that age indexation began when the eligibility age was initially established and show how it would have changed by 2004. We then use projected mortality estimates to forecast the effect of age inflation on eligibility ages to 2050. We also calculate age adjustments for different demographic groups to explore the effect of differences in mortality and mortality improvement on age inflation.

The results indicate that, on average, historical adjustment of eligibility ages for age inflation would have increased ages of eligibility by approximately 0.15 years annually. The adjustments implied by improvements in female mortality are smaller than those calculated using male mortality improvement, and differences in mortality improvement across race are not as large as the differences in the base level of mortality. Estimates of projected mortality show that future adjustments would be lower, approximately 0.08 years per annum, indicating that a lower rate of mortality improvement is implicit in Social Security's intermediate estimates of projected mortality. This slowing in the rate of improvement is far from agreed upon among U.S. demographers, and Social Security mortality projections have underestimated mortality improvements in the past.

The idea of indexing nominal ages to generate real ages requires an appropriate metric for the indexation. While we have used four such metrics, another appealing one would be to index age by the change in disability-free life expectancies. We briefly examined the state of knowledge about the evolution of active (or disability-free) life expectancies. There is some evidence that active life expectancies have been growing as rapidly as total life expectancies. However, in our opinion, the evidence is not sufficiently agreed upon to be used to adjust ages in government programs.

Implementing a policy that explicitly adjusts ages of eligibility for improvements in mortality would have important practical considerations. One such consideration would be the lead time that individuals would have in planning for the future. It would not be sensible to wait to announce a cohort's normal retirement age, for example, in the year they are planning to retire. One approach may be to lock in a cohort's retirement age at a predetermined time, such as when the cohort attains fifty-five years of age.

The four methods of calculating mortality-equivalent ages that we examined give different results regarding the amount of adjustment that would yield equivalent ages. Each uses a measure of mortality that summarizes a different dimension of mortality improvement, and the most appropriate measure, perhaps different than the four described here, would depend on which dimension best captures the intent of the initial legislation that defined the initial age of eligibility. In addition, the four methods we describe implicitly assume that all future improvements in mortality should be working years, rather than under the status quo where life expectancy gains have been taken as years of eligibility. It is reasonable to believe that a more appropriate treatment would be somewhere between these two extremes, where gains in life expectancy are shared between eligible and noneligible years in some manner.

In many ways, adjusting ages of eligibility for age inflation is similar to adjusting income or asset thresholds for price inflation. Prior to 1985, the parameters of the U.S. income tax code were not indexed to inflation, and high inflation rates in the late 1960s and 1970s caused "bracket creep," where more and more households were subject to high marginal tax rates because their incomes were rising in nominal terms even as their real incomes were held constant. Currently, many parameters of the income tax system are indexed to inflation to avoid this from occurring. The one major exception is the Alternative Minimum Tax (AMT), which was designed to keep taxpayers with high incomes from paying little or no income tax by taking advantage of various preferences in the tax code. Today, this tax is affecting a growing number of middle-class taxpayers. We think that the legislative intent of the AMT has been distorted due to the failure to inflation index the amount of income that can be exempted from the tax.

Adjusting government policies for age inflation would have a large impact on the number of individuals eligible to receive entitlement benefits, and consequently, on the financing of these public programs. Shultz and Shoven (2008) state that the total labor supply in 2050 would be at least 9 percent higher if workers retired with the same lengths of retirement as they do today, relative to what it would be if they retired at the same ages as today. Estimates in the literature suggest that the elderly have high labor supply elasticities (French 2005), and the effects of policies that index eligibility ages for mortality improvement on labor markets, health, and government budgets is an important area for future research.

References

Crimmins, E. M., Y. Saito, and D. Ingegneri. 1997. Trends in disability-free life expectancies in the United States, 1970–90. *Population and Development Review* 23 (3): 555–72.

Cutler, D. M., J. B. Liebman, and S. Smyth. 2006. How fast should the Social Security eligibility age rise? NBER Retirement Research Center Working Paper no. NB04-05. Cambridge, MA: National Bureau of Economic Research, July.

Cutler, D. M., and L. Sheiner. 2001. Demographics and medical care spending: Standard and non-standard effects. In *Demographic change and fiscal policy,* ed. A. Auerbach and R. Lee, 253–91. Cambridge: Cambridge University Press.

French, E. 2005. The effects of health, wealth, and wages on labour supply and retirement behaviour. *Review of Economic Studies* 72 (2): 395–427.

Fuchs, V. R. 1984. "Though much is taken": Reflections on aging, health, and medical care. *The Milbank Memorial Fund Quarterly: Health and Society* 62 (2, Special Issue, Financing medicare: Explorations in controlling costs and raising revenues): 142–66.

Human Mortality Database. 2008. University of California, Berkeley (United States), and Max Planck Institute for Demographic Research (Germany). Available at: http://www.mortality.org or www.humanmortality.de.

Lutz, W., W. C. Sanderson, and S. Scherbov. 2008. The coming acceleration of global population aging. *Nature* January: 1–4.

Manton, K. G., and V. L. Lamb. 2007. U.S. mortality, life expectancy, and active life expectancy at advanced ages: Trends and forecasts. Duke University. Unpublished Manuscript.

Manton, K. G., and K. C. Land. 2000. Active life expectancies for the U.S. elderly population: A multidimensional continuous-mixture model of functional change applied to completed cohorts, 1982–1996. *Demography* 37 (3): 253–65.

National Center for Health Statistics. 2008. National vital statistics reports: United States life tables (various years). Available at: http://www.cdc.gov/nchs/products/pubs/pubd/lftbls/life/1966.htm.

Sanderson, W. C., and S. Scherbov. 2005. Average remaining lifetimes can increase as human populations age. *Nature* 435 (June): 811–13.

———. 2007. A new perspective on population aging. *Demographic Research* 16 (January): 27–58.

Shoven, J. B. 2004. The impact of major improvement in life expectancy on the financing of Social Security, Medicare, and Medicaid. In *Coping with Methuselah: The impact of molecular biology on medicine and society,* ed. H. J. Aaron and W. B. Schwartz, 166–97. Washington DC: The Brookings Institution.

———. 2007. New age thinking: Alternative ways of measuring age, their relationship to labor force participation, government policies and GDP. NBER Working Paper no. 13476. Cambridge, MA: National Bureau of Economic Research, October.

Shultz, G. P., and J. B. Shoven with M. Gunn and G. Shah Goda. 2008. *Putting our house in order: A guide to Social Security and health care reform* New York: W. W. Norton & Company.

Social Security Administration (SSA). 2007. Social Security Act, Title II. Federal old-age, survivors, and disability insurance benefits. Available at: http://www.ssa .gov/OP_Home/ssact/ssact-toc.htm.
————. 2007. Social Security Act, Title XVIII. Health insurance for the aged and disabled. Available at: http://www.ssa.gov/OP_Home/ssact/ssact-toc.htm.

Comment   Warren C. Sanderson

The Shoven and Goda chapter is a positive one, as opposed to a normative one. It tells us how to adjust ages for increases in life expectancy and tells us what the ages represented in Social Security, Medicare, and Individual Retirement Accounts (IRA) would be if the ages in those programs were adjusted for life expectancy change starting from the date that the program began and from the current date. This chapter almost begs for a companion paper, this time a normative one. Given that we know these ages, what should we do with them? The title indicates what the authors think. They think that we should be "adjusting government policies for age inflation." But should we use the ages computed in this chapter to do the adjustment or should we do it differently? This is the basic tension in this article. We are given a tool and not told what to do with it or how to use it.

My comments are organized under five headings:

1. Some history of new age thinking.
2. New age thinking in this chapter.
3. Applications of new age thinking here.
4. New age thinking applied in new ways.
5. Terminological problems with "age inflation" and "real age."

Some History of New Age Thinking

Shoven (2007) introduced the term "new age thinking" and I like it very much. It refers simultaneously to new thinking about age and to thinking about what some people are calling a new age segment, the time after retirement but before the ravages of old age become severe enough to seriously reduce the quality of life. The phrase new age thinking is not used in the chapter. Perhaps one reason for this is that, as the authors understand, their thinking about age is not exactly new.

Compare, for example, the quotation from (Steuerle and Spiro 1999) with one in the current chapter:

> If, in studies of the economy, past and present currencies are made equivalent by adjusting dollars for inflation, why shouldn't age be adjusted for

Warren C. Sanderson is professor and cochair of economics at Stony Brook University.

life expectancy in labor force studies of the elderly? Today's sixty-five-year-olds can expect to live longer than they did in the past and, in this sense, are younger than sixty-five-year-olds were sixty years ago. In 1997, men turning sixty-five could anticipate another sixteen years of life; in 1940, men who could expect to live this long were sixty years old. While there is no perfect way to make past and present ages equivalent, given the comparability between the life expectancies of sixty-five-year-olds today and sixty-year-olds in 1940 (and assuming that equivalent life expectancy indicates a similar ability to work), studies of labor force participation that contrast the two may offer details not apparent in the traditional chronological measure. (1)

It is commonly agreed upon that government programs such as tax systems, welfare programs, and retirement programs must adjust for price inflation to account for the fact that a fixed amount of dollars can buy items of different values from one time period to the next. Few would argue that a $10,000 income in 1970 is the same in real terms as a $10,000 income in 2008, and most government programs explicitly take this difference into account. In fact, the year-to-year adjustments that are needed to keep systems in line with their initial intentions are often automatic. When comparing U.S. economic statistics for different time periods, economists and policy analysts state the figures in "real dollars" or "dollars of constant purchasing power" rather than using unadjusted nominal dollars. Just like a dollar in 1950 is not the same unit as a dollar in 2008, we argue that a year of age or a year since birth is not a constant unit of age. (Shoven and Goda, chapter 4, this volume)

Indeed, new age thinking has a reasonably long pedigree. I do not know when the idea of adjusting Social Security for increases in life expectancy was first broached, but more academic studies of adjusting age for life expectancy change goes back at least to Ryder (1975). There, Ryder suggested that old age should not be considered to start at age sixty-five, but rather at some age associated with a fixed remaining life expectancy. Ryder suggested people in age groups with remaining life expectancies of ten years or less be considered old. Method 1 (in this chapter), for adjusting ages for changes in life expectancy is a natural extension of this idea.

Fuchs (1984) was the first person to see the formal equivalence of adjustment of nominal quantities for price change and the adjustment of age for life expectancy change. He followed the standard economic nomenclature and called conventional age "nominal age" and age, after the adjustment for life expectancy change, "real age." People of the same real age had the same remaining life expectancy. People of the same nominal age had lived the same number of years.

The insights of Ryder and Fuchs went undeveloped. They were sporadically reinvented as illustrated by the quotation from Steuerle and Spiro (1999) earlier. In Sanderson and Scherbov (2005) we independently reinvented the concept of age based on remaining life expectancy yet again. This is method 1 in the chapter. We now call this age "prospective age" in order to emphasize that it is a forward-looking measure as opposed to conventional or retrospective age, which is a backward-looking measure. I will discuss later why I think that the term prospective age is preferable to real age.

We applied the concept of prospective age to the demographic histories and forecasts for Germany, Japan, and the United States. We showed that there were historical periods or likely future periods where the countries exhibit aging as measured by increases in the conventional median age and simultaneously increased youthfulness as measured by decreases in their prospective median ages. In addition, we did calculations there equivalent to method three in the current chapter.

Three papers (written by Sanderson and Scherbov [2007a, 2007b] and Lutz, Sanderson, and Scherbov [2008]) have now come out that deepen our understanding not only of prospective age, but also other ways of adjusting age for life expectancy change; more papers are in the works. Shoven and Goba understand that their contributions here are not conceptually original. The contribution of their chapter is in the actual calculations that they make for important government programs.

New Age Thinking in This Chapter

The chapter suggests four methods for adjusting age for life expectancy change:

1. Remaining life expectancy is matched.
2. Mortality risk is matched.
3. Percentage of life expectancy at birth is matched.
4. Percentage of remaining life expectancy at twenty is matched.

In concept, adjusting the age at receipt of a full Social Security pension or at the onset of Medicare coverage using method one is utility-reducing. Tables 4.1, 4.2, and 4.3 in the chapter show that the ages produced by methods two, three, and four are even higher than those produced by method one, and therefore reduce utility even more. I will address why method one reduces utility in the next section.

Even putting aside the problem of utility-reducing reforms, I do not see the rationale for methods two, three, and four. For Social Security and Medicare the periods of pay-in and pay-out are relevant. Method one is clearly more appropriate in that case. I see no reason why method two would be used. Moreover, mortality risks are less stable than life expectancies, and so adjusting for them would make for more noisy policies. Method four seems to have some merit, but we need to remember that life expectancy at age twenty has increased faster than life expectancy at older ages. Life expectancy at the age computed using method four actually decreases as life expectancy at twenty increases. From my perspective, only method one should be used in policy reform discussions. The other three are interesting in a pedagogical sense because they show concretely why they should not be used.

Two base years are considered:

1. The year the program was introduced.
2. The current year.

Using the year the program was introduced is illustrative, but not very useful. They show that if we were to adjust the ages in the public programs for life expectancy changes starting from the year of program initiation, we would have to make large discontinuous changes in those programs today. This teaches us why we would not want to use ages adjusted for life expectancy changes computed from the beginning of the program forward. When we use the program's introduction date as the base year, we might be subtly introducing the notion that the policymakers at that time really had a life expectancy-adjusted age in mind, and that being true to their programs would require large discontinuous changes in ages. Alternatively, we can think that subsequent policymakers, by keeping the ages in the programs constant, were also making a statement about policy. I do not see a public policy rationale for favoring the views of one group of decision makers over another. In terms of the continuity of policy, it is certainly best to view age changes based on current policies.

This chapter is a positive one. It does not provide policy prescriptions. From a policy perspective, however, only one of the eight figures is useful—method one, starting from current conditions.

Applications of New Age Thinking Here

The eight computations are applied to the Social Security program, Medicare, and Individual Retirement Accounts. These applications are interesting from a policy viewpoint, but incomplete. The main problem with them is that all of them are utility-reducing. Let us take a simplified Social Security system as an example. When normal pension ages, Social Security tax rates, and benefit payments are fixed, each generation pays into the system for a fixed number of years, but, as life expectancies rise, each generation gets a longer and longer period of payout. Each generation gets a better deal from the Social Security system, but the risk is that the system could go bankrupt. Alternatively, when life expectancies at the normal pension age are fixed, along with Social Security tax rates and benefit payments, each generation has a reduced utility from the pension system. This is because there is an ever increasing length of the pay-in period and a fixed average length of the pay-out period. This is exactly what happens with Shoven and Goba's method one. Successive generations get lower and lower utility from the Social Security system.

Social Security and Medicare reforms based on all the methods presented in this chapter are utility-reducing. This is the most important problem with the chapter. As a strictly positive contribution, the authors can calculate whatever they wish. On the other hand, our interest in the chapter depends on how relevant the numbers are. If we would never wish to employ any of the methods because they reduce the utility of successive generations, then how intriguing are these numbers? Would it not be better to provide numbers that we might possibly use in policy discussions?

New Age Thinking Applied in New Ways

If none of the methods offered in the chapter are useful for policy analysis, then should we give up on new age thinking? The answer is certainly no, but to justify it, I need to demonstrate how new age thinking can be used in the policy debate.

The normal pension age is now undergoing a phase of rapid increase. People born in 1937 had a normal pension age of sixty-five. That age rises by two months per year through people born in 1943, who can receive a normal pension at age sixty-six. This is followed by a pause in the increase through the cohort of 1954. Next comes another phase of rapid increase by two months per year until the normal pension age becomes constant at sixty-seven for those born in 1960 and beyond. There is little rhyme or reason to this stair-step pattern. The fixed normal pension age of sixty-seven eventually leads to the bankruptcy of the Social Security system around 2042. Method one, on the other hand, would lead to a more rapid and continuous rise in the normal pension age, and would be progressively utility-reducing. Is there not some middle ground?

A rough projection based on the rates of changes of life expectancies at older ages experienced in the United States in the last half century suggests such a middle ground. A Social Security reform that would increase the normal pension age by half a year for every additional year of life expectancy at age sixty-five would quite closely approximate the current situation up to the cohort of 1960, and then produce a steady upward movement in the normal pension age. This is not the place to discuss the benefits and drawbacks of this reform. It is just important to notice that it can be relatively easily implemented because it does not cause discontinuities in normal pension ages, it uses new age thinking, and it does not involve any of the four methods suggested in this chapter.

Clearly, new age thinking can be a useful tool in policy dialogue regarding U.S. entitlement programs. I think that a bit more orientation in this chapter toward potentially useful reforms would have made it more exciting.

Terminological Problems with Age Inflation and Real Age

I think that the terms age inflation and real age as used in this chapter will be confusing to many noneconomists and that they should not be used. In order to assess the reactions of noneconomists to the terms, I shared the Shoven and Goda paper with Wolfgang Lutz. He is one of the foremost demographers of his generation, a colleague, and a frequent coauthor. Here is what he wrote:

> While the comparison to inflation is understandable with respect to the need for some adjustment of existing systems, it seems to be flawed under different perspectives and overall I think it is inappropriate.

What followed this quotation was an analysis of why it was inappropriate. Rather than reproduce that here, I will combine some of his ideas with mine and hope that the mixture is coherent. When we do inflation adjustment for monetary aggregates such as gross domestic product (GDP) and personal income, we recognize that the underlying unit of measure, say dollars, is getting less valuable over time because of price increases. Because of this, we need more dollars after inflation to buy the same bundle of goods. When we talk about age inflation, what is becoming devalued? The unit of measure of age is years. So, by analogy, the value of additional years must be going down as life expectancy rises. To have the same number of "effective" years, we would need to have more of them. However, to get more future years, we would need a lower real age, not a higher one. This seems to lead to a contradiction. Age inflation seems to imply lower ages over time, not higher ones.

Even putting this apparent contradiction aside, the argument by analogy seems to have problems. Why should the value of my sixty-fifth-year, for example, be lower to me when my life expectancy was eighty-six than it would be when my life expectancy was eighty-five? There are answers to all these issues. They begin by realizing that the premise of the previous argument is wrong. Age inflation does not mean that anything is really inflated. Age inflation is technically time deflation. As life expectancies at older ages increase, the number of years ahead of us, at any fixed age, increases. This is analogous to price decreases that increase the value of the money that we have. To compensate for having more years ahead of us, we have to take away some years. This is done by increasing the real age. Thus age inflation is due to a form of time deflation.

Most people will be frustrated and confused with this argument. The terms age inflation and time deflation as well as the murky concept of revaluing years will hinder our discussion of important aspects of new age thinking, not enhance it.

What about the term real age? Does it make our discussions of new age thinking any easier? I do not think so. There is already a term for this in the literature. It is prospective age. The term prospective age has the advantage that it does not immediately lead us back to the quandary of age inflation. There is also another problem with the term real age. Not all aspects of life should be analyzed in life expectancy-adjusted terms. The fecundity of a thirty-five-year-old woman in 2000 was not that different from the fecundity of a thirty-five-year-old woman in 1900, despite the increase in life expectancy. It is better to think of age as having two components: retrospective or conventional age, and prospective age. The different components could have different weights in answering different questions.

Communicating concepts involving the adjustment of age for life expectancy change to nontechnical audiences is a difficult challenge, but it is a challenge that we must overcome if we are to make those concepts part of the policy debate. For this reason, we must be careful in our choice of expressions. In my opinion, the terms age inflation and real age will only muddle the discussion and therefore we should stay away from them.

The Shoven and Goda chapter is a good one. It shows us what some ages in important public programs would be if they were adjusted for increases in survival rates at older ages. The chapter virtually demands a companion piece saying what should be done with the ages that were computed here. The current chapter would have been even better if the authors had had this companion paper in mind while they were writing this one.

References

Fuchs, V. 1984. Though much is taken: Reflections on aging, health, and medical care. *The Milbank Memorial Fund Quarterly: Health and Society* 62 (2): 142–66.

Lutz, W., W. Sanderson, and S. Scherbov. 2008. The coming acceleration of global population ageing. *Nature* 451 (February): 716–19.

Ryder, N. 1975. Notes on stationary populations. *Population Index* 41: 3–28.

Sanderson, W. C., and S. Scherbov. 2005. Average remaining lifetimes can increase as human populations age. *Nature* 435 (June): 811–13.

———. 2007a. A near electoral majority of pensioners: Prospects and policies. *Population and Development Review* 33 (3): 543–54.

———. 2007b. A new perspective on population aging. *Demographic Research* 16: 27–57.

Steuerle, C. E., and C. Spiro. 1999. Adjusting for life expectancy in measures of labor force participation. Available at: http://www.urban.org/publications/309271.html.

Old Europe Ages
Reforms and Reform Backlashes

Axel Börsch-Supan and Alexander Ludwig

5.1 Introduction

While aging is global, there are marked international differences in the speed and the extent of the aging processes. Even within the industrialized countries, differences are large. Europe and Japan have already a much older population than North America. Italy and Germany, in turn, are aging faster than France and Great Britain. Italy and Germany are projected to shrink in population size; even more dramatic is the shrinkage of the labor force between 2010 and 2035 when the German and Italian baby boom generations will retire. To the extent that labor force shrinkage precedes population shrinkage, these countries will face steeply falling support ratios (workers per consumers). One likely implication is slower economic growth and, in the worst case, stagnating or falling standards of living if the force of aging is stronger than the force of productivity growth.

This chapter has two broad aims. First, it shows that pension and labor market reforms have the potential to mitigate much of the negative implications of population aging. Hence, there is a good reason to bear the short-run costs of reforms in exchange for the long-run benefits. Second, the chapter models potential backlashes to reform in order to provide a more realistic

Axel Börsch-Supan is director of the Mannheim Research Institute for the Economics of Aging, and a research associate of the National Bureau of Economic Research. Alexander Ludwig is professor of macroeconomics at the University of Cologne, and is affiliated with the Mannheim Research Institute for the Economics of Aging.

This chapter was prepared for the NBER Conference on Demography and the Economy, Yountville, California, 11–12 April 2008. We thank Alan Auerbach, Francesco Billari, John Pencavel, Sam Preston, Warren Sanderson, Syl Schieber, John Shoven, Guido Tabellini, and Michele Tertilt for helpful comments on an earlier version. Financial support was provided by the Deutsche Forschungsgemeinschaft, the Land Baden Württemberg, and the German Association of Insurers. The usual disclaimer applies.

assessment of what might be the outcome of the politically complicated reform process in Europe.

The chapter is part of a research agenda that analyzes the aging process and its macroeconomic implications in continental Europe, focusing on its three largest countries—France, Germany, and Italy, the core of Old Europe. These countries have large public budgets and pay-as-you-go financed social security systems. Their unsustainability has already received prominent attention. In addition, these countries have labor markets characterized by low participation rates, high unemployment, and high wages. They are particularly vulnerable to the challenges of globalization due to the high tax and contribution burden in total labor compensation. In spite of these problems, France, Germany, and Italy have been remarkably resistant to labor market and pension reform. If governments manage to push such reforms through parliament, workers may thus react adversely and undo at least some of the expected effects of the reforms. Thus the main questions posed in this chapter are: What can pension and labor market reforms ideally achieve? What are possible behavioral reactions to reform policies? Which direction will they take and how large are they? And, ultimately, can Old Europe maintain its high living standards even if behavioral reactions offset some of the current reform efforts?

Some behavioral reactions will strengthen reform. A good example is raising the statutory retirement age. It has direct effects on the labor supply by bringing older individuals to the labor market. Indirect effects emerge from endogenous labor supply reactions; for example, through incentive effects generated by the tax and contribution burden that actuarially unfair social security systems impose on households. Raising the retirement age will lower social security contributions in such pension systems. In response to rising net wages, labor supply may then increase at all ages.

There are, however, also behavioral effects that weaken policy reforms. To take up the same example, older workers, now forced to work longer, may exploit part-time opportunities given by the pension system. In some countries (e.g., Finland and Germany), such opportunities led to a very early transition to part-time work with the perverse result that in some sectors hours supplied actually decreased in response to pension reform. Along the same line, encouraging female labor supply—for example, through public provision of day care facilities—may precipitate a decrease in male labor supply. This within-household substitution would be perfectly rational if households desire joint leisure and joint household production.

Little is known about these behavioral reactions. Therefore, one of the key issues taken up in this chapter is to model and calibrate behavioral reactions to reform. Which behavioral reactions will strengthen, and which will weaken reform policies? What are their quantitative effects?

We will build a simple model of reforms and reform backlashes into an overlapping generations (OLG) model of the Auerbach, Kotlikoff, and Skinner (1983)/Auerbach and Kotlikoff (1987) type, extended to a multicountry version (Börsch-Supan, Ludwig, and Winter 2006).[1] As a particular feature of our model, we add to the model the distinction between exogenous labor supply components (as key results of labor market and pension reform) and endogenous labor supply components (in order to represent possible reform backlash). To keep the language simple, we call the exogenous labor supply component "labor force participation," and the endogenous labor supply component "working hours." This language is metaphorical as we are well aware that both labor force participation and working hours have endogenous as well as exogenous components.

The metaphorical language chosen comes from our thinking of labor market and pension reforms as lifting institutional constraints. Typical constraints are a minimum labor market entry age generated by the school system, constraining the labor force participation of the young; an early labor market exit age generated by the pension system, effectively constraining the labor force participation of the old; and inflexible working hours and unavailable day care facilities, constraining female labor force participation. This view of lifting restrictions motivates our modeling strategy and the language behind it: labor market and pension reforms are represented by exogenous changes of labor supply at the extensive margin (the number of working persons in an economy).

Households then are modeled to respond to the changes of labor supply by changing their working hours (the intensive margin of labor supply). Endogenous hours supply may increase, for example, if distorting social security taxes and contributions decline as an implication of pension reform. The opposite reaction is also possible: endogenous hours supply may decrease in response to an exogenous change of the number of working persons if there is intrahousehold substitution between the number of persons working and the hours worked by each person.

Another important feature of our model is its multicountry nature. No country in continental Europe is even approximately modeled by a closed economy. France, Germany, and Italy have large export sectors and considerable foreign direct investments. These provide a second source of opportunities during the global aging process: not all income needs to come from domestic production, and the gross national product (GNP) may become substantially larger than the gross domestic product (GDP) if foreign direct investments create large returns. We compliment France, Germany, and Italy as countries that save more than they invest, with the United States representing the rest of the world currently absorbing the continental European savings.

---

1. Similar multicountry OLG models have been developed, among others, by Feroli (2002); Henriksen (2002); Brooks (2003); Domeij and Floden (2006); Attanasio, Kitao, and Violante (2006, 2007); and Krüger and Ludwig (2007).

While this feature is important for a credible quantification of our pension and labor market reform analysis, it is not the main focus of this chapter. We refer to a sister paper, Börsch-Supan, Ludwig, and Winter (2006), which analyzes the resulting international capital flows and the associated rate of return developments, including the "asset meltdown hypothesis."

The key results of our chapter rest on a set of three-way comparisons that are best imagined by a two-by-two-by-two table. The first dimension reflects labor market policies. One extreme is the complete failure to adapt those institutional restrictions that keep labor force participation so low in France, Germany, and Italy. The result is unchanged low labor force participation rates by age and gender, also in the future. The polar case, for some an extreme, is the adaptation of all societal systems from kindergarten to retirement policies to increase age- and gender-specific labor force participation rates across the board.

As a second dimension, we model two extreme positions of pension policy. One extreme is a fully funded, voluntary private accounts system with no distortions and perfect intertemporal consumption smoothing. The other extreme is a pay-as-you-go pension system with flat benefits financed by a contribution that is perceived as a pure tax with the associated labor supply distortions.

Finally, the third dimension in these comparisons isolates behavioral effects. One extreme is a fixed hours supply by each working individual. As in the polar case, we derive a supply function of working hours that is responsive to wages net of taxes and contributions, but also to household labor participation.

Our chapter shows that direct quantity and indirect behavioral effects are large. They both significantly affect economic growth and living standards. Due to strong interaction effects between pension system and labor markets, a smart combination of pension policy and adaptation of institutions related to the labor market can do more than each policy in isolation. We show that they can offset the effects of population aging on economic growth and living standards. On balance, however, behavioral effects dampen such reform efforts. Taking positive and negative behavioral effects into account, a combination of many policy measures is necessary in order to keep per capita consumption from falling behind the secular growth path.

The rest of the chapter is structured as follows. Section 5.2 briefly sets the demographic background. Section 5.3 describes the current labor market situation and our labor market reform scenarios. Section 5.4 presents the multicountry computational general equilibrium model with a combination of exogenous and endogenous labor supply components. Section 5.5 delivers our main results in the two-by-two-by-two table set up. We vary the institutional framework of labor markets and pensions in order to investigate the interactions between pension and employment policies and the behavioral reactions to pension and labor market reform. Since higher old-age labor force participation raises issues of age-specific productivity, they are briefly addressed in section 5.6. Section 5.7 concludes.

5.2 Demography

While the patterns of population aging are similar in most countries, timing and extent differ substantially. The United States is considerably younger and will age later and to a slower extent than the European Union (EU), especially Germany and Italy. This is most graphically depicted in the changing population pyramids of our four countries between 2000 and 2050; see figure 5.1.

The differences are startling. While the U.S. population pyramid in 2050 features the normal large base, Germany and Italy have strongly inverted population pyramids. The French pyramids change little between 2000 and 2050, with relatively small differences in cohort sizes up to age seventy. These differences can largely be attributed to different fertility rates (France and the United States have fertility rates close to the replacement level; see table 5.1), while Germany and Italy lose about a third of their population from generation to generation due to fertility rates that are below 1.4.

Life expectancy also differs remarkably among the four countries. This is accentuated in the healthy life expectancy, a measure developed by the World Health Organization (WHO) based on functional ability. It measures the expected age without functional limitation as defined by a set of disability indicators. Healthy life expectancy in France is almost four years higher than in the United States. Note that in Europe healthy life expectancy is about ten years higher than the average retirement age, providing some room for an increase in retirement age; see section 5.3.

We compute the future demography of the four countries based on three key assumptions. First, we provide projections of mortality based on a Lee-Carter decomposition, using past mortality rate changes derived from the Human Mortality Database (2008). Table 5.1 shows the resulting life expectancies in 2050 (column [5]). They coincide with the current United Nations (UN) projections for Germany and the United States, but are slightly higher for France and Italy (the UN has age eighty-five compared while our projections yield ages eighty-six and eighty-seven, respectively).

Second, we assume that fertility rates are exogenous and remain constant as given by table 5.1. Third and similarly, we assume constant and exogenous migration flows, based on the current medium variant of the UN projections (the net migrants per year are France, 100,000; Germany, 150,000; Italy, 135,000; and the United States, 1,100,000), which is about the long-term average. It is important to note that these migration flows are small relative to the decline in the labor force projected in section 5.3.

Figure 5.2 shows the total population aged fifteen years and over, which will be the base of our projections and simulations. It reflects the stark

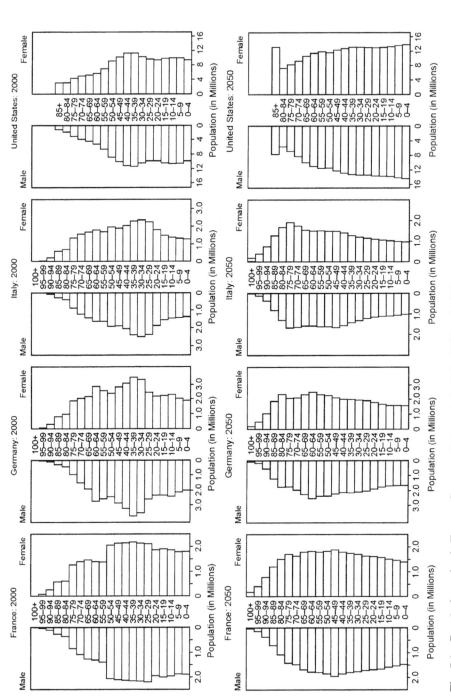

Fig. 5.1 Population aging in France, Germany, Italy, and the U.S., 2000 and 2050

Source: U.S. Bureau of the Census, International Database, http://www.census.gov/ipc/www/idb/pyramids.html.

Table 5.1   **Fertility rates and life expectancy**

	Total fertility rate	Life expectancy at birth	Healthy life expectancy	Life expectancy in year 2050
France	1.89	80.3	71.3	86
Germany	1.34	79.0	70.2	84
Italy	1.29	80.4	71.0	87
U.S.	2.10	77.8	67.6	83

Sources: European Commission and U.S. Census (2008); OECD Health Data 2007; WHO (2007); and own computations.

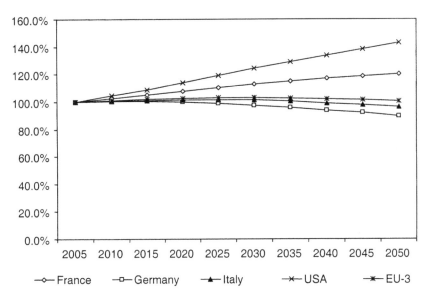

Fig. 5.2   Population fifteen years and older, indexed to 2005 = 100 percent
Source: Own projection based on assumptions detailed in text.

differences among the population pyramids that we have seen in figure 5.1. There will be population growth in France and the United States, but significant decline in Germany and a somewhat smaller decline in Italy after 2020, mainly due to the higher expected migration to Italy. The fifth line represents the aggregate of France, Germany, and Italy, which we will call EU-3 in order to represent the three largest continental European countries.

Truly remarkable is the decline of the working age population (aged twenty to sixty-four; see figure 5.3). Relative to total population aged fifteen and older, the United States will lose about 10 percent of their working age individuals between 2005 and 2050. In Italy, the loss is more than twice as high with 22 percent. France is closer to the United States and Germany closer to Italy, reflecting the fertility rates in table 5.1.

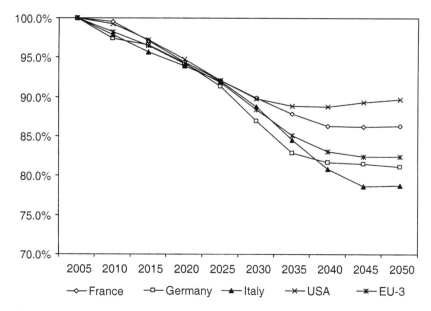

Fig. 5.3   Working age population as share of total population aged fifteen and over, 2005 = 100 percent

Source: Own projection based on assumptions detailed in text. Working age is age 20 to 64.

5.3   Employment and Labor Market Reforms

Working age population is not equal to employment. The demographic differences, in particular those between Italy and the United States, are dramatically amplified by the differences in labor force participation. Figure 5.4 shows the percentage of individuals employed in the population aged fifteen and older. This is a variant of the "support ratio" reflecting the number of workers per adult consumer. The United States' support rates are much higher than the European ones. In Europe, Italy stands out with the lowest support ratio. Unlike its demographic position, France shares the low labor force participation of continental Europe; current French labor force participation rates are actually lower than the German ones.

Figure 5.4 is based on the assumption of constant age- and gender-specific labor force participation rates. Given this assumption, Germany has about the same low support ratio in 2005 that the United States will have after 2040. In this sense, Germany is one generation ahead of the United States when it concerns the macroeconomic balance between individuals in production and individuals who consume.

Figure 5.4 also shows that the decline of the support ratio, given the assumption of no behavioral changes, will be more pronounced in the three European countries than in the United States (24.3 percent versus 15.0 per-

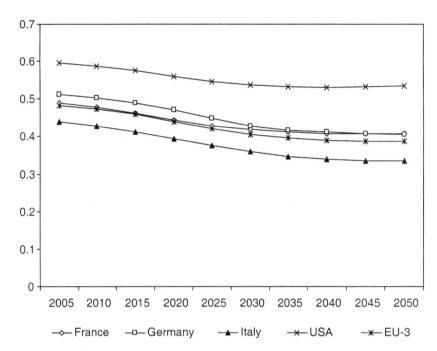

Fig. 5.4   Employed persons as share of total population aged fifteen and over, not indexed

Source: Own projection based on 2005 labor force participation rates.

cent between 2005 and 2050), aggravating the current differences of the support ratios among the four countries.

Aggregate employment is a result of labor market entry age, female labor force participation, unemployment rates, and labor market exit age, to
name the four most important parameters. These parameters are strongly
governed by institutional restrictions. Labor market entry age, for example,
is a function of the school system. Germany has regulations that generate
late entries into the school system, a long duration in high schools and
universities, and thus a late labor market entry age. Similarly, female labor
force participation is a function of institutions such as kindergarten and
afternoon school, which tend to be provided by public entities in Europe.
Unemployment is a function of the duration and generosity of unemployment compensation. Labor market exit, finally, is strongly governed by
pension regulations that effectively make the early eligibility age also the
effective age of labor market withdrawal. Our main point is, that from an
individual's point of view, labor supply has important exogenous components that restrict possible endogenous labor supply decisions.

It is unlikely that these exogenous components remain unchanged over the course of population aging and the general change of society over the next two decades. We therefore define two polar scenarios representing the potential changes in the institutional framework restricting households' labor supply decisions:

- In the status quo scenario (STATQUO), age- and gender-specific labor force participation rates will remain as they are at baseline in 2005; this was the scenario underlying figure 5.4.
- The labor market reform scenario (LREFORM) includes four reform steps:

  - RETAGE: an increase in the retirement age by two years.
  - JOBENTRY: a decrease in the job entry age by two years.
  - FEMLFP: an adaptation of female labor force participation rates to those of men.
  - UNEMP: a reduction of unemployment to 40 percent of its current level.

The increments are motivated by actual policy proposals: in Germany, the statutory retirement age has been raised from sixty-five to sixty-seven years in a series of transitions until about 2020; in France and Italy, similar steps will follow with some delay. The change in the European high school and university system (the so-called Bologna process) is expected to decrease duration in schooling by about two years. Finally, 40 percent of current unemployment represents the conventional estimate of the Non-Accelerating Inflation Rate of Unemployment (NAIRU) (Ball and Mankiw 2002).

These reform steps will be phased in linearly between 2010 and 2050. The increase in retirement age (the decrease in the job entry age) is modeled as a shift of the distribution of labor force participation rates by age to the right (to the left, respectively), thereby increasing the flat part of the distribution in the middle (see figure 5.5).

Overall, these reform steps do not appear to be overly radical; in fact, their combination would lead in 2040 to labor force participation rates fairly similar to those in Denmark today. Nevertheless, attempts to actually execute reforms with those goals have faced stiff opposition in France and Italy, and more recently, and to a somewhat lesser extent, also in Germany.

Figure 5.6 displays the resulting trajectories of the number of working individuals. Each reform step is additive to the one before; hence, the trajectory labeled UNEMP corresponds to the LREFORM scenario of all four reform elements implemented.

The trajectories are very different across countries. France can easily compensate the slightly declining number of individuals of working age by a combination of two or three of the aforementioned policy changes, while Germany has no chance to offset the loss in working age population even with a combination of all four measures.

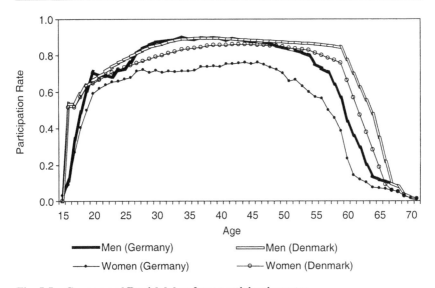

Fig. 5.5   German and Danish labor force participation rates

Source: Own computations based on the German Mikrozensus (www.destatis.de) and Statistics Denmark (www.statbank.dk).

The three countries also differ in the efficacy of the four policy parameters. Note in particular Italy, with a large jump if female labor force participation adapts to that of men. This is due to the very low female labor force participation currently in Italy. The irony is, of course, that because Italy's pool of hitherto unused labor capacity (in particular women) is so large, tapping it provides a very large opportunity to counteract the effects of population aging. Italy, while aging more than Germany, is thus much better off than Germany, which has less room to increase labor force participation.

Lower labor input as indicated in these figures will most likely slow down Germany's, and possibly also Italy's, GDP growth.[2] However, since total population will also decline, this does not necessarily imply that standards of living will fall. Figure 5.7 therefore divides the number of working persons by the population aged fifteen and older, our support ratio. The main message is that a combination of the four policy scenarios can in all countries, more or less also in Germany and Italy, stabilize these countries' support ratio. This is a very important message: lifting labor market constraints and tapping into the pool of currently unused labor can offset the force of aging in the three countries of Old Europe.

2. Given the large share of labor in output and the history of total factor productivity, it is unlikely that productivity growth and capital accumulation can overcompensate the decline in labor force.

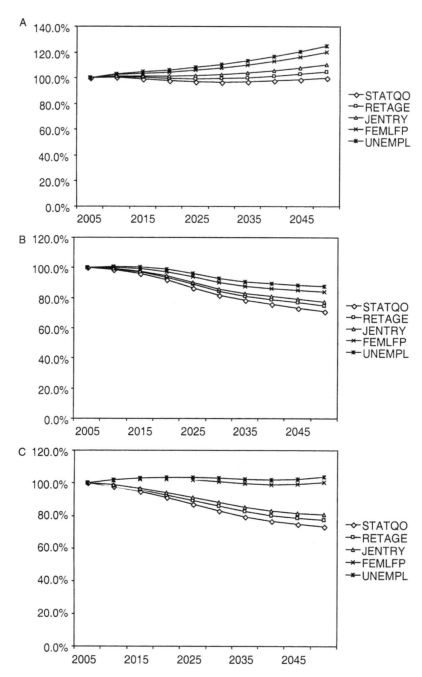

Fig. 5.6   Employment, indexed to 2005 = 100 percent: *A*, **France;** *B*, **Germany;** *C*, **Italy**

Source: Own calculations.

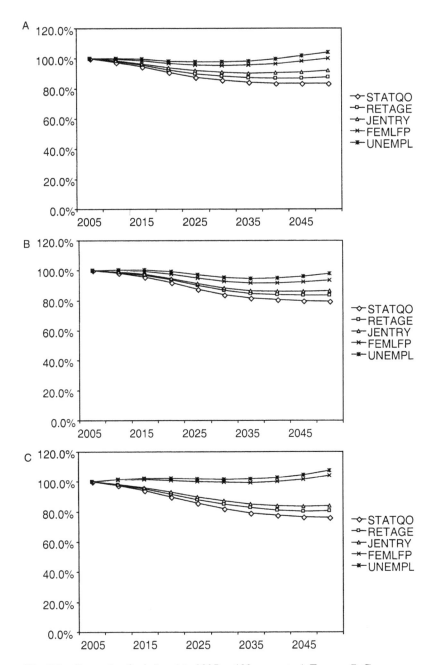

Fig. 5.7 Support ratio, indexed to 2005 = 100 percent: *A*, France; *B*, Germany; *C*, Italy

Note: Employment as share of population age fifteen and over, own calculations.

5.4   A Dynamic Open-economy Macroeconomic Model with Exogenous Labor Force Participation and Endogenous Hours Supply

We now construct a dynamic open-economy macroeconomic model that allows us to analyze the effects of the labor market reforms described in the previous section on the GDP and consumption per capita in an aging Europe. As described in the introduction, labor supply has an endogenous and an exogenous component. While we treat the reforms and the resulting variation in employment numbers as exogenous, households in our model endogenously adjust hours worked and may thus counteract parts of the labor market reforms.

Our main assumptions on this interplay between the exogenous variation of employment numbers and hours worked are as follows: We model the decision of a household with preferences over consumption and leisure. Total labor supply of a household of age j as derived from the household's optimization is the product of exogenous employment numbers l_j, and the endogenous decision on hours worked at age j, h_j. The crucial difference between the two labor supply components is that hours worked may not exceed the time endowment (which we normalize to one), while employment numbers l_j can take any positive value.

As the age-specific employment l_j is exogenously increased, for example, due to an increase in the retirement age, the household endogenously decreases hours worked, h_j. In the absence of any constraints, the two components of labor supply are perfect substitutes such that the exogenous variation of l_j leaves the labor supply of the household unaffected. However, the exogenous variation of l_j affects total effective labor supply for those households for whom the time endowment constraint is binding. As a consequence, the exogenous employment variation of l_j has some effect on aggregate effective labor supply, but the overall effect is substantially smaller than in an alternative specification of our model with fully exogenous labor supply where h_j is restricted to one.

5.4.1   Demography

Time in our model is discrete and extends from $t = 0, \ldots, T$. Each model period t reflects a time interval of five years. Our demographic projections, however, are more detailed with an annual periodicity. These detailed demographic projections form the background of our analysis. Demography is taken as exogenous. It represents one of the main driving forces of our simulation model, in addition to exogenous changes in labor supply restrictions and pension policy changes.

Households in our model economies enter economic life at age fifteen, which we denote by $j = 0$. The maximum age is one hundred years. Accordingly, the maximum economic age, denoted by J, is eighty-five. We assume that households give birth between ages $0, \ldots, jf$, the age of menopause.

Accordingly, in each country i, the size of population of age j in period t, $N_{t,j,i}$, is given recursively by

(1) $\qquad N_{t+1,j+1,i} = N_{t,j,i}\,\varsigma_{t,j,i}\quad$ for $j > 0\quad$ and $\quad N_{t+1,0,i} = \sum_{j=0}^{jf} f_{t,j,i} N_{t,j,i}$

where $\varsigma_{t,j,i}$ denotes the age-specific conditional survival rate, and $f_{t,j,i}$ the age-specific fertility rate. The resulting total fertility rates and life expectancies have been summarized in table 5.1.

5.4.2   Production

The production sector in each country consists of a representative firm that uses a Cobb-Douglas production function given by

(2) $\qquad\qquad Y_{t,i} = F(\Omega_{t,i}, K_{t,i}, L_{t,i}) = \Omega_{t,i}K_{t,i}^{\alpha}L_{t,i}^{1-\alpha},$

where $K_{t,i}$ denotes the capital stock and $L_{t,i}$ is aggregate effective labor supply of country i at time t; α is the capital share and $\Omega_{t,i}$ is the technology level of country i growing at the exogenous rate g.

The firm's problem is static such that wages and interest rates are given by

(3) $\qquad\qquad\qquad w_{t,i} = \Omega_{t,i}(1-\alpha)k_t^{\alpha},$

(4) $\qquad\qquad\qquad r_t = \alpha k_t^{\alpha} - \delta,$

where k_t is the capital stock per efficient unit of labor and δ is the depreciation rate of capital.

5.4.3   Households

An exogenous fraction $l_{t,j,i}$ of each household supplies work. This fraction of the household endogenously decides on the hours of work, $h_{t,j,i}$. The other fraction of the household, $1 - l_{t,j,i}$, does not work and fully enjoys leisure. Accordingly, total labor supply of a household is given by the product of the two components, $l_{t,j,i} \cdot h_{t,j,i}$, and total leisure is therefore $1 - l_{t,j,i} \cdot h_{t,j,i}$, whereby we restrict time endowment to one.

The household derives utility from consumption $c_{t,j,i}$ and leisure $1 - l_{t,j,i} \cdot h_{t,j,i}$, and the household's per period utility function is given by

$$u(c_{t,j,i}, 1 - h_{t,j,i} \cdot l_{t,j,i}) = \frac{1}{1 - \theta}(c_{t,j,i}^{\phi}(1 - l_{t,j,i}h_{t,j,i})^{1-\phi})^{1-\theta}.$$

The maximization problem of a cohort born in period t at $j = 0$ is given by

(5) $\qquad\qquad \max\sum_{j=0}^{J}\beta^j \pi_{t,j,i} u(c_{t+j,j,i}, 1 - l_{t+j,j,i} h_{t+j,j,i}),$

where β is the pure time discount factor. In addition to pure discounting, households discount future utility with their unconditional survival probability in period, $\pi_{t,j} = \Pi_{k=0}^{j} s_{t+k,k}$.

A feature of our model is uncertainty about the time of death expressed in the term $\pi_{t,j,i}$ in equation (5). We assume that accidental bequests resulting from premature death are taxed by the government at a confiscatory rate and used for otherwise neutral government consumption.[3] We do not include intended bequests in our model.

Labor productivity changes over the life cycle according to age-specific productivity parameters ε_j. Hence, the age-specific wage is $w_{t,j,i} = w_{t,i} \cdot \varepsilon_j$.

Denoting total assets by $a_{t,j,i}$, maximization of the household's intertemporal utility is subject to a dynamic budget constraint given by

$$(6) \quad a_{t+1,j+1,i} = a_{t,j} (1 + r_t) + \lambda l_{t,j,i} h_{t,j,i} w_{t,j,i} (1 - \tau_{t,i}) + (1 - \lambda) p_{t,j,i} - c_{t,j,i},$$

where $\lambda = 1$ for $j = 0, \ldots jr$ and $\lambda = 0$ for $j > jr$ and jr is the exogenous retirement age, $\tau_{t,i}$ is the contribution rate to a pay-as-you-go (PAYG) financed public pension system, and $p_{t,j,i}$ is pension income; see following.

Furthermore, maximization is subject to the constraint that hours worked are positive and may not exceed one, hence,

$$(7) \quad\quad\quad\quad\quad\quad 0 \le h_{t,j,i} \le 1.$$

In the variant of our model with fully exogenous labor supply we replace the constraint (7) with the constraint that $h_{t,j,i} = 1$ for all t, j, i.

5.4.4 Pensions and Pension Reform

The only purpose of the government in our model is to organize a prototypical continental European public pension system that is pay-as-you-go financed and provides flat (i.e., not earnings-related) pension benefits. We assume that the budget of the pension system is balanced in all t,i such that

$$(8) \quad\quad \tau_{t,i} w_{t,i} L_{t,i} = \sum_{j=jr+1}^{J} p_{t,j,i} N_{t,j,i} = \rho_{t,i} w_{t,i} (1 - \tau_{t,i}) \sum_{j=jr+1}^{J} N_{t,j,i},$$

where $\rho_{t,i}$ denotes the net replacement rate and $\tau_{t,i}$ the contribution rate of the pension system in t,i. Households consider the contributions as pure taxes.

The main policy parameter is the net replacement rate ρ; the contribution rate τ responds passively to balance the pension system's budget. If ρ is large, public pensions crowd out private saving through the households consumption/saving decision given by equations (5) and (6). Moreover, since the benefits are not related to individual earnings, we consider the contributions to the pension system as pure taxes, with the associated labor supply distortions that work through the households labor supply decision given by equations (5), (6), and (7).

---

3. An alternative assumption would be to redistribute accidental bequests to the population according to some scheme. The redistribution would, however, not affect our results much, and we therefore opted for this simplifying assumption.

If $\rho = 0$, all old-age provision will be private savings. This represents the textbook life cycle model in which intertemporal consumption smoothing over the life cycle provides the retirement income through saving in young age and dissaving after retirement.

Pension reform is modeled as a reduction of the net replacement rate ρ. We will consider two polar cases:

- FLATSS: maintaining the current country-specific replacement rates also in the future ($\rho_{t,i} = \rho_{2005,i}$ for $t > 2005$).
- SAVING: abolishing the public pension system altogether ($\rho_{t,i} = 0$) so that all age provision is private savings.

5.4.5   Equilibrium

Given initial capital stocks $K_{0,i}$, a competitive equilibrium of the economy is defined as sequences of disaggregate variables for the households, $\{c_{t,j,i}, l_{t,j,i}, h_{t,j,i}, a_{t,j,i}\}$; sequences of aggregate variables, $\{C_{t,i}, L_{t,i}, K_{t,i}\}$; prices for labor as well as contribution rates to the pension system, $\{w_{t,i}, \tau_{t,i}\}$; in each country i; and a common world interest rate, $\{r_t\}$, such that:

1. Given prices and initial conditions, households maximize lifetime utility in equation (5) subject to the constraints in equations (6) and (7).

2. Factor prices equal their marginal productivities as given in equations (3) and (4).

3. Government policies satisfy equation (8) in every period.

4. All markets clear in all t,i.

$$L_{t,i} = \sum_{j=0}^{J} \varepsilon_j l_{t,j,i} N_{t,j,i} \text{ for all } t,i$$

$$\sum_{i=1}^{I} K_{t+1,i} = \sum_{i=1}^{I} \sum_{j=0}^{J} a_{t+1,j+1,i} N_{t,j,i}$$

$$\sum_{i=1}^{I} \sum_{j=0}^{J} c_{t,j,i} N_{t,j,i} + \sum_{i=1}^{I} K_{t+1,i} = \sum_{i=1}^{I} \Omega_{t,i} K_{t,i}^{\alpha} L_{t,i}^{1-\alpha} - (1-\delta) \sum_{i=1}^{I} K_{t,i}.$$

5.4.6   Numerical Implementation

Our timeline has four periods: a phase-in period, a calibration period, a projection period, and a phase-out period. First, we start calculations 110 years before the calibration period begins with the assumption of an "artificial" initial steady state in 1850. The time period between 1960 and 2004 is then used as a calibration period in order to determine the structural parameters of the model. Our projections run from 2005 through 2100.[4] The phase-out period after 2100 has two parts: a transition to a steady-state

---

4. Results are displayed through the year 2050 to show the main period of population aging.

population in 2200, and an additional one-hundred-year period until the macroeconomic model reaches a final steady state in 2300.

We determine the equilibrium path of the overlapping generations model by using the modified Gauss-Seidel iteration as described in Ludwig (2004). The algorithm searches for equilibrium paths of capital to output ratios, and, in case there are social security systems, pension contribution rates in each country.

5.4.7   Calibration

The current version of the chapter features a calibration that is based on an ad hoc choice of parameters by reference to other studies. In future versions of the chapter we will specify certain calibration targets and determine deep structural model parameters by minimum distance methods. In particular, we will emphasize a careful calibration of the consumption weight in the utility function, φ, that determines the relative preference for labor versus leisure and thereby indirectly, the number of households at the constraint with $h_j = 1$. We currently set $\varphi = 0.66$, which corresponds with the value determined by minimum distance methods in Börsch-Supan, Ludwig, and Winter (2006).

The structural model parameters are summarized in table 5.2. These parameter values refer to an annual periodicity of the model.

5.5   Results

We structure our results by investigating three dimensions, each with two polar assumptions:

- Labor market reforms: no reform at all, resulting in future labor force participation rates that equal the current ones (STATQUO, abbreviated SQ) versus the implementation of all four reform steps described in section 5.3 (LREFORM, abbreviated RF).
- Pension reform: a prototypical pension system of continental Europe, purely pay-as-you-go, providing flat social security benefits financed by distorting contributions (FLATSS, abbreviated) versus a fully

Table 5.2	Structural model parameters	
	α: capital share in production	0.4
	g: growth rate of labor productivity	0.015
	δ: depreciation rate of capital	0.05
	Ω_t: technology level	0.05–0.07
	β: discount factor	0.99
	θ: coefficient of relative risk aversion	2
	φ: consumption share parameter	0.66

funded, voluntary private accounts system that generates no distortions (SAVING, abbreviated SV), as described in subsection 5.4.5.
- Labor supply reaction: fixed hours supply (EXOGENOUS, abbreviated EX) versus endogenous supply of working hours (ENDOGENOUS, abbreviated EN), as described in the households optimization problem, subsection 5.4.3, equations (5) to (7).

This set up yields a two-by-two-by-two table of underlying assumptions displayed in table 5.3. The eight resulting combinations are labeled: for example, by "FL-SQ-EX" to denote a flat benefit pay-as-you-go social security system (FL) with status quo labor force participation (SQ) and an exogenously given hours supply (EX); by "SV-RF-EN" to denote a fully funded private savings based old-age provision system (SV) with a comprehensive labor market reform (RF) and an hours supply that reacts endogenously to aging and policy changes (EN), and so forth.

On the following pages, we develop how the outcome variables of our general equilibrium model emerge from the three exogenous changes that drive our model:

- The demographic aging process in the background.
- Lifting of labor supply restrictions as described in section 5.3.
- A fundamental change in the type of pension system.

We begin with figures that display the evolution of employment, the supply of hours, total labor supply, wages, and domestic capital stock. We then present the evolution of our two target variables, GDP and consumption per capita.

Table 5.3   **Setup of scenarios**

	Extensive margin: Labor market regime			
	Constant age- and gender-specific labor force participation (STATQUO, abbreviated SQ)		Increasing age- and gender-specific labor force participation (LREFORM, abbreviated LF)	
	Intensive margin: Hours' supply			
Pension system	EXOGENOUS hours supply (abbrev. EX)	ENDOGENOUS hours supply (abbrev. EN)	EXOGENOUS hours supply (abbrev. EX)	ENDOGENOUS hours supply (abbrev. EN)
Pay-as-you-go with flat benefits (FLATSS, abbrev. FL)	FL-SQ-EX	FL-SQ-EN	FL-RF-EX	FL-RF-EN
Fully funded voluntary accounts (SAVING, abbrev. SV)	SV-SQ-EX	SV-SQ-EN	SV-RF-EX	SV-RF-EN

All figures refer to the aggregate of France, Germany, and Italy (EU-3). The United States is modeled in the background with similar changes in retirement age and female labor force participation, but no other exogenous policy changes.

All figures have the same design (cf. table 5.3). The first diagram in each figure shows all eight combinations of the scenarios. The following three smaller panels show the differences in each of the three directions in order to identify interaction effects.

5.5.1   Extensive Margin: Employment

Figure 5.8 corresponds to figure 5.6 in section 5.3 and depicts the evolution of labor supply at the extensive margin; that is, the exogenously given number of persons who participate in the labor market: $L_{t,i} = \sum_{j=0}^{J} l_{t,j,i} N_{t,j,i}.$

The STATQUO scenario is marked by diamonds. It shows a steady decline of the number of employed persons. The decline is about 20 percent between 2005 and 2050.

This is very different from the LREFORM scenario (marked by triangles). The increase in labor force participation due to all four reform steps—earlier entry in, and later exit from, the labor market, more women working and less unemployed—more or less stabilizes employment in the EU-3 area. Labor supply declines only slightly after 2015 but increases again after 2035, the peak of the aging process in continental Europe. Except for the time between 2015 and 2035, when the losses in employment created by the retirement of the baby boom generation are very large, the effects of labor market reforms and migration just compensate the aging effects.

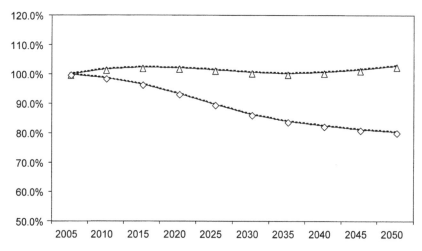

Fig. 5.8   Employment, indexed to 2005 = 100 percent, EU-3

5.5.2   Intensive Margin: The Supply of Hours
         for Given Labor Force Participation

The supply of working hours now reacts to the exogenous change in labor force participation according to the household's maximization problem as specified in subsection 5.4.3. We distinguish two cases: households that are constrained by the time endowment limit (equation [7] in section 5.4.3), and households that are not constrained.

Given the calibration parameters, about 58 percent of households are not constrained in 2005, mainly middle-aged households. The difference between France and Germany on one side, and Italy on the other side, is large: in France, 67 percent of all households are unconstrained, in Germany 63 percent, while only 43 percent of Italian households can work as much as they would like. These households fully undo exogenous policy changes by adjusting their working hours inversely, since for them hours h and persons l are perfect substitutes (equations [5] and [6] in section 5.4.3). One might think of these households as a couple. In the status quo regime, one person was restricted to work while the other person worked as much as the household needed for consumption and saving. Once the restriction for the first person was lifted, however, the couple distributes the work more equally between the two persons without increasing total hours supplied by the household.

Figure 5.9 shows this from a microeconomic perspective; that is, on the level of an individual representative household of each age class, separately for each country. For unconstrained households (hours less than one), the hours (marked by squares) respond inversely to the changes in participation (diamonds) when moving from the status quo (left panels) to the LREFORM regime (right panels).

The remaining 42 percent of households have been constrained under the labor market policy regimes in 2005. This is the majority in Italy, where 57 percent of all households are constrained, and roughly a third in France (33 percent) and Germany (37 percent). These households are shown in figure 5.9 as those households that have an hours supply of exactly one: the very young and the old. Releasing these constraints generates more hours supply when the policies are phased in over time. This is visible in the lower number of households on the hours = 1 line in the LREFORM scenarios (right panels) than under STATQUO labor force participation (left panels).

Taking both participation and hours together yields total labor supply of the household (marked by triangles in figure 5.9). It is much higher for the younger and older age groups in the LREFORM scenario as compared to the STATQUO scenario, but remains unchanged for the unconstrained middle-aged households, which perfectly substitute between participation and hours supply.

Figure 5.10 turns to the macroeconomic view. It shows the aggregate

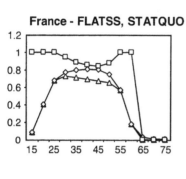

France - FLATSS, STATQUO

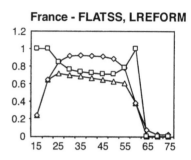

France - FLATSS, LREFORM

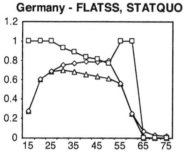

Germany - FLATSS, STATQUO

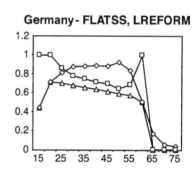

Germany- FLATSS, LREFORM

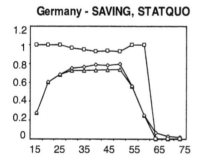

Germany - SAVING, STATQUO

Germany - SAVING, LREFORM

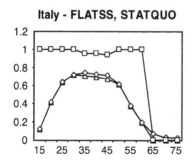

Italy - FLATSS, STATQUO

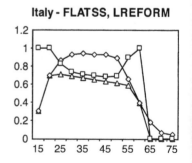

Italy - FLATSS, LREFORM

Fig. 5.9   Household labor force participation, hours supply and total labor supply

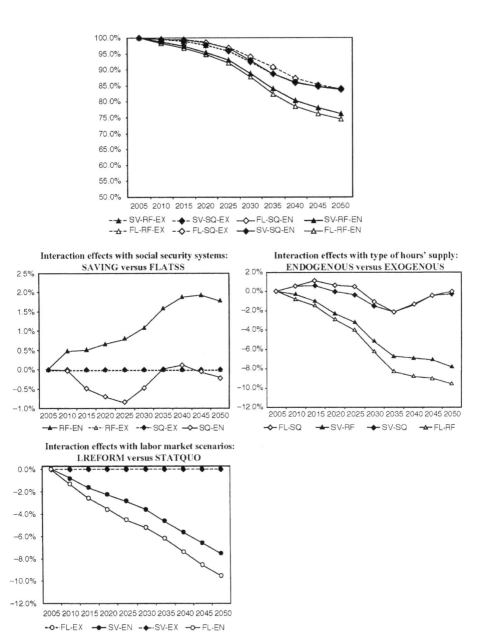

Fig. 5.10 **Hours for fixed labor force participation, indexed to 2005 = 100 percent, EU-3**

supply of working hours: $H_{t,i} = \sum_{j=0}^{J} h_{t,j,i} N_{t,j,i}$ for a labor force participation of one in all working-age households (aged twenty to sixty-four). Hours are normalized to 100 percent in 2005 within each scenario. Hence, they are adjusted for any level effects generated by pension and labor market policies that create cross-country differences already in 2005.

Figure 5.10 shows the hours result for the eight scenarios defined in table 5.3. Population aging generates declining hours in all scenarios. There is, of course, no difference among the four scenarios with exogenous hours supply as this is fixed to one. It can be interpreted as the baseline that reflects the decline in working-age population without any reaction in supplied working hours.

The reaction of the endogenous hours supply differs by labor market and pension scenario. Hours are much lower in the LREFORM scenarios (triangles) than under constant labor force participation rates (STATQUO, diamonds).

There are interesting interaction effects between labor market and pension reform. Without labor market reform, hours supply is almost identical in the FLATSS and SAVING pension scenarios; actually, hours supplied are a bit lower in the pension reform scenario. This relation reverts when the labor reforms are put in place. If labor market and pension reform concur, hours supply is higher than in the case when labor markets are reformed without a pension reform.

A microeconomic perspective of this interaction effect is given in figure 5.9 for the case of Germany. A comparison between the second and the third left panels shows that the hours reduction is much smaller in a funded pension system than in a flat-benefits pay-as-you-go system. This reflects the negative incentive effect of high distorting taxes. Under the LREFORM scenario (right panels), fewer households are constrained by labor market institutions. More age groups, therefore, substitute hours for participation within a household. Since the hours reduction is much smaller in the funded pension system, more total labor supply remains.

Another way to understand the interaction effects is first taking differences in the direction of each dimension of the two-by-two-by-two table 5.3. This is done in the three smaller panels of figure 5.10 labeled "interaction effects." The first panel shows the impact of a radical social security reform. Hours increase under a funded system vis-à-vis the pay-as-you-go system if exogenous labor force participation also increases. The difference is zero if hours are exogenous, and very small, but negative if labor force participation remains at status quo.

The second panel displays the difference between higher and unchanged exogenous labor force participation. Hours react negatively because of intrahousehold substitution between hours and labor force participation. This effect offsets some, but not all, of the higher labor force participation as we will see in the following subsection. The offsetting effect is higher in a distorting pay-as-you-go system. We may interpret the additional difference between the two lines in the second interaction effect as an incentive effect due to distorting taxes, while the difference between the horizontal axis and the lines denoted by SV is the substitution effect between hours and labor force participation.

The third panel summarizes these effects as it displays the difference between endogenous and exogenous hours supply under the four combinations of pension and labor market regimes while the two former graphs can be interpreted as differences in differences. Quite clearly, there is a strong and beneficial interaction between changing the pension system and lifting labor market restrictions. This is an important result of our chapter.

5.5.3   Putting All Together: Total Effective Labor Supply

Total labor effective supply is the product of working persons (figure 5.8) and hours per person (figure 5.10), adjusted for age-specific productivity:

$$L_{t,i} = \sum_{j=0}^{J} \varepsilon_j l_{t,j,i} h_{t,j,i} N_{t,j,i}.^5$$

Its evolution under the eight scenarios is displayed in figure 5.11. If hours are exogenous, there is no difference between figures 5.8 and 5.11, and there is no difference between the two pension scenarios. Hence, the lines for FL-RF-EX and SV-RF-EX at the very top overlap as well as the lines representing FL-SQ-EX and SV-SQ-EX at the very bottom. This is also visible in the first panel on interaction effects.

If hours are endogenous, the increase in the number of working persons in the LREFORM scenario is only partially reduced by the decline in hours supply that we have seen in figure 5.10. Figure 5.11 is the aggregate picture representing the total labor supply of the various age groups depicted in figure 5.9 (triangles).

The first panel on interaction effects shows again the strong interaction between pension reform and labor market reform: relative to the current pay-as-you-go system, total labor supply increases strongly after 2020 in the LREFORM scenario, while it declines if labor force participation remains unchanged.

5.5.4   Hourly Wage Rate

The hourly wage rate is depicted in figure 5.12. It more or less reflects the supply of total effective labor with some additional effects due to capital accumulation; see the following subsection.

The hourly wage increases more in the STATUSQUO (diamonds) than in the LREFORM (triangles) scenario, reflecting relative scarcity. It increases much stronger under a funded system (denoted by SV) than under pay-as-you-go (denoted by FL). The additional capital accumulation lowers inter-

---

5. See section 5.6. All graphs in section 5.4 are based on a flat age-productivity profile ($\varepsilon = 1$). Aggregate results are not sensitive to the age-productivity profile.

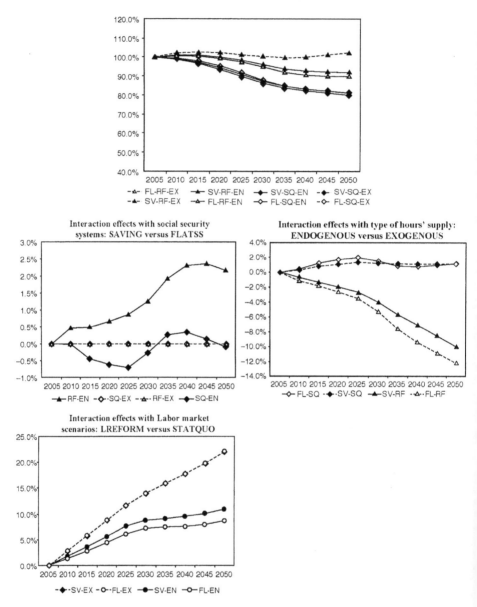

Fig. 5.11   Total labor supply, indexed to 2005 = 100 percent, EU-3

ests and raises labor productivity, thus also the wage rate. Finally, the wage rate increases more when hours are exogenous (dashed lines). This effect is very small when labor force participation rates do not change (STATQUO), but it is substantial in the LREFORM scenario, when the hours' reaction is large.

Considering the massive decline in total labor supply, the hourly wage

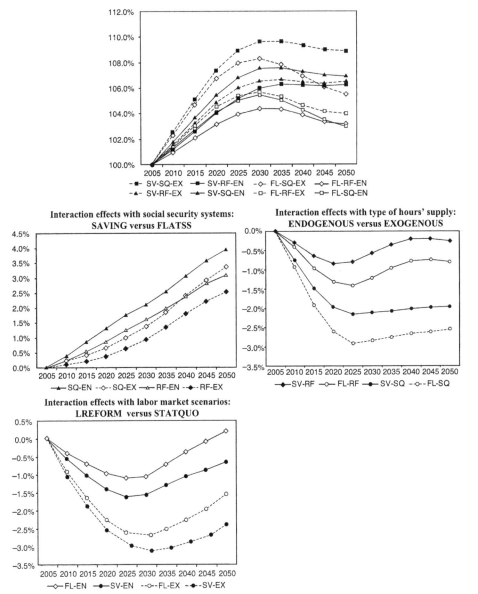

Fig. 5.12   Hourly wage rate, indexed to 2005 = 100 percent, EU-3

rate reacts somewhat dampened, with an elasticity of about 0.5 (compare figures 5.11 and 5.12).

5.5.5   Capital Accumulation

Figure 5.13 depicts the evolution of the combined domestic capital stock of France, Germany, and Italy. As expected, capital accumulation is much

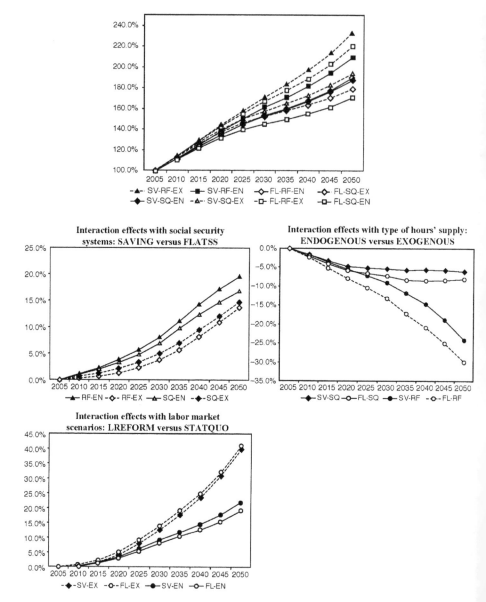

Fig. 5.13   Domestic capital stock, indexed to 2005 = 100 percent, EU-3

higher under a funded pension system than in a pay-as-you-go system, as can be seen in the first panel of interactions. There is also substantially more capital accumulation in the high labor force participation scenario (LREFORM) as compared to constant participation (STATQUO). This is visible in the second panel on interaction effects. Finally, the third panel shows that capital accumulation is higher if endogenous hours supply is not dampening the effect of a higher labor force participation.

Combining these three effects yields the top diagram of figure 5.13. Capital accumulation is highest under a fully funded system with high labor force participation and no dampening effect of endogenous hours (SV-RF-EX). It is lowest in a pay-as-you-go system with status quo labor force participation and the full force of negative incentive effects (FL-SQ-EN).

5.5.6   GDP Per Capita

Our first target variable is economic growth, measured as the change in GDP per capita, net of exogenous growth in total factor productivity. This is displayed in figure 5.14. Economic growth relative to secular productivity growth is very much affected by the combination of pension and labor market policies. With exogenous hours, growth is highest and always positive when labor supply restrictions are released and pensions are financed by a funded system. In turn, growth (after adjusting for total factor productivity [TFP] increases) is lowest and always negative under the opposite combination of policies. This is a strong message: in spite of aging, economic growth can be as high as historically given by the estimated long-run growth of total factor productivity. It can even be increased by a smart combination of pension and labor market policies. However, it can also secularly decline behind the path, which we have experienced in the past.

The quantities are large: the difference between the best and the worst scenario is about 20 percent in 2040, and 30 percent in 2050. This must be seen in comparison to total factor productivity growth, which is about 90 percent over the period from 2005 to 2050, almost doubling output.[6] Remaining at status quo in terms of labor market and pension policy will "eat up" about a third of productivity growth. Reform backlash is about half of this: it reduces the effect of labor market reform on GDP per capita to about half the size with unchanged hours supply.

The eight output paths in figure 5.14 can be derived as a straightforward combination of labor and capital inputs displayed in figures 5.11 and 5.13. Output per capita is unequivocally higher in a fully funded pension system without distorting taxes as compared to a pay-as-you-go pension system with flat benefits. Output per capita is similarly clearly higher when labor market restrictions are removed (LREFORM) than in the status quo scenario. The latter two findings are clearly seen in the first two small panels below the large diagram.

The third panel shows the interaction between pension and labor market policies in the case of endogenous supply of working hours. Endogenous hours supply reduces growth relative to a situation when households cannot substitute more persons by less hours. This is shown by the two lines at the

---

6. The growth path with this productivity increase, without population aging and reform effects, is represented by the horizontal 100 percent line in figure 5.14.

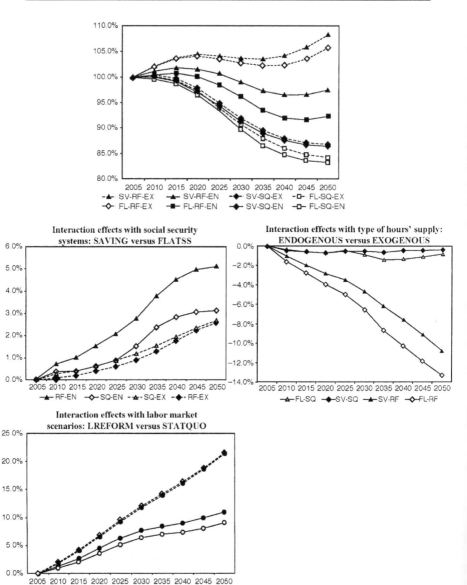

Fig. 5.14   GDP per capita, indexed to 2005 = 100 percent, EU-3

bottom of this graph (FL-RF and SV-RF). The effect, however, is smaller when the pension system is fully funded (SV-RF).

5.5.7   Consumption Per Capita

Finally, figure 5.15 displays our second target variable, living standards measured by consumption per capita. As we did for output, we normalize

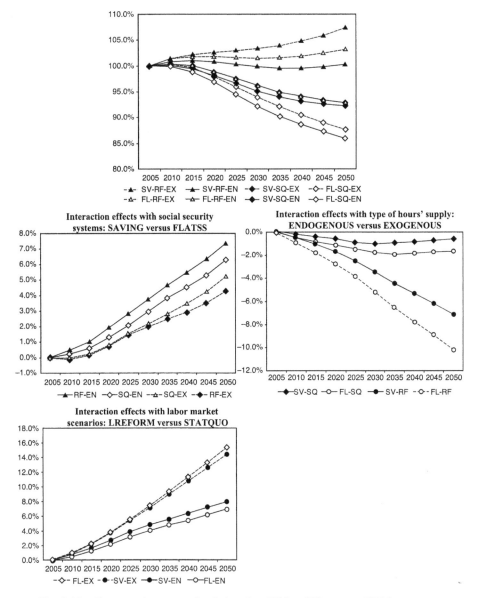

Fig. 5.15   Consumption per capita, indexed to 2005 = 100 percent, EU-3

consumption per capita by secular total productivity growth. The evolution of living standards very much parallels that of GDP per capita; there are no major deviations in the growth patterns of output and consumption as it concerns the relative position of the eight scenarios.

Saving in young age and dissaving in old age, however, smoothes some of the effects that we have seen in figure 5.14. A notable example is the evolution of living standards in the fully funded pensions, high labor force participation, and endogenous hours supply scenario (SV-RF-EN). Living standards remain very close to the secular growth path (the horizontal line), while the associated GDP per capita exhibited a stronger increase until 2020, followed by a strong decline.

This shows that a smart combination of labor market and pension policies can stabilize living standards in continental Europe in spite of population aging and an adverse behavioral reaction to the structural policy changes. In turn, this stabilization needs more than a half-hearted pension reform or a few adjustments in labor market restrictions. All labor market policies described in section 5.3 are needed in addition to a secular pension reform; other policy scenarios imply that living standards in continental Europe will grow slower than what we have experienced in the past. Living standards will not decline because secular productivity growth is still stronger than aging. Living standards, however, will decline relative to all other countries that age less than continental Europe.

5.6 Productivity Issues

If labor productivity is age-dependent, a shift in the age structure will also bring about a change in aggregate productivity, even if age-specific productivity were to remain constant. Moreover, if labor productivity declines strongly after, say, age sixty, an increase in retirement age will not have much effect on aggregate output. This brief section provides a gross estimate of the approximate magnitude of this effect.

This is not a simple task, however, as there is no reliable data available on age-specific labor productivity; see the review by Skirbekk (2004). Barth, McNaught, and Rizzi (1993) conclude from a survey of human resource executives in 406 organizations that "Older workers were consistently rated as having more positive attitudes being more reliable and possessing better skills than the average worker; they were rated worse than the average worker when it comes to health care costs, flexibility in accepting new assignments, and suitability for training." Hutchins (2001) questions the usefulness of such an employer survey to address these issues because of justification bias. Kotlikoff and Wise (1989) evaluate confidential data originating from a major U.S. service enterprise in which output is well defined. They provide two estimates that can be used to proxy productivity. One measure uses age- and seniority-specific earnings of sales staff that can be measured by the sale of insurance contracts; hence, a kind of piece rate. Corrected for seniority, the age profile of these piece rates is relatively flat. Their second measure is the entry salary of clerks. This profile is much more hump shaped. Both measures are likely to suffer from selection effects. Börsch-Supan, Düzgün, and Weiss (2008) use another approach. They used confidential data on error rates in a large assembly line-style car manufacturing factory. Output and

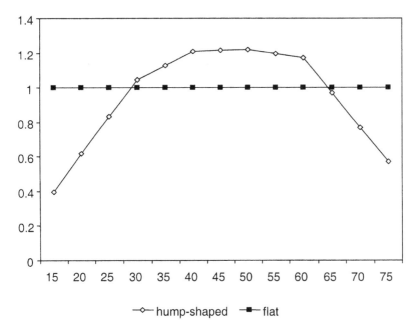

Fig. 5.16   Hump-shaped age productivity profile

production times are perfectly controllable in this environment, permitting a direct estimate of productivity. They find that age and experience effects cancel, such that the resulting productivity profile is essentially flat, with reliable observations until about age sixty-three.

How do these microeconomic differences translate into macroeconomic differences? In order to get some feeling, we underlie our simulations with two alternative age-productivity profiles (in our model represented by ε_j, see subsection 5.4.3). One profile is flat; the other imposes the sharp hump shape depicted in figure 5.16. It features a strong decline of productivity after age sixty. We treat these age profiles as exogenous.

Figure 5.17 describes what difference it makes whether the age productivity profile is flat or whether it is hump-shaped. Figure 5.17 is computed under the assumptions of exogenous hours supply and the current pay-as-you-go system. We display the two extreme employment scenarios, STATQUO and LREFORM. In spite of the strong hump shape of figure 5.16, there is not much difference in the resulting GDP per capita; a surprising result.

5.7   Conclusions

We have simulated a set of far-reaching pension and labor market policies and investigated their impact on production and consumption per capita in three large continental European countries. A new feature of our compu-

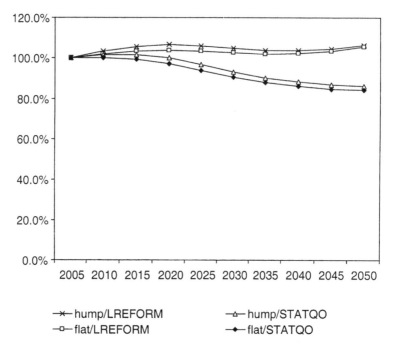

Fig. 5.17   GDP per capita, indexed to 2005 = 100 percent, different productivity assumptions

tational general equilibrium model is a combination of exogenous changes of labor supply at the extensive margin (metaphorically represented in our model by the number of working persons), and endogenous responses of labor supply at the intensive margin (metaphorically called working hours). We think of exogenous changes as lifting institutional restrictions generated by the school system, actuarially unfair pension systems, inflexible working hours, and unavailable day care facilities. The endogenous component of labor supply ("hours" chosen by the household members) reacts to the exogenous component of labor supply ("working persons" freed from labor market restrictions), but also to social security taxes and to the aging process itself and its repercussions.

Our chapter shows that direct quantity and indirect behavioral effects are large. They both significantly affect economic growth and living standards. Due to the strong interaction effects between pension system and labor markets, a smart combination of pension policy and adaptation of institutions related to the labor market can do more than such policies in isolation. We show that they could easily offset the effects of population aging on economic growth and living standards if there were no endogenous behavioral reactions. On balance, these behavioral effects dampen reform efforts, thus representing reform backlashes in our model. Taking behavioral effects into account, a combination of many policy measures is necessary in order to keep per capita consumption from falling behind the secular growth path. If these measures are taken, Old Europe can maintain her high living standards in spite of aging. This is an important message for the never-ending reform debate on the European continent.

The key to our approach—the combination of an exogenous variation of employment rates with endogenous hours choice—has its advantages and disadvantages. It provides a theoretically consistent way to model the subtle balance between policy changes and individual reactions. From an empirical point of view, this approach produces a lot of pressure to get the calibration right in order to achieve a realistic number of households that are constrained by labor market restrictions (expressed less metaphorically: the balance between what is exogenous and what is endogenous in labor supply). The current version of the chapter features a calibration that is based on an ad hoc choice of parameters by reference to other studies. In future versions of the chapter, we will specify certain calibration targets and determine deep structural model parameters by minimum distance methods, as we have done in earlier work.

From a theoretical point of view, we do not model a motive for households to actually participate in the labor market. An alternative approach making the metaphorical distinction more realistic would be to model the decisions endogenously at both margins. This could be done by accounting for home production and preferences for leisure goods as in Greenwood and Vandenbroucke (2005), and by explicitly modeling the institutions that determine households labor market participation decision; for example, along the lines of Garibaldi and Wasmer (2005) and Guner, Kaygusuz, and Ventura (2008). We speculate that removing these frictions would lead to stronger total labor supply reactions than in our model. Such extensions of our model are subject to future research.

References

Attanasio, O. P., S. Kitao, and G. L. Violante. 2006. Quantifying the effects of the demographic transition in developing economies. *Advances in Macroeconomics* 6 (1): article 2. Available at: http://www.bepress.com/bejm/advances/vol6/iss1/art2.
———. 2007. Global demographic trends and Social Security reform. *Journal of Monetary Economics* 57 (1): 144–98.
Auerbach, A. J., and L. J. Kotlikoff. 1987. *Dynamic fiscal policy.* Cambridge, MA: Cambridge University Press.
Auerbach, A. J., L. J. Kotlikoff, and J. Skinner. 1983. The efficiency gains from dynamic tax reform. *International Economic Review* 24 (1): 81–100.
Ball, L., and N. G. Mankiw. 2002. The NAIRU in theory and practice. *Journal of Economic Perspectives* 16 (4): 115–36.

Barth, M., W. McNaught, and P. Rizzi. 1993. Corporations and the aging workforce. In *Building the competitive workforce: Investing in human capital for corporate success,* ed. P. H. Mirvis, p. 156–200. Hoboken, NJ: John Wiley & Sons.

Börsch-Supan, A., I. Düzgün, and M. Weiss. 2008. Labor productivity in an aging society. In *Frontiers in pension finance and reform,* ed. D. Broeders, S. Eijffinger, and A. Houben. Cheltenham: Edward Elgar.

Börsch-Supan, A., A. Ludwig, and J. Winter. 2006. Aging, pension reform, and capital flows: A multi-country simulation model. *Economica* 73:625–58.

Brooks, R. 2003. Population aging and global capital flows in a parallel universe. *IMF Staff Papers* 50 (2): 200–21.

Deardorff, A. V. 1985. Trade and capital mobility in a world of diverging populations. In *Population growth and economic development: Issues and evidence.* ed. D. G. Johnson and R. D. Lee. Madison, WI: University of Wisconsin Press.

Domeij, D., and M. Floden. 2006. Population aging and international capital flows. *International Economic Review* 47:1013–32.

European Commission. 2008. Eurostat. Available at: http://ec.europa.eu/eurostat.

Feroli, M. 2003. Capital flows among the G-7 nations: A demographic perspective. Finance and Economics Discussion Series no. 2003-54. Washington, DC: Board of Governors of the Federal Reserve System.

Garibaldi, P., and E. Wasmer. 2005. Equilibrium search unemployment, endogenous participation, and labor market flows. *Journal of the European Economic Association,* 3 (4): 851–82.

Greenwood, J., and G. Vandenbroucke. 2005. Hours worked: Long-run trends. In *The new Palgrave dictionary of economics,* 2nd edition, ed. L. E. Blume and S. N. Durlauf. Available at: http://dictionaryofeconomics.com/article?id=pde 2008_T000238>doi:10.1057/9780230226203.0748.

Guner, N., Kaygusuz, R., and G. Ventura. 2008. Taxation, aggregates and the household. IZA Discussion Paper no. 3318. Bonn: Institute for the Study of Labor.

Henriksen, E. R. 2002. A demographic explanation of U.S. and Japanese current account behavior. Carnegie Mellon University, Graduate School of Industrial Administration. Unpublished Manuscript.

Human Mortality Database. 2008. Available at: http://www.mortality.org.

Hutchins, R. M. 2001. Employer surveys, employer policies, and future demand for older workers. Paper prepared for the Roundtable on the Demand for Older Workers. The Brookings Institution, Washington, DC.

Kotlikoff, L., and D. Wise. 1989. Employee retirement and a firm's pension plan. In *The economics of aging,* ed. D. A. Wise, 279–334. Chicago: University of Chicago Press.

Krüger, D., and A. Ludwig. 2007. On the consequences of demographic change for rates of return to capital, and the distribution of wealth and welfare. *Journal of Monetary Economics* 54 (1): 49–87.

Ludwig, A. 2004. Improving tatonnement methods for solving heterogeneous agent models. Mannheim Research Institute for the Economics of Aging Discussion Paper no. 04058. Mannheim: University of Mannheim.

Skirbekk, V. 2004. Population aging and productivity. Max Planck Institute for Demographic Research. Working Paper.

U.S. Census Bureau, Population Division. *International database.* 2008. Available at: http://www.census.gov/ipc/www/idb/.

World Health Organization (WHO). 2007. *Healthy life expectancy.* Available at: http://www.who.int/whosis/indicators/2007HALE0/en/.

Comment   Alan J. Auerbach

This chapter is the latest in a series by the authors utilizing a multicountry, computable general equilibrium model that features international capital flows and a rich characterization of demographic variables. In earlier work, the model has been used to consider the macroeconomic effects of aging and the role of pension reform in improving welfare and macroeconomic performance. The present effort focuses on a related question: whether a Europe that is "old" both in history and in population can prosper even as the strong demographic transition already under way continues. The answer is a provisional "yes," and figure 5.15 shows the keys to success. The authors suggest that the following measures, in some combination, could keep per capita consumption rising even as these countries' populations age:

1. Adopt labor market reforms aimed at increasing labor force participation.
2. Adopt a funded public pension plan.
3. Force people to work.

The last prescription, of course, is problematic. A reduction in hours—among those already working—in response to labor market reforms is a natural part of the household decision-making process; there is no easy way to prevent it, and a government seeking to maximize welfare, rather than simply output, would not want to. But even the other prescriptions are not so simple. How to adopt labor market reforms that have proved so difficult in the past is certainly a challenge, and the benefits of a funded pension plan cannot be magically obtained without a painful transition to funding that has left most countries seeking other options. Let me expand a little on these points.

How can labor market reforms be adopted? The authors characterize a suite of labor market changes that might be accomplished by Old Europe, including increases in labor market participation by the elderly, the young, and women, along with a reduction in the unemployment rate. The fact that an existing advanced European country—Denmark—already has these characteristics is a good start in thinking about what might be possible elsewhere. But it is only a start. The chapter does not specify what actual policy reforms might accomplish these changes in the labor market, nor does it provide evidence that all of these reforms would be welfare-improving, even if they were feasible. For example, Italy's lower labor force participation rate among women may reflect some difference in social or cultural values,—that

Alan J. Auerbach is the Robert D. Burch Professor of Economics and Law and director of the Robert D. Burch Center for Tax Policy and Public Finance at the University of California, Berkeley, and a research associate of the National Bureau of Economic Research.

is, in preferences—and overriding these preferences could be detrimental to social welfare. Without a fuller specification of the nature of the existing constraints on labor markets and the costs of relaxing them, it is hard to know whether, and at what social cost, the labor market changes considered here could be accomplished.

Achieving pension reform. The chapter shows that the transition to an older society has less severe macroeconomic consequences when a funded pension system is in place. This is a lesson from the authors' earlier simulation studies, and it makes perfect sense. To continue servicing a pay-as-you-go (PAYG) public pension system as the old-age dependency ratio increases, a country must increase marginal tax rates on workers, thereby worsening labor market distortions. Under a funded system, of course, this will not happen, as workers provide for their own future retirement through contributions that are linked to future benefits.

But *getting* to a funded system is different from starting with one. The capital accumulation needed in transition must come at the expense of some generations, and this requirement has posed a very high political obstacle that has left countries in search of alternatives. The recent pension reforms in Sweden and Germany are illustrations of attempts to achieve greater financial stability and intergenerational equity without departing from the PAYG framework. It might make sense for the authors to consider a more achievable pension reform within the PAYG format as they search for options for Old Europe; for example, changes that would increase the linkage between an individual's taxes and benefits and thereby lessen the perceived tax burden of pension contributions.

Interpreting the Results

As already mentioned, the chapter uses a multicountry, general equilibrium simulation model the authors have developed in prior work. Because development of the model is not this chapter's primary focus, there is relatively little discussion of the various parameter choices made in the calibration process. One does not want to get bogged down reviewing all aspects of the model, but it would be useful if Börsch-Supan and Ludwig provided further elaboration as to the model's key parameters. In particular, on which parameters do the chapter's main result critically hinge, and how certain are we about the values chosen?

In qualitative terms, most of the chapter's findings make sense, although some would benefit from further elaboration. For example, one might have expected that, with a hump-shaped productivity profile, an increase in elderly workers would lead to a less productive labor force, at least relative to the productivity that one would observe if productivity profiles were flat with respect to age. As figure 5.17 shows, however, the opposite result occurs. Presumably, this is because of the shape and location of the hump—in particular, that productivity does not fall off so fast to make the declines in older age offset the increases at slightly lower ages.

Another example of at least one reader's difficulty in interpreting the results is in figure 5.10, where, as in other figures in the chapter, the authors use what might be characterized as a graphical difference-in-differences approach to report the effects of policies. I think, by the way, that this method of analysis is a useful and innovative way of looking separately at the many pieces of a complicated whole, but it does not eliminate the complexity of the results, which often must be traced to a series of interacting factors. The first lower panel of figure 5.10 shows the marginal impact on hours of having a public pension system. As discussed earlier, we would expect a favorable outcome, but this is actually what we observe only if labor market reforms are also implemented; that is, hours of work are higher for a funded pension plan than for the status quo under the labor market reform labor force assumptions, but not under the status quo labor force assumptions.

Conclusions

In summary, this is a chapter that barrages the reader with many interesting findings. Some are quite intuitive, while others are less so. Such less intuitive findings can be where the payoff lies in using such models, for by understanding where these findings come from we gain a better understanding of how different factors interact. But much of the chapter's findings derive from its assumptions, in particular those about what labor market reforms might deliver. We can see quite clearly from the chapter's results that these reforms could matter in a big way for future economic performance. But we do not know any more than before what has kept these reforms from being adopted, or how they might be achieved in the future. Thus, the chapter shows that Old Europe *can* prosper. But whether it *will* remains a very open question.

6

The Final Inequality
Variance in Age at Death

Shripad Tuljapurkar

6.1 Introduction

Demography and economics shape many aspects of the lives and decisions of individuals as well as the structure and welfare of populations. An important and persistent demographic shift that occupies much attention around the world is the aging of many national populations, driven by changes in the rates of birth, death, or migration. An ongoing decline in death rates is a common factor that drives aging in all industrialized nations and many of the world's developing regions. Birth rates and migration also influence aging, but their importance varies between countries. The twentieth century was the first period in history in which humans experienced a sustained decline in death rates that resulted, in the now-rich nations, in a doubling of human life expectancy at birth and a 50 percent increase in the remaining life expectancy of people at age sixty-five. These changes expanded human life cycles in time and precipitated changes in the pattern of individual lives and in relationships between generations. Economic and demographic analyses of aging work at one or both of these levels. For individuals and families, the stretching of lives affects decisions about the level and timing of life-cycle events such as schooling, work, savings, and retirement. For populations, aging has meant changes in flows of labor and money and challenges related to education, annuities and pensions, insurance, and health care. Analyses at both levels require an understanding of how long people live, the differences between individuals in life spans, and

Shripad Tuljapurkar is the Morrison Professor of Population Studies and a professor of biological sciences at Stanford University.
This research has been supported by grants from the U.S. National Institute of Aging and by the Morrison Institute for Population and Resource Studies at Stanford University.

the rates at which these are changing. One dimension of mortality that has been extensively studied is life expectancy, the average span of life, which is the key statistic used to describe mortality and health conditions. Many studies have examined trends and forecasts of life expectancy, while others have examined the effect of inequalities in wealth, income, or education on health by studying differences in life expectancy between groups that differ in these characteristics.

This chapter focuses on a second dimension of mortality, the variation in lifespan between individuals and groups of individuals. We begin by asking whether the length of life should be measured starting at birth or at some later age. To answer this question, we first show that in today's industrialized countries, childhood mortality is so low that we should focus on differences in the length of adult life. To measure such differences, we define the age at adult death and its variance, following Edwards and Tuljapurkar (2005). This variance and aggregate life expectancy describe two distinct dimensions of the distribution of life (and death) within populations. Next, we present and discuss historical trends in this variance and compare trends across countries. We then discuss the relationship between the pattern of adult death and socioeconomic inequalities, in factors such as education and income, using data from the United States. Finally, we examine the effect of variance in adult death on simple economic measures in an overlapping generations setting.

6.2   Death and Inequality

The modern rise in the length of life began about the time of the Industrial Revolution and has continued ever since. Figure 6.1 illustrates the gains in life expectancy at birth (e_0) and at age sixty-five (e_{65}) using data for Sweden from 1950 to 2000. Over that period, e_0 increased by about 12 percent and e_{65} by about 33 percent. Mortality here is measured using period death rates observed in particular calendar years; for each year, we compute quantities such as the average age at death that describe a hypothetical cohort of individuals who experience those over their lives. The higher proportional increase in e_{65} compared to e_0 resulted from two factors. First, mortality in Sweden at young ages is now so low that further reductions have relatively little leverage on life expectancy. Second, reductions in mortality are, over time, occurring at older ages than in the past. To gain further insight into these two factors, we next examine the probability distribution of the age at death.

The age pattern of mortality is described by an age-specific mortality rate $\mu(a)$, and the probability of living to at least age a is the survivorship $l(a)$. The probability that an individual dies at age a is described by the density $\phi(a) = \mu(a)l(a)$. Figure 6.2 displays this density for Sweden in 1950 and in 2000. The risk of dying at young ages is concentrated in the first year of life

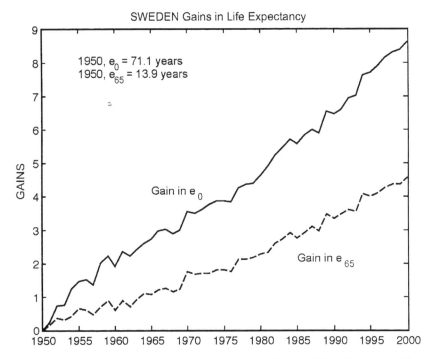

Fig. 6.1 Gains in period life expectancy between 1950 and 2000 at birth (e_0, solid) and at age 65 (e_{65}, dashes) for Sweden, both sexes combined

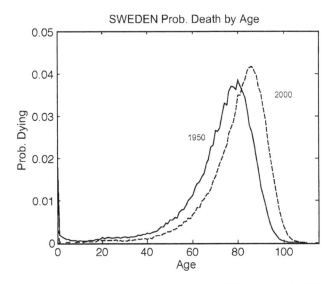

Fig. 6.2 Probability distribution of age at death in 1950 (solid) and 2000 (dashed) for Sweden, both sexes combined

and has fallen steadily in the past fifty years. For example, in Sweden in 2000, less than 0.4 percent of deaths in the period life table occur at ages under ten years. Beyond age ten, death is increasingly likely, with over 85 percent of all deaths concentrated in a range of twenty years or so around a sharply defined modal age that is slightly higher than the life expectancy at birth. It is the variation in this age range that describes the bulk of variation in "adult" death. An individual who survives his or her first year of life is most likely to die as an adult (over age ten), and differences between individual ages at death are largely differences in the age of adult death.

Based on these observations, Edwards and Tuljapurkar (2005) define adult death as death occurring after age ten. The probability distribution of the age of adult death is derived from $\phi(a)$ in figure 6.2 as the conditional distribution given that death occurs after age ten. The shape of the conditional distribution is the same as that of ϕ. The variance of this conditional distribution is defined to be the variance in the age at adult death, denoted here by S_{10}^2. The value of S_{10} measures the dispersion in age at adult death. We cannot measure this dispersion by the variance of the full distribution ϕ because the size of that variance is always strongly affected by the infant mortality peak even when infant mortality is as small as it is in figure 6.2. Our choice of ten years is somewhat arbitrary, but any age near the minimum of the full distribution (see figure 6.2) serves equally well. Figure 6.3 shows the effect of using different cutoff ages of ten and twenty years on the standard deviation of the age at adult death, using data for Sweden from 1951 to 2000. The two curves shown track each other closely, and the values are very close over the period.

The measure S_{10} describes the extent of inequality in the age at death. Why do we call this an inequality? There is considerable current interest in the role of socioeconomic inequalities as determinants of inequalities in health outcomes (e.g., Marmot 2005). Health is not easily defined or measured, but mortality risk is widely used as an indicator of health, and age at death is, of course, a primary health outcome variable. In this context, our S_{10} is an appropriate measure of inequality in health outcomes. We note that a different way of describing inequality in adult death is to use percentiles of the death distribution, as suggested by Victor Fuchs in his comments on this chapter. Such percentiles have previously been used by Wilmoth and Horiuchi (1999) in a discussion of the possible compression of age at death. We believe that S_{10} is in many ways a natural measure and is particularly useful in thinking about the nature of risk, but percentiles can provide useful additional insights.

The distribution of adult deaths is the large concentrated mass of the distribution in figure 6.2. A rough approximation to the distribution is a normal centered on the modal age at death with a standard deviation of S_{10}, and we use this approximation later in this chapter. It is worth comparing the actual distributions in figure 6.2, or their normal approximations, to two stylized distributions of death that have been used by economists. The first, dating back to early work (Yaari 1965; Blanchard 1985) on overlapping generation models, assumes that the probability of death is independent of age (panel A of figure 6.4) and leads to a most unrealistic exponential distribution of the age at death. The second (Futagami and Nakajima 2001) assumes that all adults die at the same age (panel B of figure 6.4). Our discussion suggests that a more realistic treatment of the age distribution of human deaths

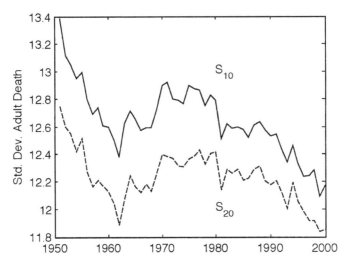

Fig. 6.3 The effect of defining "adult" death as deaths over age 10 or 20. The solid line shows S_{10}, and the dashed line shows S_{20}, as defined in the text, for Sweden from 1950 to 2000, both sexes combined

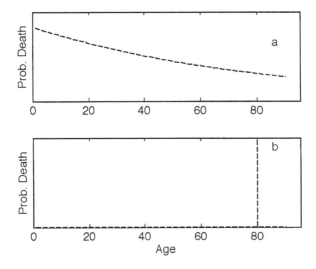

Fig. 6.4 Stylized probability distributions of age at death: A, Age-independent probability of death; B, All deaths at one age

should use e_0, which is close to the modal age of adult death, as a measure of location and S_{10} as a measure of dispersion.

6.3   Historical Inequality in Adult Death

Historical changes have increased the average age at death e_0 in most countries. We now examine the corresponding historical change in the dispersion in adult death measured by S_{10}. The nature of change in S_{10} will tell us whether mortality improvement means that both the average and the variance in adult age at death change together. In other words, are we compressing inequality in age at adult death while also delaying death?

Figure 6.5 plots S_{10} versus life expectancy e_0 for Sweden from 1900 to 1950. Time turns out to run from left to right across the plot. There were fluctuations in both e_0 and S_{10}, but the overall negative correlation between them was very high. In this period, S_{10} fell to 50 percent of its 1951 value, decreasing at 0.22 years per calendar year, whereas e_0 grew to nearly 150 percent of its value in 1951, increasing at 0.4 years per calendar year. In the years 1951 to 2000, as shown in figure 6.6, the negative correlation between S_{10} and e_0 weakened somewhat. Life expectancy continued to increase, albeit at a slower pace, at about 0.2 years per calendar year. But S_{10} decreased much more slowly and with significant fluctuation, at about 0.022 years per calendar year.

In the first half of the twentieth century, mortality declines clearly acted as a "rising tide" that reduced inequality in age at adult death across the

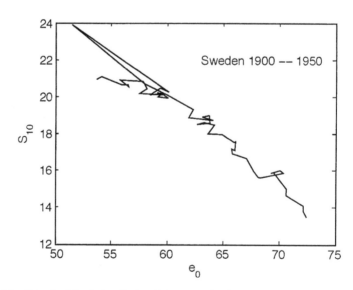

Fig. 6.5   Standard deviation S_{10} in adult age at death plotted against life expectancy at birth e_0 from 1900 to 1950 for Sweden, both sexes combined

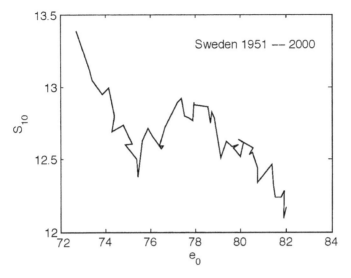

Fig. 6.6 Standard deviation S_{10} in adult age at death plotted against life expectancy at birth e_0 from 1951 to 2000 for Sweden, both sexes combined

population as a whole. In terms of the distribution of age at death (recall figure 6.2), the mass of adult deaths moved to later ages while also being compressed. In the second half of the twentieth century, progress against mortality continued, so the mass of deaths continued its march to older ages, but the compression of inequality slowed considerably. It is important to recognize that the compression of mortality inequality contains an important message about the extent of variation in mortality between individuals. There is great interest in the effect of risk factors as predictors of individual mortality risk, and the notion that individual behavior can strongly affect age at death is widespread. Indeed, the argument is often made that the distribution of risk factors shapes the distribution of deaths (e.g., Mokdad et al. 2004). History tells us, however, that the total variance in adult death, which includes the contributions of all risk factors, has declined substantially over time and indeed continues to do so. We return to the predictive value of risk factors later in this chapter.

6.3.1   International Trends and the Future

How do these historical patterns for Sweden compare with what has happened in other countries? The slowdown in the decline of S_{10} in Sweden since about 1960, seen in figures 6.5 and 6.6, is partially mirrored across the industrialized world. A comprehensive and recent comparison across all Organization for Economic Cooperation and Development (OECD) countries has been published by the OECD (2007). We focus on a subset of the OECD countries from 1960 onward as shown in figure 6.7, which is redrawn

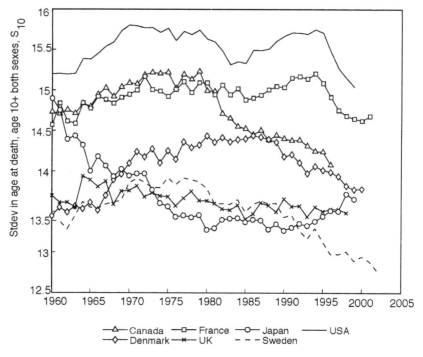

Fig. 6.7   Conditional standard deviations in the age at death, S_{10}, in seven high-income countries since 1960

Source: Data for both sexes combined are taken from the Human Mortality Database (http://www.mortality.org).

from the data used by Edwards and Tuljapurkar (2005). The strikingly highest and steadiest curve in the plot is for the United States, which had the highest level of mortality inequality among these countries (and, indeed, across the industrialized world) over the entire period. Canada displayed a level of inequality and a lack of trend similar to the United States from 1960 to 1980, but after that, S_{10} in Canada has fallen significantly. The sharp contrast between recent trends in S_{10} in these two countries is plausibly due to the widespread availability of national health services in Canada after 1980. For the entire period shown in figure 6.7, there is one country whose S_{10} is just below that for the United States and shows the same absence of overall trend. That country is France. Given the widespread public commentary in each country that they are least likely to resemble each other, this is quite a surprise.

The United Kingdom, Sweden, and Denmark started out with similar levels of inequality in 1960. Sweden and the United Kingdom changed little through the 1980s, but Sweden's S_{10} then declined, whereas the United Kingdom had a modest increase. Denmark is another surprise, with an increase in S_{10} through the 1980s and higher inequality at the end of the period than it had in 1960. Japan, as is often the case in such comparisons, is strikingly distinctive, with a notable decrease in inequality from 1960 (when Japan and the United States had similar levels of S_{10}) till 1990 (when Japan and Sweden were tied with the lowest inequality). In the most recent decade, Japan's S_{10} has actually increased. Victor Fuchs (in his comments on this chapter) has examined this recent trend in Japan using percentiles of the distribution of age at death. To see why percentiles matter, look again at figure 6.2. The distribution of age at death around the mode has a left skew, as is typical of most human history, which means that much of the inequality we discuss here is driven by early deaths. But for recent years in Japan, Fuchs finds that the probability of dying at ages above the mode (use figure 6.2 as a guide) has increased relative to the past, thus changing the skewness of the distribution. As a result the inequality in age at death in Japan may be increasing because there is a higher chance of living to old ages past the mode. This explanation marches with the known fact that the number of centenarians in Japan is increasing very rapidly with time (Robine, Saito, and Jagger 2003).

Bongaarts (2007) recently proposed an interesting model of mortality change to be used in making forecasts. He argues that life expectancy simply increases at some steady rate per year and that the shape of the distribution of adult deaths, based on $\phi(a)$, does not change with time for deaths over age twenty-five years. In his view, the mass of adult deaths, as shown in our figure 6.2, simply translates to later ages at some steady rate, but with the dispersion of the mass constant. He arrived at his model using rather different arguments about the nature of senescence, and so our historical analysis provides a test of his assumptions. It is clear from figure 6.7 that his approximation is plausible for trends in the United States since 1960; it may also be plausible for some other, but not all, countries in recent decades. His model would clearly not be correct as a description of historical change prior to 1960.

6.4   The Sources of Variance in Adult Death

We turn now to a different question: what causes differences in mortality within a country between groups that are distinguished by characteristics such as income, education, race, or other factors that we expect to influence mortality risk? This question has become particularly important in recent discussions about the relationships between mortality and socioeconomic inequality measured in various ways (Mokdad et al. 2004; Marmot 2005). Typically, analyses of such relationships have focused on the effect of a particular risk factor on either life expectancy or relative mortality rates. Controlling for differences in other likely risk factors, a successful analysis detects a difference in the e_0 corresponding to differences in the particular factor in question. Such studies measure what we call the variance *between* groups that are distinguished by particular explanatory factors. But we have found that such relationships can be studied in a different and more informative way by asking how socioeconomic factors affect the variance of adult age at death both *between* groups and *within* groups.

We consider a decomposition of a population into subgroups based on differences in socioeconomic variables and use results from Edwards and Tuljapurkar (2005). They considered the effects of education and income, both factors that are well known to be correlated with mortality rates and average age at death, as well as of sex, race, and certain causes of death. We focus on the effects of education, which is a much more stable socioeconomic measure for adults than is income. Data were taken from the U.S. National Longitudinal Mortality Study, a panel study of over half a million individuals who were interviewed around 1980 and then tracked for nine years. Socioeconomic data were observed only at the beginning of the period, and the analysis used only mortality in the first year of the sample. To keep comparisons simple, the analysis considered only two socioeconomic strata, with individuals sorted according to whether they are high school graduates, roughly two-thirds of the sample. Life tables were constructed for both sexes combined in each group, and smoothed distributions of ages at death were constructed and used to estimate conditional means and variances.

Figure 6.8 (redrawn using the data from Edwards and Tuljapurkar 2005) plots distributions of age at adult death by educational status. The plot lists for each group the values of the conditional mean age at death M_{10} and the within-group standard deviation S_{10}. Clearly, adults in the lower stratum not only have shorter average life spans, but also are subject to greater variability. As adults, high school graduates live an average of five years longer than their less-educated counterparts, while enjoying a standard deviation that is two years lower. But the variance between these groups (approximately the square of the difference in M_{10}, so ≈ 25) is an order of magnitude smaller than the variance within groups (the average of the variances, so ≈ 225). This huge difference reflects the considerable overlap between the two distributions in figure 6.8. Even if everyone in the United States had a high school diploma, S_{10} would remain fairly high, at 14.6, which is only a year lower than the value for the United States as a whole. Clearly, education matters, but it matters more to averages and rather less to inequality, and, thus, matters less to the predictive power of education about the age of death. A similar result is found when looking at age at death as a function of household income (Edwards and Tuljapurkar 2005).

These results lead to broad conclusions about analytical strategies for future research and about policy conclusions from existing research. The analytical strategy used to study the effects of socioeconomic inequality needs to focus on mortality inequality and not just on average outcomes. For example, it would be useful to search for risk factors that best separate groups, that is, that maximize the ratio of between-group variance to within-

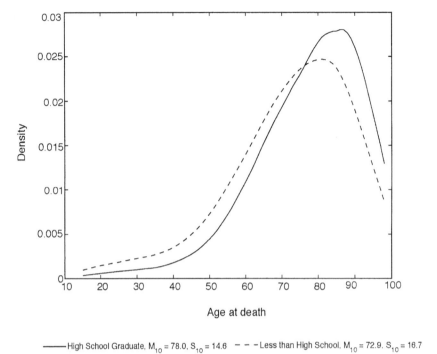

Age at death

———High School Graduate, M_{10} = 78.0, S_{10} = 14.6   – – –Less than High School, M_{10} = 72.9. S_{10} = 16.7

Fig. 6.8   Distributions of ages at death by educational group in the United States in 1981

Source: Data are constructed from a life table derived from deaths observed in the first year of the U.S. National Longitudinal Mortality Study.

Notes: Education was observed at the beginning of the period. M_{10} is the mean age at death above age ten, equal to e_{10} + 10. Data have been smoothed using a kernel density estimator.

group variance in adult age at death. It would be useful to ask whether the roughly constant inequality in age at death in the United States can be explained by changes in socioeconomic inequality. In other countries where S_{10} has fallen over time, we should ask whether the effect of mortality decline has been to reduce the within-group variances for all groups or just the variances within particular groups. In terms of policy, the results show clearly that reducing some kinds of socioeconomic inequality will have little or no effect on inequality in age at death.

6.4.1   Economic Theory and Variance in Adult Death

Our variance S_{10} is simply the dispersion of the random age at death, call it T, across adult individuals in a population. We can approximate the distribution of adult deaths by a normal distribution around the modal age at death, call it μ, with a standard deviation $\sigma = S_{10}$. This approximation undershoots the true left-skewed distribution at ages below μ and overshoots the true distribution at ages much over μ, but it is reasonable for seeing how variance in T affects lifetime income, consumption, and utility.

Suppose that wages are fixed at some value W and an individual works starting at some age a_s (upon leaving school or college, say) until the earlier of death or retirement at age a_r. For a given interest rate r, expected lifetime earnings are

$$I = WE \int_{a_s}^{(T^\wedge a_r)} dse^{-rs} = \left(\frac{W}{r}\right)[e^{-ra_s} - Ee^{-r(T^\wedge a_r)}].$$

Here E indicates an expectation over the distribution of age at death T, which we take to be a normal distribution as in the preceding. The exact expressions here are messy, but they are closely approximated by

$$I = \left(\frac{W}{r}\right)\{e^{-ra_s} - l(a_r)e^{-ra_r} - [1 - l(a_r)]e^{-r\mu + (1/2)r^2\sigma^2}\}.$$

This is sensible: when retirement occurs at an age well below the modal age at death μ, uncertainty in death has little effect on lifetime income. As age at retirement increases toward μ, the dispersion σ in T translates into dispersion in lifetime income. There is a trade-off between μ and σ, in that

$$\frac{\partial I}{\partial \sigma} = -r\sigma \frac{\partial I}{\partial \mu}.$$

For an interest rate of 0.03, and σ; 14, which is typical of industrialized countries, the multiplier is 0.42; in developing countries with σ; 25, the multiplier is 1. So the effect of increasing μ by a year is about the same as decreasing σ by half a year in industrialized countries and by a year in developing countries.

Lifetime consumption also depends on T. In simple overlapping generations models (Blanchard 1985) with constant relative risk aversion (CRRA) utility, the optimal consumption at age x is a function

$$c(x) = c_0 e^{kx}, \text{ where } k = \frac{(r - \theta)}{\gamma},$$

where r is interest rate, θ is the discount rate, and γ is the coefficient of risk aversion. Lifetime consumption then depends on e^{kT}, and we have

$$Ee^{kT} = e^{k\mu + (1/2)k^2\sigma^2}.$$

So inequality in T translates into inequality in lifetime consumption. This fact suggests that it would be useful to incorporate uncertainty in T into analyses of the benefits of increasing lifespan.

Lifetime utility depends on consumption in these settings, and in the CRRA model, utility at age x is proportional to $c(x)^{(1-\gamma)}/(1 - \gamma)$. Expected lifetime utility averages over the variation in T and, thus, also depends on

σ. The effect of σ on lifetime consumption depends on the factor k, but the effect on lifetime utility depends on the product $k(1-\gamma)$, being modified by the level of risk aversion. Li (2005) has explored these connections in more detail by studying the equilibrium of a simple closed economy model with adult deaths distributed normally as in the preceding.

6.5   Conclusion

This chapter has shown that the variance in age at adult death is a useful and important dimension of mortality change. Trends in this variance are informative about the speed and the age pattern of mortality change. The decomposition of this variance with respect to risk factors provides useful insights into the explanatory power of different factors that are correlated with mortality. Historical and economic analyses can benefit from an examination of variance in age at death in addition to the traditionally important study of life expectancy.

References

Blanchard, O. J. 1985. Debt, deficits and finite horizons. *Journal of Political Economy* 93:223–47.

Bongaarts, J. 2005. Long-range trends in adult mortality: Models and projection methods. *Demography* 42:23–49.

Edwards, R., and S. Tuljapurkar. 2005. Inequality in life spans and a new perspective on mortality convergence across industrialized countries. *Population and Development Review* 31 (4): 645–74.

Futagami, K., and T. Nakajima. 2001. Population aging and economic growth. *Journal of Macroeconomics* 23:31–44.

Li, Q. 2005. Essays on asset pricing, consumption and wealth. PhD diss., Stanford Univ.

Marmot, M. 2005. Social determinants of health inequalities. *Lancet* 365:1099–1104.

Mokdad, A. H., J. S. Marks, D. S. Stroup, and J. L. Gerberding. 2004. Actual causes of death in the United States, 2000. *Journal of the American Medical Association* 291:1238–45.

OECD. 2007. *Society at a glance: OECD social indicators—2006 edition.* Paris: Organization for Economic Cooperation and Development.

Robine, J.-M., Y. Saito, and C. Jagger. 2003. The emergence of extremely old people: The case of Japan. *Experimental Gerontology* 38:735–39.

Wilmoth, J. R., and S. Horiuchi. 1999. Rectangularization revisited: Variability of age at death within human populations. *Demography* 36:475–95.

Yaari, Menahem E. 1965. Uncertain lifetime, life insurance, and the theory of the consumer. *Review of Economic Studies* 22:137–50.

Comment   Victor R. Fuchs

In this chapter, Shripad Tuljapurkar uses mean age of death (derived from a period life table) to measure life expectancy (e_0) and the standard deviation of the age of death distribution to measure inequality. He focuses on "adult" mortality by limiting the standard deviation to the distribution of deaths from age ten on (S_{10}). He uses data from the United States, Sweden, and a few other high-income countries. His principal empirical findings are the following:

- Life expectancy at birth has increased appreciably since the Industrial Revolution, albeit at a slower pace in recent decades.
- Inequality in mortality, measured by S_{10}, has decreased; the rate of decrease has slowed in recent decades.
- Over time, there is a negative correlation between life expectancy (e_o) and inequality (S_{10}); the correlation has weakened in recent decades.
- Inequality in length of life is greater in the United States than in a subset of Organization for Economic Cooperation and Development (OECD) countries. Furthermore, there has been very little decline in S_{10} in the United States since 1960, unlike several other OECD countries that show substantial declines.
- While there is a correlation between education and age of death in the United States, the variation in length of life in the United States is much greater than the variation in length of life across education groups. It appears that socioeconomic disparities in general can explain only a small part of the inequality in length of life.

Comments

The mean and standard deviation are well-established statistics to describe a distribution. They are familiar and have desirable mathematical properties. But they are not the only statistics that are easily calculated; other measures can provide additional insights into questions about inequality in length of life. Life expectancy can be represented by the median age of death rather than the mean. Inequality can be described by the interquartile range rather than the standard deviation. Attention to the median and the interquartile range yields results that are at times similar to those of Tuljapurkar, but are at times strikingly different.

Victor R. Fuchs is the Henry J. Kaiser Jr. Professor of Economics and of Health Research and Policy, emeritus; a senior fellow of the Freeman Spogli Institute for International Studies; a core faculty member at the Center for Health Policy/Center for Primary Care and Outcomes Research (CHP/PCOR) at Stanford University; and a research associate of the National Bureau of Economic Research.

Assistance from Hal Ersner-Hirshfield with the preparation of this comment is gratefully acknowledged.

Because the United States has a large heterogeneous population, inequality is calculated for whites in each of the fifty states.[1] Each state is treated as if it were a separate demographic entity to make more appropriate comparisons between the states and foreign countries, many of which also have relatively small populations. The comparison is limited to whites because of the large black-white differential in length of life (about five years), the large variation across states in the percentage of the population that is black, and the fact that the percentage black is much larger in the United States than in the other countries.

Within-state inequality of U.S. whites is significantly greater ($p < .001$) than within-country inequality in twenty-one "Western" countries.[2] This result adds support to Tuljapurkar's finding that inequality in the United States is greater than in other countries. Unlike Tuljapurkar's results, however, the mean interquartile range in the states (as well as in the other Western countries) declined from 1970 to 1980 and from 1980 to 1990. Between 1990 and 2000, the mean interquartile range for the twenty-one countries fell by an additional 0.8 years. State data are not available for 2000, but for U.S. whites as a whole, the decrease from 1990 to 2000 was 0.9 years. This suggests that the gap between the states and other countries was probably about the same in 2000 as in 1990.

The greater inequality in the United States is also evident in the ages at which 25 percent, 50 percent, and 75 percent of the cohort are dead, according to period life tables. By comparing the fifty states with the twenty-one countries at these different levels of survivorship, we find that the greater inequality in the United States, is the result of two disparate phenomena. The age at which 25 percent of the cohort is dead is substantially lower in the states than in the other countries, indicating higher mortality rates in the states at younger ages. By contrast, the age at which 75 percent of the cohort is dead is *higher in the states* than in the other countries, indicating lower mortality rates in the states at older ages. Both the relatively higher U.S. mortality rates at younger ages and the relatively lower rates at older ages explain the greater inequality in length of life in the states. It should also be noted that the age at which 50 percent of cohort is dead is similar in the states as in the countries. That is, white median life expectancy in the average state was about the same as median life expectancy in the average Western country in 2000.

Tuljapurkar's finding of a negative correlation between inequality and life

---

1. National Center for Health Statistics, *U.S. Decennial Life Tables for 1969–71*, volume 2, *State Life Tables* (Rockville, MD: National Center for Health Statistics, 1985); *U.S. Decennial Life Tables for 1979–91*, volume 2, *State Life Tables* (Hyattsville, MD: National Center for Health Statistics, 1985); *U.S. Decennial Life Tables for 1989–91*, volume 2, *State Life Tables* (Hyattsville, MD: National Center for Health Statistics 1998).

2. "Western" countries are Australia, Austria, Belgium, Canada, Denmark, England, Finland, France, Germany (West), Iceland, Italy, Japan, Luxembourg, the Netherlands, New Zealand (non-Maori), Norway, Portugal, Spain, Sweden, Switzerland, and Taiwan.

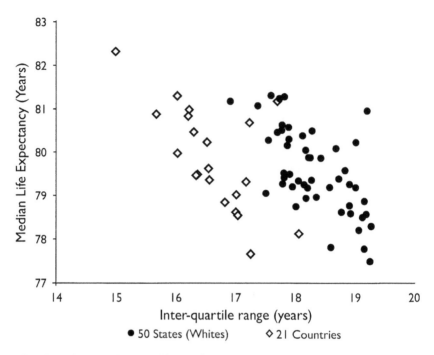

Fig. 6C.1   Scatter diagram of inequality and life expectancy, 50 states (whites) and 21 Western countries, 1990

expectancy over time is also evident in cross section using the interquartile range for inequality and the median age of death for life expectancy. The correlation across the fifty states is −0.63, and for the twenty-one countries, it is −0.64. (See figure 6C.1). This relationship between inequality and life expectancy results from the fact that death rates at younger ages (captured by the age at which 25 percent of a cohort is dead) drives both life expectancy and inequality. The correlation with median life expectancy is almost perfect: $r = 0.98$ for the states and 0.96 for the countries. Its greater importance for inequality than the age at which 75 percent is dead can be seen in figure 6C.2. All these results can be traced to the greater variability of death rates at younger ages than at older ages across states and across countries. The coefficient of variation (standard deviation divided by the mean) across the states for the age at which 25 percent is dead is 1.7 percent; for the age at which 75 percent is dead is only 0.8%. Across the countries, the coefficients are 2.1 percent and 1.2 percent, respectively.

In calling attention to the large inequality in length of life that still prevails in the United States—and other high-income countries—Tuljapurkar is on the right track; the matter could be put even more strongly. Consider the following situation in the United States. The mean age of death of white college graduates is no more than four or five years greater than that of white high

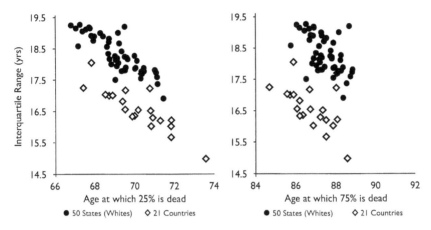

Fig. 6C.2   Scatter diagrams of relationship between interquartile range and age at which 25% is dead and 75% is dead, 1990

school dropouts. By contrast, the mean age of death of the one-fourth of white cohort who live the longest is about twenty-five years greater than the mean age of death of the one-fourth who have the shortest lives. A major challenge for social and medical scientists is to explain this inequality in length of life. A good starting point would be to explain differences in the age at which 25 percent is dead across states and across countries.

7

Demographic Trends, Housing Equity, and the Financial Security of Future Retirees

James M. Poterba, Steven F. Venti, and David A. Wise

About 80 percent of households with heads at retirement age own a home. Aside from Social Security and dedicated retirement saving, home equity is the primary asset of a large fraction of these homeowners. Thus, the financial security of many older households depends importantly on the value of their homes. Venti and Wise (1990, 2001, 2004); Megbolugbe, Sa-Aadu, and Shilling (1997); and Banks et al. (2010) show that housing equity tends to be withdrawn when households experience shocks to family status like entry to a nursing home or death of a spouse. If, as these analyses suggest, housing equity is conserved for a "rainy day," then the value of housing can have important implications for the reserve of wealth in the event of such shocks.

In a series of earlier papers—Poterba, Venti, and Wise (2007a, b, 2008, 2009)—we considered the retirement asset accumulation of future retirees. In particular, we considered the implications of the transition from a pension system dominated by employer-provided defined benefit plans to a system dominated by 401(k) plans and personal retirement accounts. We

James M. Poterba is the Mitsui Professor of Economics at the Massachusetts Institute of Technology, and president and chief executive officer of the National Bureau of Economic Research. Steven F. Venti is the DeWalt Ankeny Professor of Economic Policy and a professor of economics at Dartmouth College, and a research associate of the National Bureau of Economic Research. David A. Wise is the John F. Stambaugh Professor of Political Economy at the Kennedy School of Government at Harvard University, and area director for Aging at the National Bureau of Economic Research.

This research was supported by the National Institute on Aging through grant #P01 AG005842 and by the U.S. Social Security Administration (SSA) through grant #10-P-98363-1-04 to the National Bureau of Economic Research (NBER) as part of the SSA Retirement Research Consortium. The findings and conclusions expressed are solely those of the author(s) and do not represent the views of SSA, any agency of the Federal Government, or the NBER. We are grateful to Tom Davidoff for comments on an earlier draft of the paper.

concluded that future retirees in the United States were likely to have substantially greater retirement assets than current retirees. In this chapter, we begin to develop a parallel analysis of home equity, the other key asset of a large proportion of households. We consider how trends in housing equity could affect the well-being of future elderly.

To structure the analysis, we distinguish two phases of housing equity accumulation. The first phase is the home equity that households have on the eve of retirement. The second phase is the trend in home equity *after* retirement. With these two phases in mind, there are two key goals of the analysis. The first goal is to understand the extent of uncertainty about home equity at older ages, given the home equity that households have at retirement. That is, how much home equity will be available to households when the "rainy day" arrives? The second goal is to explore how one might project the trend in the home equity of younger cohorts as they approach retirement.

The second goal is a difficult issue to address with any degree of certainty, as past attempts to project home prices have demonstrated. To understand the difficulty of projecting home prices, we begin this chapter by describing the change (or persistence) over time in relationships between age and home ownership and home values. We illustrate how projections based on past empirical regularities can lead to substantial errors in projections. Nonetheless, although we recognize that any projections are extremely uncertain, we consider whether some "what if" scenarios based on the relationship of home equity to household wealth might be used to make informed judgments about the housing equity of future retirees.

While our focus is on the possible effect of housing equity on the financial security of future elderly, our discussion of housing equity is necessarily related to prior work on demographic trends and housing prices. Substantial attention was first drawn to this issue by Mankiw and Weil (1989), and their paper elicited responses from many reviewers. McFadden (1994) and Hoynes and McFadden (1997) also consider the effect of demographic change on future house prices. Demographic change is, of course, not the only explanation for changes in house prices. Poterba (1991) considers the role of construction costs, the after-tax cost of home ownership, as well as demographic change. Glaeser, Gyourko, and Saks (2005) investigate the possibility that restrictive zoning has resulted in rapid price increases in some cities. More recently, Shiller (2008) discusses some of the causes of the recent spike in house prices observed in some regions of the United States since 1998.

To put the importance of housing equity in perspective, we begin in this introduction with data on home equity relative to other assets of households near retirement. The following tabulation shows the dollar values of housing equity and other assets, calculated from responses to questions in the Health and Retirement Study (HRS), which included households with a member aged fifty-one to sixty-one in 1992. Although housing equity represents about 15 percent of total wealth for all households in 2000, it represents about 33 percent of nonretirement assets. For about half of all households, housing equity represents over 50 percent of nonretirement assets. Because of the apparent special nature of home equity—as a reserve of last resort for many families—it may have a particularly important effect on the resources available to older families in the event of shocks to family status, such as entry into a nursing home, other health shocks, or death of a spouse (see table 7.1).

In the first four sections of the chapter, we explore the relationships between age, home ownership, and home values in recent decades. The goal is to understand how projections based on the historical stability of these relationships can easily go astray. We show both cohort and cross-section representations of the data and consider which relationships changed over time and which ones have remained relatively unchanged for several decades. In section 7.1, we present cohort and cross-section descriptions of trends in home ownership by age. We find that the profiles of ownership by age changed little between 1984 and 2004—for couples, single men, and single women separately. In section 7.2, we combine the profile of home ownership by age with demographic projections to obtain projections of the aggregate *number* of homes in future years. These projections suggest that the total number of homes will continue to grow through 2040, but at a declining

Table 7.1   **Mean assets of Health and Retirement Study households in 2000**

	Dollar amount		Percent of total wealth	
Asset category	All households	Homeowners	All households	Homeowners
Retirement assets	370,748	415,357	53.93	52.34
Social Security wealth	174,865	188,185	25.44	23.71
Defined contribution pension wealth	94,118	108,038	13.69	13.61
401(k) assets	31,885	35,876	4.64	4.52
IRA and Keogh assets	69,879	83,258	10.16	10.49
Other nonretirement-nonhousing assets	212,928	249,420	30.97	31.43
Housing equity	103,820	128,843	15.10	16.23
Total wealth	687,497	793,620		

	All households	Homeowners
Percentage of households with housing equity greater than a specified percentage of total wealth		
>25%	22.7	26.7
>50%	5.4	5.4
>75%	2.8	2.1
Percentage of households with housing equity greater than a specified percentage of nonretirement wealth		
>25%	70.1	83.0
>50%	50.2	58.5
>75%	30.6	34.4

rate. In section 7.3, we discuss the *value* of housing by age given ownership. Unlike the stable pattern for home ownership, we find that the real value of housing roughly doubled between 1984 and 2004—for couples, for single men, and for single women. In section 7.4, to check our estimates of home values, we combine demographic data with ownership rates and home value given ownership to develop estimates of the aggregate value of housing between 1984 and 2004. Over these years, our estimates correspond closely to Flow of Funds Accounts (FFA) estimates of aggregate housing value. The increase in home values is likely the result of many factors that affect housing markets, including demographic trends, changes in financial market returns, and changes in consumer preferences for housing relative to all other goods. The wide historical variation in house values suggests that it is likely to be very difficult to forecast the future value of homes based on the past age profile of home values and projections of future demographic structure.

In the next two sections, we explore the relationship between household wealth on the one hand and home values, mortgage debt, and home equity on the other hand. In particular, we draw attention to the stability of the empirical correspondence between home equity and household wealth (which we return to more formally in section 7.8). In section 7.5, we consider the relationship between nonpension wealth and home equity between 1984 and 2004, based on cross-section comparisons. We find that the ratio of home values to wealth increased somewhat between 1984 and 2004, while the ratio of mortgage debt to wealth increased substantially. On net, the ratio of home equity to wealth was essentially the same in 2004 as in 1984. This ratio did vary over the intervening years, largely as a function of stock market values. In section 7.6, we consider cohort descriptions of home values, home equity, and mortgage debt, as well as the relationship between home equity and nonpension wealth. We find that the home values and home equity of successively younger cohorts increased very substantially over the 1984 to 2004 period. But the mortgage debt of younger cohorts also increased. Because the percent increase in equity was less than the percent increase in home values and the percent increase in mortgage debt was much greater than the percent increase in home values, the ratio of equity to home value decreased for successively younger cohorts, and the ratio of mortgage debt to home value increased. Thus, younger cohorts will approach retirement with more home equity than older cohorts, but also with more mortgage debt. In spite of the large changes in the ratios of home equity to home value, the cohort data also show that the age profile of the ratio of home equity to nonpension wealth remained strikingly stable over the 1984 to 2004 period.

In section 7.7, given home equity at retirement, we use simulation methods to illustrate the potential effect of changes in home prices on the home equity of households as they age. For illustration, we consider two cohorts—one attaining retirement age in 1990 and the other in 2010—whose members entered retirement with very different levels of home equity. For each of these cohorts, we simulate home equity late in retirement by randomly drawing future house price changes from the historical distribution of price changes. The younger cohort is projected to have substantially more home equity late in retirement. However, both cohorts face a moderate risk of a decline in real home equity following retirement.

In section 7.8, we explore the relationship between home equity and non-pension wealth more formally, with the goal of understanding whether projections of future trajectories for household wealth might be helpful in projecting the home equity of future retirees. We find that over the 1984 to 2004 period—during which mortgage rates declined by half, home prices fluctuated substantially, and household wealth doubled—the ratio of home equity to total wealth remained surprisingly stable. The stability in this empirical relationship prompts us to raise the possibility that it might be used to judge the likely home equity of future cohorts of retirees.

In section 7.9, we summarize our findings and discuss future research plans.

7.1   Trends in Home Ownership

We begin with a cohort description of home ownership. The data are from the Survey of Income and Program Participation (SIPP). The SIPP asks each household respondent if the housing unit in which they are living is owned or rented. If the unit is owned, then up to three owners can be designated. We use this information to classify each person as an owner, a renter, or living in a unit owned by another person. We also distinguish "families" within a living unit using the same rules as the tax code. Thus, for example, a house owned by a married couple also containing their adult son contains two "families" in our analysis: a married couple (owners) and a single male (a nonowner living in a unit owned by another person). Our analysis focuses on home owners.

The SIPP is a series of short panels that survey respondents for thirty-two to forty-eight months. New panels were introduced in most years between 1984 and 1995 and every four years after 1996. We disregard the short time series component of the SIPP and treat survey data in each calendar year as independent cross sections. We make use of data on home ownership for seventeen years: 1984, 1985, 1987, 1988, 1991 to 1995, and 1997 to 2004. From the random samples from each for these years, we create cohort data. For example, to trace the average home ownership rate of the cohort that attained age forty in 1984, we calculate the ownership rate for persons aged forty in the 1984 cross section, aged forty-one in the 1985 cross section, aged forty-three in the 1987 cross section, and so forth. The last observation for this cohort will be at age sixty in 2004. We follow the same procedure for all cohorts that are between the ages of twenty-one and eighty at anytime between 1984 and 2004. For most cohorts, this procedure yields seventeen observations. However, fewer observations are available for some older cohorts (attaining age eighty before 2004) and for some younger cohorts (attaining age twenty-one after 1984).

The home ownership rates of couples from selected cohorts are shown in figure 7.1. The data show essentially no cohort effects, except at older ages. The cohort data suggest that cross-section data for any year would look much like the pieced-together cohorts. For example, the 1984 data for different ages lie essentially on the age-ownership profile described by the cohort data. So do the data for 2004, the last year for which SIPP data are available. (See also figures 7.2 and 7.3) The cross-section data for 1984 and 2004 are shown for couples, single men, and single women in figures 7.4, 7.5, and 7.6, respectively. The ownership rates by age changed very little for couples between 1984 and 2004, except perhaps at older ages—eighty and above. The ownership rate of single men aged sixty and younger was about the same in 2004 as in 1984, but for those over sixty, the ownership rate was higher in 2004 than in 1984. The ownership rate of single women changed little between 1984 and 2004. Because of the increasing proportion of single persons at younger ages, however, the number of all "households" (single persons and couples) who owned homes declined at younger ages between 1984 and 2004, as shown in figure 7.7. On balance, ownership rates at older ages were somewhat higher in 2004 than in 1984.

Considering both the cohort and the cross-section data, it appears that the ownership rate of older households will likely be higher in future years than it is today.

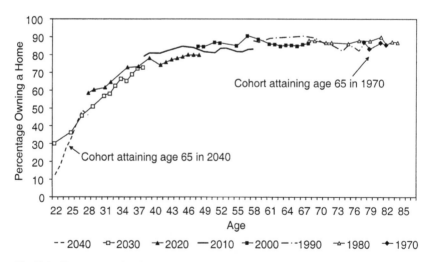

Fig. 7.1   Percent owning for two-person households: Eight selected cohorts identified by year members of cohort attain age 65

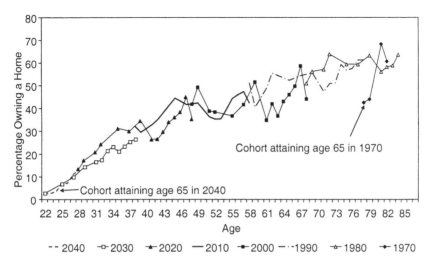

Fig. 7.2   Percent owning for single males: Eight selected cohorts identified by year members of cohort attain age 65

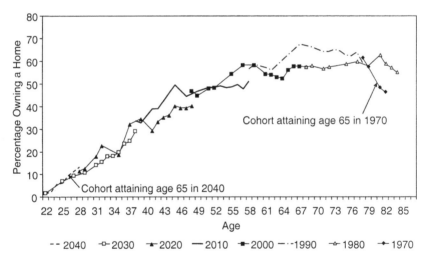

Fig. 7.3   Percent owning for single females: Eight selected cohorts identified by year members of cohort attain age 65

7.2   The Aggregate Number of Homes

The previous section showed that the age profile of homeownership for couples, single males, and single females changed little between 1984 and 2004. We combine these age profiles with demographic data on the number of couples and single persons at each age in each year to obtain projections

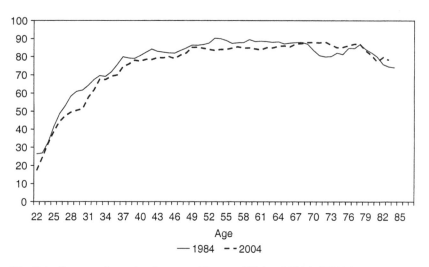

Fig. 7.4   **Percent of couples that owned homes, 1984 and 2004, SIPP data**

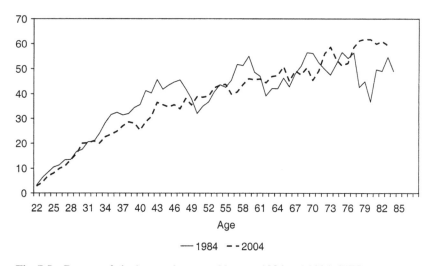

Fig. 7.5   **Percent of single men that owned homes, 1984 and 2004, SIPP data**

of the aggregate number of home owners (or the number of owner-occupied homes) in each year.

Projections are shown for the years 1982 to 2040 in figure 7.8. These projections use the 2004 age profiles of homeownership shown in figures 7.4, 7.5, and 7.6. Thus, the projections show what homeownership would be if the age profile of home ownership was the same as the 2004 profile over the entire period. The projection uses population forecasts by age, year, gender, and marital status that were provided by the Office of the Actuary of the Social

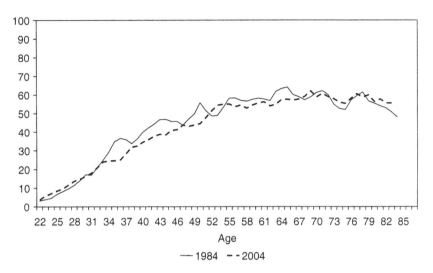

Fig. 7.6   Percent of single women that owned homes in 1984 and 2004, SIPP data

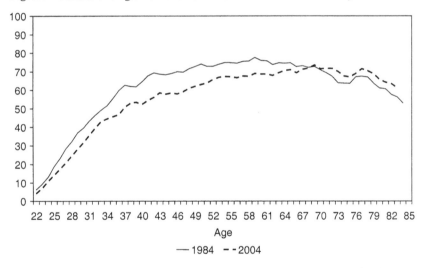

Fig. 7.7   Percent of all households that owned homes in 1984 and 2004, SIPP data

Security Administration.[1] In each year and for each age, the SIPP ownership rate for couples is weighted by the number of couples in the population to

1. Population estimates for 1980 to 1999 are from the U.S. Census. Population projections from the Social Security Administration (SSA) are used for the years 2000 through 2040. The two sources differ slightly in coverage. The Census data exclude persons in the military and persons living abroad. These two groups are included in the SSA data. We have adjusted the SSA data by the ratio of Census estimates to SSA projections in the year 2000 for each of the gender and marital status groups.

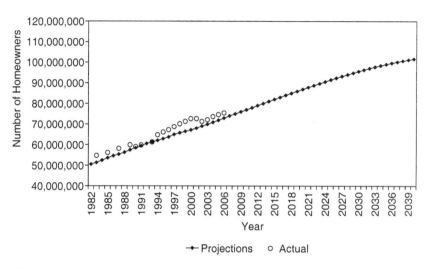

Fig. 7.8   **Projected and actual number of owner-occupied units**

obtain an estimate of the number of couple homeowners. A similar calculation is made at each age for each year for single males and for single females.
The projected aggregate number of homeowners shown in figure 7.8 is the
sum over all ages and over all demographic groups in each year.

The projected number of homeowners mirrors the pace of underlying
demographic change. For the years 1982 to 2006, the figure also shows the
actual number of owner-occupied housing units obtained from the Census
estimate of the housing inventory in each year. The two series are quite
close although there is more fluctuation in the Census series. The projected
number of homes increases essentially linearly from about 51 million in 1982
to about 102 million in 2040.

The projections suggest a substantial slowdown in the rate of increase in
the number of homeowners. Figure 7.9 shows the implied rate of growth
which declines from about 2 percent in the early 1980s to about half a percent by 2040. The figure also shows the "actual" growth rates implied by the
Census estimates of the number of home owners. On average, the decline in
the growth rate implied by the Census data essentially matches the decline
implied by the projections. And the decline in the projected growth rates after
2006 essentially continues the path of decline between 1982 and 2006.

7.3   The Value of Owned Homes and Housing Equity

The preceding data show that the profiles of home ownership by age for
couples, single men, and single women changed little between 1984 and 2004.
But the value of homes and home equity increased substantially over this
time period. Figures 7.10, 7.11, and 7.12 show the age profiles of the value

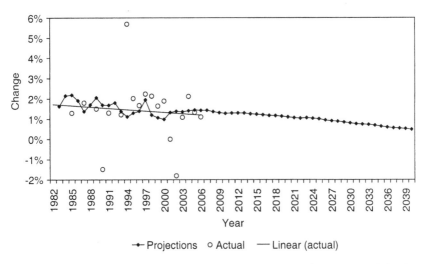

Fig. 7.9   Projected and actual percent change in the number of owner-occupied units

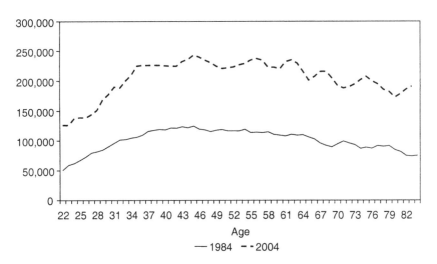

Fig. 7.10   Home value given ownership, couples, 1984 and 2004 (in year 2000 dollars)

of homes by age for couples, single men, and single women, respectively. For each of the groups, the home values (in 2000 dollars using the gross domestic product [GDP] price deflator) increased approximately twofold between 1984 and 2004. For households between ages sixty and seventy, real home values of couples increased by 110 percent, home values of single men increased 136 percent, and home values of single women increased 93 percent.

In addition, home equity increased substantially for each of the groups.

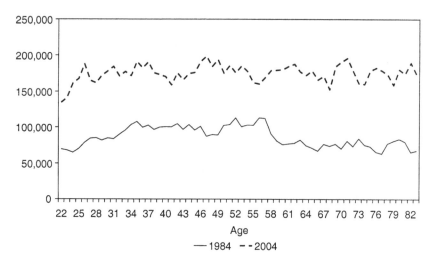

Fig. 7.11   Home value given ownership, single males, 1984 and 2004 (in year 2000 dollars)

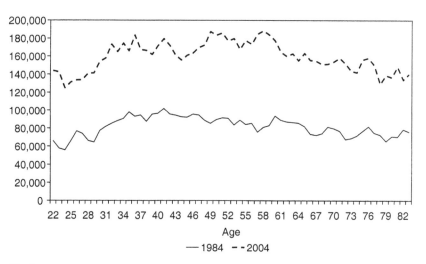

Fig. 7.12   Home value given ownership, single females, 1984 and 2004 (in year 2000 dollars)

The age profiles of home equity for couples, single men, and single women are shown in figures 7.13, 7.14, and 7.15, respectively. For households between sixty and seventy, real home equity increased by 95 percent for couples, 119 percent for single men, and 77 percent for single women. Figure 7.16 shows the differences in the profiles of home values given ownership for couples between 1970 and 2000. The differences are even greater than the differences between 1984 and 2004.

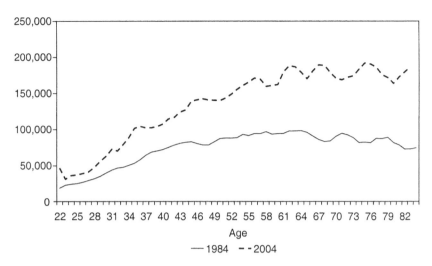

Fig. 7.13   **Home equity given ownership, couples, 1984 and 2004 (in year 2000 dollars)**

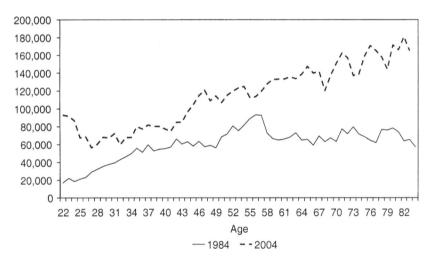

Fig. 7.14   **Home equity given ownership, single males, 1984 and 2004 (in year 2000 dollars)**

There are several possible reasons for the increase in home values and home equity between 1984 and 2004. One explanation is that household investment patterns changed over this time period and that households chose to invest more in housing assets. Another is that home prices increased so that both home values and home equity increased while owners remained in the same home. In sections 7.5 and 7.7, we find that the increase in housing equity and housing values is strongly correlated with the increase in household wealth over this time period. This is consistent with either the hypoth-

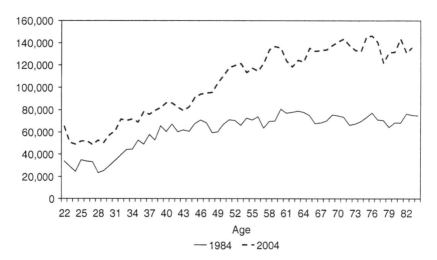

Fig. 7.15   Home equity given ownership, single females, 1984 and 2004 (in year 2000 dollars)

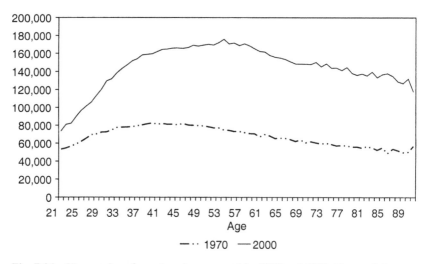

Fig. 7.16   Home value of couples given ownership, 1970 and 2000, Census data (in year 2000 dollars)

esis that (a) a broad-gauge increase in asset values, triggered for example by falling risk premiums or required returns, resulted in rising stock, housing, and other asset values, or (b) that increases in nonhousing asset values stimulated greater housing demand and thereby increased house values.

These data highlight the difficulty of projecting home prices and home values based on past empirical relationships, as many projections have done. Projections based on the profiles of home values, or home equity, by age in 1984, for example, would be far from the mark in 2004. These results also have implications for the oft-made suggestion that personal retirement accounts such as 401(k) plans and individual retirement accounts (IRAs) were funded in part by increasing home equity loans and reducing home equity. In this case, however, these data are not by themselves definitive. As discussed more fully in the following, as home equity increased, so did mortgage debt. In principle, home equity loans could have been used to fund 401(k) and other personal accounts. Greenspan and Kennedy (2009), however, show that increasing home equity loans and home refinancing in recent years were used largely to pay off short-term debt. Thus, home equity loans were apparently not used in large part to fund personal retirement accounts.

7.4   The Aggregate Value of Housing and Home Equity between 1984 and 2004

To check our results on home ownership and home values, we predict the aggregate value of housing based on our data and compare our estimates with FFA aggregate data. We find a close correspondence between our estimates and the FFA aggregates. Our calculations for the 1984 to 2004 period are based on the observed pattern of home values and home ownership by age. We cannot assume, however, that the profile of home values by age will remain stable in the future. Thus, we are not confident that the method we have used here could be used to make reliable projections for future years.

The preceding data show that the home value of owners increased substantially between 1984 and 2004 based on SIPP data. The increase between 1970 and 2000, based on Census data, was even greater. Now we want to consider the change in the aggregate value of housing between 1984 and 2006. To do this, we build upon the estimates produced in section 7.3. There we combined SIPP estimates of ownership by age in 2004 with population estimates for each year to obtain an estimate of the number of homes (or homeowners) for each year 1984 through 2006. Separate calculations were made for each gender and marital status group because these groups had different ownership profiles and because these groups experienced different rates of population growth over the period.

The next step is to assign housing values to the estimated population of owners in each year. Because housing values changed so much between 1984 and 2004, we use separate age-home value profiles for each year that they are available in the SIPP. These profiles are shown in figure 7.10, figure 7.11, and figure 7.12 for two of the years, 1984 and 2004, but we have estimates for fifteen of the twenty-one years between 1984 and 2004.

The results are displayed as square markers in figure 7.17. For comparison, we have also graphed the market value of household real estate from the FFA. The trends are strikingly similar for the two series although our projec-

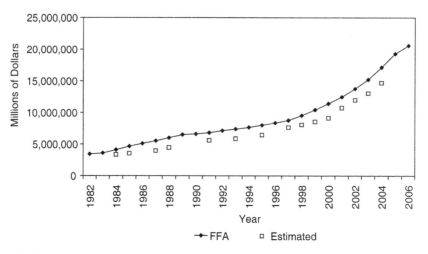

Fig. 7.17   Projected and actual aggregate value of owner-occupied homes

tions lie below the FFA estimates. This is likely the result of differences in coverage between the two series. The FFA data include several components (farm houses, second homes that are not rented, vacant homes for sale, and vacant land) that are not contained in our projections.

7.5   Home Value, Home Equity, and Household Wealth between 1984 and 2004

Various commentators have suggested a range of different explanations for the nationwide increase in home values between 1984 and 2004. Glaeser, Gyourko, and Saks (2004) suggest that land use restrictions constraining the supply of housing in key markets has played a role in rising house prices. Green and Wachter (2008) point to major changes in the home finance system and falling mortgage rates that reduced the user cost of housing, which stimulated the demand for housing. Real incomes rose over this period as well. Himmelberg, Mayer, and Sinai (2005) discuss the role of expectations of continued real house price appreciation. These factors, and others, may have offset the downward effect of demographic pressures on house prices that Mankiw and Weil (1989) identified in their projections.

One potential explanation of rising house values is that they were the result of rising demand for housing assets, driven in turn by rising nonhousing wealth. It is difficult to test this potential explanation for the observed pattern because housing values and other asset values are simultaneously determined in general equilibrium. As a first step in considering this explanation for rising house values, one must explore the relationship between housing wealth and nonhousing wealth. To do that, we begin by comparing wealth in 2004 with wealth in 1984 and the ratio of home values to wealth and the ratio of home equity to wealth in these two years. We show that wealth in 2004 was much higher than wealth in 1984. In addition, we show that both the ratio of housing value to wealth and the ratio of home equity to wealth were about the same in 2004 as in 1984. Differences between the two years were largely concentrated among young households. The ratio of mortgage debt to wealth was greater in 2004 than in 1984, essentially at all ages. We then consider the ratio of home value to wealth, the ratio of home equity to wealth, and the ratio of mortgage debt to wealth in each of the intervening years for which SIPP data are available between 1984 and 2004. We find in particular that the ratios vary with the stock market fluctuations over this period although the ratio of home equity to wealth was essentially the same in 2004 as in 1984.

Figure 7.18 shows that at each age mean total nonpension wealth, including housing equity, increased between 1984 and 2004. Over all ages, mean wealth increased 69.1 percent between 1984 and 2004 (in year 2000 dollars). Figure 7.19 shows that at each age, nonpension wealth excluding home equity also increased between 1984 and 2004. Over all ages, this measure of wealth increased 58.8 percent between 1984 and 2004.

We are particularly interested in the relationship between home values and home equity on the one hand and household wealth on the other. Figure 7.20 shows that the ratio of home value to wealth was somewhat higher in 2004 than in 1984 at ages forty and over but was substantially higher in 2004 than in 1984 for younger ages. Figure 7.21 shows that the ratio of mean home mortgage to household wealth increased between 1984 and 2004 for all ages. Figure 7.22 shows that, on balance, the ratio of home equity to wealth was very similar in 1984 and 2004, except at ages thirty and younger. Thus, due to an increase in mortgage levels, the ratio of home equity to wealth

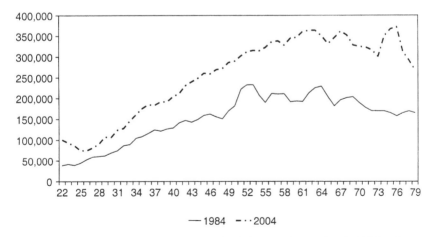

Fig. 7.18   Mean total nonpension wealth (including housing equity) in 1984 and 2004 (in year 2000 dollars)

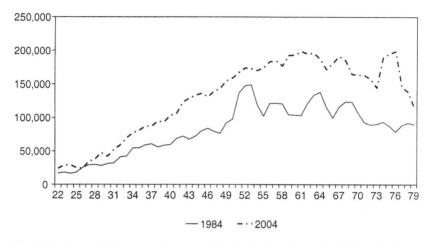

Fig. 7.19   Mean total nonpension wealth (excluding housing equity) in 1984 and 2004 (in 2000 dollars)

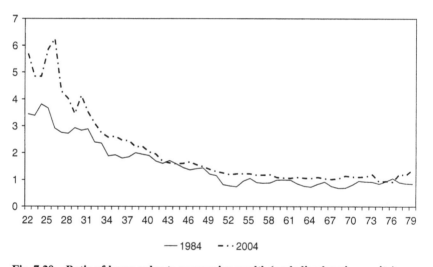

Fig. 7.20   Ratio of house value to nonpension wealth (excluding housing equity)

remained the same when the ratio of home values to wealth increased. This is the "home equity extraction" process that was widely cited as a factor supporting consumer spending during the decade between 1995 and 2004. Sinai and Souleles (2008) focus their analysis of house values and mortgage debt among older households on the degree to which households increased borrowing in response to rises in house prices.

Although the ratio of home equity to wealth was about the same in 2004 as in 1984, except at younger ages—which we suspect can be attributed to the explosion of subprime mortgages—there were substantial changes in

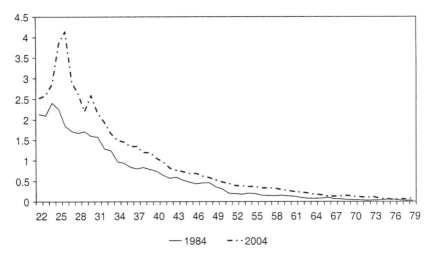

Fig. 7.21   Ratio of mortgage debt to nonpension wealth (excluding housing equity)

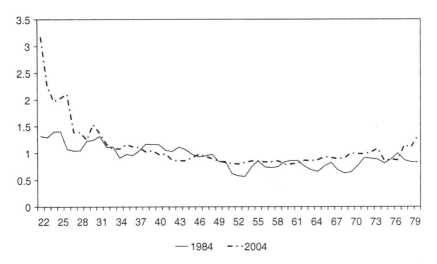

Fig. 7.22   Ratio of home equity to nonpension wealth (excluding housing equity)

household wealth over the intervening years, as well as changes in the ratio of home equity to household wealth. To understand these changes, we consider household wealth and the ratios of home value, mortgage debt, and home equity to wealth for each of the years between 1984 and 2004. We consider the changes in each of these ratios for four geographic regions— midwest, northeast, south, and west. Figure 7.23 shows nominal nonhousing wealth in each of the four regions. There was a substantial increase in all of the regions, especially beginning in 1995. On average there was about a

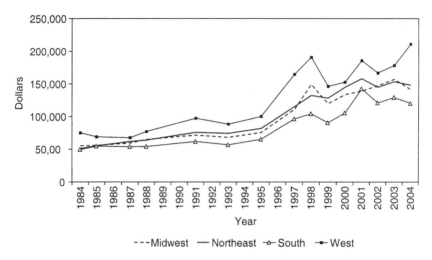

Fig. 7.23   Mean nominal nonhousing wealth for owners, by region, 1994 to 2004, SIPP data

threefold increase in wealth over this period. The pattern of increase was essentially the same in each of the regions.

Figure 7.24 shows that the ratio of housing value to wealth varied over the period, with a dip about at the peak of the stock market bubble. Home values, however, were higher at the end than at the beginning of the period. Figure 7.25 shows that the ratio of mortgage debt to wealth increased over the period in all geographic regions. Figure 7.26 shows that the net effect was a ratio of home equity to wealth that was, on average, about the same in 2004 as in 1984. Like the ratio of home value to wealth, home equity also changed over intervening years, with a dip at about the peak of the stock market bubble. Although the ratio tends be higher in the northeast and the west, the basic trend is the same in all four regions. We return to more formal analysis of this "regularity" in section 7.8.

Figure 7.27 shows the ratios of home value, mortgage debt, and home equity to wealth for all regions combined. The combined data show the ratio of home value to wealth followed the wealth profile over the period, with a dip when stock market values reached their peak. The ratio of home value to wealth was somewhat higher in 2004 than in 1984. The ratio of mortgage debt to wealth, however, also increased substantially over the period, from 0.182 to 0.246, an increase of 35 percent. On net, the ratio of housing equity to wealth followed a pattern similar to the ratio of home value to wealth. But the ratio of home equity to wealth was essentially the same in 2004 as in 1984—0.462 versus 0.491.

Table 7.2 shows summary data, including these same ratios, for homeowners aged sixty to seventy. Total wealth, home value, and home equity

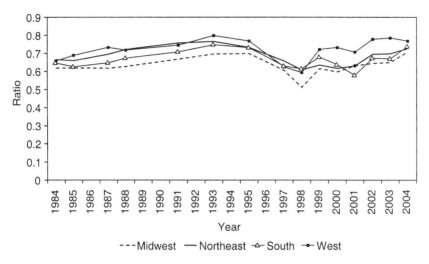

Fig. 7.24   Ratio of home value to nonpension wealth for owners, by region, 1984 to 2004, SIPP data

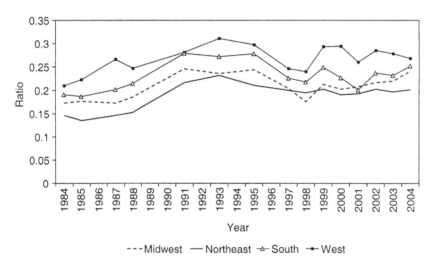

Fig. 7.25   Ratio of mortgage debt to nonpension wealth for owners, by region, 1984 to 2004, SIPP data

all increased substantially between 1984 and 2004 (in 2000 dollars)—72.5 percent, 107 percent, and 91 percent, respectively. Of the $147,355 increase in wealth, $102,222, about 69 percent, was accounted for by the increase in home values. Of the increase in home value, $78,137, or 76 percent, was reflected in home equity, and $24,085, or 26 percent, was offset by an increase in mortgage debt.

The growth in mortgage debt to home value at ages sixty to seventy likely

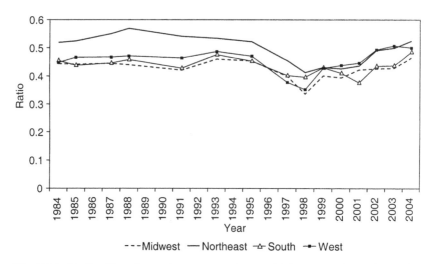

Fig. 7.26   Ratio of housing equity to nonpension wealth for owners, by region, 1984 to 2004, SIPP data

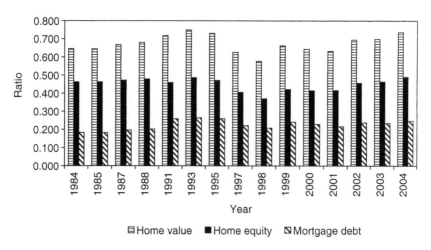

Fig. 7.27   Ratio of home value, home equity, and mortgage debt to nonpension wealth for owners, all regions, 1984 to 2004, SIPP data

reflects the run-up in late-age refinancing and the resulting residual mortgage debt on the household balance sheet at older ages. These data bring to the fore the question of the balance between housing equity and the mortgage debt of future retirees. To explore this question further, we consider in the next section cohort data on home values, home equity, and mortgage debt.

Table 7.2   Means and percentage changes for all owners aged 60 to 70, 1984 and
                 2004, in year 2000 dollars

Measure	1984	2004	Change
Total wealth ($)	203,343	350,698	147,355
House value ($)	95,661	197,883	102,222
Home equity ($)	86,032	164,169	78,137
Mortgage debt ($)	9,629	33,714	24,085
Ratio to wealth			
House value	0.470	0.564	0.094
Home equity	0.423	0.468	0.045
Mortgage debt	0.047	0.096	0.049
Ratio to home value			
Home equity	0.899	0.830	–0.070
Mortgage debt	0.101	0.170	0.070

7.6   Cohort Description of Home Values, Home Equity,
Mortgage Debt, and Wealth

The data description in the last section is based on changes in the cross-section profiles of wealth, home values, mortgage debt, and home equity. Here we consider the cohort profiles of these same measures. These descriptions help to inform the possible financial implications of housing equity and housing debt for future retiree cohorts.

Figure 7.28 shows the increase in the mean home value of homeowners for selected cohorts. As described in section 7.1, each cohort is observed in fifteen of the years between 1984 and 2004. The figure presents profiles for cohorts attaining age sixty-five in 1970, 1980, 1990, 2000, 2010, 2020, 2030, and 2040. All values in this figure and subsequent figures have been converted to year 2000 dollars using the GDP implicit price deflator. The sharp acceleration in the rate of growth of real home values over the last eight years of data (beginning in about 1995) are common to all but the oldest cohorts and are largely year (time) effects, rather than cohort effects. The vertical differences between the cohort profiles represent "cohort effects." The combination of year effects and cohort effects leads to large differences in the home values of different cohorts at the same age. For example, the cohort retiring in 2010 had mean home value of $208,766 when observed at age fifty-nine in 2004, and the cohort retiring in 1990 had only $103,416 when observed at the same age twenty years earlier. The difference—the "cohort effect"—is shown in the figure. Without exception, more recent cohorts (those retiring later) have substantially higher home value at each age than earlier cohorts.

Mortgage debt also increased for successively younger cohorts, as shown in figure 7.29. In this case, there are also substantial cohort effects—each

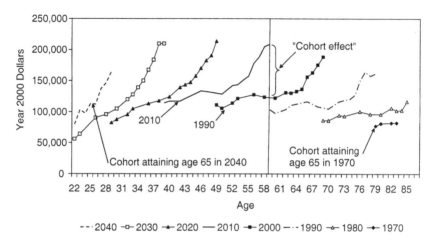

Fig. 7.28   Mean house value for homeowners: Eight selected cohorts identified by year cohort attains age 65

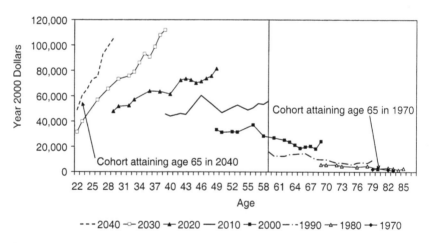

Fig. 7.29   Mean mortgage debt for homeowners: Eight selected cohorts identified by year cohort attains age 65

successively younger cohort has more mortgage debt than the cohort ten years earlier. For older cohorts, mortgage debt fell as the cohort aged. Figure 7.30 shows home equity profiles for the same cohorts and reflects the net effect of the increase in home values and the increase in mortgage debt. As is the case with home value, younger cohorts have substantially more home equity at each age than older cohorts. In each of these figures, the vertical line at age fifty-nine is intended to emphasize the large differences between home values, mortgage debt, and home equity at age fifty-nine, depending on the year in which the cohort attained age fifty-nine. The 2010 cohort attained age fifty-nine in 2004, the 2000 cohort in 1994, and the 1990 cohort in 1984.

Over the 1984 to 2004 period, the rate of growth of mortgage debt exceeded that of home value. As a consequence, successively younger cohorts have lower ratios of home equity to value, but higher ratios of mortgage debt to value, as shown in figures 7.31 and 7.32, respectively. Within each cohort, the ratio of home equity to value increased with age. But there are also cohort effects. On balance, the ratio of home equity to home value is lower for each successively younger cohort. For all cohorts, the mortgage debt

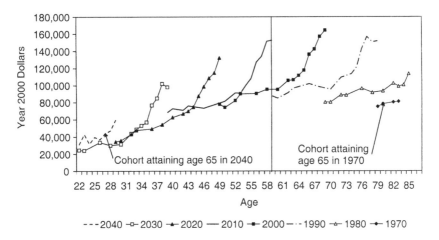

Fig. 7.30   Mean home equity of homeowners: Eight selected cohorts identified by year cohort attains age 65

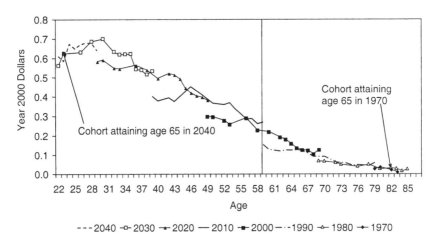

Fig. 7.31   Mortgage debt to house value ratio for homeowners: Eight selected cohorts identified by year cohort attains age 65

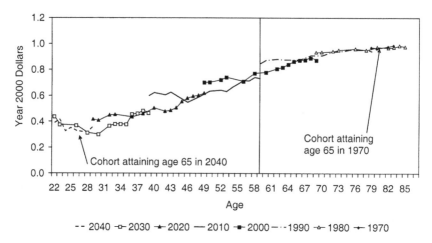

Fig. 7.32   **Home equity to house value ratio for homeowners: Eight selected cohorts identified by year cohort attains age 65**

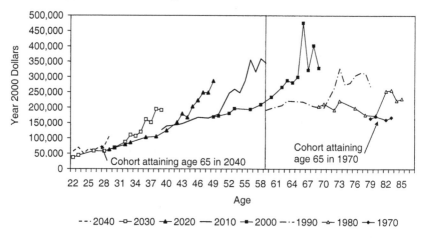

Fig. 7.33   **Mean total wealth of homeowners: Eight selected cohorts identified by year cohort attains age 65**

burden declines steadily with age. Again, though, there are some noticeable cohort effects.

In the following, we will consider in more detail the implications of the data in figures 7.28 to 7.32. But for future reference, we also show here the relationship between household wealth and home equity. Figure 7.33 shows total wealth (home equity plus nonpension wealth) profiles for the same set of cohorts. The increase in wealth corresponding to the stock market run-up is evident. For example, households that attained age fifty-nine in 2004 had much more wealth than households who attained age fifty-nine in 1984 (in year 2000 dollars).

Home equity increased over the same period. It is striking that with very large increases in wealth, home values, and mortgage debt, the trend of the ratio of home equity to wealth was quite stable over the period. Indeed, there appear to be no systematic cohort effects in the profile of home equity to wealth, as shown in figure 7.34, although there are substantial within-cohort fluctuations. We return to this regularity in the following.

To understand the implications of these trends, we begin by examining data for persons who attained age fifty-nine in different years. Figure 7.35 shows the average home value, the average equity, and the average mortgage

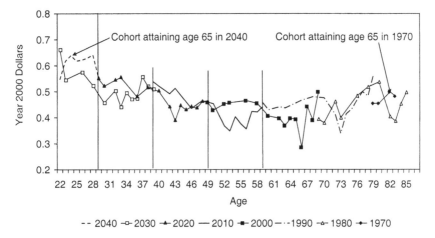

Fig. 7.34   Home equity to wealth ratio for homeowners: Eight selected cohorts identified by year cohort attains age 65

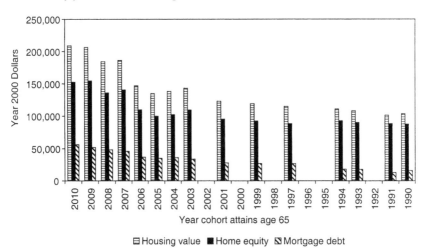

Fig. 7.35   Housing value, home equity, and mortgage debt at age 59, by cohort (year attains age 65)

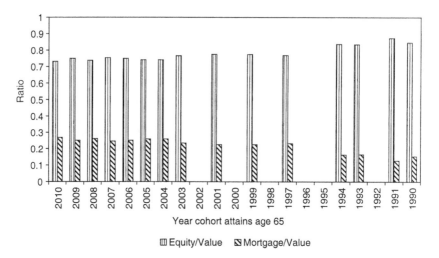

Fig. 7.36   Ratio of home equity to value and ratio of mortgage debt to value at age 59, by cohort (year attains age 65)

debt at age fifty-nine for the cohorts that attain age fifty-nine between 1990 and 2010. Figure 7.36 shows the ratio of equity to home value and the ratio of mortgage debt to home value for these same cohorts. Average real home value nearly doubled over this period. But real home equity increased by only a factor of 1.7. Real mortgage debt increased by a factor of 3.5. Thus, as figure 7.36 shows, the ratio of home equity to home value declined, and the ratio of mortgage debt to value increased.

One of the reasons we have constructed the summary measures presented in the preceding is to gain some insight regarding the home equity positions of future retirees. It is clear that the answer to this question must depend on the unknown future path of house prices and that it also depends on the behavior of homeowners before and after retirement. In the next section, we use historical house price data—subject to the usual concern that the future price paths may not be the same as the past—to project the housing equity at older ages for those who are currently near retirement. In the following section, we use various statistical tools to examine the relative constancy of the ratio of home equity to total wealth in more detail. We consider the implications of this relative constancy for our home equity projections.

7.7   Simulation of Home Equity as Cohorts Age

To understand the implications of fluctuations in home prices on the home equity of households after retirement, we use for illustration the very different home value, home mortgage, and home equity profiles of the cohorts that attained age fifty-nine in 1990 and 2010. To increase the sample sizes, we combine the SIPP data for ages fifty-seven to sixty-one and refer to the result as "age 59." The top panel of table 7.3 shows the average values for all homeowners in each cohort. (The table shows data for the R2000 cohort—the cohort that attains age sixty-five in 2000—as well as the R1990 and R2010 cohorts. The graphical analysis that follows only shows the R1990 and the R2010 cohorts.) The lower panels show data for homeowners in the bottom quintile of the total wealth distribution, those in the 3rd quintile and those in the 5th quintile of the wealth distribution. Moving from older to younger cohorts (left to right in the table), the decrease in the ratio of home equity to home value and the increase in the ratio of mortgage debt to home value are much more pronounced for poorer households than for the wealthier households.

To understand the implications of these trends, suppose that the home equity that households in each cohort have at age fifty-nine is the home equity that the households in these cohorts will have as they enter retirement. We would like to consider the expected level of future home equity and, in

Table 7.3   Home value, home equity, mortgage debt, and ratios of equity and mortgage debt to equity, at age 59 for three cohorts, attaining age 65 in 1990, 2000, and 2010 (year 2000 dollars)

Wealth quintile and measure	Cohort attaining age 65 in:		
	1990	2000	2010
All			
Home value	105,365	121,968	208,960
Equity	89,867	92,428	154,074
Mortgage	15,498	29,540	54,885
Equity to value	0.853	0.758	0.737
Mortgage to value	0.147	0.242	0.263
1st wealth quintile			
Home value	28,855	40,949	76,964
Equity	14,049	12,249	26,289
Mortgage	14,806	28,700	50,674
Equity to value	0.487	0.299	0.342
Mortgage to value	0.513	0.701	0.658
3rd wealth quintile			
Home value	82,801	90,732	147,082
Equity	69,496	66,555	100,221
Mortgage	13,305	24,177	46,860
Equity to value	0.839	0.734	0.681
Mortgage to value	0.161	0.266	0.319
5th wealth quintile			
Home value	169,928	200,583	349,741
Equity	150,393	162,958	281,877
Mortgage	19,535	37,626	67,864
Equity to value	0.885	0.812	0.806
Mortgage of value	0.115	0.188	0.194

particular, the distribution of home equity as these homeowners age and house prices change. Previous work, including Venti and Wise (1990, 2001, 2004); Megbolugbe, Sa-Aadu, and Shilling (1997); and Banks et al. (2010) suggests that home equity tends to be saved for a "rainy day" and used when there is a shock to family status, such as the death of a spouse, entry into a nursing home, or the household faces large medical costs. Because home equity is the largest nonpension asset of a large fraction of households, we are interested in the level of home equity when the "rainy day" arrives. What is the risk that changing home prices place on the "rainy day" assets of retirees?

We begin with observed home values of households approaching retirement, at age fifty-nine. We then simulate the distribution of home values (and, thus, home equity) over the next twenty years. We compare the home equity over this age range for members of the cohort retiring in 1990 (R1990) with the home equity of households over the same age range in the cohort retiring in 2010 (R2010). Members of the R1990 cohort were aged fifty-nine in 1984, the year of the first SIPP survey. The R2010 cohort was age fifty-nine in 2004, the year of the latest SIPP survey. For each of these cohorts, the baseline levels of home value, home equity, and mortgage debt are shown in the first and third columns of table 7.3. The figures in section 7.6 highlight the differences in the home values, home mortgages, and the home equity of these two cohorts.

To simulate the home prices that households in each of these cohorts will face in the future, we use the historical distribution of changes in home values *by state* for each year from 1975 to 2006, based on the Office of Federal Housing Enterprise Oversight (OFHEO) house price index. For each cohort, we assume that future changes in house values after age fifty-nine are uncertain. For a household in a given state, possible price changes are determined by random draws (with replacement) from the historical distribution of price changes in that state. Thus, for example, to simulate the distribution of home prices at age sixty-four, we draw five values at random (with replacement) from the historical distribution of changes in home prices for that state. From these five changes, we calculate the average home price at age sixty-four. We assume that each person in a given state faces the same sequence of price changes. We repeat this process 10,000 times to produce a distribution of future home prices and report the results for ages sixty-four, sixty-nine, seventy-four, and seventy-nine. For each age, we calculate the expected home value. Home equity is obtained by subtracting mortgage debt from home value at each age. We assume that the mortgage debt observed at age fifty-nine declines by 9.1 percent per year, which is the observed rate of mortgage payoff for households aged fifty-nine to seventy-nine in the SIPP. As shown in table 7.3, mortgage debt is only about 26 percent of home value at age fifty-nine in 2004. This declines to about 4 percent by age seventy-nine, on average. Because we simulate price changes 10,000 times for each cohort, we are able to obtain rather precise estimates of low levels of home equity in the tails of the distributions.

Our analysis is likely to understate the riskiness of home equity for individual households because we assume that all houses appreciate or depreciate at the statewide rate. In practice, households own individual houses, and their experiences may differ from the state means. A similar point arises with regard to financial assets, where individuals hold specific and sometimes poorly diversified portfolios, but simulations impute marketwide returns.

Our illustrative simulated results begin with the actual distribution of the home equity of homeowners at age fifty-nine in R1990 and the R2010 cohorts. We choose these cohorts for illustration because, as figure 7.28 shows, the home equity of these two cohorts as they approached retirement were very different—$89,867, on average, for the 1990 cohort and $154,074 for the 2010 cohort, both in year 2000 dollars.

We walk through the simulation procedure we follow with the aid of several figures. The OFHEO home price index we use is shown in figure 7.37 for the United States as a whole, together with two other indexes. One is the National Association of Realtors (NAR) index, which corresponds very closely to the OFHEO index. The other is the Case-Shiller index. The Case-Shiller index shows much greater price fluctuations than the other two. It is a dollar-weighted index based on price changes in twenty large metropolitan areas. The OFHEO index is nationally representative, but only includes "conforming" mortgages that are purchased by Fannie Mae or Freddie Mac (currently less than $417,000). Because we use the OFHEO indexes by state, the fluctuation in the actual values we use is much greater than the national

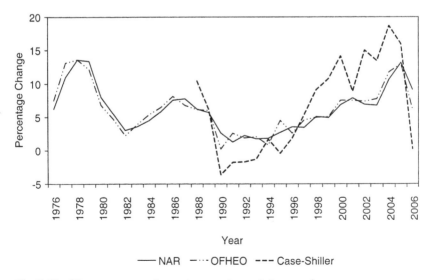

Fig. 7.37   Three measures of year-to-year change in house prices

OFHEO index. The national average year-to-year house price increase was 5.2 percent between 1980 and 2006. The standard deviation of the national price changes is 3.1. However, the standard deviation at the state level is more than twice as large, 6.3 percent. Moreover, the change in house prices at the national level was positive in every year between 1980 and 2006, but at the state level, double-digit house price declines were common in the slumps of the early 1980s and the early 1990s.

Because we are interested in this chapter in the risk that price fluctuations pose for the home equity of homeowners, it is of some interest to compare home price fluctuations with the fluctuation in the returns on financial assets. Figure 7.38 shows that since 1976 home prices have fluctuated less than stock and bond returns. With respect to the total assets of retirees, it is also of interest that home price fluctuations are negatively correlated with the return on stocks and bonds over this period. The correlations are shown in table 7.4. The correlations between the OFHEO home price index and the returns on stocks and bonds is around –0.20.

The starting point for our simulations is the actual distribution of the home equity of homeowners at age fifty-nine. Cumulative distributions of the home equity at age fifty-nine for the 1990 and 2010 cohorts are shown in figure 7.39. It is evident that home equity at age fifty-nine was much larger for the R2010 cohort (households observed at age fifty-nine in 2004) than for the R1990 cohort (households observed at age fifty-nine in 1984). In particular, the upper percentiles of the distribution were much larger for the R2010 than for the R1990 cohort. The top panel of table 7.5 shows selected percentiles of the distribution of actual home equity at age fifty-nine. The

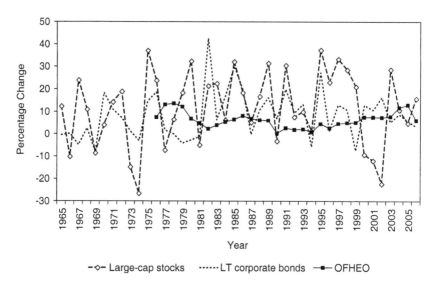

Fig. 7.38   Returns on stocks, bonds, and housing

Table 7.4   Correlation between stock and bond returns and change in home prices for 1976 through 2006

Series	Large company stocks	Long-term corporate bonds	Long-term government bonds	NAR repeat sale % change	OFHEO % change
Large company stocks	1.00				
Long-term corporate bonds	0.26	1.00			
Long-term government bonds	0.24	0.96*	1.00		
NAR repeat sale % change house prices	−0.24	−0.35*	−0.32*	1.00	
OFHEO % change	−0.18	−0.22	−0.18	0.95*	1.00

Note: NAR = National Association of Realtors index; OFHEO = Office of Federal Housing Enterprise Oversight house price index.
*Significant at the 10 percent level.

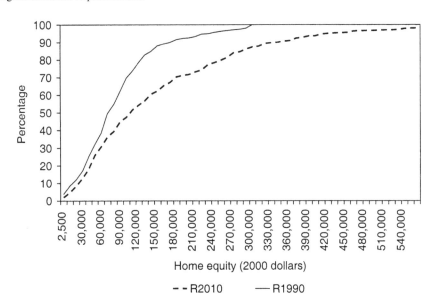

Fig. 7.39   Cumulative distribution of actual home equity for households aged 59, 1990 and 2010 cohorts

90th percentile of the R2010 cohort was almost 98 percent larger than the 90th percentile of the R1990 cohort. The 10th percentile was only 32 percent larger. (Table 7.5 summarizes several additional results that will be referred to as we proceed.)

The distribution of home equity, calculated as the difference between home value and mortgage debt, is affected to some extent by the top-coding of both home value and mortgage debt. The effect of top-coding is essentially limited to the upper tail of the distribution of home equity and leads to some underestimation of the number of households with very high levels

Table 7.5   Percentiles of actual home equity at age 59 and projected home equity at age 79, all households and households in the 1st and 5th home equity quintiles (year 2000 dollars)

| Measure | Cohort retiring in: | | % change 1990–2010 |
	1990	2010	
All households			
Actual home equity at age 59			
10th percentile	20,690	27,407	32.5
50th percentile	75,372	111,454	47.9
90th percentile	173,085	342,585	97.9
Mean	89,867	154,074	71.4
Projected home equity at age 79			
10th percentile	36,929	65,456	77.2
50th percentile	113,646	202,408	78.1
90th percentile	333,610	805,527	141.5
Mean	159,538	341,848	114.3
Households in the 1st home equity quintile			
Actual home equity at age 59			
10th percentile	0	6,395	NA
50th percentile	20,690	28,320	36.9
90th percentile	36,947	45,678	23.6
Mean	19,361	26,067	34.6
Projected home equity at age 79			
10th percentile	10,639	31,742	198.4
50th percentile	39,079	85,879	119.8
90th percentile	105,019	218,587	108.1
Mean	53,742	112,450	109.2
Households in the 5th home equity quintile			
Actual home equity at age 59			
10th percentile	133,010	274,068	106.1
50th percentile	173,085	338,930	95.8
90th percentile	295,578	566,407	91.6
Mean	191,620	372,496	94.4
Projected home equity at age 79			
10th percentile	158,706	351,263	121.3
50th percentile	292,742	702,397	139.9
90th percentile	603,983	1,512,243	150.4
Mean	346,824	840,871	142.4

of home equity. The number of home equity values that are affected by the top-coding of either home value or mortgage debt is described in figures 7B.1 and 7B.2.

Figure 7.40 shows the simulated cumulative distribution of projected home equity at age seventy-nine, twenty years after actual values of home equity were observed at age fifty-nine. The simulated distributions at age seventy-nine together with the actual distributions at age fifty-nine are shown in figure 7.41. It is apparent that the average simulated home equity

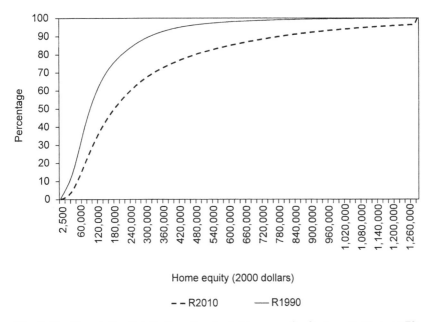

Home equity (2000 dollars)

- - R2010   —— R1990

Fig. 7.40   Cumulative distribution of projected home equity for households aged 79, based on initial home equity at 59, 1990 and 2010 cohorts

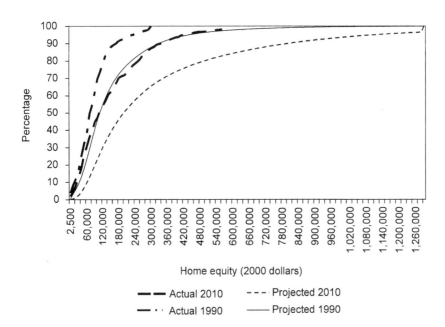

Home equity (2000 dollars)

—— Actual 2010   - - - Projected 2010

—·· Actual 1990   —— Projected 1990

Fig. 7.41   Cumulative distribution of actual home equity at age 59 and projected home equity at age 79, 1990 and 2010 cohorts

at seventy-nine is much greater than actual home equity at fifty-nine for both the R1990 and the R2010 cohorts. In addition, equity at age seventy-nine is much larger for the R2010 cohort than for the R1990 cohort—the mean for the 2010 cohort is $341,848 and for the 1990 cohort is $159,538, as shown in the second panel of table 7.5. The increase of the simulated *average* over the actual average at age fifty-nine arises because, on average, prices increased in each year over the 1976 to 2006 period, from which the random prices were drawn. These figures pertain to the distribution of home equity across households for the two cohorts. In the following, we consider the distribution of the *gains and losses* of individual homeowners.

Although home equity at age seventy-nine is simulated for the 1990 cohort, the actual distribution of home equity at age seventy-nine is also observed for the 1990 cohort because members of this cohort were observed at age fifty-nine in 1984 and at age seventy-nine in 2004. The simulated distribution corresponds quite closely to the actual distribution. The 10th, 50th, and 90th percentiles are $41,110, $118,763, and $319,746, respectively, for the actual distribution and $36,929, $113,646, and $333,610 for the simulated distribution. The mean of the actual distribution is $153,659 and for the simulated distribution is $159,538. Recall that the "historical" price changes were drawn from the period 1975 through 2006 and, thus, include most of the years over which the 1990 cohort aged from fifty-nine to seventy-nine (the years 1984 to 2004).

The distributions of actual and simulated equity shown in the preceding pertain to all homeowners. The difference between the actual distribution at age fifty-nine and the simulated distribution at age seventy-nine, however, differs greatly by equity level. This is most easily seen by considering the pdf of simulated equity at age seventy-nine. The pdf for all homeowners is shown in figure 7.42, for both the 1990 and the 2010 cohorts. While it is clear that the average equity at age seventy-nine is greater for the 2010 than for the 1990 cohort, both distributions are concentrated around the mean for each cohort. The same is true for the pdf of equity values for homeowners in the 1st quintile of home equity values, as shown in figure 7.43. The distributions for the 5th quintile of home values are very different (see figure 7.44). In particular, the proportion of high-equity values is much more pronounced for homeowners in the 2010 cohort than for those in the 1990 cohort. Thus, the simulations suggest that when the 2010 cohort attains age seventy-nine, a much larger fraction of homeowners will have very substantial home equity than was the case for seventy-nine-year-old homeowners in the 1990 cohort.

Given home equity at ages near retirement, we are interested in the extent of uncertainty about home equity at older ages when many homeowners will choose to use home equity to meet "rainy day" expenses. The uncertainty about future home values will increase with age. To illustrate the extent of

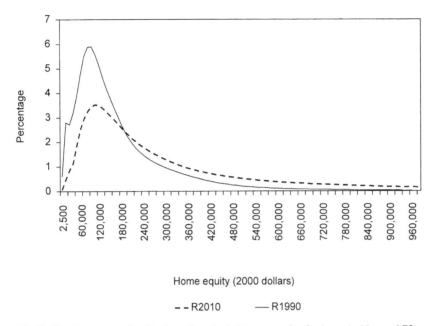

Fig. 7.42   Frequency distribution of projected home equity for households aged 79, based on initial home equity at 59 for the 1990 and 2010 cohorts

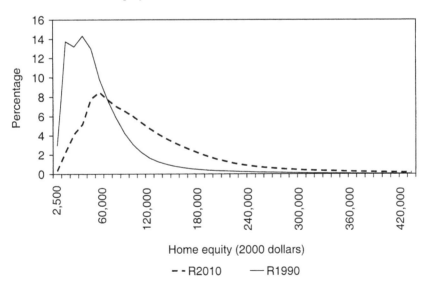

Fig. 7.43   Frequency distribution of projected home equity for households aged 79, based on actual home equity at age 59, 1990 and 2010 cohorts (1st quintile at age 59)

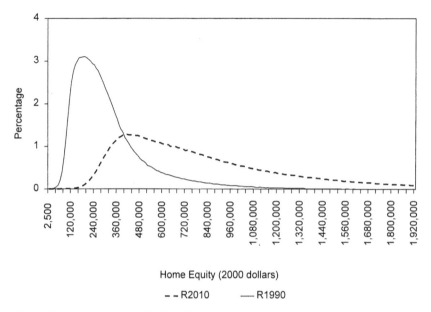

Home Equity (2000 dollars)

- - R2010   —— R1990

Fig. 7.44   Frequency distribution of projected home equity for households aged 79, based on actual home equity at age 59, 1990 and 2010 cohorts (5th quintile at age 59)

the increase, we have simulated the distribution of home equity at five-year intervals, following actual observed home equity at age fifty-nine. The 10th, 50th, and 90th percentiles of these simulated distributions are shown for all homeowners in figure 7.45. Two features of the distributions stand out. The first is the large increase in the 90th percentile for the 2010 cohort over the 90th percentile for the 1990 cohort as the cohort ages. The second is the substantial overlap in the distributions for the two cohorts. For example, at all ages, including the distribution of actual values at age fifty-nine, the 10th percentile for the 2010 cohort is well below the 50th percentile of the 1990 cohort. And the 90th percentile of the 1990 cohort is well above the 50th percentile for the 2010 cohort.

Analogous data for the 1st and the 5th quintiles are shown in figures 7.46 and 7.47, respectively. The features of these figures are like the figure for all homeowners, except that the overlap between the distributions for the 1990 and the 2010 cohorts is much less for the 5th quintile than for the 1st quintile.

The illustrations discussed in this section suggest that, *on average,* households in both the R1990 and the R2010 cohorts will have more home equity at age seventy-nine than they had when they approached retirement, at age fifty-nine. Nonetheless, although most households will have more equity at

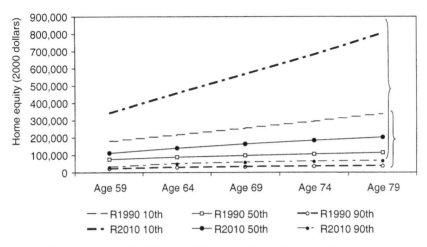

Fig. 7.45   Projected 10th, 50th, and 90th percentiles of home equity based on actual equity at age 59, cohorts retiring in 1990 and 2010, all homeowners

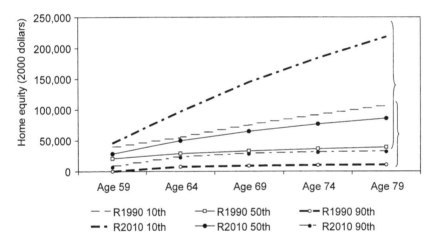

Fig. 7.46   Projected 10th, 50th, and 90th percentiles of home equity based on actual equity at age 59, cohorts retiring in 1990 and 2010, 1st quintile

seventy-nine than at fifty-nine, some households will have less. Recall that for our simulations, future home price changes are drawn from the historical distribution of price changes in that household's state. The state distributions include price decreases as well as price increases. Figure 7.48 shows the cumulative distribution of the percent changes in home equity over the twenty-year projection period over all households in our sample. The figure illustrates that there is a noticeable probability that some households will experience a fall in home equity, even though home equity will increase

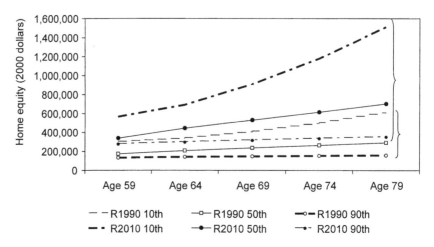

Fig. 7.47   Projected 10th, 50th, and 90th percentiles of home equity based on actual equity at age 59, cohorts retiring in 1990 and 2010, 5th quintile

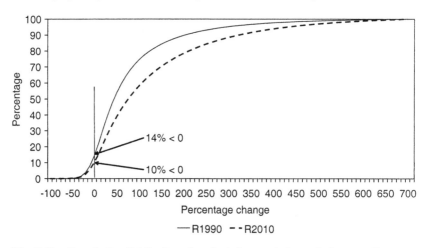

Fig. 7.48   Cumulative distribution of projected percent change in home equity between ages 59 and 79, cohorts attaining age 65 in 1990 and 2010

substantially for most households, even under the assumptions underlying these simulations. For the 1990 cohort, home equity will decline between ages fifty-nine and seventy-nine for almost 14 percent of households. For the 2010 cohort, equity will decline for about 10 percent of households.

Of course, as recent turmoil in the housing market has made clear, there can be substantial changes in average home values even in the short run. To address the potential implications of this "macro risk," we have obtained simulations for the R2010 cohort trying to incorporate recent changes in house values. To do this, we make two changes in the procedure described in the preceding. First, we take house prices in 2008, when the R2010 cohort was aged sixty-three, as a base for simulation (instead of age fifty-nine). To establish the distribution of prices in 2008, we assume that between 2004 and 2006 home prices increased in each *state* according to the OFHEO index—an average increase of 12.96 percent in 2005 and 6.10 percent in 2006, at the national level. We further assume that home prices were flat in 2007 and fell 10 percent in 2008. (The outstanding mortgage balance is assumed to decline at the same rate described in the preceding.) Second, we add three home price changes to the sample of prices from which price changes were drawn for the simulations above—zero percent for 2007, minus 10 percent for 2008, and minus 5 percent for 2009.

Figure 7.49 shows the percentiles of home prices at ages fifty-nine, sixty-four, sixty-nine, seventy-four, and seventy-nine under these assumptions. The increase in median home prices between age fifty-nine and seventy-nine is about $66,000, compared to an increase of almost $91,000 based on the assumptions underlining figure 7.45. At the 10th percentile, the increase is about $30,000, compared to about $38,000 in figure 7.45; at the 90th percentile, the increase is about $330,000, compared to $463,000 in figure 7.45.

Figure 7.50 shows that under these assumptions, almost 19 percent of households experience a decline in home equity between ages fifty-nine and seventy-nine, compared to about 10 percent under the prior assumptions, underlying the cumulative distributions for both cohorts in figure 7.48. For comparison, figure 7.50 also shows the distribution for the R1990 cohort, which is the same as the distribution shown in figure 7.48.

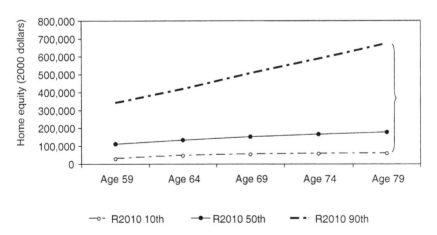

Fig. 7.49   Projected 10th, 50th, and 90th percentiles of projected home equity for the R2010 cohort, based on actual equity at age 59 adjusted for changes in home prices between ages 59 and 63 (2004 and 2008), all households

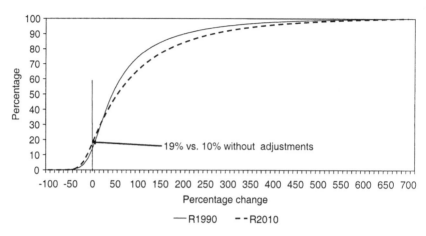

Fig. 7.50   Cumulative distribution of percent change in home equity between 59 and 79 for the R1990 and R2010 cohorts, adjusted for changes in home prices between ages 59 and 63 (2004 and 2008) for the R2010 cohort, all households

7.8   Further Evidence on the Consistency of the Ratio of Home Equity to Wealth

The simulations in section 7.7 illustrate how housing equity at older ages can fluctuate, given the home equity held by households approaching retirement. These simulations compare the distribution of home equity for two cohorts—attaining age fifty-nine in 1984 and 2004—a period over which home prices and home equity increased substantially. But what might the level of home equity at retirement be for cohorts that will retire ten or twenty or thirty years from now? Are there any "what if" assumptions that could be used to speculate about future levels of home equity at retirement? The cross-section data in section 7.5 suggest that nonhousing wealth and home equity are strongly related. The cohort data in figure 7.34 suggests relatively small cohort effects in the ratio of home equity to total (nonpension) wealth over a broad span of cohorts, attaining age sixty-five between 1970 and 2040. In this section, we consider additional data on the relationship between housing equity and wealth. We then present regression analyses to help to understand this regularity more fully.

Figure 7.51 shows the ratio of home equity to (nonpension) wealth by wealth quintile for owners for the years 1984 through 2004. The figure also shows the average of the ratio over all quintiles. Two features of the figure stand out. One is that the fluctuation over time in the average is determined almost entirely by the fluctuation in the ratio for the 5th quintile. The households in the 5th wealth quintile hold the bulk of financial wealth. As stock wealth peaked in the late 1990s, the ratio of home equity to wealth declined. The second feature of the data is the quite modest fluctuation over time for households in the 2nd through 4th quintiles. The ratios for the 1st quintile

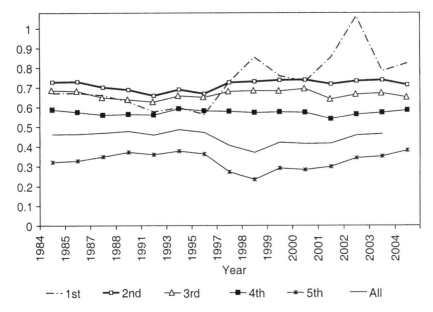

Fig. 7.51   Ratio of home equity to wealth, by wealth quintile (ratio of means)

show a large increase, with substantial fluctuation, beginning in the mid 1990s. The increase may be the result of the subprime mortgage explosion. The ratio is sensitive to nonpension wealth in the denominator, and many households in this quintile have little or no wealth other than housing equity, which may explain the substantial fluctuation.

Figure 7.52 shows several percentiles of the distribution of real home equity. The 5th percentile was close to zero for all years between 1984 and 2004. The 50th percentile and the mean increased substantially over the period. The increase at the 95th percentile was especially large, over three-fold. The increase in home equity kept pace with the increase in wealth so that the ratio of equity to wealth showed little variation over the 1984 to 2004 period. This is true for the 5th, the 50th, and the 95th percentiles, as well as the mean, as shown in figure 7.53. The percentiles in this figure, as well as the mean, are based on the average of ratios and are, thus, not dollar-weighted. The average in figure 7.51, on the other hand, is based on the ratio of means and, thus, the trend is affected by aggregate dollar values.

Finally, figure 7.54 shows the age profile of the ratio of home equity to wealth for selected years for which the SIPP data are available. The average over all years for which SIPP data are available is also shown. The key feature of the data is that, although there is random variation across ages in a given year, the age profiles of the ratio of equity to wealth are very similar across the years between 1984 and 2004. Overall, the ratio is high at young ages, bottoms in the fifties, and then increases at older ages. The age profile

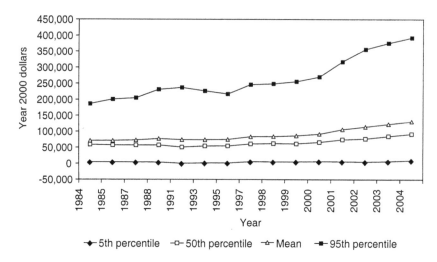

Fig. 7.52   Percentiles of home equity by year (in 2000 dollars)

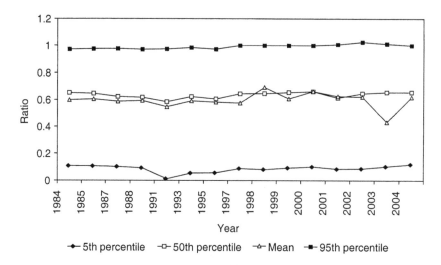

Fig. 7.53   Percentiles of the ratio of home equity to wealth, by year (ratio of means)

of equity to wealth in figure 7.54 is very similar to the cohort-based profile shown in figure 7.34. The similarity of the two figures is consistent with limited cohort effects in the cohort data.

To explore further whether forecasts of future nonhousing wealth might be used to speculate about future trends in home equity, we present some simple regression summaries of the relationship. In large part, the regression analysis is used to formalize the relationships shown in the preceding figures. Suppose that there is, on average, some "desired" proportion of

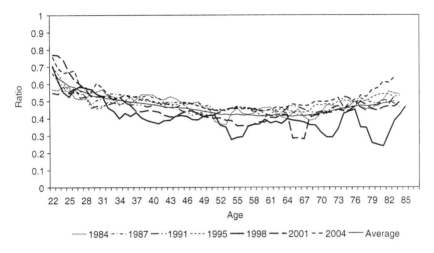

Fig. 7.54   Ratio of home equity to wealth by age and by year (ratios of means)

wealth in housing equity. At the household level, this desired proportion may vary by age, wealth, income, or family status. We consider the proportion of wealth in home equity at a point in time. We recognize that the costs of changing houses and adjusting leverage after purchasing a home may create differences for some households between their observed home equity position and their desired position. The net difference, averaged over all households, could be positive or negative. The disequilibrium may be especially large when there are abrupt changes in nonhousing wealth or when there are house price shocks affecting a particular household. Households are likely to be more able to adjust housing equity than their housing stock because they can refinance the mortgage on the existing home or take out a home equity loan on the existing house.

More formally, we analyze variation across households in the proportion of wealth that is in housing. We describe this relationship as having the form

$$E_i = [f(X_i)] \cdot W_i + \varepsilon_i,$$

where E is the housing equity of person$_i$ in year, W_i is total wealth of person$_i$—housing equity plus other nonpension wealth—and X_i is a vector of personal attributes of person$_i$. We begin with a simple ANOVA specification:

$$E_i = (c + \text{age}_{ai} + \text{wealth}_{wi} + \text{income}_{yi} + \text{familytype}_{fi} + \beta\text{children}) \cdot W_i + \varepsilon_i,$$

where c is a constant term. There are age effects for each age from twenty-four to eighty-four, wealth effects (indicated by wealth quintiles), income effects (indicated by income quintiles), family type effects (couple, single male, single female), and the number of children. The age, wealth, income, and family type effects are all normalized by setting the sum of each of the effects equal to zero. Thus, the estimated effects should be interpreted as deviations from the estimated value of $_c$, the mean of the proportion of wealth in home equity, over the whole sample.

We estimate this specification for each of the years between 1984 and 2004 for which the SIPP collected housing data. One might think that the mortgage rate (by state) should be included as a covariate in the regressions. Figure 7.55 shows the decline in mortgage rates between 1984 and 2004. The decline likely contributed substantially to the increase in home prices over this time period. We are interested, however, in the extent to which the equity proportion of wealth adjusted to the increase in home values, whether due to the decline in mortgage rates or to other factors.

For each year, seventy-two parameters are estimates. The estimated results for 1984, 1995, and 2004 are shown in tables 7A.1 to 7A.3. The comparative results for all years are shown in several figures.

The key result is in figure 7.56, which shows the estimated overall average equity to wealth ratio in each year, as well as the 95 percent confidence interval for the estimate. The average is close to 0.60 in each year, which corresponds closely to the mean and 50th percentile shown in figure 7.53. (The values in figure 7.53 are ratios of means, however, whereas the estimates in figure 7.55 reflect means of proportions, controlling for covariates.) Recall that over this period, mortgage rates declined by almost 70 percent, and real household nonhousing-nonpension wealth increased by almost 75 percent. Both trends would suggest an increase in the demand for housing and pre-

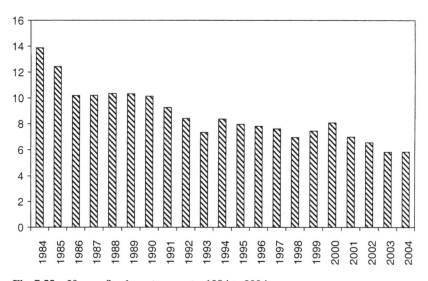

Fig. 7.55   30-year fixed mortgage rate, 1984 to 2004

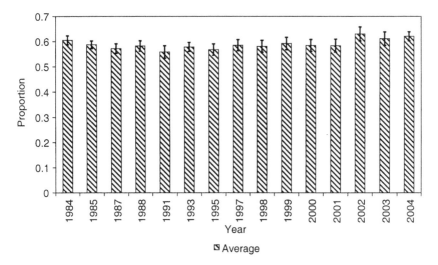

Fig. 7.56   Estimated overall average equity proportion of wealth and 95% confidence interval, by year

sumably an increase in home values. Indeed, average real home values almost doubled between 1984 and 2004. Yet, judging by the confidence intervals, the proportions of wealth in equity over the 1984 to 2001 period were typically not significantly different one from the other. The estimates show an increase in the equity proportion of wealth after 2001, but the estimates for 2002 to 2004 are often not statistically different from the estimates for many of the preceding years. Thus, it would seem that substantial active behavioral adjustments in home equity—through refinancing, home equity loans, and new purchases—were necessary to maintain a relatively constant proportion of wealth in home equity.

Although the overall average ratio of equity to wealth is rather consistent over the entire period, there is some variation over time for households in some wealth and income categories, especially high-wealth households. For example, figure 7.57 shows the estimated ratios of equity to wealth for households in the 5th wealth and 5th income quintiles and for households in the 3rd wealth and the 3rd income quintiles. Perhaps most noticeable is the pattern of equity to wealth ratios for households in the 5th quintiles. The bulk of stock market equity is held by households in these quintiles. With the run-up in the stock market in the late 1990s, the ratio of equity to wealth declined in this quintile and then increased as the stock market slumped. There is some variation over time for households in the 3rd quintiles as well, but the relative fluctuations from year to year are much less than for the wealthiest households. In addition, there seems to be little correspondence between the ratio of home equity to wealth for these households and trends in the stock market.

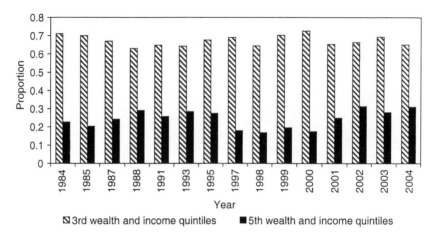

Fig. 7.57   Estimated equity to wealth ratio for households in the 3rd wealth and income quintiles and in the 5th income and wealth quintiles, by year

The estimated household type effects are shown in figure 7.58. These effects vary somewhat from year to year but typically show that the proportion of wealth in home equity is highest for single women, presumably reflecting in part the home equity of widows. The proportion is lowest for single men.

There is considerable fluctuation in the estimated age effects—across ages in a given year and across years for a given age. But there is no systematic variation across years. The average of the estimated age effects (one for each age) is shown in figure 7.59, together with the estimated effects for a few illustrative years. Except for the very young ages, the average profile is flat. This is in contrast to the U-shaped profiles shown in figures 7.34 and 7.54. The estimated profile in figure 7.59 controls for wealth and income quintile as well as for marital status and the number of children, whereas the values in figure 7.54 are not adjusted for covariates. These estimates suggest that given the covariates, the ratio of home equity to nonpension wealth varies little with age.

Finally, the estimated age effects by year can be used to consider whether there are cohort effects in the age profile of the ratio of wealth to home equity. We have estimated age effects for each of the years. Age effects by cohort can be determined by following (diagonally) through the effects by year. For example, suppose we start with the age effect of persons aged twenty-five in 1984. The cohort that is twenty-five in 1984 is twenty-six in 1985, twenty-eight in 1987, and so forth. This cohort can be followed through age forty-five in 2004. The cohort effect for a year can be added to the average proportion for that year to obtain the equity proportion of wealth for each age for each cohort. The age profiles of these equity proportions for selected

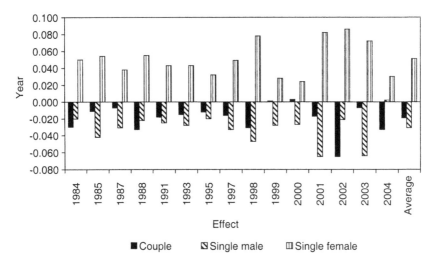

Fig. 7.58 Estimated household type effects, by year

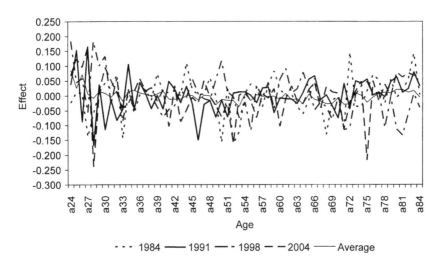

Fig. 7.59 Estimated age effects for selected years and the average effect over all years

cohorts are shown in figure 7.60. Cohort effects are not evident. These are the same cohorts shown in figure 7.34. There are two differences, however. The values in figure 7.34 are the ratio of mean of equity to the mean of wealth, whereas the estimates in figure 7.60 reflect average proportions. And the proportions in figure 7.60 are controlling for covariates—wealth quintile, income quintile, and family type. The proportions for each age, for each of the cohorts in figure 7.60, cluster around 0.60, although because some of the age effects are based on a small number of data points, some of the

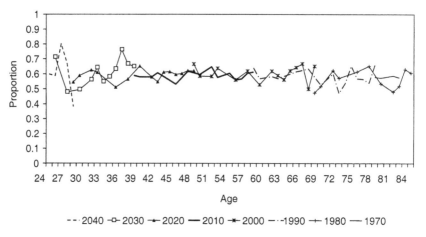

Fig. 7.60   Ratio of home equity to wealth for eight selected cohorts (identified by year cohort attains age 65), controlling for covariates

estimates fluctuate rather broadly, especially for the youngest cohorts. These proportions, when compared to the proportions in figure 7.34, suggest that the profile of proportions by age in figure 7.34 are explained by the variation in wealth and income by age.

The regression estimates show that the proportion of wealth accounted for by home equity did not vary much over the 1984 to 2004 period, even though home values and household wealth varied enormously over this period. Perhaps more important, after controlling for household wealth and household income, there are essentially no important cohort effects in the proportion of wealth allocated to home equity. Again, this is true even though home values and household wealth varied enormously over this period. Our results are in many ways complementary to the findings of Sinai and Souleles (2008), who emphasize the growth in household net worth over the 1983 to 2004 period, using data from the Survey of Consumer Finances (SCF). They find that younger elderly increased their housing debt to offset some of the rise in house values and invested some of the proceeds from the debt in other assets. This finding is consistent with our finding of a rather constant *ratio* of home equity to nonpension assets—after controlling for covariates—over this period. Sinai and Souleles also emphasize that net worth increased more than home equity, which is not inconsistent with a constant ratio of home equity to nonpension assets that we emphasize. And while we emphasize the uncertain home equity that will be available to retirees as they age, Sinai and Souleles emphasize the proportion of housing equity that older households can actually tap through reverse mortgages and is thus available to finance consumption at older ages.

A key question, then, is whether projections about household wealth in the future might be used to make informed judgments about future values of home equity. In several other papers, we have made projections of pension wealth though 2040. These projections show very large increases in 401(k) assets at retirement. But for a large fraction of households, home equity comprises a large proportion of nonpension wealth. And this wealth seems in large part preserved for use in the event of shocks to family status such as the death of a spouse or entry into a nursing home. Thus, to present a more complete picture of the assets of future retirees, it is necessary to make informed judgments about future home equity. Perhaps the consistency of the ratio of equity to wealth may help. The current turmoil in the housing market and the potential for further declines in home values, however, raises the question: will the ratio of equity to wealth continue to persist over the next five of six years. If so, this would give further support for projections based on assumptions about household wealth.

7.9   Summary and Future Work

Housing equity accounts for a large share of the nonpension assets for a large fraction of retirees. We considered first how home ownership, housing equity, and housing value have changed in recent decades and, in particular, how home equity of households approaching retirement age has changed. We find that the age profile of home ownership rates has been stable over the past two decades. This suggests that the prediction of the effect of demographic trends on the *number* of owned homes can be made with some confidence. On the other hand, there have been very large increases in the *value* of owned homes and home equity over the past two or three decades. Thus, attempts to forecast the future value of homes based on the past age profile of home values can easily miss the mark.

We examined cohort data on home value, mortgage debt, and home equity for cohorts attaining age sixty-five between the late 1970s and 2040. We used simulation methods to illustrate the potential effect of changes in home prices on the home equity of households as they age. We compare the distributions of home equity of two cohorts—one attaining retirement age in 1990 and the other in 2010—whose members entered retirement with very different levels of home equity. Our interest is in the home equity available to households when they experience a health or other shock to family status and would like to tap into their home equity. Even though recent retirees have more mortgage debt than past retirees, they are also likely to have more home equity at older ages than past retirees had. We emphasize that although, on average, the home equity of households is likely to increase as they age, for the cohorts reaching retirement age in 1990 and 2010, a noticeable proportion of households will have less home equity at older ages than they did when they retired (in real terms). Our results are based on a simulation methodology that uses the historical distribution of state-level house price changes to project changes in house prices in the future.

There is, of course, the possibility that the United States will experience future price changes outside of the historical range. Bordo (2005) shows that the past record of house prices in the United States is unusually stable when compared to other major developed countries and that a future price change outside of the recent historical range has occurred frequently in other countries.

Finally, we considered the correlation between home equity and total non-nonpension wealth in both cross-sectional and cohort data. We find that the ratio of home equity to nonpension wealth has been remarkably stable over time. We pursued analysis of this relationship using more formal regression analysis to control for other household attributes. Over the years between 1984 and 2004, we find very little change in the average proportion of household wealth allocated to home equity. There was, however, some variation in this ratio across household wealth and income categories, especially the wealthiest households. This was also a period during which the number of homeowners was increasing but at a declining rate. In addition, we find very small differences in the ratio of equity to wealth among cohorts attaining retirement age as early as the late 1960s and as late as 2040. One interpretation of these two facts is that the increase in household wealth over the period led to an increase in the dollar value of resources allocated to housing and this wealth-induced demand offset the declining rate of increase of the demand for new homes that was associated with demographic change and that might otherwise have led to a decline in home values and, thus, in housing equity. This empirical regularity leads us to consider whether projections of the home equity of future retirees might be based on forecasts of the wealth of future households.

The analysis in this chapter raises several questions for future work. In related work, we dealt with the accumulation of 401(k)-like assets through 2040. We concluded that the accumulated pension wealth of persons aged sixty-five in 2040 would likely be much larger than the pension wealth of persons retiring now. We also concluded that that aggregate pension assets in the economy would increase severalfold between now and 2040. Given the accumulation of these retirement assets, how might the build-up of home equity and mortgage debt affect overall financial well-being of future retirees? We will want also to address this question, recognizing the negative correlation between price movement in housing on the one hand and stock and bond returns on the other hand.

Appendix A

Table 7A.1   **Home equity regression for 1984**

Variable total wealth	Coefficient	Standard error	t-statistic
	0.605	0.009	66.1
a25	0.013	0.069	0.2
a26	0.009	0.043	0.2
a27	−0.138	0.031	−4.4
a28	−0.060	0.033	−1.8
a29	0.012	0.032	0.4
a30	0.043	0.030	1.5
a31	0.023	0.024	1.0
a32	0.072	0.029	2.5
a33	−0.144	0.014	−10.1
a34	0.022	0.022	1.0
a35	−0.059	0.013	−4.5
a36	0.003	0.016	0.2
a37	0.021	0.015	1.5
a38	−0.015	0.012	−1.2
a39	0.075	0.022	3.4
a40	0.008	0.015	0.5
a41	0.012	0.013	0.9
a42	0.017	0.014	1.2
a43	0.001	0.014	0.1
a44	0.111	0.016	6.8
a45	0.020	0.014	1.4
a46	0.004	0.012	0.3
a47	0.006	0.013	0.5
a48	0.061	0.017	3.6
a49	0.000	0.014	0.0
a50	−0.158	0.006	−26.1
a51	0.032	0.013	2.5
a52	−0.162	0.005	−34.8
a53	−0.122	0.006	−21.1
a54	0.009	0.012	0.8
a55	0.040	0.011	3.7
a56	0.031	0.011	2.7
a57	−0.037	0.008	−4.8
a58	0.036	0.011	3.4
a59	0.083	0.012	6.9
a60	0.023	0.012	2.0
a61	−0.001	0.009	−0.2
a62	0.006	0.011	0.5
a63	−0.037	0.007	−5.2
a64	−0.061	0.007	−8.2
a65	−0.014	0.010	−1.4
a66	0.059	0.014	4.1
a67	−0.021	0.014	−1.5
a68	−0.131	0.005	−24.3

(continued)

Table 7A.1 (continued)

Variable total wealth	Coefficient	Standard error	t-statistic
a69	−0.015	0.013	−1.1
a70	−0.002	0.012	−0.2
a71	−0.108	0.008	−13.0
a72	0.146	0.019	7.8
a73	−0.034	0.018	−1.8
a74	−0.038	0.012	−3.1
a75	0.017	0.020	0.8
a76	0.072	0.021	3.4
a77	0.053	0.017	3.0
a78	−0.026	0.015	−1.8
a79	0.055	0.024	2.3
a80	−0.006	0.023	−0.3
a81	0.020	0.029	0.7
a82	0.055	0.031	1.7
a83	0.143	0.042	3.4
a84	0.004	0.016	0.2
q2	0.119	0.016	7.7
q3	0.085	0.012	7.3
q4	0.002	0.010	0.2
q5	−0.279	0.009	−30.0
i2	0.048	0.006	8.8
i3	0.020	0.005	4.1
i4	0.002	0.004	0.4
i5	−0.100	0.003	−30.0
No. of children	0.025	0.002	15.8
Single male	−0.020	0.005	−4.2
Single female	0.050	0.005	10.7
No. of observations	12,148		
$F(72, 12{,}076)$	479.18		
Prob > F	0		
R^2	0.7407		
Adjusted R^2	0.7392		
Root MSE	47,080		

Note: MSE = mean squared error.

Table 7A.2   Home equity regression for 1995

Variable total wealth	Coefficient	Standard error	t-statistic
	0.568	0.012	48.9
a25	−0.115	0.112	−1.0
a26	0.057	0.065	0.9
a27	−0.017	0.064	−0.3
a28	0.107	0.069	1.6
a29	−0.073	0.044	−1.6
a30	−0.151	0.044	−3.4
a31	−0.066	0.027	−2.4
a32	−0.068	0.031	−2.2
a33	0.028	0.030	0.9
a34	−0.084	0.022	−3.8
a35	−0.010	0.023	−0.5
a36	−0.024	0.023	−1.0
a37	−0.006	0.022	−0.3
a38	−0.035	0.020	−1.8
a39	0.085	0.019	4.5
a40	0.002	0.015	0.1
a41	−0.051	0.016	−3.3
a42	−0.015	0.016	−1.0
a43	−0.056	0.014	−4.0
a44	−0.004	0.016	−0.3
a45	−0.025	0.015	−1.7
a46	0.027	0.015	1.8
a47	−0.026	0.013	−2.0
a48	−0.085	0.010	−8.8
a49	0.029	0.016	1.8
a50	−0.030	0.013	−2.4
a51	0.023	0.014	1.6
a52	−0.038	0.013	−3.0
a53	0.013	0.015	0.9
a54	0.037	0.015	2.5
a55	0.028	0.012	2.2
a56	0.017	0.014	1.2
a57	−0.032	0.014	−2.3
a58	0.001	0.014	0.1
a59	−0.039	0.012	−3.3
a60	−0.072	0.010	−7.2
a61	−0.058	0.012	−4.9
a62	0.022	0.014	1.6
a63	0.029	0.013	2.2
a64	−0.077	0.010	−7.6
a65	0.038	0.014	2.6
a66	−0.009	0.010	−0.9
a67	−0.034	0.012	−2.9
a68	0.035	0.014	2.6
a69	−0.041	0.013	−3.2
a70	0.050	0.014	3.5
a71	−0.013	0.015	−0.8

(continued)

Table 7A.2 (continued)

Variable total wealth	Coefficient	Standard error	t-statistic
a72	−0.011	0.015	−0.7
a73	0.050	0.018	2.8
a74	0.037	0.013	2.8
a75	0.101	0.016	6.3
a76	0.027	0.018	1.5
a77	0.024	0.014	1.7
a78	0.084	0.017	4.9
a79	−0.033	0.018	−1.9
a80	0.053	0.023	2.3
a81	0.161	0.027	6.0
a82	0.014	0.026	0.5
a83	−0.006	0.014	−0.5
a84	−0.033	0.021	−1.6
q2	0.110	0.019	5.7
q3	0.089	0.014	6.2
q4	0.026	0.012	2.1
q5	−0.233	0.012	−19.9
i2	0.020	0.005	3.8
i3	0.019	0.005	4.1
i4	−0.040	0.004	−9.2
i5	−0.060	0.004	−17.2
No. of children	0.022	0.002	11.4
Single male	−0.020	0.005	−4.3
Single female	0.032	0.005	6.8
No. of observations	11,585		
$F(72, 11,513)$	452.28		
Prob $> F$	0		
R^2	0.7388		
Adjusted R^2	0.7372		
Root MSE	53,321		

Note: MSE = mean squared error.

Table 7A.3   **Home equity regression for 2004**

Variable total wealth	Coefficient	Standard error	t-statistic
	0.621	0.009	68.0
a25	0.125	0.057	2.2
a26	0.096	0.078	1.2
a27	0.163	0.059	2.8
a28	−0.239	0.028	−8.5
a29	0.016	0.045	0.4
a30	0.095	0.031	3.0
a31	0.052	0.036	1.5
a32	0.011	0.023	0.5
a33	−0.042	0.023	−1.9
a34	−0.024	0.019	−1.3
a35	0.014	0.018	0.8
a36	0.058	0.019	3.0
a37	0.016	0.017	0.9
a38	0.028	0.017	1.7
a39	−0.018	0.014	−1.3
a40	0.020	0.016	1.3
a41	−0.104	0.012	−8.3
a42	0.034	0.013	2.6
a43	−0.088	0.011	−8.2
a44	−0.048	0.010	−4.8
a45	−0.005	0.011	−0.5
a46	−0.026	0.011	−2.5
a47	0.051	0.013	4.0
a48	−0.003	0.010	−0.3
a49	−0.033	0.010	−3.4
a50	−0.071	0.009	−7.8
a51	−0.025	0.010	−2.5
a52	−0.161	0.007	−22.9
a53	0.002	0.009	0.2
a54	0.014	0.010	1.4
a55	−0.018	0.009	−2.1
a56	−0.074	0.008	−8.9
a57	0.007	0.009	0.8
a58	−0.008	0.010	−0.8
a59	0.024	0.012	2.0
a60	−0.104	0.008	−13.7
a61	−0.010	0.010	−0.9
a62	0.033	0.010	3.2
a63	−0.019	0.009	−2.1
a64	−0.027	0.011	−2.5
a65	0.021	0.012	1.7
a66	0.045	0.011	4.1
a67	−0.043	0.011	−4.1
a68	0.031	0.010	3.0
a69	0.013	0.012	1.1
a70	0.009	0.012	0.8
a71	−0.112	0.010	−11.6

(*continued*)

Table 7A.3   (continued)

Variable total wealth	Coefficient	Standard error	t-statistic
a72	−0.020	0.012	−1.7
a73	0.016	0.013	1.2
a74	0.049	0.015	3.3
a75	−0.217	0.005	−41.4
a76	0.051	0.012	4.1
a77	−0.018	0.011	−1.6
a78	0.039	0.014	2.8
a79	0.000	0.015	0.0
a80	0.080	0.020	3.9
a81	0.063	0.018	3.6
a82	0.077	0.020	3.9
a83	0.068	0.015	4.4
a84	0.068	0.010	6.5
q2	0.094	0.015	6.2
q3	0.044	0.011	3.9
q4	−0.004	0.010	−0.4
q5	−0.256	0.009	−28.0
i2	0.044	0.004	10.5
i3	−0.015	0.004	−4.0
i4	−0.024	0.003	−7.2
i5	−0.054	0.003	−19.2
No. of children	0.011	0.002	7.0
Single male	0.002	0.004	0.6
Single female	0.030	0.004	8.6
No. of observations	21,663		
$F(72, 21,591)$	795.77		
Prob $> F$	0		
R^2	0.7263		
Adjusted R^2	0.7254		
Root MSE	95,170		

Note: MSE = mean squared error.

Appendix B

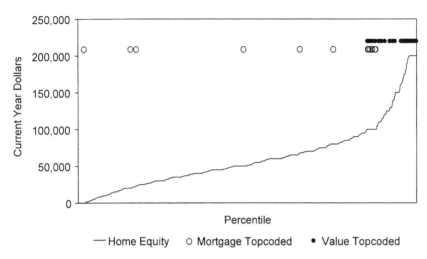

Figure 7B.1   Top-coding, cumulative distribution of equity for R1990

Figure 7B.2   Top-coding, cumulative distribution of equity for R2010

References

Banks, James, Richard Blundell, Zoe Oldfield, and James Smith. 2010. Housing price volatility and downsizing in later life. In *Research findings in the economics of aging,* ed. D. Wise, 337–79. Chicago: University of Chicago Press.

Bordo, Michael. 2005. U.S. housing boom-busts in historical perspective. Paper prepared for conference, Housing Bubbles, Indiana State University, Indianapolis.

Glaeser, Edward, Joseph Gyourko, and Raven Saks. 2005. Why is Manhattan so expensive? Regulation and the rise in housing prices. *Journal of Law and Economics* 48:331–69.

Green, Richard, and Susan Wachter. 2008. The housing finance revolution. In *Housing, housing finance, and monetary policy.* Kansas City, MO: Federal Reserve Bank of Kansas City.

Greenspan, Alan, and James Kennedy. 2009. Sources and uses of equity extracted from homes. *Oxford Review of Economic Policy* 24 (1): 120–44.

Himmelberg, Charles, Christopher Mayer, and Todd Sinai. 2005. Assessing high house prices: Bubbles, fundamentals, and misperceptions. *Journal of Economic Perspectives* 19 (4): 67–92.

Hoynes, Hilary, and Daniel McFadden. 1997. The impact of demographics on housing and nonhousing wealth in the United States. In *The economic effects of aging in the United States and Japan,* ed. M. Hurd and N. Yashiro, 153–94. Chicago: University of Chicago Press.

Mankiw, N. Gregory, and David Weil. 1989. The baby boom, the baby bust, and the housing market. *Regional Science and Urban Economics* 19:235–58.

McFadden, Daniel. 1994. Demographics, the housing market, and the welfare of the elderly. In *Studies in the economics of aging,* ed. D. Wise, 225–88. Chicago: University of Chicago Press.

Megbolugbe, Issac, Jarjisu Sa-Aadu, and James Shilling. 1997. Oh yes, the elderly will reduce housing equity under the right circumstances. *Journal of Housing Research* 8 (1): 53–74.

Poterba, James. 1991. House price dynamics: The role of tax policy and demography. *Brookings Papers on Economic Activity,* Issue no. 2: 143–203. Washington, DC: Brookings Institution.

Poterba, James, Steven Venti, and David A. Wise. 2007a. Pension assets of the baby boom cohort: The effects of shifting from defined benefit pension plans to 401(k) plans. *Proceedings of the National Academy of Sciences* 104 (3):

———. 2007b. The rise of 401(k) plans, lifetime earnings, and wealth at retirement. NBER Working Paper no. 13091. Cambridge, MA: National Bureau of Economic Research.

———. 2008. New estimates of the future path of 401(k) assets. In *Tax policy and the economy.* Vol. 22, ed. J. Poterba, 43–80. Chicago: University of Chicago Press.

———. 2009. The decline of defined benefit retirement plans and asset flows. In *Social Security policy in a changing environment,* ed. J. Brown, J. Liebman, and D. Wise, 333–79. Chicago: University of Chicago Press.

Shiller, Robert. 2008. Understanding recent trends in house prices and home ownership. In *Housing, housing finance, and monetary policy.* Kansas City, MO: Federal Reserve Bank of Kansas City.

Sinai, Todd, and Nicholas S. Souleles. 2008. Net worth and housing equity in retirement. In *Recalibrating retirement spending and saving,* ed. J. Ameriks and O. Mitchell, 46–77. New York: Oxford University Press.

Venti, Steven, and David Wise. 1990. But they don't want to reduce housing equity. In *Issues in the economics of aging,* ed. D. Wise, 13–32. Chicago: University of Chicago Press.

———. 2001. Aging and housing equity. In *Innovations for financing retirement,* ed. O. Mitchell, Z. Bodie, P. B. Hammond, and S. Zeldes, 254–81. Philadelphia: University of Pennsylvania Press.

———. 2004. Aging and housing equity: Another look. In *Perspectives in the economics of aging,* ed. D. Wise, 127–80. Chicago: University of Chicago Press.

Comment   Thomas Davidoff

This chapter forecasts the distribution of future home equity among retirees. This involves projecting the joint distribution of future homeownership rates, home prices, and equity to value ratios. The most noteworthy findings are that households face a wide range of plausible home equity changes, with an interquartile range of approximately zero to almost 200 percent for twenty-year changes in real value. The authors also find that the ratio of average home equity to average total nonpension wealth by age and by wealth quintile has been almost constant over the last two decades, despite large changes in leverage and asset values.

I have three sets of comments. The first considers the forecasts in the context of an equilibrium model. Second, the forecasting methodology has important, albeit offsetting, biases. Third, it is not clear what we learn about sufficiency of retirement savings from the distribution of feasible home equity levels.

What, If Anything, Would a Model Tell Us?

The forecasts of future home equity center around current debt-to-equity ratios and home values and home price appreciation over the last three decades. Simulations based on relatively recent history may not reflect the true distribution of future home purchases, leverage, or prices. Investors in real estate and mortgage backed securities have learned that the hard way over the last two years. For that reason, it would be nice to appeal to a dynamic stochastic general equilibrium model of home prices and mortgage demand into which different paths for some underlying fundamental, such as productivity, could be planted. Unfortunately, such a model would be either intractable or incapable of matching many empirically relevant moments.

Forecasting home prices based on an economic model based on some kind of rational expectations would involve forecasting future discounted

Thomas Davidoff is an assistant professor in the Sauder School of Business at the University of British Columbia.

"dividends" from homes. Two major problems with this approach are that the dividends that homes offer their owners are not observable and that the appropriate discount rate for housing dividends is difficult to characterize.

The dividends to owner housing are not observable because homeowners do not pay themselves rent. The market rent for units comparable to owner homes may not reflect a dividend in any meaningful way. Rental units are typically different from owner units, and changes in rent will partly reflect demand for rental, as opposed to owner, units. Also, the utility flow to an owner may not change when market rents change. For these reasons, we do not know the time series relationship between, say, gross domestic product (GDP) and dividends to homeowners.

The appropriate discount rate for housing is difficult to evaluate for a variety of reasons. The discount rate might be decomposed into a riskless rate, a risk premium, and expected growth. The risk premium is problematic in part because home equity is commonly, but not always, held until death. The option structure induced by the availability of remaining in the home implies that older owners may not be risk averse toward home price variability. Sinai and Souleles (2005) show that for younger owners, variability in housing prices may make a home more valuable for hedging purposes. Given that economists do not have the tools to assess what the right price level is for housing, it is unrealistic to expect a model to deliver an accurate expectation of growth even in a single housing market. Calibrating a distribution for price growth by location is far beyond the current state of economic science. Van Nieuwerburgh and Weill (2006) calibrate differences in housing costs in a much simplified model.

With these caveats in mind, it is reasonable to think that home values should be highly correlated in a long time series with something like discounted GDP. Indeed, I find that over the last three decades, at a five-year horizon, changes in the national Office of Federal Housing Enterprise Oversight (OFHEO) repeated sale home price index have had a correlation of .3 with changes in GDP divided by the ten-year treasury rate minus lagged Consumer Price Index (CPI) growth, when both series are deflated by the nonhousing CPI.

Particularly given the results on the constancy of the ratio of home equity to total nonpension wealth, it would be interesting to compare plausible distributions of home equity under the authors' methodology to forecast distributions based on a constant ratio of home equity to wealth and estimated values of wealth based on simply discounted GDP. One might then recognize that there are a range of multipliers of this value that housing markets would apply, depending on the heat of the market, and depending on how elastic supply is in a given market. An approach along these lines would have the benefit of time series for GDP, interest rates, and inflation that are more than twice as long as the OFHEO series and include the Depression years.

Interestingly, changes to the Standard & Poor's (S&P) 500 index have also been highly correlated with discounted GDP over long horizons, but negatively correlated with changes in home values (as the authors observe). It bears mention that the recent extreme event of rapidly decreasing home prices has been matched by a large drop in stock market values. Any future work that tries to estimate a joint distribution of housing and total wealth must decide whether to trust intuition, which says that there should be a positive correlation between stocks and housing, or our own eyes, which have seen a negative correlation for as long as we have data. Coastal housing prices have drifted away from home prices in the rest of the country over the last two decades. Presumably, this has to do with changes in the wage premium to education driving up demand for locations blessed with amenities and agglomeration opportunities. Whether this trend continues or reverses will have important effects on the distribution of both wealth and home equity. Assuming that the next T years will look like the past three decades, as the authors do, assumes that growth in home prices across regions will continue to diverge.

A problem in applying standard models to equilibrium in housing markets is the empirical retention of home equity late into life among the elderly. One would expect to see transitions into rental status, smaller homes, or at least home equity borrowing among older households with high levels or changes to the ratio of home equity to wealth. As the authors have shown in previous work, such transitions have been the exception rather than the rule in recent decades. The fact that older homeowners have retained home equity is presumably part of the reason the demographics-based prediction of Mankiw and Weil (1989) went awry.

A question in forecasting future home equity is, thus, whether households will become more like life-cycle consumers facing complete markets. If so, we would expect to see much reduced equity to debt ratios in the future. The reverse mortgage market has grown rapidly in percentage terms recently, but on a small base. All the results in the paper rely on an assumption that there will not be major growth in that market, or that if there is, it will be accompanied by considerable price appreciation. In particular, the authors assume that homeowners will reduce mortgage debt at a rate matching historical average amortization. Historical data do not include jumps in home equity borrowing among the elderly, but it does not seem right to assign such a jump zero probability.

The constancy of the ratio of home equity to wealth over time, shown visually in figures 7.51 through 7.54 is intriguing. Part of what makes the result interesting is the fact that there is considerable cross-sectional heterogeneity in the ratio. Home value is nonhomothetic in wealth, and the ratio of home equity to total wealth is, too. The equity to wealth ratio is decreasing in wealth, but constant within wealth deciles over time, despite growing wealth by quantile. A natural justification for these results is that home values were rising relative to overall wealth. This is true for the majority of households with limited stock market wealth.

The absence of large cohort effects in the ratio of home equity to wealth is noteworthy. This nonrelationship appears to mask numerous offsetting effects: cohorts are becoming wealthier, nonhousing assets are growing in value, older households have lower housing value to other asset ratios, older households are less leveraged than other households, and later cohorts are becoming more leveraged. That these and other effects have offset historically does not mean that they will in the future.

A mechanism that also seems to be at work is that leverage has increased with time as the lending market became (until the last few months) looser and looser. This looseness doubtless had significant effects on housing values (see, e.g., Ortalo-Magné and Rady 2006). Following the logic of Artle and Varaiya (1978), we would expect homes to be more valuable to buyers anticipating the ability to cash out capital gains through reverse mortgages. The elasticity of price with respect to elder borrowing capacity would have to be large for current ratios of equity to wealth to withstand a large increase in borrowing after retirement.

Calibrating a Future Home Price Distribution

The authors use historical changes in OFHEO home prices by state to calibrate a distribution of future home price changes. In particular, the distribution of T year changes in log home prices for households in a given state is obtained by drawing a sum (with replacement) of historical one-year OFHEO price changes in that state. Even assuming that the three decades of data available to the authors have reflected the true distribution of price changes going forward, there are significant biases to the volatility and, possibly, mean of the distribution based on the OFHEO data and sampling approach.

There is downward bias in the volatility of forecast home values because state average price changes are less volatile than metropolitan home prices, which are, in turn, less volatile than changes in value in neighborhoods and individual homes. The move from metropolitan means to individual results is particularly problematic, given the large magnitude of home improvement expenditures (thousands of dollars per year, on average, with wide variance) and stochastic depreciation. Possibly operating in the opposite direction is the fact that home price changes are serially correlated. National home prices, and particularly prices in large coastal cities, have followed two up-and-down cycles over the life of the OFHEO data. If we believe that home prices cannot deviate too far from fundamental values before correcting, large price swings may show up in simulations that would be unlikely to occur if longer horizon draws were taken. In the authors' defense, there are only two long cycles to draw from over the last thirty years, and we just witnessed an almost uninterrupted decade-long run-up in prices.

As the authors recognize, the OFHEO data, which is confined to repeated sales of new homes, exhibits less volatility than the Case-Shiller data. The latter data is less geographically representative but includes homes of very high and low value that may have more price volatility than homes that are subject to conventional mortgages. While the repeated sale methodology deals better with problems of composition than a median home index, if home builders sell disproportionately in down markets (as they cannot wait for higher prices as well as homeowners who receive a dividend), then excess depreciation of new homes will bias volatility of a repeated sales index downward.

What Does Home Equity Tell Us about Retirement Readiness?

The authors observe that home equity is rarely spent absent death of a spouse or entry of a household member into long-term care. In the case of bequests, it is not clear that more home equity is better than less. Heirs may be worse off, not better off, if home prices rise. In the case of long-term care, prices are correlated cross sectionally with housing prices. If the elasticity of care costs with respect to housing prices is large (incorporating effect of labor costs on both), then again utility may be lower in high price states than low. One way to think about this is that rather than the national CPI for all goods, housing should be deflated by by regional CPI (where available), for all nonhousing goods. Oddly, the two sets of series are sufficiently highly correlated that this likely induces little bias.

Another consideration is that older homeowners have some ability to time the sale of their homes. Given serial correlation in prices, it is not impossible to believe that older owners could avoid selling during market troughs. In that case, the distribution of future home equity may be downward biased.

In summary, the authors have presented a strikingly wide range of plausible home equity wealth values for future retirees. They have also documented the intriguing fact that home equity to wealth ratios are quite stable across time and cohorts. The difficulty of modeling equilibrium in housing markets leaves us with little choice but to assume that the future will look like the past, but there are good reasons to think that it may not. Chief among these reasons are growth in the home equity lending market both before and after retirement; the recent volatility of housing prices, unmatched in the last three decades; and the divergence of coastal from noncoastal housing prices. The authors have identified an important task for future researchers: providing a justification for the near constant equity to wealth ratio in the face of major and imperfectly correlated changes to nonhousing wealth, home prices, and leverage.

References

Artle, Roland, and Pravin Varaiya. 1978. Life-cycle consumption and homeowner-ship. *Journal of Economic Theory* 18 (1): 38–58.

Mankiw, Gregory, and David Weil. 1989. The baby boom, the baby bust, and the housing market. *Regional Science and Urban Economics* 19:235–58.

Ortalo-Magné, Francois, and Sven Rady. 2006. Housing market dynamics: On the contribution of income shocks and credit constraints. *Review of Economic Studies* 73: 459–85.

Sinai, Todd, and Nicholas Souleles. 2005. Owner occupied housing as insurance against rent risk. *Quarterly Journal of Economics* 120 (2): 763–89.

Van Nieuwerburgh, Stijn, and Pierre-Olivier Weill. 2006. Why has house price dispersion gone up? New York University and University of California at Los Angeles, Working Paper.

Aging Populations, Pension Operations, Potential Economic Disappointment, and Its Allocation

Sylvester J. Schieber

8.1   Introduction

Much has been written about population aging and its economic implications. A great deal of this discussion has focused on the retirement systems that exist in various parts of the world and how they will fare under the aging phenomenon. Some analysts conclude that we must radically modify many of the retirement systems now in operation in order to deal with new economic realities that are unfolding before us.

There are many instances where the adjustment of pension policy to address the population aging issue has been to move systems that have been traditionally financed on a pay-as-you-go basis more toward being funded. A case can be made that the United States did this in the early 1980s when policymakers adopted legislation that resulted in the build-up of the Social Security trust funds from nearly nothing in 1983 to more than $2 trillion today. Chile did this when it abandoned its traditional pay-as-you-go defined benefit pension for an individual account program in the early 1980s. Australia followed suit in the 1990s. Sweden did not go as far as Australia or Chile but implemented a pension reform that included a 2.5 percent of covered payroll mandatory defined contribution account for all workers. Canada followed the U.S. lead in the 1990s, to an extent, by increasing the funding of its national pension during its post-World War II baby boom generation's working career but took a very different path on how the accumulating assets

Sylvester J. Schieber is retired from Watson Wyatt Worldwide and currently works as an independent consultant.

The analysis and conclusions presented here are the author's and should not be attributed to anyone else. I wish to thank Steven Nyce of Watson Wyatt Worldwide for his help with various computations presented throughout the chapter and Steven Venti for helpful comments on the chapter at the time of its presentation.

would be invested. Germany also moved toward greater pension funding, but more passively, by limiting the cost of their pay-as-you-go national pension with the implication that reduced future benefits under the new cost constraint would result in workers saving more to meet their own retirement needs in the future.

While many countries have changed their course on funding their retirement systems, it is not always clear that the economic results are as straightforward as they might seem on the surface. In the next section of the chapter, we explore the alternative economic perspectives of pension funding. From a microeconomic perspective, many workers may not discern any practical effect from the restructuring of the approach to financing their pensions. Even from a macroeconomic perspective, there are questions over whether some of the move toward pension funding that has arisen in recent years is more cosmetic than real.

In virtually every case in which a country has adopted policies in recent years to increase the funding of their future retirement claims, a major motivation has been to ameliorate the economic implications of population aging. Axel Börsch-Supan (this volume) shows that moving to a savings based retirement system improves the economic outlook that even rapidly aging countries face. To date, however, there has been relatively little analysis of whether pension funding has the potential to provide the sort of economic growth that citizens in many of the developed countries of the world have come to expect. In the third section of this chapter, we explore some of the implications of diverse demographic scenarios under pay-as-you-go versus funded pension systems.

A fundamental economic issue that population aging may pose in many societies is that their labor forces will grow more slowly in the future than in the past. This slower labor force growth has two important implications. First, labor force growth rates are one of the primary drivers that underlie economic growth. Slower labor force growth will mean slower economic growth and diminished contributions to improving living standards that have been realized in virtually all developed economies of the world since the end of World War II. Second, a growing aged population in the face of a stable or diminished workforce implies significant increases in aged dependency. The combination of these forces will limit future growth in living standards in the developed economies of the world. In the fourth section of the chapter, we explore how the pension systems may be used to allocate the economic disappointment that aging societies will face unless they can find policies that will grow the economic resources available to them.

If our economies cannot meet public expectations about economic performance, the method for allocating the disappointment is an important policy issue. In that regard, pension policy may play a significant role although other means of partially addressing the matter may be available to policymakers. Many retirement systems have been structured traditionally to provide retirees with increasing levels of benefits linked to growing wages or workers' productivity levels. If total output in an economy is unsatisfactory but retirees are allocated benefits directly correlated to rising worker productivity, then workers and their dependents will be disappointed. Our ability to encourage workers to achieve even higher levels of productivity may be significantly limited if we cannot reward them for the added contribution. On the other hand, if we let workers enjoy the fruits of their rising productivity rates, we run the risk that retirees' standards of living might actually fall from one generation to the next. If neither outcome is viewed as satisfactory, one alternative is to encourage higher levels of labor force participation from all segments of the population beyond normal school ages.

Some societies may attempt to address the aging issue by shifting from pay-as-you-go financing of their pension systems to prefunded arrangements. Our analysis suggests that some countries face such significant demographic shifts toward older populations that this will offer little practical relief. In these cases, the whole concept of retirement that has persisted over much of the past century may need to be revisited.

8.2 Retirement Plans as a Consumption Allocation Mechanism

Retirement systems are income transfer mechanisms that facilitate the distribution of goods and services produced by workers to the elderly, nonworking members of a society. At a given point in time, the utilization and productivity of labor and capital limit the total output in an economy. Workers receive their share of output in the form of wages. Owners of capital receive their share of output in the form of returns on their investments. Retirees can receive a share of output either through their ownership rights of capital or from transfers from the wages paid to workers.

In the first type, the capital-based retirement system, workers accumulate their ownership of capital during their working career. They do so by saving a portion of their earnings along with employer contributions and letting the total savings accumulate with interest until they retire. During retirement, retirees liquidate their assets to finance their consumption needs. In this regard, the retirement plan is a mechanism to transfer consumption rights across time periods. This intertemporal transfer of consumption is accomplished by the buying and selling of assets. Accruing pension liabilities are "funded" as the rights to future pension benefits are earned in defined contribution plans. In funded defined benefit plans, they are approximately funded on the basis of actuarial estimates of what is required to meet future obligations as they are earned.

Financing retirees' consumption through intergenerational transfers can take place either on an informal basis or through more formal arrangements. The informal arrangements are typically worked out within families, where a younger generation commits to support its elders when they are no longer able to work. Governments generally sponsor formal arrangements although some employers sponsor retirement plans that are intergenerational rather than intertemporal transfer mechanisms. These plans are known as pay-as-you-go plans because they take money from current workers' production and transfer it to current retirees.

In both capital-based and pay-as-you-go plans, workers forego some current earnings and, thus, some portion of consumption during the earning period to finance retirement consumption. In funded retirement vehicles, workers do this by purchasing assets that earn returns while held and that are sold in retirement. In pay-go retirement systems, workers do it by surrendering a share of their earnings, which are then transferred to retirees.

8.2.1   Retirement Savings and Personal Wealth Accumulation

To show how alternative pension financing structures operate from a worker's perspective, consider an example of a worker who begins a career at age twenty-five earning $35,000 per year. Assume this individual has perfect foresight and knows that his pay will increase 4 percent per year until he reaches age sixty-five, when he will retire and receive a pension that is 70 percent of his disposable income. His disposable income is his total wage minus what he has to contribute to a pension in order to finance his retirement income. To simplify the process of determining how much the worker should save, we assume he knows that he will live to be 81.5 years of age. We also assume the worker anticipates receiving an annual rate of return on his assets of 5 percent per year.

If everything goes according to plan, this worker will earn roughly $161,600 in his last year of employment. After his retirement savings are put aside, his disposable income will be approximately $135,700 that year. As it turns out, this worker will need to save 16 percent of his annual earnings each year in order to fulfill his work and retirement plans. If he does that, he should be able to receive an annuity of $113,100 per year for each year of retirement, 70 percent of his final year's earnings, or about 83 percent of disposable income in his final year of work. This pattern of asset accumulation and net balances are reflected in figure 8.1.

Over the working period, the worker's steady saving plus interest accruing on accumulated assets gradually accelerates the growth in assets. From a macroeconomic perspective, contributions to the plan are reflected as savings accruing in the economy. After retirement, the assets are steadily depleted over the worker's remaining lifetime and run out when he dies. Net savings over the worker's lifetime, in this example, are zero. Had he wished to leave a bequest to heirs, the worker would have had to save more during his working life or spend less during retirement.

If the same worker described in the preceding is covered by a pay-go retirement plan, the dynamics of his accumulating retirement wealth are considerably different than in a funded pension plan. First, his annual contributions to the retirement system are paid out to current retirees. Second, rather than becoming part of an accumulation of capital that can be invested in the economy, in most cases his contributions merely purchase an entitlement to a benefit at retirement age. The pattern of this transaction is reflected in figure 8.2, which turns out to be a mirror image of figure 8.1. In this case, the "accumulated savings" from the worker's perspective is the sum of the obligations owed to the worker. It grows on a gradually accelerating basis until the worker reaches age sixty-five and then is paid off over the remainder of his lifetime as annual retirement benefits.

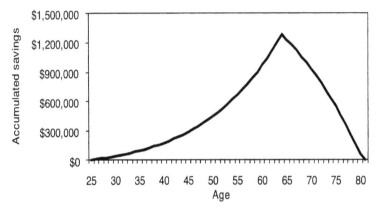

Fig. 8.1   Accumulated savings of a hypothetical worker participating in a funded pension plan
Source: Calculated by the author.

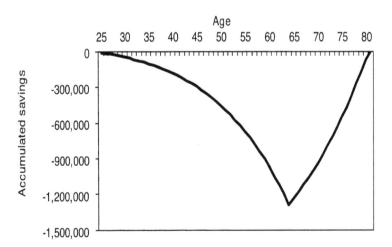

Fig. 8.2   Accumulated savings of a hypothetical worker participating in a pay-as-you-go pension plan
Source: Calculated by the author.

Table 8.1   **Pension operations from a worker's perspective under alternative financing mechanisms**

	Pay-as-you-go plans	Funded plans
Workers	Contribute taxes from wages	Save from wages to buy assets
Net effect while working	Reduces consumption during work life	Reduces consumption during work life
Retirees	Receive benefits from workers' current taxes	Receive interest and sell assets to workers
Net effect while retired	Use benefit income to finance consumption	Use asset income to finance consumption

Source: Developed by the author.

Pay-as-you-go retirement plans are intergenerational transfer mechanisms. In this case, workers contribute to the plan while working to support contemporary retirees. By contributing to the system during the working career, workers earn "rights" when they retire to have the next generation support their consumption needs. Paul Samuelson, the Nobel laureate economist, characterized these latter plans as "consumption loan" devices (Samuelson 1958). The theory is that when workers pay the payroll tax to support such systems, they forego consumption at the time with the implied understanding that they will be repaid when they reach retirement age.

From the perspective of the worker, the accumulation of pension rights through a pay-go social security system is no different than accumulating wealth through personal savings or a funded pension. The operations of the two types of plans are summarized from a worker's perspective in table 8.1. In both cases, the worker gives up consumption during the working career and stores the value of that foregone consumption in a personal retirement portfolio that is cashed in to support consumption during the retirement period.

The suggestion that these two types of plans are essentially the same in terms of their consumption effects from a worker's perspective is not to suggest that they may have very different real and perceived legal and political risks associated with them. In terms of the dynamics of an individual accruing benefit rights during a working career and receiving benefits during retirement, there is little practical difference. Indeed, there have been many economic analyses of the economic status of individuals approaching retirement that have treated social security wealth, pension, and retirement plan savings and other personal wealth as equivalent (Moore and Mitchell 2000; Poterba, Venti, and Wise 2007).

8.2.2   Retirement Wealth Accumulation and National Savings

Over the years, there has been a considerable body of economic research developed regarding the implications of pay-go pensions for national savings rates, most of it developed by U.S. economists in the context of the U.S. Social Security program. For example, in 1974, Martin Feldstein estimated that for each $100 increase in social security wealth in the United States, private saving was reduced by $2.10 (Feldstein 1974). Shortly after his study was released, Dean Leimer and Selig Lesnoy, two analysts working for the U.S. Social Security Administration, discovered a computation mistake in Feldstein's analysis, which they corrected, and extended the computation period. Their estimate was half of Feldstein's and was statistically equivalent to zero (Leimer and Lesnoy 1982). In other words, Leimer and Lesnoy concluded that Social Security had no effect on U.S. savings rates. Feldstein subsequently argued that the difference in results of the two analyses was because Leimer and Lesnoy extended the data series to 1974, without taking into consideration the program changes adopted in 1972 (Feldstein 1982). In 1996, Feldstein updated the model and estimated that a $1 increase in Social Security wealth reduced savings by two to three cents. While two or three cents may seem trivial, Feltstein estimated that the U.S. Social Security system reduced personal saving by $416 billion in 1992, compared to $248 billion of actual savings—a reduction of 63 percent of potential personal saving (Feldstein 1996).

The matter of whether our Social Security program contributes to national savings was somewhat muddied when Congress adopted the provisions in 1983 that have led to a substantial buildup in the trust funds. Table 8.2 shows that since the passage of the 1983 funding requirements, tax revenues flowing into the Social Security trust funds has consistently exceeded expenditures under the program. How this asset buildup is interpreted also is important for thinking about the implications of alternative ways to deal with the program's projected financing shortfalls.

In some circles, the 1983 amendments to the Social Security Act have been regarded as "funding" a portion of the baby boomers' retirement benefits. Since that time, the Social Security trust fund assets have grown from $31 billion in 1984 to $2,048 billion at the end of 2006, although 47 percent of that growth has been government-credited interest on the accumulating assets, which are held in long-term Federal Government bonds. Despite the substantial growth in the Social Security trust funds over the last twenty years, there has been a considerable debate over whether the accumulating trust fund assets have added to the level of national savings. This debate centers on how holding the accumulating trust fund entirely in government bonds affects the government's other fiscal operations.

The analysts who argue that the U.S. accumulating trust fund has not added to national savings contend that the U.S. government has run larger deficits in its other fiscal operations due to the accumulating trust fund. That is, having the surplus annual revenue available to Social Security relieves policymakers from having to raise funds elsewhere to finance other government operations. A special commission established by President George W.

Table 8.2   U.S. Social Security cash flows and Federal Government unified budget operations for selected years (in billions of U.S. $)

| | U.S. Social Security trust fund operations | | | U.S. Government unified budget operations | | |
Year	Tax revenues	Current expenditures	Net surplus	Current receipts	Current expenditures	Surplus or (–) deficit
1984	183.1	180.4	2.7	1,112.5	1,256.6	–144.1
1985	197.5	190.6	6.9	1,213.5	1,366.1	–152.6
1986	212.8	201.5	11.3	1,289.3	1,459.1	–169.8
1987	225.6	209.1	16.5	1,403.2	1,535.8	–132.6
1988	255.2	222.5	32.7	1,502.2	1,618.7	–116.5
1989	276.7	236.2	40.5	1,626.3	1,735.6	–109.3
1990	301.1	253.1	48.0	1,707.8	1,872.6	–164.8
1991	307.8	274.2	33.6	1,758.8	1,976.7	–217.9
1992	317.2	291.9	25.3	1,843.7	2,140.4	–296.7
1993	327.7	308.8	18.9	1,945.8	2,218.4	–272.6
1994	350.0	323.0	27.0	2,089.0	2,290.8	–201.8
1995	364.8	339.8	25.0	2,212.6	2,397.6	–185.0
1996	385.7	353.6	32.1	2,376.1	2,492.1	–116.0
1997	413.9	369.1	44.8	2,551.9	2,568.6	–16.7
1998	439.9	382.3	57.6	2,724.2	2,633.4	90.8
1999	471.2	392.9	78.3	2,895.0	2,741.0	154.0
2000	504.8	415.1	89.7	3,125.9	2,886.5	239.4
2001	529.1	438.9	90.2	3,124.2	3,056.4	67.8
2002	546.3	461.7	84.6	2,980.7	3,224.0	–243.3
2003	546.9	479.1	67.8	3,012.8	3,426.4	–413.6
2004	568.7	501.6	67.1	1,880.3	2,293.0	–412.7
2005	607.8	529.9	77.9	2,153.9	2,472.2	–318.3
2006	642.5	555.4	87.1	2,407.3	2,655.4	–248.2
2007				2,568.2	2,730.2	–162.0

Sources: U.S. Social Security Administration, *2008 Annual Report of the Board of Trustees of the Federal Old-Age and Survivors Insurance and Federal Disability Insurance Trust Funds,* and U.S. Office of Management and Budget, *Fiscal Year 2009 Budget of the U.S. Government, Historical Tables.*

Bush to make recommendations on Social Security reform fell into this camp. They acknowledged the theoretical possibility that the trust fund accumulation could add to national savings but concluded that the reality since the passage of the 1983 funding legislation had taught the "nation a clear lesson about how unlikely this is as a practice. The availability of Social Security surpluses provided the government with an opportunity to use these surpluses to finance other government spending, rather than saving and investing for the future" (President's Commission to Strengthen Social Security 2001, 38).

Diamond and Orszag (2004), two economists and noted participants in the debate over U.S. Social Security reform, reach the opposite conclusion. They looked at congressional attempts to reduce federal budget deficits throughout the 1980s and early 1990s that ultimately resulted in surpluses toward the end of the century. On the basis of the efforts to reduce the unified budget deficits, Diamond and Orszag conclude that it is plausible that U.S. policymakers were not raiding the Social Security surpluses to finance other government operations. In addition, they note that if policymakers were pursuing such a policy, financing general government operations with payroll taxes would have imposed a greater burden on lower-wage workers than financing such operations out of the more progressive U.S. federal income tax. Given that people with lower incomes generally have higher marginal propensities to consume, such a policy would have reduced disposable income for people with high marginal propensities to consume and raised it for people with high marginal propensities to save. The net result would have been to increase the national saving level and reduce consumption levels accordingly.

To some extent, it is impossible to know whether the U.S. Social Security trust fund balance represents wealth that will benefit future generations because the answer partly depends on unobservable or counterfactual behavior. Smetters (2003) argues, however, that by comparing variations in the financing of other government functions to the accumulation in the retirement system over time, we can tell whether the systematic growth in the pension trust funds has been paralleled by changes to the other balances. He devised an empirical test to see what happened in the United States. The logic of his model is that if the accumulating trust fund has not added to national savings, each dollar of growth in the trust fund should be offset by a dollar increase in the deficit. If the growing pension balances are being saved, then there should be no change in other government net deficits as the pension surplus grows. In his favored specification of the model utilizing data from 1949 through 2002, Smetters found that for every dollar added to the trust funds, the other government net deficits increased by $2.76. He concludes that not only are the accumulating Social Security surpluses spent elsewhere in government, but that they act as some sort of accelerator to deficit financing of other government operations.

Nataraj and Shoven (2004) expanded and updated Smetters's analysis. They note that Smetters only looked at the implications of U.S. Social Security trust fund accumulations on other federal fiscal operations. They widened the analysis to include all U.S. government trust funds because the Social Security trusts represent only about half of all government trust funds, and there was considerable correlation between their accumulations over time. In their preferred estimate, Nataraj and Shoven found that a dollar increase in the total federal trust funds increased federal deficits in other operations by $1.73, a result that was not statistically different from one. Carrying the analysis further, they broke their analytical period into two periods, 1949 to 1969 and 1970 to 2003. This split was important because in 1970, the U.S. government modified its budgeting procedures to explicitly combine the trust fund and other government operations into budget considerations on a unified basis. Before then, each had been considered separately. For the period before the budgets were unified, Nataraj and Shoven found that the accumulating trust funds were not statistically associated with the deficits run in other government operations. After 1970, the accumulating trust funds did lead to added deficits in other government operations, once again statistically on a dollar-for-dollar basis.

Bosworth and Burtless (2004) extended this sort of analysis in another way with two different groups of government entities. First they considered the pension systems sponsored by state governments in the United States for their own employees. At the end of 2000, these state pensions held approximately $2.3 trillion in assets, about half the amount held by private employer plans at that time. In this case, they found that as the pension funds increased their holdings by $100, the deficits in the states' nonpension accounts increased by about $8, an amount statistically equivalent to zero. These state systems are significantly different from the federal Social Security system in that they are not considered in the unified budget context of the federal program. In addition, many of these systems have funding requirements, with contributions held in strictly segregated, trusteed accounts and invested in broadly diversified real assets. Finally, many U.S. state governments have strict balanced budgeting provisions embedded in their constitutions. State-level pension systems in the United States operate much like ordinary funded pensions offered by private-sector employers operating their plans under U.S. legal funding requirements.

In the second part of their analysis, Bosworth and Burtless studied the pension funding in national pension systems and the government deficits associated with other government operations. They had data on thirteen Organization for Economic Cooperation and Development (OECD) countries from the period 1970 through 2000. They found that a 1 billion currency unit increase in social insurance trust funds increased the government deficit in other operations by 1.26 billion currency units. After adjustments for autocorrelation in their data series, this dropped to 0.57 billion currency units. When they limited the analysis to five countries whose policies require them to fund a portion of their national pensions—Canada, Denmark, Finland, Japan, and Sweden—they estimated the offset at 0.64 billion currency units after adjusting for autocorrelation. In any event, the authors concluded that a unit increase in national pension funding significantly increased net deficits in other government operations.

In the case of employer-sponsored funded retirement plans, there has been an economic debate over whether the tax-preferences accorded retirement savings results in added savings in the economy. For example, Engen, Gale, and Scholz (1996) conclude that tax incentives favoring retirement savings have profound effects on whether savings are in tax-preferred accounts or traditional savings forms but have little or no effect on the level of saving. Subsequently, Gale (2005) conceded that tax incentives for retirement savings did have some marginal effect on savings levels but were largely concentrated on higher earners who did not need them and were largely tax shelters rather than saving stimulants. On the other side of this debate, Poterba, Venti, and Wise (1993, 1995, 1996) evaluate contributions to individual retirement accounts (IRAs) and 401(k) plans from a variety of perspectives and consistently conclude that most of the savings in these plans represent net additions to personal savings.

To date, the statistical studies of the effects of pension saving in funded pensions on personal savings rates are no more conclusive than those examining the savings effects of the pay-as-you-go Social Security pension system. In both cases, there is a general consensus among economists that these plans do reduce other personal savings but probably not dollar for dollar. Because the pay-go systems do not compensate for the reductions in personal savings with the accumulation of real assets, these plans lead to an absolute reduction of savings within the total economy. In the case of funded plans, plan participation should raise savings rates because a unit of pension accrual is matched by a unit of actual savings, and there is only a partial reduction in personal savings.

What would the U.S. government have spent, and, for that matter, what would tax collections have been, without access to Social Security's cash-flow surpluses over the last twenty-five years or so? No one knows with absolute certainty, but, that debate notwithstanding, the debate over whether Social Security has affected national savings has been focused too narrowly. In a broader context, the implications of operating a funded versus pay-go pension system are relatively clear. Once again, the U.S. example is a good one because the United States has a relatively large funded pension system that runs parallel to its Social Security system, and there is reasonably good data on both systems that can be compared over time.

A pension system's aggregate contribution to national savings is the extent to which its assets cover its net obligations. It is not the net of the annual contributions into a trust fund minus the payout of current benefits and administrative expenses. It is the extent to which accruing obligations in the plan are covered by the assets in the plan. In the case of private pensions, actuaries are required to estimate the accrued benefit obligations in private plans at each valuation, and plan sponsors are required to report the results to the Federal Government. These periodic tallies of assets and obligations in plans can be used to track the contributions of the system to national savings. Along similar lines, the Social Security actuaries have calculated something they have labeled the "maximum transition cost" for that system in recent years. The actuaries report that this measure "represents the transition cost for continuing the Social Security program in a different form, with all payroll taxes for work after the valuation date credited to the new benefit form. The maximum transition cost is equivalent to the unfunded accrued obligation of plan designed to be fully advance funded at the time of plan termination" (Goss, Wade, and Schultz 2008, 3). The tally of assets in the system and the accruing obligations allows us to assess the net effect Social Security is having on national saving.

The results of the Social Security liability calculations and funding levels are presented in the left-hand set of columns in table 8.3. The table shows that while trust fund assets in the Social Security system grew by nearly $1.5 trillion between 1996 and 2006, while total obligations increased by $8.3 trillion over that same period, with unfunded obligations climbing by $6.9 trillion. Some people look at the trust fund growth and conclude that between 1996 and 2006, Social Security contributed $1.5 trillion to U.S. saving but completely ignore the added $6.9 trillion of obligations created for future generations of workers to bear.

To put the results in table 8.3 in perspective, consider a household that begins a year with a bank account balance of zero, runs up a $20,000 debt over the year and, at year-end, has $5,000 in its bank account and a note for the $20,000 loan. No one would say that this household has saved $5,000. Yet that is exactly the logic behind the claim that the U.S. Social Security program's trust fund accumulation is adding to national savings. In the house-

Table 8.3	Social Security and private pension obligations, trust fund assets, and over (under) funding (in billions of U.S. $)					
	Social Security			Private pensions		
Year	Plan obligations	Trust fund assets	System overfunding	Plan obligations	Trust fund assets	System overfunding
1996	9,492.5	567.0	−8,925.5	4,508.4	4,540.5	32.0
1997	9,381.8	655.5	−8,726.6	5,150.3	5,307.2	156.9
1998	10,274.8	762.5	−9,512.3	5,985.1	6,165.0	179.9
1999	11,066.8	896.1	−10,170.7	6,957.1	7,164.1	207.0
2000	11,879.3	1,049.4	−10,829.9	6,704.9	7,286.6	581.8
2001	12,919.5	1,212.5	−11,707.0	6,634.4	6,954.3	319.8
2002	13,539.8	1,378.0	−12,161.8	7,658.0	5,958.3	−1,699.7
2003	14,160.1	1,530.8	−12,629.3	7,454.1	7,154.8	−299.3
2004	15,183.0	1,686.8	−13,496.2	8,488.9	8,007.5	−481.4
2005	16,397.5	1,858.7	−14,538.8			
2006	17,803.7	2,048.1	−15,755.6			

Sources: Social Security trust fund balances are drawn from *The 2007 Annual Report of the Board of Trustees of the Federal Old-Age and Survivors Insurance and Federal Disability Insurance Trust Funds;* the estimated underfunding is unpublished data from the Office of the Actuary, U.S. Social Security Administration; private pension plan assets are derived U.S. Pension Benefit Guaranty Board's *Pension Insurance Data Book* for various years for private defined benefit plans and from the Federal Reserve Bank's *Flow of Funds* data for various years for defined contribution assets and individual retirement account balances; private pension plan obligations for defined benefit plans also are taken from the *Pension Insurance Data Book,* and defined contribution plan and individual retirement account obligations were calculated as the equivalent of assets.

hold described in the preceding, it is clear that their net financial position has deteriorated by $15,000 over the year—that is, the growth in total liabilities minus the net increase in cash in hand. One could claim that the household would have been $5,000 deeper in debt if it had spent the money rather than putting it in the bank, but it makes no sense to consider the $5,000 as savings in the face of the much larger debt it has accrued.

The U.S. Social Security system has had a steadily growing balance in its trust fund accounts over the past two decades, but its underfunding has grown steadily as well. The accumulated funding can be considered saving only to the extent that had the assets not grown, the level of dissaving would have been even higher. The contention by some that accruing Social Security benefits have not reduced workers' other savings would still leave Social Security having a net negative effect on national savings if unfunded obligations are taken into account.

In contrast to Social Security, the private pension system in the United States is largely funded. The private system comprises three elements: employer-sponsored defined benefit plans, employer-sponsored defined contribution plans, and individual retirement accounts. In 1974, the U.S. Congress adopted legislation meant to secure private pensions for workers. For defined benefit plans, these requirements mean that benefits must be funded at roughly the same rate that benefits are earned by participants and that unfunded liabilities must be amortized over a specified schedule. Defined contribution plans and individual retirement accounts are fully funded by the nature of the plans—that is, the obligation of the plan equals its value.

The three right-hand columns of table 8.3 reflect the growing obligations and assets in the U.S. private pension system and correspond with the three columns to their left for Social Security. In this case, private pension obligations in the United States were fully funded on an aggregate basis over most of the period. This does not mean that all defined benefit plans were fully funded; indeed, some were underfunded, but the overfunding in some plans more than offset the underfunding in others. In a national savings context, it is the aggregate balances that are important. In 2002, the system slipped into an underfunded status generally due to declining asset values in the financial markets. In addition, the value of liabilities also increased in defined benefit plans because the interest rates used to calculate full funding requirements fell to historic lows. Some of that underfunding was corrected by a rebound in the financial markets and higher contributions from plan sponsors after 2002.

There has been some chronic underfunding of private defined benefit plans even after the passage of the Employee Retirement Income Security Act (ERISA) in 1974. The Pension Protection Act (PPA) of 2006 has established new funding and disclosure rules for both single-employer and multiemployer pension plans. It increased the funding requirements for single-employer defined benefit plans generally requiring that sponsors fund 100 percent of the present value of all benefits accrued as of the beginning of a plan year. Funding shortfalls can be amortized over seven years. In the case of multiemployer plans, the legislation shortens the amortization period for unfunded liabilities to fifteen years and created a condition labeled as "endangered status" where a plan is less than 80 percent funded. Plans in this status are required to file a ten-year funding improvement plan during which they are required to improve their funding status by one-third and to avoid an accumulated funding deficiency.

The funding requirements for private employer pensions are meant to ensure that the plans will generally hold assets at least equal to liabilities. If that goal is not achieved because of fluctuations in either asset or liability values, the system is intended to encourage accelerated saving for assets to catch up to the level of liabilities. Even though unfunded liabilities did increase in the private system toward the end of the period shown in table 8.3, between 1996 and 2004, private pension assets grew by $3.5 trillion, from $4.5 trillion to $8.0 trillion, while excess funding dropped by $500 billion. In other words, from 1996 to 2004, private pensions made net contribution to national wealth of $3.0 trillion. At this writing, the Pension Benefit Guaranty Corporation (PBGC) has not yet published the accumulated obligations or funding levels among their insured plans for 2005 and 2006, but the Federal Reserves' *Flow of Funds* reports suggest that private retirement assets increased another $1.5 trillion between 2004 and 2006.

The preceding discussion suggests that from 1996 to 2004, aggregate pension saving in Social Security fell $4.6 trillion because obligations outstripped asset accumulations significantly, while net private pension savings rose by roughly $3.0 trillion because asset growth largely kept up with accruing obligations. Although all economists may not agree on the rate at which pension saving is offset by personal saving, most of them agree there is some offset and some believe it is so substantial that the marginal positive effects on saving are not worth the tax preferences accorded such savings. Still, at the end of the day, no one denies that the accumulated wealth in these plans is savings, whereas most of what is accruing in Social Security is consumer loan obligations.

8.3   Pension Finance and Savings under
Alternative Demographic Scenarios

We noted earlier that, from the perspective of the worker, the accumulation of pension rights through a pay-go social security system is little different than accumulating wealth through personal savings or a funded pension. The previous section of this discussion suggested that many countries are facing the prospect that their economic performance in coming years will be disappointing to the resident populations and that the pension systems will be used to allocate that disappointment. In that discussion, there was no distinction made between countries that have been almost solely reliant on pay-as-you-go retirement systems, such as Germany, Italy, and Sweden, versus those with considerable funding in their retirement systems, such as Canada, the United Kingdom, and the United States, or countries that are attempting to move toward almost full funding of their national retirement systems, such as Australia and Chile.

The demographic composition of a nation's population can affect the potential provision of income for the retiree population under both types of plans. In the case of plans financed on a pay-go basis, the cost of benefit provision is driven directly by the ratio of retirees to workers who finance benefits. As populations age, this "dependency ratio" is expected to rise significantly. In the case of pay-as-you-go retirement systems, if lawmakers determine that the cost of financing the benefits defined in current law is more than workers can bear, they will likely reduce benefits in some fashion, which may put strains on the economic security of people depending on the benefits. In the case of funded plans, the demographic composition of society may also be important. When the baby boomers retire, they will begin to sell off their private retirement assets. The dependency ratio that is important in determining how much pay-go retirement plans cost also defines the relative number of sellers and buyers of assets. We face a future where we will have relatively more domestic sellers of assets compared to buyers than at any time in modern history.

Schieber and Shoven (1997) painted a scenario where the sell-off of baby boomers' defined benefit pension assets has the potential to depress financial market prices, which could put strains on the economic security of people depending on the benefits of pension savings. Specifically, Schieber and Shoven projected private employer contributions to defined benefit plans based on actual contribution rates during the early 1990s and assumed that workers would claim benefits in accordance with benefit formulas then in place when they reached retirement eligibility. Their results suggested that savings in these plans would gradually decline as the baby boomers retired under their base assumptions and turn negative in the mid-2020s. They acknowledged that this scenario was untenable as the trust funds would ultimately run out of assets given the contribution and accrual rates that persisted in private plans in the late 1980s and early 1990s. Still, their results raised the specter that the retirement of the baby boom generation could lead to negative savings.

More recently, James Poterba (2004) has concluded that, aside from the automatic decline in the value of defined benefit pension assets as workers age, other financial assets decline only gradually during retirement. He suggests that when the pattern of asset accumulation and selling by age is used to project asset demands in light of the future age structure of the U.S. population, the results do not suggest a sharp decline in asset demand between 2020 and 2050. Looking at the U.S. situation, however, may be misleading because of the relatively favorable demographics that it faces. It might also be misleading because the significant reliance on pay-as-you-go retirement plans significantly reduces the need to cash out assets for many retirees. Full dependence on funded retirement systems would likely change the dynamics of asset decumulation during retirement for many people covered under existing social security pension systems.

In the following discussion, we simulate how pay-as-you-go pensions versus funded pensions would operate under the evolving demographics in three countries with very different population profiles—India, Italy, and the United States. These three countries were chosen because their population profiles are expected to evolve in significantly varied fashions. The simulations help to clarify the importance of demographics on the issues being analyzed.

The model used in this analysis is not a general equilibrium model with built-in feedback and behavioral responses to the evolving economic outcomes under the alternative demographic scenarios. Still, the estimates of economic dependency due to population aging that we model in the various cases link closely with those of other assessments of pay-as-you-go pensions. We are simply applying our estimates of evolving aging dependency to both pay-as-you-go and funded pensions for comparisons in order to show the orders of magnitude of potential swings in important economic variables given a set of demographic scenarios that are tied to population projections associated with actual countries under alternative formulations of retirement systems.

In our modeling of the retirement systems, everyone starts working at age twenty-five and earns $35,000 in their first year of employment. There is no inflation. As workers age, they receive a 2 percent pay raise each year until they retire at age sixty-five, 1 percent related to general productivity improvement rates across the economy and 1 percent related to the individual's own productivity associated with experience. Under this set of assumptions, average wages in the economy grow by 1 percent per year. That is, a twenty-five-year-old worker would earn 1 percent more in 2006 than a similarly situated worker earned in 2005 and so on. We assumed that workers would earn average wages for their cohort and that all working-age citizens would work full time until death or retirement at age sixty-five. This latter assumption, while not very realistic, will not bias the analytical results as long as a relatively constant proportion of each working-age group is actually employed over time. We assumed that life expectancy was equivalent to rates that persisted in the United States in 2000 as estimated by the U.S. Social Security actuaries.

The example assumes that workers' annual contributions to their pension are 13.9 percent of pay over their forty-year careers and that those assets accrue annual returns of 4 percent. Retirees receive benefits worth 70 percent of their final earnings. Some analysts contend that this level of

Table 8.4   **Quasi-retirement income replacement rates for selected countries (%)**

| | Percentage of mean disposable income of people ages 65–74 compared to: | | | |
| | People aged 51–64 | | People aged 41–50 | |
Country	Mid-1980s	Mid-1990s	Mid-1980s	Mid-1990s
Canada	82.4	86.9	78.2	86.6
Finland	77.6	75.5	69.2	71.6
Germany	78.1	84.4	75.5	78.2
Italy	76.4	78.7	77.8	78.1
Japan	82.3	79.6	84.8	81.8
The Netherlands	83.1	80.7	85.2	78.9
Sweden	76.1	76.1	73.6	80.3
United Kingdom	70.4	74.1	59.9	65.0
United States	82.2	79.9	84.3	83.6

Source: OECD (2001, 22).

retirement income exceeds the level needed for many individuals to maintain their preretirement standard of living, but it is not inconsistent with the level of income realized by retirement-age populations across many of the developed economies of the world as shown in table 8.4. The table shows mean disposable income of people ages sixty-five to seventy-four, people who would be largely retired in most developed countries, relative to mean disposable income of people at younger, working ages.

India, Italy, and the United States had highly varied demographic profiles over the past half century. The total fertility rate in India in 1950 was around 6.0 but has declined steadily to around 2.5 in 2000. The United States was in the early part of its postwar baby boom in 1950, but by the late 1960s, the total fertility rate had dropped to under 2.0, where it hovered for several years before rebounding to around the 2.1 replacement rate toward the end of the century. Italy did not have a significant postwar baby boom, and its total fertility rate dropped from around 2.5 in the mid 1960s to about half that by 2000. In the simulations we are doing here, workers begin their careers at age twenty-five and work steadily until retiring at age sixty-five. These variations in past fertility rates will play a significant role in determining the relative size of the working and retiree populations for decades to come.

The cost of a pay-as-you-go pension is simply the product of the retiree dependency ratio—the ratio of retirees to workers—and the ratio of average pension benefits to average wages of workers. For the three countries under study, dependency ratios are projected to increase significantly (figure 8.3). Despite the fact that we used a U.S. 2003 period life table in developing these simulations, the dependency ratios we project here are in relatively

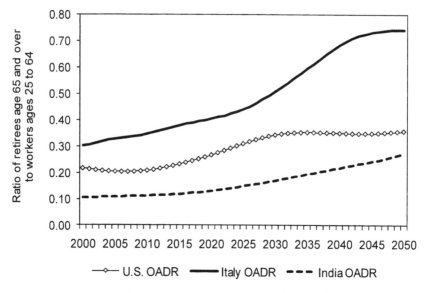

Fig. 8.3   Simulated retiree dependency ratios for India, Italy, and the United States
Source: Derived by the author.

close alignment with the United Nations (UN) population projection of the relative size of the working-age population, ages twenty to sixty-four, to the retirement-age populations in the three countries for 2030. Using the UN *World Population Prospects* 2000 revision for our baseline population estimates, we estimated an aged dependency ratio for Italy of 0.506 in 2030, of 0.157 for India, and 0.365 for the United States (Nyce and Schieber 2005, 70).

In our simulated model, retirees' benefits will always be 70 percent of workers' average wages in the year before they retire. People start working at age twenty-five and retire at age sixty-five. In a pay-as-you-go system, variations in the cost of total benefits over time will be driven purely by the dependency ratio. This is a reasonable characterization of a typical national retirement pay-as-you-go retirement system. The cost of a pay-as-you-go retirement system financed by taxing workers' earnings can be reflected as the ratio of total benefits paid to retirees relative to workers' total wages. That ratio approximates the payroll tax required to support system.

In developing any set of projections of population composition, certain assumptions are required. We used fertility and immigration assumptions from the UN *World Population Prospects* 2000 revision in developing our projections. In subsequent revisions, both fertility and immigration assumptions have been increased under the UN's projections. Between 2005 and 2050, the 2006 UN estimated total fertility rate in Italy is ranges between 7 and 15 percent higher than estimated in 2000. Immigration rates for Italy in the UN's 2006 estimates are generally more than double the rates estimated in 2000. For the purposes of this exercise, the immigration assumptions are more important over much of the period than fertility rates in projecting aged dependency. By definition, aged dependency is the number of retirees divided by the working population. Increases in fertility today will not affect the number of workers for another twenty years or so. Higher immigration, which tends to be concentrated among younger working-age individuals, on the other hand, can have an immediate effect on aged dependency rates. Using the 2006 UN demographic projections, the number of people in Italy over the age of sixty-five divided by the number ages twenty to fifty-nine results in a ratio of 0.73 in 2030. By comparison, the 2000 projections yield a ratio of 0.78. This difference may be significant in a statistical context but would only raise the Italian pay-as-you-go pension cost projections by 3 to 4 percentage points in 2030. For other reasons, discussed in the following, we have reason to believe our projections of aged dependency and pension costs may already be low compared to other estimates, so we do not believe changing the assumptions would significantly alter the conclusions derived here. For the longer term, fertility assumptions become very important, and we believe the assumption that assumptions that Italy's fertility rate will increase markedly relative to recent history without a rationale for it doing so is questionable in making projections of this sort.

Figure 8.4 shows the estimated payroll tax rates that would be required to support future benefit payouts from our hypothetical pay-as-you-go systems in India, Italy, and the United States under our assumptions and demographic projections. The direct linkage between the dependency ratios and the cost of benefits in these systems is clear. There is a highly correlated

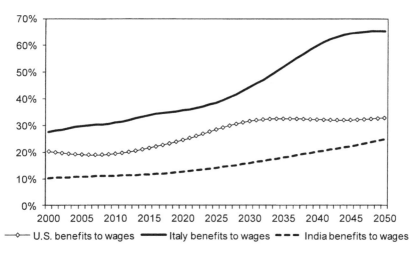

Fig. 8.4   Simulated pension payroll tax rates for India, Italy, and the United States
Source: Developed by the author.

correspondence between the dependency distributions in figure 8.4 and the cost distributions in figure 8.4. The Indian and, potentially, the U.S. scenarios could conceivably be supportable in many developed countries. Yet in the U.S. case, the rapid run-up in tax rates between 2010 and 2030 to support a pay-go financed program could create significant burdens on workers as the full benefit of their improving productivity is siphoned off to support the growing retiree population due to rising pension and health costs (Schieber 2008). The Italian scenario, however, would appear to be unsupportable in any event, which is why a number of countries, including Italy, have embarked on pension reforms. In many cases, an element of the pension reform has been a shift in the direction of funding pension obligations.

Given Italy's demographics, the problem with its pay-as-you-go pension system is that workers likely would be neither able nor willing to support it. In most developed countries, older people vote at much higher rates than younger ones, which could inspire policymakers to protect their interests. However, in Italy and some other countries, the costs of these systems would become so burdensome that workers likely would not pay them. Workers could choose to work outside the formal economy, scale back their work efforts, or immigrate to an economy with more tolerable tax burdens.

The simplifying assumptions used in developing these projections give rise to the question of whether the cost projections presented in figure 8.4 are reasonable. Börsch-Supan, Köke, and Winter (2005) have simulated the cost of pay-as-you-go pension systems in France, Germany, and Italy through 2030 and estimate that the cost of the Italian system would be 62 percent of the national wage bill that year compared to the estimate of 44 percent presented in figure 8.4. This suggests our results are conservative compared to projections that others are presenting.

The Italian system would be more expensive than estimated here under a projection of its recent historical operations because labor force participation rates among the adult population are significantly lower than in our simulations and because most workers in Italy retire much earlier than we have simulated. Given recent age-gender labor force participation rates, Nyce and Schieber (2005, 63) estimate that the Italian dependency ratio of retirees to active workers in 2030 will be about twice the level estimated in the simulations presented in figure 8.3. The cost of the actual pension system in Italy would be ameliorated somewhat relative to the simulation result presented in figure 8.4 because our simulations are based on a benefit that is larger relative to preretirement earnings than the Italian system provides.

A funded pension may not fully ameliorate the adverse economic effects of demographics like those in Italy. As noted earlier, pensions are simply devices retirees use to make a claim on the goods and services available in the economy. In a funded pension, retirees claim their share of these goods and services by selling off assets they accumulated during their careers to work-

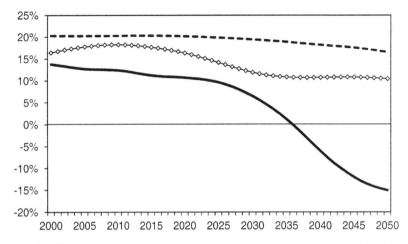

Fig. 8.5 **Simulated savings rates through a funded pension system for India, Italy, and the United States assuming work begins at age 25 and retirement at age 65**
Source: Developed by the author.

ers. In simulating the funded version of the pension systems in this analysis, we assumed that workers had been covered by a funded pension over their entire careers. In this scenario, if too many assets were sold too quickly, it would portend the collapse of asset values.

Figure 8.5 illustrates the implications of alternative demographic outlooks by showing the contributions that funded pensions would make to national savings. The national savings rate in the simulation results presented here is the amount of workers' pension contributions—which would be 13.9 percent of their pay—plus the interest income on assets, minus benefit payouts. National income is the sum of all wages paid to workers plus the sum of all interest paid on savings. The national savings rate is the aggregate of savings divided by total income.

In the United States, the contribution to national savings from a funded pension system under the simulations would peak at about 18 percent around 2010 and then gradually decline thereafter. This corresponds with the anticipated retirement of the baby boom generation in the United States. The deterioration of savings rates from the simulation would settle out by roughly 2035 at just over 10 percent. However, savings rates continue to decline at a more gradual pace reflecting the persistently low rates of fertility anticipated over the coming decades. All in all, even under a funded pension system, the United States could see its national savings rate associated with a fully funded pension system cut in roughly half from their peak by the mid-2030s.

As significant as the shift in potential savings rates might appear in the United States, the shift would be far more pronounced in Italy, which is already approaching the demographic conditions that the United States will face a quarter century from now. Over the next fifteen years or so, the last large cohorts of working-age people will pass over the retirement age used in these simulations. At that juncture, the long-term implications of extremely low fertility rates would take their toll even on a funded pension system. By roughly 2035, a fully funded pension system in Italy would no longer be adding to national savings. And by 2050, the sell-off of assets would be equivalent to 15 percent of national income.

Figure 8.6 shows the estimated pattern of savings in France, Germany, Italy, and the Netherlands, where savings at each age are stated as a percentage of the savings held by forty-year-olds. In explaining the differences across the various countries, Börsch-Supan, Köke, and Winter (2005) focus on the differences in the pension plans that operated in the various countries. In the Netherlands, the declining levels of savings at higher ages reflects the draw-down of their funded pensions. If reliance on funded pensions at the individual level results in savings rates declining and even turning negative at advanced ages, then it would seem extremely high aged dependency could lead to negative savings rates in the aggregate at some point.

In terms of aggregate savings rates, the pattern of saving in Germany that Börsch-Supan (2004) projected under their pre-2002 pension reforms is shown in figure 8.7. These results were for a closed economy projection, which corresponds with the nature of the projection in figure 8.5, although his open-economy projections are not all that different. While Borsch-Supan projects a significant decline in the German national savings rate related to their population aging, it is not nearly the magnitude that we are projecting here. The relative structure of the retirement systems may be an important

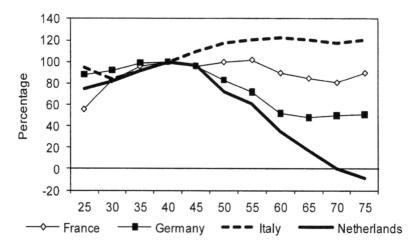

Fig. 8.6   Cohort-corrected savings rates by age for various countries
Source: Börsch-Supan, Köke, and Winter (2005, 95).

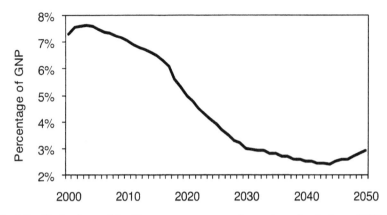

Fig. 8.7   Projections of the German aggregate savings rate under their pre-2002 pension system
Source: Börsch-Supan (2004, 33).

consideration here. Börsch-Supan, Köke, and Winter (2005, 93) estimate that funded pensions systems in France, Germany, and Italy comprised 5 percent or less of household wealth in 2000 compared to 38 percent in the Netherlands, 22 percent in the United Kingdom, and 24 percent in the United States.

Yet in Germany and other countries with large public pension systems, there was considerable private saving going on in recent decades. If their pension systems had been funded, added savings outside the pension systems would likely have also been the norm. Would the Germans have saved outside a funded pension system at comparable levels they saved outside their pay-as-you-go system? Even if they did, the net swing in the German savings rate would be much larger than that shown in figure 8.7 because the direct saving and dissaving related to the retirement system would overlay other saving, positively affecting the rate during the positive demographic period and negatively affecting it during the period of high aged dependency.

The point here is that demographic conditions in some nations could result in economic chaos unless retirement patterns change radically, regardless of how retirement systems are organized and financed. It is unlikely that payroll tax rates of over 60 percent, or even 50 percent, are sustainable—yet current projections suggest some countries would have to increase taxes to these levels to support their pay-as-you-go retirement systems. The alternative—trying to weather the demographic storm with a funded pension system—may not be much better. But the funded pension plan offers one safety valve that the pay-as-you-go plan does not from a macroeconomic perspective. The assets accumulated in a funded pension can be invested in other economies around the world and can allow a nation to diversify its demographic risks accordingly. Indeed, the prospect of increased savings related to the move toward funded pensions in a number of aging countries will face declining demand for capital where workforces are not only aging but shrinking.

Countries like Canada, Germany, and Sweden have adopted new pension policies in recent years with the intention of increasing the funding of accruing pension obligations with an eye toward increased investing of pension assets in foreign markets. But in many countries, there are still biases toward investing close to home and political resistance to use foreign capital markets to help ameliorate the longer-term implications of population aging. An editorial in the *Washington Post* (Myerson 2004, A19) a while back made the case that the burden of proof was on policymakers "to demonstrate how private investment in a global economy creates jobs here at home. And why the hell our tax policy should boost income in Bangalore, not Baltimore."

Shifting to a funded retirement system without also adopting incentives to boost workforce participation could ultimately lead to large declines in national savings rates or even to negative savings rates in some developed economies. Even if these economies do not collapse under the crushing pressure of aged dependency, the resources needed to support publicly financed pensions will put tremendous strain on all other facets of government expenditures.

8.4   Economic Operations and Limitations in Aging Societies

Under assumptions that the economies discussed in the preceding section were closed to foreign trade and exchange, the operations of pay-as-you-go versus funded pensions for individual workers, as summarized in table 8.1, would aggregate up for the total economy. Focusing on the Italian case, the high rates of payroll taxes under the pay-as-you-go pension scenario almost certainly would lead to reduced standards of living for those working and their dependents. But the rates of asset sales implied in the funded pension scenario would require workers to save outside of their retirement saving at such high rates that their consumption rates would almost certainly have to fall relative to levels achieved by earlier cohorts of workers. Any alternative that would allow working-age people to save less and to increase their standards of living would suggest significant reductions in living standards for retirees because the value of their savings would be reduced. The pension system, then, will be the fulcrum for allocating the economic disappointment.

The rate of growth of gross domestic product (GDP) in an economy is the sum of labor force growth and the growth in worker productivity. For the United States, the decade-by-decade levels of real output (GDP), total labor supply (billions of hours), and productivity (GDP per hour) measures are shown in table 8.5 from 1950 through 2006. The growth rates in the table are the decade-by-decade compound annual growth rates, except for the 2000s, where they reflect the first six years of the decade and were derived from the base data. The GDP growth rates shown in the table vary slightly from the sum of the growth rates in the labor supply and productivity measures due to rounding of the various base measures. While it is not shown in the table, the combination of a growing labor force and improving worker productivity has resulted in a steady increase in standards of living in the United States as measured by per capita GDP.

The labor force growth rates shown in table 8.6 and those in any economy depend on the demographics of the society and the labor force behavior of the working-age individuals in it. There are a variety of factors that contribute to worker productivity improvement rates. To a considerable extent,

Table 8.5   **Levels and growth rates in U.S. gross domestic product (GDP), total labor supply, and output per hour**

| Year | GDP (in billions of 2000$) | Labor supply (billions of hours worked) | GDP per hour ($) | Compound annual growth rate from prior to current year in: | | |
				GDP (%)	Labor supply (%)	GDP per hour (%)
1950	1,777.3	122.4	14.5			
1960	2,501.8	134.6	18.6	3.48	0.95	2.50
1970	3,771.9	157.3	24.0	4.19	1.57	2.58
1980	5,161.7	185.0	27.9	3.19	1.63	1.53
1990	7,112.5	219.9	32.3	3.26	1.75	1.48
2000	9,817.0	257.9	38.1	3.28	1.60	1.64
2006	11,319.5	261.7	43.3	1.43	0.15	1.29

Source: Office of the Chief Actuary, U.S. Social Security Administration.

Table 8.6   **Compound annual growth in gross domestic product per capita for various Organization for Economic Co-operation and Development countries over selected decades**

Country	1960s	1970s	1980s	1990s
Austria	4.05	3.54	2.07	1.74
Canada	3.07	3.04	1.56	1.64
France	4.47	2.66	1.84	1.34
Germany	3.71	2.70	2.10	2.33
Italy	4.97	3.10	2.16	1.44
Japan	9.01	3.25	3.51	1.07
The Netherlands	3.74	2.08	1.62	2.31
Sweden	3.91	1.60	1.87	1.39
Switzerland	3.23	1.19	1.54	0.18
United Kingdom	2.29	1.81	2.47	1.88
United States	2.92	2.25	2.16	2.25

Source: Nyce and Schieber (2005, 165).

they are dependent on the other factors of production—the level of capital stock that workers utilize in their jobs and the level of technology imbedded in it. In addition, they are also dependent on the innate abilities of the workers themselves—their health status, education levels, and possibly their age. The latter may be more important in some types of work than others. Rates of productivity improvement also depend on labor practices. Finally, managerial practices, how work is structured, workers compensated, and the like are important.

In an historical context, the combination of labor productivity improvements and labor force growth have resulted in steady decade-to-decade economic growth and rising standards of living in all the economies of the developed world. The rates vary somewhat from decade to decade and from country to country, but GDP per capita consistently increased across the last four decades in all developed nations, as reflected in table 8.6.

Long-term patterns of the sort reflected in table 8.6 tend to create expectations of further improvements in living standards. Most people hope for increasing prosperity, if not for themselves, then for their children and grandchildren. And certainly most young adults aspire to improve their lot. Improving the status of generations across time typically implies economic expansion. So while most people may aspire to increasing output per capita, that may become increasingly difficult to achieve given the demographic developments ahead.

The history of labor force growth that has persisted over virtually the whole period since the beginning of the industrial revolution in what we consider today to be the highly developed economies of the world is likely to be reversed in the relatively near future. Assuming that people continue to conform to the working patterns of recent years, the aging populations may create workforce contractions in several countries during this decade or next. Börsch-Supan (2004) has estimated that the German labor force will contract from 36 million workers in 2010 to around 32 million by 2025. Clark, Ogawa, and Matsukura (2008, 3) estimate that the Japanese labor force peaked at 67.9 million workers in 1998 and dropped to 66.4 million workers in 2004. They conclude that "if age specific labor force participation rates remain constant, the labor force will reflect the smaller, older population and the rate of decline in the labor force will tend to exceed the rate of decline of the population." They estimate that the labor force could decline by 2.2 percent between 2005 and 2010 and another 7.1 percent between 2010 and 2020 (Clark, Ogawa, and Matsukura 2008, table 5). Given the age structures and normal life expectancies in the developed countries, where labor forces are expected to contract, they are likely to do so prior to the contraction of national populations. This may be occurring in Italy, Japan, Sweden, and Switzerland this decade and accelerate in the next, while also spreading across a number of other countries as well.

Assuming that recent age-gender employment levels would persist into the future, Nyce and Schieber (2005) estimated that in the 2010s, roughly two out of every three developed countries will experience a reduction in labor supply under projections using recent demographics and labor force participation patterns. Even in Australia, Ireland, and the United States, which are expected to have relatively persistent labor force growth in the coming years, labor supply growth rates during the 2010s will be half to one-quarter those of the 1990s (Nyce and Schieber 2005, 183). Employers in the developed countries may face considerable challenges in finding sufficient numbers of talented employees to run their operations. If labor force growth rates slow to the levels anticipated in some of these countries, the result could be economic stagnation or even economic decline, depending on the severity of the workforce contraction.

If population aging leads to slower or negative growth of labor supplies in the developed economies and that slows economic growth, declines in rates of improvement in living standards will follow. This would not necessarily occur if total population growth were slowing to the same rate as labor force growth or contracting in the cases where the labor force will be getting smaller. But the populations in virtually all of these countries will not begin to contract for some time due to their evolving demographic structures. The problem is that labor force contraction due to increasing numbers of retirees associated with aging populations precedes population decline. The standard of living is determined by the distribution of output across the whole population. If the rate of improvement in living standards is slowed due to the demographic transition underway, then the loaded question many societies will have to answer is who will bear the brunt of the slowdown. The character of the retirement systems in many countries will likely have a lot to do with how they answer that question.

In order to demonstrate the implications of the changing demographics in developed countries, Nyce and Schieber (2005) projected the levels of output in the developed economies of the world on the basis of assumptions that labor productivity improvement rates achieved in recent years would persist in the future and that labor force participation patterns by age and gender of the working age population at the beginning of the century would persist over the next couple of decades. In this manner, it is possible to estimate how changing demographics would alter economic performance for countries dependent upon their own domestic capacity. The results suggest that population aging would lead to a slowdown in the historical growth rates in standards of living. This was especially the case in the 2010s projection series. If this outcome is ultimately realized, then the question the developed societies face is who bears the brunt of the slowdown in improving living standards. The answer to this question: it depends on pension policy.

In many countries, retirement benefit levels are tied to workers' productivity levels through some form of wage indexing. Even where pension benefits are tied to general growth in income levels or to price indexing, the disproportionate growth in the cost of health benefits consumed by retirees tends to increase the cost of total retiree benefits at rates approaching those of wages. If retirees largely depend on pensions that grow with worker productivity or wages, pension systems will insulate retirees from the slowing economic growth resulting from population aging and slower labor force growth. As retirees become a larger share of the population, they potentially could divert more of the benefits of productivity growth—meaning higher standards of living—from the active workforce. This would place a growing real burden on workers and their dependents.

In order to show the implications of slower economic growth resulting from population aging and to show the potential from alternative policies for dealing with it, Nyce and Schieber (2005) considered two scenarios for how policymakers might allocate the economic disappointment of slowing improvement in standards of living. In the first scenario, they assumed that retirees would receive pensions that grow at the rate of growth in wages. After retirees received their share of the national output on this basis, the residual improvement in workers' living standards were estimated from distributing what would be left in national output. In the second scenario, the allocation process was reversed: workers were assumed to benefit fully from their improving productivity, and the residual was then divided among the retiree population.

The results of the simulations for the 2010s from the first scenario simulation are presented in table 8.7 for a selected set of countries. The results suggest that workers could end up seeing their incomes grow significantly slower than their productivity improvement rates if existing pension policies

Table 8.7   Annual growth in workers' per capita income levels assuming the elderly population's income grows at the rate of growth in worker productivity

Country	2010–2020	
	Worker productivity improvement rate	Growth rate in workers' per capita income
Australia	2.05	1.61
Canada	1.50	0.87
Denmark	2.07	1.70
France	1.23	0.63
Germany	1.49	0.95
Italy	1.54	1.00
Japan	1.12	0.76
Spain	1.31	0.88
Sweden	2.49	2.24
Switzerland	0.65	0.12
United Kingdom	1.93	1.48
United States	1.48	1.10

Source: Nyce and Schieber (2005, 189).

in many countries are carried forward despite population aging. In interpreting the results of the table, it is important to keep in mind that the results show a marginal loss of income relative to productivity improvement over and above whatever level of taxes workers are already bearing.

In the abstract, the allocation of output along the lines suggested in table 8.7 is no better or worse than any other suggested distribution of output. The potential issue likely to arise, however, is that with the slowdown in growth or even shrinkage of the labor supply, the primary factor driving economic growth will be improving worker productivity. Workers may be less than enthusiastic about increasing their levels of output when they are losing ground in their own living standards relative to those who have withdrawn from the workforce.

The eventual situation in many countries may be much worse than the scenario depicted in table 8.7 suggests because the results of the analysis presented here focus only on added pension claims related to population aging and extra health claims may add as much or more cost related to population aging than pension costs (Costello and Bains 2001; Nyce and Schieber 2005). The disincentives that high taxes on labor create are a concern—workers simply are not willing to work harder indefinitely if they are not rewarded for their efforts. If we lose the benefits of continued improvement in worker productivity levels, the implications of population aging could become even direr than suggested here.

Several countries have already taken actions or proposed ways to limit the liabilities that pension systems will place on workers. In the United States, President George W. Bush suggested that the indexing of initial Social Security pensions might not be directly linked to average wage growth in the future for all workers. Several other countries, including Germany, Italy, Japan, and Sweden have already adopted a range of measures to restrict the growth of their retirement systems.

To the extent that policymakers limit the implications of population aging on pension costs, it will protect workers, at least partially, from the demographic transition that is underway. Insulating workers from the economic implications of changing demographics, however, has the potential to adversely affect standards of living for the elderly, probably through erosion in their benefits. To see the implications of this scenario, consider the results presented in table 8. Here, workers and their dependents are assumed to realize improvements in their consumption rates consistent with improving productivity, and that the residual of total output would be allocated to retirees. In this case, the news is contained in the right-hand column of table 8.8. Where the entry has a negative sign, it suggests that standards of living among the elderly will be falling.

The results suggest that if policymakers respond to population aging by simply driving down the income levels of the elderly, there could be significant declines in standards of living among the elderly across much of

Table 8.8   Annual growth in per capita income levels for the elderly population assuming workers' income increases at the rate of increase in productivity with the residual

| | 2010–2020 | |
Country	Worker productivity improvement rate	Growth rate in retirees' per capita income
Australia	2.05	–0.12
Canada	1.50	–1.28
France	1.23	–0.82
Germany	1.49	–0.38
Italy	1.54	–0.05
Japan	1.12	–0.30
Spain	1.31	–0.50
Sweden	2.49	1.11
Switzerland	0.65	–1.65
United Kingdom	1.93	0.31
United States	1.48	–1.05

Source: Nyce and Scheiber (2005, 191).

the developed world over the next decade. The phenomenon could become widespread. The prospect of solving the aging challenge by pushing more and more elderly into substandard income levels is likely to be regarded as unacceptable by many policymakers. The significant benefit adjustments to pension systems that have already been adopted in a number of countries suggest that this scenario may actually be embedded in current policy in a number of cases.

8.5   Can Pension Funding Trump Population Aging?

Earlier we raised the question of whether it made much difference whether a country facing a demographic situation similar to Italy's had a pay-as-you-go or funded retirement system. Ultimately, it may not, but it is likely that a funded pension system would offer countries facing dramatic increases in their aged dependency levels more options for dealing with its demographic outlook than a pay-as-you-go system. A funded pension system might relieve some of the pressures associated with population aging due to the fact that such systems have to adjust to market conditions more rapidly than politically directed pay-as-you-go systems. To the extent that aging would lead to significant sales of assets under a funded pension system, asset prices could decline and diminish the proceeds being paid to the owners, prompting them to work longer to make up for the loss in retirement savings value.

In this regard, it is possible that the organization of funded pension systems will play a significant role in how quickly they respond to demographic pressures. A system organized like the Canadian national defined benefit plan, where a portion of the benefit obligation is being funded but the benefit structure is still defined by legislative fiat, may not be as responsive to excess benefit claims as the Australian system that is essentially organized as a capital accumulation device with actual benefit payout being determined at the point an individual worker retires. In the former case, it is possible that political pressure will allow funding ratios to be depleted while corrective legislation is considered. In the latter case, the ruthless arithmetic of life expectancy and available resources to support it will dictate benefit adjustments in real time.

Potentially, the greatest advantage that funded pensions offer is to give countries an option to tap outside productivity by investing in global financial markets that a pay-as-you-go system cannot. While capital flows have increased in recent years, there is still reason to be concerned about home bias in investing patterns including the investment of pension assets that will reduce the effectiveness of pension funding as a mechanism for dealing with population aging. If Italy and other developed countries had funded their national pensions as they were maturing and invested in other economies around the world with an eye toward future labor availability, the sell-off of significant pension assets due to population aging would be relatively inconsequential for the home economy.

If a country needs to augment the productivity of its workforce to generate sufficient output for its society, the ability to do so with a traditional pay-as-you-go financing scheme is extremely limited. Funded pensions, on the other hand, have significant potential in allowing countries to diversify their demographic risks because capital can move across borders relatively freely. The returns on capital invested outside of the owner's home country create the prospect of tapping the productivity of foreign labor that is otherwise hard to achieve.

In the final analysis, however, countries do not face an instantaneous choice between funded or pay-as-you-go retirement systems. Those that are largely dependent on pay-as-you-go financing face the prospect of higher taxes or lower benefits as they work out the allocation of the economic disappointment they are facing. They may buffer the longer-term ramifications of prior policies by moving toward greater funding of future pension promises, but someone has to bear the burden of the outstanding consumer loans. If the workers are given the burden, they pay twice—once to cover the old pay-as-you-go obligations at the same time they bear the cost of prefunding their own retirement income claims. If the retirees are given the burden, they end up with less income in retirement than they expected when they paid their part of the consumer loan bargain. Any transition from a pay-as-you-go pension system to a funded one is necessarily a long-term undertaking that involves substantial cash-flow support while it is underway. Accomplishing such a transition at the point that aged dependency is already challenging general economic prosperity is likely to be doubly daunting.

In the German case, policymakers tried to split the hair. They put a limit on the payroll tax claim they would allow the national retirement plan to make, which meant some reduction in pension benefits for current retirees that will increase over time and gave workers tax incentives to save to make up for the implicit reductions in benefits that follow. From the perspective of making claims on foreign workers, it is going to be a long time before there are sufficient assets in Germany's added pension funding to provide any significant buffer for the excessive levels of aged dependency that they face now and over the next couple of decades. It is likely that a key component of the answer to the aging challenge that Germany and most developed countries face today is to increase the numbers of workers in their domestic economies. That almost certainly means that workers will have to remain employed later in life than was generally the case at the end of the twentieth century.

References

Börsch-Supan, Axel. 2004. Global aging, issues, answers, more questions. University of Michigan Retirement Research Center, Working Paper no. 2004-084.

Börsch-Supan, Axel, F. Jens Köke, and Joachim K. Winter. 2005. Pension reform, savings behavior, and capital market performance. *Journal of Pension Economics and Finance* 4:87–107.

Bosworth, Barry, and Gary Burtless. 2004. Pension reform and saving. Paper presented at a conference of the International Forum of the Collaboration Projects, Tokyo, Japan.

Clark, Robert L., Naohiro Ogawa, and Rikiya Matsukura. 2008. Population decline, labor force stability. Paper presented at the Low Fertility Conference, University of St. Gallen, St. Gallen, Switzerland.

Costello, Declan, and Mandeep Bains. 2001. *Budgetary challenges posed by ageing populations.* Brussels, Belgium: Economic Policy Committee, European Economic Commission.

Diamond, Peter A., and Peter R. Orszag. 2004. *Saving Social Security: A balanced approach.* Washington, D.C.: Brookings Institution.

Engen, Eric M., William G. Gale, and John Karl Scholz. 1996. The illusory effects of savings incentives on saving. *Journal of Economic Perspectives* 10 (4): 113–38.

Feldstein, Martin. 1974. Social Security, induced retirement, and aggregate capital accumulation. *Journal of Political Economy* 82 (4): 905–26.

———. 1982. Social Security and private savings: Reply. *Journal of Political Economy* 90 (3): 630–42.

———. 1996. Social Security and private savings: New time series evidence. *National Tax Journal* 49 (2): 151–64.

Gale, William G. 2005. The effect of pensions and 401(k) plans on household saving and wealth. In *The evolving pension: Trends, effects and proposals,* ed. W. G. Gale,

J. B. Shoven, and M. J. Warshawsky, 103–21. Washington, DC: Brookings Institution.

Goss, Steve, Alice Wade, and Jason Schultz. 2008. *Unfunded obligations and transition cost for the OASDI program.* Actuarial Note no. 2007, 1. Baltimore, MD: Office of the Chief Actuary, Social Security Administration.

Leimer, Dean R., and Selig D. Lesnoy. 1982. Social Security and private savings: New time series evidence. *Journal of Political Economy* 90 (3): 606–29.

Moore, James F., and Olivia S. Mitchell. 2000. Projected retirement wealth and savings adequacy. In *Forecasting retirement needs and retirement wealth,* ed. Olivia S. Mitchell, P. Brett Hammond, and Anna Rappaport, 68–94. Philadelphia: University of Pennsylvania Press.

Myerson, Harold. 2004. Good for investors, bad for the rest. *Washington Post,* January 14, 2004.

Nataraj, Sita, and John B. Shoven. 2004. Has the unified budget destroyed the Federal Government trust funds? Paper presented at conference sponsored by the Office of Policy, Social Security Administration and Michigan Retirement Research Consortium, Washington, DC.

Nyce, Steven A., and Sylvester J. Schieber. 2005. *The economic implications of aging societies: The costs of living happily ever after.* Cambridge, UK: Cambridge University Press.

Organization for Economic Cooperation and Development (OECD). 2001. *Ageing and income.* Paris: OECD.

Poterba, James. 2004. The impact of population aging on financial markets. NBER Working Paper no. 10851. Cambridge, MA: National Bureau of Economic Research.

Poterba, James, Steven Venti, and David A. Wise. 1993. Do 401(k) contributions crowd out other personal saving? NBER Working Paper no. 4391. Cambridge, MA: National Bureau of Economic Research.

———. 1995. The effects of special saving programs on saving and wealth. NBER Working Paper no. 5287. Cambridge, MA: National Bureau of Economic Research.

———. 1996. How retirement savings programs increase saving. *Journal of Economic Perspectives* 10 (4): 91–112.

———. 2007. New estimates of the future path of 401(k) assets. NBER Working Paper no. 13083. Cambridge, MA: National Bureau of Economic Research.

President's Commission to Strengthen Social Security. 2001. *Strengthening Social Security and creating personal wealth for all Americans: Final report of the President's Commission to Strengthen Social Security.* Washington, DC: U.S. Government Printing Office.

Samuelson, Paul A. 1958. An exact consumption-loan model of interest with or without the social contrivance of money. *Journal of Political Economy* 66: 467–82.

Schieber, Sylvester J. 2008. The end of the golden years. *Milken Quarterly Review* (2nd quarter): 54–64.

Schieber, Sylvester J., and John B. Shoven. 1997. The consequences of population aging on private pension fund saving and asset markets. In *Public policy toward pensions,* ed. Sylvester J. Schieber and John B. Shoven, 219–46. Cambridge, MA: MIT Press.

Smetters, Kent. 2003. Is the Social Security trust fund worth anything? University of Pennsylvania. Unpublished Manuscript.

Comment   Steven F. Venti

The demographic transition to an older population has enormous implications for the well-being of future workers and retirees. In this chapter, Sylvester Schieber shows how this transition will affect economic growth, how it will stress pension systems, and how countries with different pension systems will be able to cope with the consequences. He finds that aging economies will be hard pressed to maintain past levels of economic performance, and living standards will likely fall for some segments of the population in some economies, regardless of how the pension system is financed. A move to a funded system can possibly provide limited relief from the harmful effects of population aging. He also shows that if current levels of living standards are unsustainable, then the organization of the pension system will be an important determinant of how "economic disappointment" will be shared by future generations. I broadly agree with Syl Schieber's assessment of the effect of the demographic transition on economies and pension systems. In the following, I will comment briefly on the key issues raised in the chapter. My focus is on how little we know about behavioral and political responses to the kinds of demographically induced stresses that Schieber identifies. I will also consider, in more detail, the likelihood of one particular consequence of population aging—an "asset meltdown"—that may occur when older households sell assets to finance retirement consumption.

Schieber begins with a review of the conventional literature on the effect of pension systems employing a variety of financing mechanisms—from complete pay-as-you-go to fully funded—on national saving. He argues that the focus on national saving is incomplete and advocates a broader approach that tracks the change over time of the difference between the accruing obligations of a pension system and its assets. Such an approach is currently used in the United States to assess the funding status of defined benefit pension plans. When applied to the entire U.S. pension system (public and private), Schieber shows that the U.S. retirement system is going progressively deeper into debt—increases in Social Security trust fund assets and private-sector pension saving are more than offset by skyrocketing Social Security system liabilities. Thus, the positive spin typically placed on the excess of Social Security tax revenue collected over benefits paid out misdirects attention from the fact that the health of our pension system is rapidly deteriorating. Schieber is correct to try to get analysts, legislators, and the general public to focus more on the increase in unfunded promises in the system.

Schieber next shows that aging stresses economies regardless of how pen-

Steven F. Venti is the DeWalt Ankeny Professor of Economic Policy and a professor of economics at Dartmouth College, and a research associate of the National Bureau of Economic Research.

sions are financed. He presents results based on a simple but powerful model that uses the population structure of three countries at very different stages of the demographic transition (Italy, the United States, and India) to show how each country will fare in the future if each had either a benchmark pay-as-you-go system or a funded system. The results strikingly show how aging places a heavy burden on future workers and retirees that is independent of the funding mechanism. As the population ages, taxes must increase or benefits fall in pay-as-you-go systems or savings rates must fall in funded systems. (These are just two of many outcomes affected by aging.) As Schieber notes, the burdens he projects are so great that they will never occur. Behavioral and political responses will prevent the worst from happening. The likelihood that these responses will be large highlights for the need for models that can account for these responses. Such models, though in the early stages of development, (see, for example, Börsch-Supan and Ludwig in this volume) simulate the effects of aging in an overlapping generations framework, allowing for more than one country, a realistic pension sector, and explicit demographics. Such models are, for example, capable of assessing whether international capital flows can blunt the negative effect of aging on saving in funded systems. The models can also incorporate labor supply and productivity responses to higher taxes in a pay-as-you-go system— behavioral responses that may exacerbate future burdens. These models can also evaluate different political reform scenarios designed to lessen the effects of aging. In sum, Schieber's projections of where we are headed— given current pension systems and current demographic trends—implicitly makes a very strong case for further development of models that incorporate political and behavioral feedback.

The other key points Schieber makes are well supported by the evidence he presents. He makes the case that population aging will inevitably result in slower growth of living standards. There is really no way out of this without massive increases in labor force participation or productivity increases. It is clear that future retirees will be working longer than current retirees. Even so, future generations will likely face "economic disappointment." Although how a pension system is financed may have little effect on the level of disappointment we may face, Schieber shows us how the pension system is likely to play a very important role in determining how this disappointment is allocated between the generations.

As noted in the preceding, many of the worst projections will not occur because of political and behavioral responses that are not incorporated into simple models of the effect of demographic change on an economy. One endogenous response—cross-border capital flows—may give funded systems an important advantage over unfunded systems. If assets accumulated in funded plans are invested in other economies at different stages of the demographic transition, then an aging country may be able to diversify away demographic risk. These international capital flows may help a country with an aging population avoid an "asset meltdown." A meltdown—which has received much attention in the popular press—will occur if the older generation sells assets faster than the (smaller) younger generation can buy them, thus depressing asset prices. Support for this effect has been provided by some theoretical models, notably those that consider how the U.S. baby boom affected asset prices (Brooks 2002; Abel 2003; Geanakoplos, Magill, and Quinzii 2004). These models show that in a closed economy, high rates of saving by boomers contributed to rising asset prices in the 1990s. Presumably, the forthcoming baby bust will have the opposite effect on prices. The key feature of these models is the closed economy assumption that may be justified by the well-documented home bias observed in U.S. portfolios. In a closed economy, of course, older retirees have only the younger workers to buy their assets. Several recent models have attempted to relax the closed-economy assumption. Ludwig, Krueger, and Börsch-Supan (2007), for example, allow cross-border capital flows and find only modest effects (less than 100 basis points) of population aging on the return to capital in an open economy. Attanasio, Kitao, and Violante (2006) also find small effects. Clearly, more work needs to be done on the international diversification of demographic risk. Nonetheless, the theoretical models do suggest that "openness" may relieve some of downward pressure on asset prices expected to occur in aging societies.

One way of empirically measuring "openness" is to look at simple measures of "home bias" displayed in portfolios. Figures 8C.1 and 8C.2 present time series evidence on foreign assets held by U.S. investors and on U.S. assets held by foreign investors. The data are from the Federal Reserve Board's *Flow of Funds Accounts.* Figure 8C.1 shows U.S. holdings of foreign equities as a percent of the market value of all U.S. equities. The results show enormous growth in the "openness" of U.S. portfolios. Holdings of foreign equities increased from a little over 5 percent in 1990, to 10 percent in 2000, to 22 percent by 2007. Presumably, foreign holdings, particularly holdings in "younger" countries, will shield U.S. investors from bearing the full brunt of declines in domestic equity prices. The severity of downward pressure on asset prices will also depend on whether foreigners will buy assets sold off by older households in the United States. Figure 8C.2 shows the percentage of the market value of U.S. equities held by foreigners. Although not as striking as the result in figure 8C.1, the data indicate a steady rise in foreign holdings since the late 1990s. There is no way of knowing how large cross-border holdings have to be to relieve aging-induced downward pressure on prices, but these data do suggest that a meltdown may be less likely than it was a decade ago.

Other research findings also suggest there is little cause for concern that population aging will depress asset prices. Recall that a relatively large older population puts downward pressure on asset prices because older households sell their assets to finance retirement consumption. However, the latter

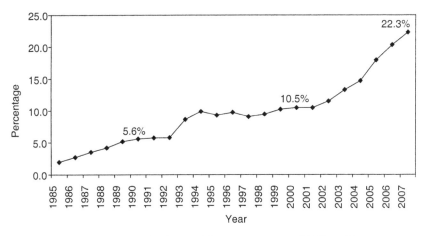

Fig. 8C.1   U.S. holdings of foreign equities as percentage of U.S. equities

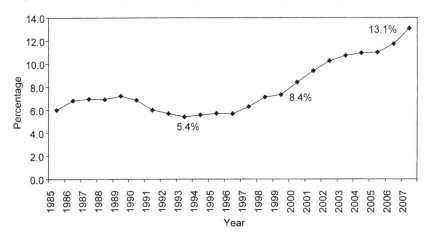

Fig. 8C.2   Foreign holdings of U.S. equities as percentage of U.S. equities

part of this statement—that the old want to sell assets—doesn't square too well with the empirical evidence on age-wealth profiles. In most European and Asian countries, and to a lesser extent the United States, household wealth is not observed to decrease at older ages, thus suggesting that older persons in aging populations may not sell-off assets to the extent predicted by the life-cycle model (see Börsch-Supan 2003). Other empirical work more directly examining the link between population aging and the return to capital has delivered mixed results (Poterba [2004] surveys the literature). Perhaps the most comprehensive analysis in Poterba (2004) looks at the relationship between a variety of demographic indicators and asset returns using U.S. data for the period 1926 to 2003. He concludes that there is little evidence that past changes in the demographic composition of the U.S.

population has had any effect on asset returns, thus casting doubt on the hypothesis that future changes in demographics will impact future returns.

Finally, Schieber and Shoven (1997) and Poterba, Venti, and Wise (2008) construct simulation models of the pension sector in the United States. The models, which are based on Social Security Administration (SSA) demographic forecasts, project balances held in pension plans in future years. The results suggest that the rate of growth and perhaps even the levels of assets will decline in the future as the population ages but that the declines are not projected to be large enough to trigger a meltdown. Thus, overall, the existing theoretical and empirical evidence suggests, at most, only modest effects of population aging on asset prices. The possibility of an "asset meltdown" appears unlikely.

In summary, Schieber concludes that unless drastic changes are made, "economic chaos" will result. Moreover, he cautions that changes will have to be made not only to pension systems, but that "the whole concept of retirement that has persisted over the past century will have to be revisited." This is pretty strong stuff, yet the case he has made for the consequences of inaction is so convincing that behavioral and political responses are inevitable. Indeed, many of these changes are already underway. Labor force participation among older workers has increased in many of the older European countries. In several countries, participation among persons aged fifty-five to sixty-four is up over 20 percent in the last decade. This trend is, in part, driven by increases in the pension normal retirement age in many countries. Another development is the dramatic growth in projected private-sector saving in some countries. In the United States, Poterba, Venti, and Wise (2008) show that balances in 401(k) plans is expected be four to five times larger, in real dollars, in 2040 than in 2010. This additional saving is driven by three factors: modest growth in participation, the transition from a funded defined benefit system to a defined contribution system (contributions are much higher in the latter), and by an ongoing rise in the percentage of their career for which retirement-age workers have been eligible for a 401(k) retirement plan. There are many other changes underway in various countries that may also blunt demographic effects: policies to encourage the internationalization of portfolios, immigration reform, increased funding of public plans, lowering the indexation of benefits, labor market reforms, and many others. All of these are developments that should help to lessen the stress that aging societies will face in the future. However, there is still much uncertainty about how much "economic disappointment" will remain to be shared.

References

Abel, Andrew. 2003. The effects of a baby boom on stock prices and capital accumulation in the presence of Social Security. *Econometrica* 71 (2): 551–78.

Attanasio, Orazio, Sagiri Kitao, and Giovanni Violante. 2006. Quantifying the effects of demographic transition in developing countries. *Advances in Macroeconomics* 6 (1): 1–44.

Börsch-Supan, Axel. 2003. Life-cycle saving and public policy: A cross-national study in six countries. New York: Academic Press.

Brooks, Robin. 2002. Asset market effects of the baby boom and Social Security reform. *American Economic Review* 92:402–06.

Geanakoplos, John, Michael Magill and Martine Quinzii. 2004. Demography and the long-run predictability of the stock market. *Brookings Papers on Economic Activity,* Issue no. 1: 241–307. Washington, DC: Brookings Institution.

Ludwig, Alexander, Dirk Krueger, and Axel Börsch-Supan. 2007. Demographic change, relative factor prices, international capital flows, and their differential effects on the welfare of generations. NBER Working Paper no. 13185. Cambridge, MA: National Bureau of Economic Research.

Poterba, James. 2004. The impact of population aging on financial markets. In *Global demographic change: Economic impact and policy challenges,* ed. G. Sellon, 163–216. A symposium sponsored by the Federal Reserve Bank of Kansas City.

Poterba, James, Steven Venti, and David Wise. 2008. New estimates of the future path of 401(k) assets. *Tax Policy and the Economy* 22:43–80.

Schieber, S., and J. Shoven. 1997. The consequences of population aging for private pension fund saving and asset markets. In *The economic effects of aging in the United States and Japan,* ed. M. Hurd and N. Yashiro, 111–30. Chicago: University of Chicago Press.

Financing Medicare
A General Equilibrium Analysis

Orazio Attanasio, Sagiri Kitao, and
Giovanni L. Violante

9.1 Introduction

The fiscal position of the United States, given the current Social Security and health care legislation and the predicted demographic trends, is projected to worsen considerably over the next fifteen to thirty years. The main reason behind the large projected deficits of the system is the aging of the U.S. population, as the generation of the baby boomers approaches retirement. This generation, which is considerably larger than preceding ones, will enjoy longer and possibly healthier retirement, partly as a consequence of medical progress. Under current legislation, they are entitled to receive pensions, as Social Security payments, as well as health care, through Medicare, the universal health care program for the elderly. These gains, however, come at a cost that will have to be financed.

It is now clear that, under the current legislation, the fiscal problems created by Medicare are substantially larger in magnitude relative to those associated to Social Security. They are, however, much less studied in the literature. The main focus of this chapter will be on the fiscal pressure created by Medicare. Our main aim is to look at this issue within a general equilib-

Orazio Attanasio is a professor of economics at University College London, a research fellow of the Center for Economic Policy Research and the Institute for Fiscal Studies, and a research associate of the National Bureau of Economic Research. Sagiri Kitao is an economist at the Federal Reserve Bank of New York. Giovanni L. Violante is an associate professor of economics at New York University, and a research associate of the Center for Economic Policy Research and the National Bureau of Economic Research.

We would like to thank Moshe Buchinsky for his insightful discussion and the participants at the NBER conference for many helpful suggestions.

rium, overlapping-generations model calibrated to mimic the behavior of the aggregate U.S. economy.

The advantage of looking at the problem within a fully specified, structural, equilibrium model is that one can quantify the effects of rising aggregate Medicare expenditures on macroeconomic quantities (e.g., output, labor supply, and saving rates), on equilibrium prices (e.g., wages and interest rates), on the tax rate necessary to balance the government budget, and, ultimately, on household welfare.

Our model builds on the class of environments first studied by Auerbach and Kotlikoff (1987). Individuals are born as adults and are endowed with ability of generating income that depends on their skills and that evolves with age. Over the life cycle, they decide how much to work and how much to consume (and save). They are subject to medical expenditure shocks. During working ages, an exogenously given fraction of the population has employer-based health insurance, which is charged on the wage bill at an equilibrium premium. After the fixed retirement age, only some agents continue to receive supplemental coverage from employer-sponsored plans, but all are entitled to Medicare coverage and to Social Security benefits. All individuals are also covered by a safety net government program (representing Medicaid and other welfare programs), which effectively guarantees a minimal consumption, even in the face of extremely large medical expenditures.

The agents in our economy are heterogeneous in several dimensions: besides age and wealth, they differ because of their skill level (which is exogenously fixed), and their health status. The latter can take two values (good and bad health) and evolves stochastically over time according to a Markov process. Health status has an effect on individual productivity, on medical expenditures, and on mortality. Healthier individuals are more productive, have lower medical expenditures, and are less likely to die. We calibrate all these effects combining two databases, the Medical Expenditure Panel Survey (MEPS) and the Health and Retirement Study (HRS).

Armed with this framework, whose details we describe in the following, we focus on studying the effects of the two forces that will determine the evolution of the Medicare bill: changes in the demographic structure and changes in the cost of health care. As the evolution of these two factors, and especially the second, are far from certain, we simulate different scenarios and different policy responses to these scenarios. Our model provides a first step in assessing quantitative implications of these alternative policies.

In our baseline experiment, we search for the adjustment in the labor income tax needed to finance the additional Social Security and Medicare outlays. We find that the taxation of labor must increase from 23 percent to 36 percent to balance the budget in the long run. Over two-thirds of the higher taxation in 2080 is associated to Medicare.

In our baseline experiment, we assume health care inflation, in excess of productivity growth and general inflation, of 0.63 percent per year. We consider an alternative scenario where excess health care inflation is 0.86 percent per year between 2005 and 2080, close to the long-run projection of a 1 percent annual growth by the Social Security Administration (SSA). Under this scenario, the wage tax rises to 39 percent. To appreciate the macroeconomic effects of the predicted rise in medical costs, note that in the model, consumption of nonmedical services drops by 21 percent as medical expenditures (and labor taxation) eat up a larger fraction of household earnings. Moreover, the percentage of families who are recipients of social assistance doubles relative to the final steady state in the baseline simulation.

In order to let the government alleviate the fiscal pressure from Medicare, we consider three alternative reforms: (a) a rise in the Medicare premium, (b) a reduction in the Medicare coverage rate, and (c) a rise in the retirement age. Interestingly, all three experiments reduce the equilibrium wage tax in 2080 by a similar magnitude (2 percent to 3 percent relative to the baseline), and they are all welfare improving. Raising retirement age increases the aggregate labor supply and output and is shown to be the best option from the welfare perspective. Raising the Medicare premium dominates the alternative of reducing the coverage rate because it shifts the costs of the program toward the beneficiaries without increasing the expenditure uncertainty they face.

In previous work (Attanasio, Kitao, and Violante 2006, 2007), we have argued that the extent to which capital will flow in and out of the United States, in the next seventy-five years is key in determining the budgetary, macroeconomic, and welfare implications of demographic trends. Here, we confirm that our quantitative conclusions depend on the path of factor prices associated with the openness of the economy. When the United States is seen as "small" relative to the world economy, the equilibrium wage tax rate increases only to 31 percent in 2080. As households increase their savings because of life-cycle and precautionary motives, their wealth grows, but the world interest rate remains fixed. As a result, the tax-base for capital income taxation increases significantly. This, in turn, allows the government to limit the rise in labor taxation.

Several studies sharing our same approach investigate the Social Security system and its reforms (see, for instance, Huang, İmrohoroğlu, and Sargent 1997; De Nardi, İmrohoroğlu, and Sargent 1999; Kotlikoff, Smetters, and Walliser 1999, 2007; Huggett and Ventura, 1999; Fehr, Jokisch, and Kotlikoff 2008; Attanasio, Kitao, and Violante 2006, 2007; Domeij and Floden 2006; Fuster, İmrohoroğlu, and İmrohoroğlu 2007; among others).

Some recent papers have tried to estimate the overall effect of the introduction of Medicare in 1965, taking into account the general equilibrium reaction of the supply of health services (see Finkelstein 2007). Other papers have looked at life-cycle models where health shocks and medical costs play an important role (see Palumbo 1999; French and Jones 2007; De Nardi, French, and Jones 2009). Yet another set of studies looks at specific information imperfections in the market for health insurance (see, for instance, Finkelstein 2004; Brown and Finkelstein 2007, 2008; Brown, Coe, and Finkelstein 2007). However, to the best of our knowledge, the financing of Medicare and its implications have not been studied within a general equilibrium model.

The closest paper to ours is Borger, Rutherford, and Won (2008). They calibrate a model of the U.S. economy where a representative household derives utility from consumption and health status, and health depends on the purchase of medical services. Medical services, in turn, are produced by a medical sector whose productivity growth determines "health care inflation." The authors use the model to explain why the demand for medical services is expanding even though its relative price is rising. Relative to Borger, Rutherford, and Won, our model has less detail in modeling production of medical services and has no link from consumption of medical services to health status (albeit it has a link from health to medical expenditures and from health to preferences through survival rates). However, we put more structure on the household side by modeling heterogeneity in demographics, health status, and medical expenditures. Finally, the focus of our chapter is on the fiscal consequences of Medicare, a question that Borger, Rutherford, and Won do not address explicitly.

The rest of the chapter is organized as follows. Section 9.2 presents the model. Section 9.3 outlines the calibration. The results of our simulations are reported in section 9.4. Section 9.5 concludes.

9.2   The Model

9.2.1   Economic Environment

In this section, we describe the model in a stationary economic environment.

Demographics and health status: The economy is populated by J overlapping generations of households. The size of a new cohort grows at rate g. Households enter the labor market at age $j = 1$ and retire at $j = j_R$. Within a cohort, households differ by their educational attainment, indexed by e. Let η_e be the fraction of type e in each cohort.

Households face exogenous uncertainty about their health status h. Conformably with the data, we let the stochastic evolution of health status depend on education. More precisely, the health status of a household of type e and age j evolves over the life cycle according to the Markov chain $\Lambda_{e,j}^h(h', h)$ for $j > 1$, with the implied distribution $\overline{\Lambda}_{e,j}^h(h)$ at age j.

Agents of age j and education e with health status h survive into next period with probability $\pi_{e,j}(h)$. Let $\Pi_{e,j}(\mathbf{h})$ denote the probability of surviving until age j for a newborn of type e, conditional on experiencing health history $\mathbf{h} = \{h_1, \ldots, h_{j-1}\}$. Households die with certainty at the end of period

J, that is, $\pi_{e,J}(h) = 0$ for all h and e. Unintended bequests of the deceased are seized by the government.

A household's labor productivity is determined by the product of two type-specific, orthogonal components, $\varepsilon_{e,j}$ and $\omega_e(h)$. The first is a deterministic age-dependent component whose level and shape depend on type e. To model retirement, we impose $\varepsilon_{e,j} = 0$ for $j \geq j_R$. The second is a stochastic component that depends on health status h and captures the fact that a deterioration of health status may reduce labor productivity by different amounts, depending on educational level.

Preferences: Households' preferences are separable over time and state, that is,

$$U = \mathbb{E}_0 \sum_{j=1}^{J} \Pi_j^e(\mathbf{h})\beta^{j-1}u(c_j, 1 - n_j),$$

where β denotes the discount factor, c consumption, and n hours worked. The expectation operator is taken over all the possible idiosyncratic histories of health status $\mathbf{h}$.

Health expenditures and insurance: Households are subject to medical expenditure shocks. Gross (i.e., before insurance coverage) medical expenditures m are random draws from a distribution $\Lambda_{j,h}^m(m)$, with density function $\lambda_{j,h}^m$, that depends on age j and health status h. The dollar value of expenditures incurred by the household is expressed as qm, where q is the relative price of medical services to consumption. The variable q allows us to model the feature that cost inflation for medical services is projected to be higher than general inflation and productivity growth. The persistence over the life cycle in medical expenses, an important feature of the data, follows from the persistence in health status.[1]

There are three types of medical insurance coverage in the economy: employer-based insurance, Medicare, and social assistance. During the working age, some households are offered employer-sponsored health insurance that covers a fraction κ^w of gross expenditures. In addition, some of the workers are offered insurance from their previous employers throughout retirement, at coverage rate κ^{ret}. Access to employer-based health insurance is determined by a random draw at the beginning of life. Let $i \in \{0, 1, 2\}$ denote the insurance status with $i = 0$ indicating no coverage, $i = 1$ indicating employer-sponsored coverage only during the working stage, and $i = 2$ indicating employer-sponsored coverage throughout life. A draw at age $j = 1$ from the distribution $\Lambda_e^i(i)$ determines the individual state i.[2]

Employer-sponsored health insurance is administered by competitive

---

1. We implicitly take the view that the amount of health expenditures drawn m is unavoidable to have any chance of survival into next period. As a result, households always optimally choose to incur such expenditures.

2. In practice, the worker decides whether to purchase the employer-based insurance when it is offered. The majority of workers, however, take up the offer due to the subsidy provided

insurance companies that pool, separately, workers and retirees covered by employer-sponsored insurance. An agent of type $i = 1$ pays a premium p^w during work. An agent of type $i = 2$ pays the larger premium $p^w + \xi^w p^{ret}$ during work and the premium $(1 - \bar{\xi}^{ret})p^{ret}$ during retirement. The parameter $\bar{\xi}^{ret}$ represents the fraction of the retirees' health insurance premium p^{ret} covered by the firm. The firm, in turn, shifts this cost to its current workers of type 2. In this sense, the system operates with a pay-as-you-go scheme: each current worker who will receive employer-sponsored insurance as a retiree (type 2) pays the extra premium $\xi^w p^{ret}$ necessary to finance the amount $\bar{\xi}^{ret} p^{ret}$ to each current covered retiree.[3] Insurance companies incur administrative fees ϕ per unit of medical expenditure covered and, in equilibrium, they charge premiums (p^w, p^{ret}) in order to break even. As in the U.S. economy, insurance premiums are tax deductible for workers with labor income.[4]

The second form of health insurance is provided by the government through Medicare: during retirement, all households are covered by Medicare with coverage rate κ^{med} and premium p^{med}. There are administrative costs ϕ^{med} per unit of medical expenditures covered by Medicare.

Finally, the government also acts as a last-resort insurer. It runs a social assistance program that guarantees a minimum level of consumption $\bar{c}$ to every household by supplementing income with a transfer tr in the event households' disposable assets fall below $\bar{c}$. This policy provides insurance against health expenditure and survival risk—the two sources of individual uncertainty in the economy. As such, it summarizes succinctly various U.S. transfer programs such as food stamps, Temporary Assistance for Needy Families (TANF), Supplemental Security Income, and, especially, Medicaid.

Commodities, goods, and input markets: There are three commodities: (a) final goods that can be used for private consumption, public consumption and addition to the existing capital stock (investment), (b) medical services, and (c) labor services supplied by households. All markets are competitive.

Technology: There are two sectors in the economy. One sector produces the final good that can be used for private and public consumption and for investment. The other sector produces medical services. We assume that the production function in the two sectors is the same, except for the dynamics

---

by the employers and the tax benefit. See Jeske and Kitao (2009) for a model that endogenizes the health insurance decision.

3. Note that $\bar{\xi}^{ret}$ need not be equal to ξ^w because the number of retirees that the firm subsidizes is not identical to the number of workers who share the cost because of the age-dependent survival rates.

4. More precisely, employer contributions are treated as a business expense and excluded from income and payroll tax bases. Employees' share of the premium can also be tax exempt if it is offered through flexible spending plans. See Lyke (2003) for more details on the current legislation on the tax treatment.

of sector-specific Total Factor Productivity (TFP). Given competitive markets and free movement of factors across sectors, it is easy to show that the model admits aggregation into a one-sector economy. Thus, we postulate an aggregate production function

$$Y = ZF(K, N),$$

where K is aggregate capital, N aggregate labor input in efficiency units, and Z total factor productivity. The economywide resource constraint reads as

$$Y = C + K' - (1 - \delta) K + qM + G,$$

where δ is the geometric depreciation rate of the capital stock. C denotes aggregate private consumption, M aggregate expenditures on medical services (including administrative costs associated with employer-based health insurance and Medicare), and G aggregate public consumption expenditures.

Fiscal policy: The government has five different types of outlays: general public consumption G, Medicare expenses, social assistance payments, Social Security benefits, and services to public debt. We have already described the first three expenditure items.

The Social Security program is pay-as-you-go as it is in the U.S. economy. Retired households of age $j \geq j_R$ and type e receive a pension benefit b_e through the Social Security system. Benefits replace a fraction ρ_e of the average earnings across all household of type e in the cohort; that is, we have

(1)
$$b_e = \rho_e \frac{1}{j_R - 1} \sum_{j=1}^{j_R-1} \bar{y}_e(j),$$

where $\bar{y}_e(j)$ are average earnings of households of type e and age j, that is the product of four components: average hours worked by education type, $\bar{n}_e$, the wage rate per efficiency units w, and the number of efficiency units jointly determined by the age-efficiency profile $\varepsilon_{e,j}$, and the impact of health status on productivity $\omega_e(h)$.[5]

The government supplies an amount of one-period, risk-free debt D which, by no arbitrage, must carry the same return r in equilibrium as claims to physical capital.

Finally, the government collects revenues from various sources: labor income taxation at rate τ^w, consumption taxation at rate τ^c, capital income taxation at rate τ^r, Medicare premium p^{med}, and accidental bequests. In the

---

5. Modeling benefits this way strikes a compromise between realism and computational efficiency. We capture that household benefits depend on their past earnings, as in the actual system. But we posit they depend on average earnings of group e, that households take as given, instead of past individual earnings, which would require an additional continuous state variable as well as an additional effect on the labor supply decision. The dependence on economywide average earnings does not require any additional state because households in the model must forecast prices anyway to compute their decisions.

baseline economy, we treat $(\tau^c, \tau^r, p^{\text{med}}, \rho_e, D, G)$ as parameters, and we let τ^w be determined in equilibrium to balance the government budget.

Assets and financial markets: As in İmrohoroğlu (1989), Huggett (1993), Aiyagari (1994), and Ríos-Rull (1996), financial markets are incomplete in the sense that agents trade risk-free bonds, subject to a borrowing constraint, but do not have access to state-contingent insurance against individual risk.

9.2.2   Household Problem

Work stage: The timing of events is as follows. At the beginning of each period, households observe their health status h and their disposable resources ("cash in hand") x. When household resources x are not large enough to finance the minimum consumption $\bar{c}$, the government intervenes through its social assistance program with a transfer tr. Next, households make consumption and labor supply decisions. Note that these decisions are made under uncertainty about medical expenditure shocks hitting the individual later in the period. Then, labor income and capital income are earned, and the insurance premium is paid if the household is covered by health insurance ($i = 1, 2$). Then, the medical expenditure shock m is realized, a fraction κ^w of which is covered in case of coverage. The residual $(1 - \kappa^w)qm$ represents out-of-pocket expenses. Finally, the mortality shock is realized and, conditional on surviving, households enter next period with a new health status h'. We can describe the problem of working households recursively as

(2) $V(e, i, j, h, x) = \max\limits_{\{c,n\}} \{u(c, 1-n) + \beta \pi_{e,j}(h) \mathbb{E} V(e, i, j+1, h', x')\}$ WHP

subject to

$$x' = [1 + (1-\tau^r)r][x - (1-\tau^c)c + \text{tr}] + (1-\tau^w)[w\varepsilon_{e,j}\omega_e(h)n - d(i)]$$

$$- (1-\kappa^w \cdot I_{\{i>0\}})qm$$

$$d = \begin{cases} 0 & \text{if } i = 0 \\ p^w & \text{if } i = 1 \\ p^w + \xi^w p^{\text{ret}} & \text{if } i = 2 \end{cases}$$

$$\text{tr} = \max\{0, (1+\tau^c)\bar{c} - x\}$$

$$c \leq \frac{x + \text{tr}}{1 + \tau^c}$$

$$h' \sim \Lambda_{e,j}^h(h', h) \text{ and } m \sim \Lambda_{j,h}^m(m)$$

The first constraint is the budget constraint of the household, and $I_{\{\cdot\}}$ is the indicator function. The second line describes the deduction $d(i)$ on the health insurance premium. The third equation models the social assistance policy. The fourth line is the no-borrowing constraint. The laws of motion for medical expenditure shocks and health status appear in the last line. For future reference, it is also useful to define households' asset holdings as $a \equiv x - (1 + \tau^c)c + \text{tr}$.

Retirement stage: At the beginning of each period, households observe health status h and their disposable resources x. If disposable assets fall below $\bar{c}$, the government transfers the residual amount tr. Next, the household makes its consumption decision under uncertainty about medical expenditure shocks. Then, Social Security benefits are earned, the Medicare premium is paid, and the additional insurance premium is paid in case of employer-sponsored coverage ($i = 2$). Next, medical expenditure shocks m are realized, a fraction κ^{med} of which are covered by Medicare for everyone. An additional fraction κ^{ret} is covered if the household is insured through its past employer ($i = 2$). The residual represents out-of-pocket expenditures for the household. Finally, the mortality shock is realized and, conditional on surviving, households enter the next period. We can write the problem of a retired household recursively as

$$(3) \quad V_r(e,i,j,h,x) = \max_c \{u(c,1) + \beta \pi_{e,j}(h) \mathbb{E} V_r(e,i,j+1,h',x')\} \; RHP$$

subject to

$$x' = [1 + (1 - \tau^r)r][x - (1 + \tau^c)c + \text{tr}] + b_e - [1 - \kappa^{\text{med}} - \kappa^{\text{ret}} \cdot I_{\{i=2\}}] qm$$
$$- p^{\text{med}} - (1 - \bar{\xi}^{\text{ret}})p^{\text{ret}} \cdot I_{\{i=2\}}$$

$$\text{tr} = \max \{0, (1 + \tau^c)\bar{c} - x\}$$

$$c \leq \frac{x + \text{tr}}{1 + \tau^c}$$

$$h' \sim \Lambda_{e,j}^h (h', h) \text{ and } m \sim \Lambda_{j,h}^m (m)$$

9.2.3   Stationary Equilibrium

Let $s \equiv \{e, i, j, h, x\}$ be the individual state vector, with $e \in \mathcal{E}$, $i \in \mathcal{I} = \{0, 1, 2\}$, $j \in \mathcal{J} = \{1, 2, \ldots, J\}$, $h \in \mathcal{H}$, and $x \in \mathcal{X} = [\underline{x}, \bar{x}]$. Let $\mathcal{B}_{\mathcal{H}}$ and $\mathcal{B}_{\mathcal{X}}$ be the Borel sigma algebras of $\mathcal{H}$ and $\mathcal{X}$, and $P(\mathcal{E})$, $P(\mathcal{I})$ and $P(\mathcal{J})$ be the power sets of $\mathcal{E}$, $\mathcal{I}$, and $\mathcal{J}$. The state space is denoted by $\mathcal{S} \equiv \mathcal{E} \times \mathcal{I} \times \mathcal{J} \times \mathcal{H} \times \mathcal{X}$. Let $\Sigma_{\mathcal{S}}$ be the sigma algebra on $\mathcal{S}$ defined as $\Sigma_{\mathcal{S}} \equiv P(\mathcal{E}) \otimes P(\mathcal{I}) \otimes P(\mathcal{J}) \otimes \mathcal{B}_{\mathcal{H}} \otimes \mathcal{B}_{\mathcal{X}}$ and $(\mathcal{S}, \Sigma_{\mathcal{S}})$ be the corresponding measurable space. Denote the stationary measure of households on $(\mathcal{S}, \Sigma_{\mathcal{S}})$ as μ.

Given survival rates $\{\pi_{e,j}(h)\}$, fiscal variables $\{G, D, \rho_e, \tau^c, \tau^r, \text{tr}(s)\}$, and relative price of medical services q, a *stationary recursive competitive equilibrium* is a set of (a) value functions $V(s)$, (b) decision rules for the households $\{c(s), n(s)\}$, (c) firm choices $\{K, N\}$, (d) insurance premiums $\{p^w, p^{\text{ret}}\}$, (e) labor income tax rate τ^w, and (f) a measure of households μ such that:

1. Working households choose optimally consumption and labor supply by solving problem (WHP), and retired households choose optimally consumption by solving problem (RHP).

2. Firms maximize profits by setting their marginal productivity equal to factor prices

$$w = ZF_N(K, N)$$
$$r + \delta = ZF_K(K, N).$$

3. The labor market clears

$$N = \int_{\mathcal{S}|j<j_R} \varepsilon_{e,j}\omega_e(h)n(s)d\mu.$$

4. The asset market clears

$$K + D = \int_{\mathcal{S}} a(s)d\mu.$$

5. The private insurance market for working households, and retired households clears

$$p^w \int_{\mathcal{S}|j<j_R,i\in\{1,2\}} d\mu = (1 + \phi)\,\kappa^w q \int_{\mathcal{S}|j<j_R,i\in\{1,2\}} m\lambda^m_{j,h}(m)d\mu$$

$$p^{ret} \int_{\mathcal{S}|j\geq j_R,i=2} d\mu = (1 + \phi)\,\kappa^{ret}q \int_{\mathcal{S}|j\geq j_R,i=2} m\lambda^m_{j,h}(m)d\mu,$$

with all insurance companies making zero profits for the two separate pools.[6]

6. The final good market clears

$$ZF(K, N) = C + \delta K + qM + G,$$

where

$$C = \int_{\mathcal{S}} c(s)d\mu \text{ and } M = \int_{\mathcal{S}} m(s)\,d\mu + \Phi,$$

and Φ represents the total administrative costs associated with the employer-based insurance and Medicare.[7]

7. The government budget constraint satisfies

$$\tau^c C + \tau^w wN + \tau^r r \int_{\mathcal{S}} a(s)d\mu + p^{med} \int_{\mathcal{S}|j\geq j_R} d\mu + \int_{\mathcal{S}} [1 - \pi_{e,j}(h)]xd\mu$$
$$= G + rD + \int_{\mathcal{S}} \text{tr}(x)d\mu + (1 + \phi^{med})\kappa^{med}q \int_{\mathcal{S}|j\geq j_R} m\lambda^m_{j,h}(m)d\mu$$
$$+ \int_{\mathcal{S}|j\geq j_R} b_e d\mu,$$

---

6. As discussed in the preceding, each retiree pays a fraction $(1 - \bar{\xi}^{ret})$ of the premium p^{ret}, and each worker with a lifetime coverage pays a fraction ξ^w of p^{ret}, where

$$\xi^w = \bar{\xi}^{ret} \frac{\int_{\mathcal{S}|j\geq j_R,i=2} d\mu}{\int_{\mathcal{S}|j\geq j_R,i=2} d\mu}.$$

7. More precisely,

$$\Phi = \phi[\kappa^w \int_{\mathcal{S}|j<j_R,i\in\{1,2\}} m\lambda^m_{j,h}(m)d\mu + \kappa^{ret} \int_{\mathcal{S}|j\geq j_R,i=2} m\lambda^m_{j,h}(m)d\mu] + \phi^{med}\kappa^{med} \int_{\mathcal{S}|j\geq j_R} m\lambda^m_{j,h}(m)d\mu.$$

where $a \equiv x - (1 + \tau^c)c + tr(x)$, the social assistance rule $tr(x)$ is described in [WHP] and [RHP], and Social Security benefits b_e are determined as in equation (1).

8. For all sets $S \equiv (E \times I \times J \times H \times X) \in \Sigma_{\mathcal{G}}$, the measure μ satisfies

$$\mu(S) = \int_{\mathcal{G}} Q(s, S)d\mu,$$

where, for $j > 1$, the transition function Q is defined as

$$Q(s, S) = I\{e \in E, i \in I, j + 1 \in J\}\Lambda^h_{e,j}(h' \in H, h)\Pr\{x' \in X|s\}\pi_{e,j}(h),$$

with $\Pr\{x' \in X|s\}$ jointly determined by the constraint sets of problems (WHP) and (RHP), the household decision rules, and the distribution function of medical expenditures $\Lambda^m_{e,j}(m)$.

9.3 Calibration

We calibrate our model to the U.S. economy and demographics in 2005. Then we compare the stationary equilibrium of this economy to another economy that has the same set of parameter values, except for (a) the demographic structure (population growth and survival rates), and (b) the price level q of medical expenditures. This second economy is meant to represent the United States in 2080.

Demographics: Households enter the economy at the age of twenty ($j = 1$) and survive up to the maximum age of 100 ($J = 81$). They can be of either type $e = 1$ (high education) or $e = 0$ (low education). We fix the proportion of high-educated newborn η_e at 0.30. Households retire from work at the mandatory retirement age of sixty-five ($j_R = 46$). A high-education household in the data corresponds to single households where the adult holds a college degree and to married households where at least one of the spouses has attained a college degree.

In our model, survival rates $\pi_{e,j}(h)$ depend on education level e, age j, and health status h. Let $\overline{\pi}_{e,j}$ be the average (across health status) survival rate at age j for education type e. Bhattacharya and Lakdawalla (2006) have computed these survival curves by age/education demographic groups, which we use for the values of $\overline{\pi}_{e,j}$. We then combine the differentials in longevity by group with the long-run projections of the aggregate surviving rates (i.e., those averages across the entire population) formulated by the SSA (Bell and Miller 2002) in order to construct the age- and education-specific surviving rates in 2080. The key assumption we make is that the ratio between the mortality rate of the college-educated type and that of the low-education type at each age, remains constant. The left panel of figure 9.1 plots, for the high-education groups, the average survival rates

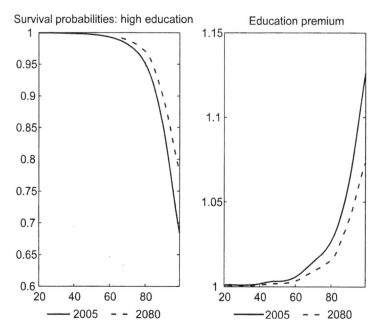

Fig. 9.1   Left panel: Survival rates by age for the college graduates in 2005 (data) and 2080 (projected). Right panel: Ratio of survival rates of college graduates to noncollege graduates by age in 2005 and 2080

$\bar{\pi}_{1,j}$ as a function age in 2005 and 2080. The right panel plots the survival differential between the two education groups, by age.[8]

In the initial steady state, we set the growth rate of the size of newborn cohorts to 1.35 percent per year in order to match an old-age dependency ratio (the ratio of the population aged sixty-five and over to that between twenty and sixty-four) of 20 percent, the observed values for the U.S. economy. According to the U.S. Census Bureau's projection, the population growth will settle at 0.69 to 0.71 percent in 2050 to 2100. We set the growth rate at 0.70 percent in the final steady state, which together with the survival probabilities in 2080 projected by the SSA implies the dependency ratio of 32.2 percent.

Preferences: Households have period utility over consumption and leisure:

$$(4) \qquad u(c, 1 - n) = \frac{c^{1-\gamma}}{1 - \gamma} + \chi \frac{(1 - n)^{1-\theta}}{1 - \theta}.$$

8. Because it is the ratio of mortality rates of high- to low-educated that we assume to be constant, the ratio of survival rates changes from 2005 to 2080.

We choose $\gamma = 2$, which implies the intertemporal elasticity of substitution of 0.5, in the middle of the range of micro estimates in the literature (see Attanasio [1999] for a survey). We set the parameter χ so that the average fraction of the time endowment allocated to market work is 0.33, which implies $\chi = 2.028$. Under this preference specification, the intertemporal labor supply elasticity is $([1 - n]/n)/\theta$. We set the average labor supply elasticity in the population to 0.50, which is a compromise between the small estimates for males and estimates for females that are above one (Browning, Hansen, and Heckman 1999). Given our target for the market work hours, this requires setting $\theta = 4$. We set the subjective discount factor β to 0.9955 so that the economy in 2005 has wealth (claims to physical capital and to public debt) to gross domestic product (GDP) ratio equal to 3.4, similar to the U.S. economy.

Technology: The aggregate production function is Cobb-Douglas in capital and effective labor:

$$Y_t = ZK_t^\alpha L_t^{1-\alpha}.$$

We set α at 0.33 to match the capital share of output and the physical depreciation rate at 0.06. Total factor productivity Z is chosen so that income per capita ($42,000 in 2005) is normalized to 1.0 in the first steady state.

Health status and survival rates: Our main source of micro data on U.S. households is the Medical Expenditure Panel Survey (MEPS). The MEPS is an ongoing annual survey of a representative sample of the civilian population with detailed information on demographics, income, labor supply, health status, health expenditures, and health insurance.

The measure of health status in MEPS is self-reported.[9] Every annual MEPS survey has three waves, and this measure is present in each one. Because health status is reported at the individual level, we face the issue of aggregating this information into the health status of a household (often composed of more than one adult) on an annual basis, while at the same time maintaining computational feasibility. We choose to define two levels of a household health status: good (h^g) and bad (h^b). First, for each spouse in the household, we compute the numerical average of the answer to the subjective health question across the three waves. We then define an individual to be in bad health that year if its average was strictly above 3. Finally, for married households, we define the household to be in bad health if at least one of the spouses was in bad health.

Table 9.1 (upper panel) reports the estimated transition function $\Lambda_{e,j}^h$ for the two education groups for ten-year age classes twenty to twenty-nine, thirty to thirty-nine, and so on. We group ages sixty-five and higher in order

---

9. The exact wording of the survey question on health status is: "In general, compared to other people of (PERSON)'s age, would you say that (PERSON)'s health is excellent (1), very good (2), good (3), fair (4), or poor (5)?"

Table 9.1   Transition probabilities between good health and bad health from MEPS and HRS, by age group and education level

| | Low education (no college) | | High education (college) | |
Age	Good	Bad	Good	Bad
Medical Expenditure Panel Survey (MEPS)				
20–29				
Good	0.9546	0.0454	0.9856	0.0144
Bad	0.4103	0.5897	0.5833	0.4167
30–39				
Good	0.9412	0.0588	0.9757	0.0243
Bad	0.3281	0.6719	0.3143	0.6857
40–49				
Good	0.9212	0.0788	0.9583	0.0417
Bad	0.2085	0.7915	0.2955	0.7045
50–64				
Good	0.8734	0.1266	0.9461	0.0539
Bad	0.1614	0.8386	0.2250	0.7750
65+				
Good	0.8630	0.1370	0.8962	0.1038
Bad	0.1386	0.8614	0.2083	0.7917
Health and Retirement Survey (HRS)				
50–64				
Good	0.8942	0.1058	0.9327	0.0673
Bad	0.2455	0.7545	0.1764	0.8236
65+				
Good	0.8925	0.1075	0.9243	0.0757
Bad	0.2113	0.7887	0.1587	0.8413

to maintain a sufficiently large sample size. This transition matrix shows that the good health status is very persistent, more so for the college-educated. The probability of a switch from good to bad health increases monotonically with age, from roughly 4.5 percent (1.4 percent) at age twenty-five to 13.7 percent (10.4 percent) beyond age sixty-five for the low-educated (for the high-educated). Also the persistence of the bad health status increases sharply with age.[10]

Figure 9.2 reports the implied fraction of households in bad health by age class and education group (solid lines) implied by the transition matrix against the empirical fractions measured directly from MEPS in each wave (stars). The fraction of households reporting to be in bad health increases sharply over the life cycle. For example, for low-educated households, it

10. The initial draw of health status for households in the model is calibrated from the MEPS data on the health status at age twenty. At this age, 98 percent of college graduates and 90 percent of high school graduates are in good health.

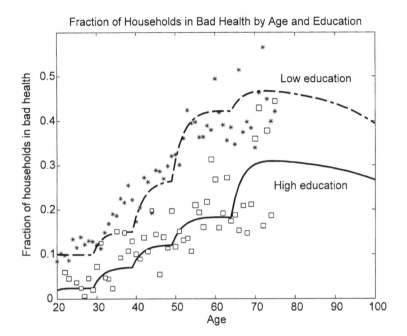

Fig. 9.2   Fraction of individuals in bad health

Notes: Stars and squares represent estimates from various waves, solid lines are model-implied fractions from the estimated transition probabilities of table 9.1.

Source: MEPS.

starts at around 10 percent at age twenty-five and reaches 45 percent beyond age sixty-five. Note that due to the small sample size, the estimates become extremely noisy after age sixty-five. The decline after age sixty-five is a natural consequence of selection: survivors are more likely to be in good health.

By design, the MEPS data do not allow to quantify the effect of health status on mortality rates. First, their panel dimension is very short. Second, individuals drop out of the MEPS sample when they become institutionalized (e.g., enter a nursing home) and are not followed thereafter. As a result, the number of individuals who are recorded as deceased in the survey is extremely small, and the sample is heavily selected. Therefore, to measure the marginal effect of bad health on mortality rates, we turn to the Health and Retirement Survey (HRS).

The main advantage of the HRS is that it focuses on a sample of older individuals (and their spouses) and follows them over a long period of time (seven waves are currently available, each contact being two years apart from the previous one). The HRS, therefore, provides the ideal sample to estimate mortality rates and how they relate to other variables. The HRS also contains a question on health status that is similar to the question asked in

MEPS.[11] We note a word of caution that the HRS asks subjective health status, while the question in the MEPS is concerned about the health status relative to others in the same age group. Therefore, in order to check their comparability, we compare the transition matrices by age in both data sets.

Before describing how we estimate the relationship between health status and mortality, we compare the distribution of health status and their persistence in the two data sets. In particular, both in the MEPS and in the HRS (between fifth and sixth waves) we use the same definition of household's "good health" and "bad health". The results from the HRS are reported in table 9.1 (lower panel). The key difference is that these are biannual transition rates, so the comparison is not immediate. From the MEPS, we can construct biannual rates and compare them to the HRS. For example,

$$\Lambda^h_{e,j}(h^b, h^b)^2 = \Lambda^h_{e,j}(h^b, h^b) \Lambda^h_{e,j}(h^b, h^b) + \Lambda^h_{e,j}(h^b, h^g) \Lambda^h_{e,j}(h^g, h^b).$$

Focusing on the oldest group among the low-educated, we obtain that $\Lambda^h_{l,65+}$ $(h^b, h^b)^2 = 0.76$ in the MEPS and 0.79 in the HRS. Overall, the similarity across the two samples is considerable, which gives us confidence in combining the two data sets.

To calibrate the effect of health status on survival probabilities, we exploit the longitudinal dimension of the HRS and model the probability of dying as a function of age, gender, and health status through a probit model.[12] As expected, the probability of dying increases with age, and it is lower for women. Being in good health decreases considerably the probability of dying. Figure 9.3 shows that this good health premium is less than 1 percent at age twenty-five, but it increases quickly up to 3.5 percent at age sixty-five. After age sixty-five, we have extrapolated the premium based on a quadratic function.

In light of these findings, we adjust our conditional survival rates as follows. Let the good health premium on survival rates at age j be denoted by survprem$_j$. Let $\bar{\pi}^{e,j}$ be the average survival rate, and $\bar{\Lambda}^h_{e,j}$ be the distribution of health status for group e at age j. Then, given values for survprem$_j$, $\bar{\pi}^{e,j}$, $\bar{\Lambda}^h_{e,j}(h^b)$, and $\bar{\Lambda}^h_{e,j}(h^g)$, the two equations

$$\bar{\pi}_{e,j} = \bar{\Lambda}^h_{e,j}(h^b)\pi_{e,j}(h^b) + \bar{\Lambda}^h_{e,j}(h^g)\pi_{e,j}(h^g)$$

$$\text{survprem}_j = \pi_{e,j}(h^g) - \pi_{e,j}(h^b)$$

allow us to determine the two unknowns $\{\pi_{e,j}(h^g), \pi_{e,j}(h^b)\}$ for each education and age (e, j) pair. When we project survival rates in the final steady-

---

11. The HRS asks each respondent the following question "Would you say your health is excellent, very good, good, fair, or poor?" with an answer from "(1) excellent, (2) very good, (3) good, (4) fair, (5) poor."

12. We also experimented with richer specifications, which entered nonlinear terms in age and interactions between age and health status. Possibly because of the limited amount of data we have, these interactions did not turn out to be significant.

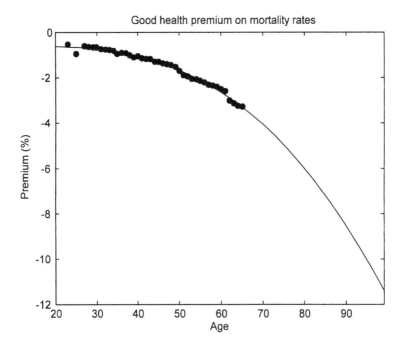

Fig. 9.3   Percentage decrease in mortality rates for an individual in good health relative to an individual in bad health, by age

Notes: Dots are data; solid line is a polynomial fit.
Source: HRS.

state, consistently with the strategy outlined in the preceding, we keep constant the estimated good health premium.

Medical expenditures and insurance: Table 9.2 reports the distribution of adult-equivalent household medical expenditures computed from the MEPS by age class and health status. In order to keep the sample size large enough, we have grouped ages into ten-year intervals twenty to twenty-nine, thirty to thirty-nine, and so on until sixty-five and above. We have also chosen to approximate the distribution by a histogram with bins corresponding to the 1st to 60th percentile, 61th to 95th percentile, and 96th to 100th percentile. Within each interval, we compute the average value and use it for our three-point grid. This approximation is guided by the findings in French and Jones (2004), who show that the vast majority of households do not spend much, but the distribution has a thin and very long tail that is generated by a small number of catastrophic events.

The table shows that, on average, old spend more than young. For example, at age sixty-five and above, households spend about four times more than at age twenty-five. A household in good health faces $1,260 of annual medical expenses at age twenty-five, but around $6,000 at age sixty-five and

Table 9.2   Gross medical expenditures in 2004 $ by age and health status: means of the 1st–60th percentiles, 61st–95th percentiles, 96th–100th percentiles, and distribution average

| | Percentiles | | | |
Age	1–60	61–95	96–100	Average
	Good health			
20–29	153	1,876	10,192	1,258
30–39	321	2,762	13,482	1,833
40–49	453	2,928	19,606	2,277
50–65	1,002	5,124	22,609	3,525
65+	2,074	8,990	33,190	6,034
	Bad health			
20–29	484	4,453	23,484	3,023
30–39	758	6,027	40,605	4,595
40–49	1,262	8,243	42,861	5,785
50–65	2,363	12,399	59,730	8,744
65+	3,946	16,194	60,556	11,063

Source: MEPS.

above. Moreover, households in bad health spend more than twice as much as those in good health. A household of age fifty in bad health has expenditures around $3,500 when in good health, but if health deteriorates, medical expenses jump to $8,700 per year. The table also shows a great skewness in the distribution: with a small probability, households face extremely large medical expenditure shocks.

It is well known that the MEPS significantly underestimates medical expenditures at the aggregate level compared to those reported in the National Health Accounts (NHA). Selden et al. (2001) report that the MEPS estimate of total expenditures in 1996 was $550 billion, while the NHA estimate exceeded $900 billion in the same year. The NHA rely on the providers' surveys while the MEPS statistics are based on households' surveys, which tend to underreport the spending and utilization of medical services. The two sources also differ in covered population and services. For example, the NHA include expenditures by individuals in institutions (e.g., nursing homes), foreign visitors, and military personnel, all of which are out of scope in the MEPS. The MEPS also excludes some sizeable service categories such as certain types of long-term mental hospital cares and skilled nursing facilities.[13]

It is important that we adjust the expenditure data from the MEPS to be consistent with the data at the national level so that we can correctly

13. For more details on the discrepancy between the two sources, see Selden et al. (2001) and Keehan et al. (2004).

assess the effect of the increase in medical expenditures on macroeconomic and fiscal variables. Therefore, we choose to proportionally adjust the individual expenditures of the MEPS by a factor of 1.48 to achieve aggregate medical expenditures equal to 13 percent of GDP in the initial steady-state economy, based on the National Health Expenditure Accounts (NHEA) data in 2004.

From the MEPS data, we are able to compute the coverage rates κ^w, κ^{ret}, and κ^{med} representing, respectively, the fraction of medical expenditures covered by private insurance for workers and retirees and by Medicare for retirees. We estimate $\kappa^w = 0.70$, $\kappa^{ret} = 0.30$ and $\kappa^{med} = 0.50$. We also verify that, in equilibrium, under our estimated Medicare coverage, Medicare costs are 2.4 percent of GDP, close to the U.S. data for 2004.

The annual Medicare premium for Part B was \$938 in 2005, or about 2.24 percent of income per capita, which puts $p^{med} = 0.0224$ according to our normalization. Because, by law, the premium is scheduled to increase enough to cover a constant fraction of Medicare Part B expenditures, we choose to adjust p^{med} in the new steady-state proportionally to the average medical expenditures of Medicare beneficiaries.[14] Finally, we set the fraction of the retiree's insurance premium paid by the employer ξ^{ret} to 0.6, based on Buchmueller, Johnson, and Sasso (2006).

We normalize $q = 1$ in the first steady state, and we set $q = 1.6$ in the final steady state, which implies a medical cost inflation rate of 0.63 percent per year over the next seventy-five years above general inflation and productivity growth, both normalized to zero in our economy. We will verify the sensitivity of our findings to the value chosen for this key parameter.

The estimates of the administrative costs associated with the private health insurance vary in the literature, and we set the parameter ϕ to 0.1 based on Kahn et al. (2005). Medicare administrative expenses account for 1.4 percent of total expenditures according to the SSA, and we set ϕ^{med} to this value.

Individual productive efficiency: The deterministic age/education-specific component $\varepsilon_{e,j}$ and the health-dependent component $\omega^e(h)$ can be all estimated from the MEPS. We first split the sample into two groups based on educational attainment. Then we run a cross-sectional regression of individual hourly wages on a constant, a cubic function of age, and the individual health status indicator.

The results are reported in figure 9.4. College education has a wage premium of 45 percent, and bad health significantly reduces individual productivity. A year of bad health reduces hourly wages by 10.6 percent for the

---

14. The implicit assumption we are making is that the fraction of total Medicare expenditures associated to Part B remains constant over time. In 2005, revenues from the premiums covered 8 percent of average medical expenditures of retirees.

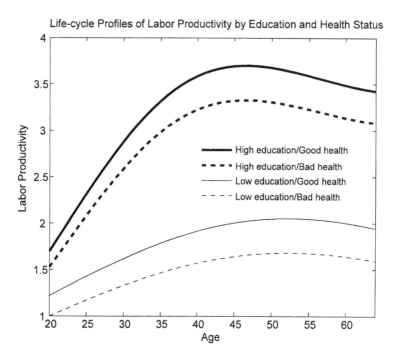

Fig. 9.4   Hourly wage-age profiles for high- and low-educated individuals in good and bad health status
Source: MEPS.

college graduates and by 19.8 percent for the noncollege graduates, relative to the earnings of workers in good health in the same education class.[15]

Government taxes, debt, and Social Security   Government expenditures G are set to 20 percent of GDP; that is the share of government consumption and gross investment excluding transfers at the federal, state and local levels (The Economic Report of the President 2004). The ratio of federal debt held by the public D to GDP is set at 40 percent, which is the value at the end of 2006. We fix the consumption tax τ^c at 5.7 percent, and the capital income tax τ^r at 40 percent based on Mendoza, Razin, and Tesar (1994).

The minimum consumption floor $\bar{c}$ is set to 10 percent of income per capita. This implies $\bar{c} = 0.10$ because income per capita is normalized to one in the first steady state. The Social Security replacement rate ρ_e is set to 0.40 for the low-educated and 0.30 for the high-educated, reflecting the

15. This education gap in the marginal effect of bad health on wages may be attributable to the different type of diseases experienced by the two groups: the low-skilled may experience illnesses that are more detrimental for work. Moreover, productivity in manual occupations, which are more common among low-educated workers, tends to be more sensitive to health deterioration.

progressivity of the system. The implied total social security outlays as a fraction of GDP are 4.5 percent in 2005.

9.4   Results

We start by contrasting the "initial steady state" calibrated to the current U.S. economy to a "final steady state," representing the U.S. economy in 2080. The final steady state differs in two important aspects: (a) the demographic structure (which in our model is summarized by the rate of growth of the population and the survival rates), and (b) the cost of health care. We will focus on changes in the labor income tax τ^w that balances the government budget, in equilibrium prices (wages and interest rates), in the saving rate, and in output. Because demographic trends worsen the budgetary position of the government with respect to both Social Security and Medicare, in one experiment we keep the Social Security outlays constant (as a fraction of GDP) to disentangle the two sources of expenditures and assess their relative importance.

We report the sensitivity of our baseline results to the key parameters. Given the uncertainty surrounding the evolution of health care costs, we consider alternative scenarios for q, and we simulate the final steady state under different assumptions for population growth in 2080.

We also run a set of simulations where the interest rate (and, therefore, the wage) is exogenously fixed, implicitly determined in the world financial markets. Given the high degree of financial integration across countries and the fast emergence of large open economies (like Russia, China, and India), which reduce the weight of the United States in the world economy, we view this set of experiments as a relevant alternative benchmark.

We then consider a set of policy experiments where the government tries to alleviate the fiscal pressure created by Medicare. In particular, we consider (a) an increase in the Medicare premium p^{med} (above what is already scheduled to happen), (b) a reduction in coverage rate κ^{med}, and (c) an increase in retirement age. We report the welfare gains of these policy reforms relative to the benchmark where only the labor income tax τ^w adjusts to balance the government budget constraint.

Last, we report two sets of robustness analysis with respect to the labor supply elasticity and generosity of the social assistance provided by the government.

9.4.1   Baseline Simulation

The second column of table 9.3 reports the results of the baseline simulation of the final steady state (the values for the initial steady state are in the first column). Besides the different demographics that raise the dependency ratio from 20 percent in 2005 to 32.3 percent, in the final steady state it is assumed that the cost of health care will be 60 percent higher ($q = 1.6$) than

Table 9.3 Results of the closed-economy simulations: baseline and sensitivity analysis

	Initial Steady State	Final Steady State						
	Baseline (q = 1.0)	Baseline (q = 1.6)	High pop. growth (1.4%)	Low pop. growth (0%)	No med. cost increase (q = 1.0)	Low med. cost increase (q = 1.3)	High med. cost increase (q = 1.9)	SS fixed at 4.5% of GDP
Labor tax rate (%)	0.230	0.357	0.315	0.411	0.308	0.331	0.388	0.318
Interest rate (%)	0.050	0.045	0.046	0.045	0.043	0.044	0.049	0.036
Wage rate	1.183	1.212	1.206	1.209	1.224	1.217	1.189	1.265
Medical expenditures (% of GDP)	0.130	0.226	0.203	0.254	0.151	0.190	0.263	0.215
Average work hours	0.329	0.368	0.364	0.374	0.340	0.354	0.381	0.368
Aggregate capital	3.000	3.301	3.367	3.154	3.146	3.218	3.232	3.772
% change from the benchmark		0.100	0.122	0.051	0.049	0.073	0.077	0.257
Aggregate labor input	0.565	0.580	0.599	0.558	0.536	0.558	0.601	0.582
% change from the benchmark		0.026	0.061	-0.012	-0.050	-0.012	0.064	0.030
Aggregate output	1.000	1.049	1.079	1.007	0.980	1.014	1.067	1.098
% change from the benchmark		0.049	0.079	0.007	-0.020	0.014	0.067	0.098
Aggregate nonmedical consumption	0.436	0.370	0.381	0.352	0.417	0.393	0.343	0.378
% change from the benchmark		-0.152	-0.127	-0.193	-0.045	-0.098	-0.213	-0.133
Fiscal outlays (all in % of GDP)								
Government expenditures	0.2000	0.2000	0.2000	0.2000	0.2000	0.2000	0.2000	0.2000
Debt service	0.0144	0.0150	0.0125	0.0181	0.0142	0.0147	0.0166	0.0116
Medicare benefit	0.0237	0.0529	0.0423	0.0661	0.0354	0.0445	0.0618	0.0505
Social Security	0.0451	0.0695	0.0546	0.0882	0.0725	0.0710	0.0680	0.0449
Social assistance	0.0032	0.0067	0.0060	0.0081	0.0028	0.0041	0.0116	0.0077
Fiscal revenues (all in % of GDP)								
Capital tax	0.0680	0.0636	0.0644	0.0641	0.0618	0.0629	0.0671	0.0554
Labor tax	0.1426	0.2121	0.1881	0.2425	0.1906	0.2007	0.2255	0.1900
Consumption tax	0.0249	0.0201	0.0201	0.0199	0.0242	0.0221	0.0183	0.0196
Bequests	0.0473	0.0400	0.0362	0.0437	0.0426	0.0415	0.0374	0.0418
Medicare premium	0.0037	0.0083	0.0066	0.0104	0.0056	0.0070	0.0097	0.0079
Social assistance recipient								
% of workers (excl. age 20)	0.0009	0.0142	0.0128	0.0168	0.0010	0.0038	0.0216	0.0108
% of retired	0.0090	0.0482	0.0380	0.0610	0.0085	0.0234	0.0886	0.0782
Dependency ratio (retired/workers; %)	20.0	32.2	25.1	41.3	32.2	32.2	32.2	32.2

Note: SS = Social Security; pop. = population; med. = medical; GDP = gross domestic product.

in the initial steady state. There are no policy changes, either in the provision of health insurance or in the provision of public pensions.[16] The government adjusts the taxation of labor income to satisfy the budget constraint.

As a consequence of the changes in these "fundamentals" between the two steady states, households accumulate more capital. The capital-output ratio jumps from 3.0 to 3.15. This change occurs for two reasons. First, households live longer and must save more for retirement. Second, because of their increased longevity and the rise in health care costs, they plan to spend more for their medical bills, especially after retirement. And, thus, savings increase both to cover these additional costs and to build a larger precautionary buffer stock of wealth to confront uncertainty in medical expenditures over the longer retirement period. Prices adjust accordingly: the interest rate falls by half a percentage point, and the wage rises.

From the point of view of government outlays, Social Security benefits grow from 4.5 percent of output to 7.0 percent, and Medicare costs rise from 2.4 percent to 5.3 percent.[17] Also, social assistance costs rise, especially because of the larger fraction of poor retirees who, when hit by large medical expenditure shocks, have not enough resources to pay their bills and resort to Medicaid. The social assistance recipients among retirees increase from 1 percent in 2005 to 5 percent in 2080. Turning to government revenues, the rise in capital stock and the fall in the rate of return offset each other in terms of revenues from capital income taxation. The taxation of labor must, therefore, increase from 23 percent to 36 percent to balance the budget.

It is interesting to note that average hours worked are 12 percent higher in the new steady state, in spite of the substantial rise in the labor income tax. The increase in labor supply occurs for two reasons. First of all, the wage rises, too, in equilibrium, which mitigates the adverse effect of the rising tax on labor supply. Second, under our preference specification, income effects slightly dominate substitution effects and, as a result of a smaller after-tax wages, hours worked rise. Compared to the large increase in average hours worked, the change in aggregate (or per capita) efficiency units of labor is moderate. The shift in the age distribution of the working age population toward older age classes induces a fall in average labor efficiency.

Social Security versus Medicare: An interesting question to ask is the extent to which our results are driven by the fiscal pressure imposed by Social Security versus Medicare. Both programs create a burden for the government budget, given the projected demographic trends. To isolate the effect

16. However, recall that the Medicare premium adjusts mechanically so that the fraction of Medicare expenditures collected as a premium is constant.

17. The SSA projects Medicare costs to rise up to 12 percent as a fraction of GDP for 2080. Our number is smaller for three reasons. First, we did not include Part D in our calculation due to lack of data in the MEPS. Second, our cost-inflation assumption in the baseline ($q = 1.6$) is more conservative than the SSA assumption. Third, as discussed, the MEPS underestimate long-term care costs, which are projected to rise very sharply.

of Medicare, we run a simulation where replacement rates ρ_e adjust so that the amount spent on Social Security payments to the elderly is kept fixed at 4.5 percent of GDP in 2080. The results of this simulation are reported in the last column of table 9.3. The answer is quite clear: most of the burden is created by Medicare. Freezing expenses on Social Security reduces the equilibrium labor income tax rate in 2080 from 36 percent to 32 percent. In other words, over two-thirds of the higher taxation in 2080 is associated to Medicare.

Sensitivity Analysis

There is considerable uncertainty over the future evolution of health care inflation and population growth. Here, we analyze how sensitive our findings are with respect to these two key inputs of our experiment.

Health care cost: Recall that in the baseline, we have assumed health care inflation, in excess of productivity growth and general inflation, of 0.63 percent per year over the next seventy-five years. We consider three alternative scenarios. One in which in 2080 q increases to 1.3 (or, 0.35 percent per year), one in which it increases to 1.9 (or 0.86 percent per year), and one where it grows at the same rate as nominal output ($q = 1$). As expected, larger health care inflation raises the labor income tax. Overall, we find that every 0.1 percent of excess health care annual inflation leads to a rise of 1 percent in the equilibrium labor income tax rate necessary to balance the budget.

Note that the economy with $q = 1.9$ is the closer to the SSA projection. Under this scenario, τ^w rises to 39 percent. To appreciate the macroeconomic effects of such a huge rise in medical costs, note that as q rises from 1 up to 1.6, savings go up monotonically for the reasons explained in the preceding. However, from $q = 1.6$ to $q = 1.9$ savings fall. The reason is that medical expenditures (and labor taxation) eat up a larger and larger fraction of household earnings who, in turn, are forced to reduce savings. Households are less self-insured and exposed to larger medical expenditure risks. Indeed, the percentage of families who are recipients of social assistance nearly doubles relative to the baseline economy.

Population growth: We solve the model for two scenarios where, in 2080, population does not grow at all and where population grows very fast (1.4 percent per year). Fast population growth reduces the dependency ratio and alleviates the fiscal burden of Social Security and Medicare. Under this scenario, the labor income tax needs to increase only to 32 percent. Under the no population growth scenario, the dependency ratio jumps to 41 percent, and the equilibrium wage tax must rise to 41 percent.

9.4.2   Alternative Policy Experiments

Changes to the Medicare premium: In the baseline economy, the Medicare premium paid by each retired household is 8.0 percent of the average medical expenditures of the retirees. These revenues finance 16 percent of the expenditures on the program, given that Medicare covers 50 percent of the expenditures. The remaining is financed through the general government budget. In order to alleviate the fiscal pressure, we consider a reform that raises the Medicare premium by factors of 2 and 3 and transfers costs from the working population to the retirees.

As shown in two columns "high med premium (×2)" and "high med premium (×3)" in table 9.4, the government will be able to reduce the labor tax rate by 1.3 percent and 2.5 percent, respectively, relative to the baseline final steady state, when we double and triple the premium. Because households anticipate larger spending for the premium after retirement, they accumulate more wealth while at work, which in turn raises the aggregate output and consumption. The labor supply and average hours of work is virtually unaffected because the substitution effect due to the lower labor tax and the income effect due to the increased wealth offset each other. As a result of these reforms, households will be better off than in the baseline scenario. The last rows of the table show sizeable welfare gains, in terms of lifetime consumption, for every education type.

Changes to Medicare coverage rate: Reducing the generosity of the Medicare program through the reduction of the coverage rate will directly lower the cost of the program. We consider policies that reduce the coverage rate from 50 percent to 40 percent and to 30 percent in the final steady state. The results are shown in two columns "lower coverage rate (40%)" and "lower coverage rate (30%)" in table 9.4.

The effects of the policy are remarkably similar to those of raising the Medicare premium discussed in the preceding. Both policies will reduce the fiscal cost of the program and lower the labor tax rate by a similar magnitude. With a lower coverage rate, households will increase the saving to better self-insure themselves against the higher out-of-pocket expenses after retirement, which also reduces the interest rate in a similar magnitude to the previous experiments.

We have, however, a very different picture in the breakdown of the fiscal outlays. On one hand, reducing the coverage rate to 40 percent (30 percent) lowers the expenditures on the Medicare from 5.3 percent of GDP to 4.2 percent (3.1 percent). On the other hand, households are exposed to a higher risk of depleting wealth because of "catastrophic" medical expenditures. Accordingly, the fraction of retirees covered by the social assistance increases from 4.8 percent to 6.5 percent (8.7 percent) in the two experiments. The spending for the social assistance program will rise from 0.67 percent of GDP to 0.79 percent (0.99 percent).

Compare the policy where the premium is tripled to the one where the coverage rate is reduced to 30 percent. They both induce virtually the same magnitude of a rise in τ^w. However, the welfare effects are very different. While increasing the premium will bring about a welfare gain of 2.11 percent of lifetime consumption, the welfare gain is only 1.48 percent if the

Table 9.4   Results of the alternative policy experiments in closed economy compared to the baseline: welfare changes reported in the last three lines

	Initial Steady State	Final Steady State					
	Baseline (q = 1.0)	Baseline (q = 1.6)	High medical premium (× 2)	High medical premium (× 3)	Lower coverage rate (40%)	Lower coverage rate (30%)	Higher retirement age (age 67)
Labor tax rate (%)	0.230	0.357	0.344	0.332	0.343	0.331	0.332
Interest rate (%)	0.050	0.045	0.042	0.039	0.042	0.039	0.044
Wage rate	1.183	1.212	1.229	1.245	1.230	1.244	1.214
Medical expenditures (% of GDP)	0.130	0.226	0.222	0.219	0.222	0.219	0.221
Average work hours	0.329	0.368	0.368	0.368	0.368	0.367	0.362
Aggregate capital	3.000	3.301	3.452	3.593	3.454	3.580	3.381
% change from the benchmark		0.100	0.151	0.198	0.151	0.193	0.127
Aggregate labor input	0.565	0.580	0.580	0.581	0.580	0.581	0.591
% change from the benchmark		0.026	0.028	0.029	0.027	0.028	0.046
Aggregate output	1.000	1.049	1.065	1.080	1.065	1.078	1.070
% change from the benchmark		0.049	0.065	0.080	0.065	0.078	0.070
Aggregate nonmedical consumption	0.436	0.370	0.373	0.375	0.373	0.375	0.381
% change from the benchmark		-0.152	-0.146	-0.140	-0.145	-0.140	-0.126
Fiscal outlays (all in % of GDP)							
Government expenditures	0.2000	0.2000	0.2000	0.2000	0.2000	0.2000	0.2000
Debt service	0.0144	0.0150	0.0138	0.0128	0.0138	0.0129	0.0149
Medicare benefit	0.0237	0.0529	0.0521	0.0514	0.0417	0.0309	0.0465
Social Security	0.0451	0.0695	0.0698	0.0700	0.0698	0.0699	0.0599
Social assistance	0.0032	0.0067	0.0069	0.0073	0.0079	0.0099	0.0063

Fiscal revenues (all in % of GDP)							
Capital tax	0.0680	0.0636	0.0609	0.0584	0.0608	0.0586	0.0633
Labor tax	0.1426	0.2121	0.2046	0.1978	0.2039	0.1972	0.1958
Consumption tax	0.0249	0.0201	0.0200	0.0198	0.0200	0.0198	0.0203
Bequests	0.0473	0.0400	0.0407	0.0412	0.0402	0.0399	0.0409
Medicare premium	0.0037	0.0083	0.0163	0.0242	0.0082	0.0081	0.0073
Social assistance recipient							
% of workers (excl. age 20)	0.0009	0.0142	0.0128	0.0120	0.0128	0.0122	0.0125
% of retired	0.0090	0.0482	0.0560	0.0665	0.0647	0.0866	0.0499
Dependency ratio (retired/workers; %)	20.0	32.2	32.2	32.2	32.2	32.2	28.0
Welfare change in final SS (relative to baseline)							
Consumption equivalent variation (%)							
All		0.00	1.17	2.11	0.96	1.48	
Low education		0.00	1.14	2.06	0.91	1.41	
High education		0.00	1.25	2.27	1.12	1.77	

Note: GDP = gross domestic product.

coverage rate declines to 30 percent. Although both policy reforms raise the saving and aggregate output and enhance welfare, households are exposed to more uncertainty under the second policy, which makes a difference in the magnitude of the welfare gain.

Changes to retirement age: The last column of table 9.4 shows the effect of postponing retirement by two years, from sixty-five to sixty-seven. We assume that households are not eligible for either Medicare or social security until sixty-seven and continue to work until this new retirement age.[18] As a result, the dependency ratio falls from 32.2 percent to 28.0 percent. The policy will lower the fiscal outlays of both Medicare and Social Security, which reduces the labor income tax by 2.5 percent compared to the baseline final steady state.

The aggregate labor supply will increase by about 2 percent relative to the benchmark final steady state, and the aggregate output will rise by about the same magnitude. Because the saving does not change much from the benchmark final steady state, the reform results in a large increase in the amount of (nonmedical) goods and services consumed. Households will be significantly better off, as shown by the welfare gain of 3.1 percent in terms of consumption equivalence.

9.4.3   Open Economy

In previous work (Attanasio, Kitao and Violante, 2006; 2007), we have argued that the extent to which capital will flow in and out of the United States in the next eighty years is crucial in understanding the budgetary, macroeconomic, and welfare implications of demographic trends. In a financially integrated economy, where the world financial markets set the interest rate, prices do not adjust (or adjust very little) to demographic changes in the U.S. economy alone because the world demographic trends are unsynchronized. For example, large economies like China and India are at a much earlier stage of the demographic transition.

Table 9.5 reports the results of our simulations done under the assumption that the interest rate is fixed at 5 percent, a value that implies that foreign-owned net assets in the United States are roughly 20 percent of GDP, based on U.S. data for 2005. The main differences with the closed-economy model are two. First, the equilibrium wage tax rate increases only to 31 percent, relative to 36 percent in the closed economy. As households increase their savings, their wealth grows as demonstrated by the huge change in the foreign asset position of the economy. However, the interest rate is fixed. As a result, the tax base for capital income taxation increases significantly. In turn, this allows the government to limit the rise in the labor income tax τ^w.

---

18. We assume the age-dependent labor productivity is constant from age sixty-four to age sixty-six.

Table 9.5   Results of the open-economy simulations: baseline and sensitivity analysis

	Initial Steady State	Final Steady State						
	Baseline (q = 1.0)	Baseline (q = 1.6)	High pop. growth (1.4%)	Low pop. growth (0%)	No med. cost increase (q = 1.0)	Low med. cost increase (q = 1.3)	High med. cost increase (q = 1.9)	SS fixed at 4.5% of GDP
Labor tax rate (%)	0.242	0.310	0.288	0.349	0.250	0.282	0.404	0.170
Medical expenditures (% of GDP)	0.130	0.234	0.209	0.264	0.159	0.198	0.264	0.241
Average work hours	0.330	0.364	0.362	0.368	0.334	0.349	0.382	0.354
Aggregate wealth/saving (% of GDP)	2.800	3.758	3.460	3.945	3.933	3.828	2.798	5.409
% change from the benchmark		0.342	0.236	0.409	0.405	0.367	-0.001	0.932
U.S. owned foreign asset (% of GDP)	-0.200	0.758	0.460	0.945	0.933	0.828	-0.202	2.409
Capital (% of GDP)	3.000	3.000	3.000	3.000	3.000	3.000	3.000	3.000
Aggregate labor input	0.567	0.572	0.595	0.547	0.527	0.550	0.603	0.556
% change from the benchmark		0.009	0.049	-0.035	-0.071	-0.030	0.064	-0.019
Aggregate output	1.000	1.009	1.049	0.965	0.929	0.970	1.064	0.981
% change from the benchmark		0.009	0.049	-0.035	-0.071	-0.030	0.064	-0.019
Aggregate nonmedical consumption	0.430	0.389	0.391	0.380	0.440	0.413	0.334	0.440
% change from the benchmark		-0.096	-0.093	-0.117	0.023	-0.040	-0.223	0.023
Fiscal outlays (all in % of GDP)								
Government expenditures	0.2000	0.2000	0.2000	0.2000	0.2000	0.2000	0.2000	0.2000
Debt service	0.0144	0.0171	0.0142	0.0200	0.0171	0.0171	0.0171	0.0171
Medicare benefit	0.0237	0.0550	0.0435	0.0689	0.0373	0.0464	0.0619	0.0566
Social Security	0.0452	0.0691	0.0543	0.0877	0.0719	0.0705	0.0680	0.0454
Social assistance	0.0033	0.0052	0.0053	0.0055	0.0026	0.0035	0.0138	0.0039
Fiscal revenues (all in % of GDP)								
Capital tax	0.0640	0.0832	0.0772	0.0869	0.0881	0.0846	0.0640	0.1162
Labor tax	0.1496	0.1833	0.1711	0.2048	0.1540	0.1701	0.2346	0.1001
Consumption tax	0.0245	0.0220	0.0210	0.0224	0.0270	0.0243	0.0179	0.0256
Bequests	0.0447	0.0492	0.0410	0.0571	0.0539	0.0512	0.0345	0.0721
Medicare premium	0.0037	0.0086	0.0068	0.0108	0.0059	0.0073	0.0097	0.0089
Social assistance recipient								
% of workers (excl. age 20)	0.0009	0.0105	0.0108	0.0108	0.0007	0.0028	0.0264	0.0043
% of retired	0.0099	0.0309	0.0285	0.0345	0.0057	0.0152	0.1058	0.0211
Dependency ratio (retired/workers; %)	20.0	32.2	25.1	41.3	32.2	32.2	32.2	32.2

Note: SS = Social Security; pop. = population; med. = medical; GDP = gross domestic product.

The key assumption behind this result is that U.S. wealth invested in foreign assets is taxed domestically.

Second, the results of the counterfactual experiment where we hold the Social Security outlays at 4.5 percent of GDP are strikingly different from the closed-economy model. Households raise their savings to finance their retirement. The fact that r does not react to the larger supply of savings pushes capital accumulation even further up so that the wealth-income ratio reaches 5.4. This is very good news for the government, as revenues from capital income taxation surge, and the equilibrium labor income tax needed to pay for the additional Medicare costs is just 17 percent, that is, a substantial drop from the 24 percent of the initial steady state.

9.4.4   Robustness Analysis

To conclude this section, we report some robustness analysis with respect to (a) the elasticity of labor supply, and (b) the level of the minimum consumption $\bar{c}$ guaranteed by the social assistance program.

Table 9.6 summarizes the effect of alternative values θ in equation (4). Given our preferences specification and the calibration target for average hours worked, values of θ equal 2, 4, and 8 imply average intertemporal labor supply elasticities of 1.0, 0.5, and 0.25, respectively. Recall that $\theta = 4$ is the benchmark. The numbers in the table represent the percentage changes in aggregate variables in the final steady state relative to the initial steady state. For each model, we recalibrate the parameters so that we match the same calibration targets discussed in section 9.3.

With a higher labor supply elasticity, hours worked increase even more, and aggregate labor supply will rise by 5.5 percent, more than twice as in the benchmark. As discussed in the preceding, under our parameterization, the income effect dominates the substitution effect and agents respond to the lower after-tax wage by working longer hours. This response is stronger under the higher elasticity of labor supply. Although there is a large difference in the labor supply response, the effect on the labor income tax base is mitigated by the fact that increase on the equilibrium wage rate is lower with a higher elasticity. Overall, the increase in the labor tax in the final steady state is surprisingly similar across parameterizations, ranging from 12 percent to 13.5 percent as we change the elasticity from 1.0 to 0.25.

Table 9.7 explores the role of the generosity of social assistance. Recall that in the baseline, calibration $\bar{c}$ is set to 10 percent of income per capita. When the consumption floor is cut to 5 percent, the precautionary saving motive is much stronger in the final steady state, and aggregate capital rises by 18.2 percent, relative to a rise of 10.3 percent in the benchmark. When social assistance is more generous and guarantees a minimum consumption of 15 percent of average income, the fiscal cost of the transition becomes more severe. As a result of the more generous benefits paid by the government, together with the lower precautionary savings that contract the fiscal

Table 9.6   Robustness analysis on the preferences parameter θ and on labor supply elasticity: each column reports percentage changes in the aggregate variables in the final steady state with respect to baseline economy

	Sensitivity analysis with respect to θ		
Value of preferences parameter θ	2	4	8
Frisch elasticity of labor supply	1.00	0.50	0.25
Labor tax rate (% points)	0.120	0.127	0.135
Wage rate	0.020	0.024	0.026
Average hours worked	0.149	0.118	0.084
Aggregate capital	0.121	0.100	0.074
Aggregate labor input	0.055	0.026	−0.006
Aggregate output	0.076	0.049	0.020
Aggregate nonmedical consumption	−0.114	−0.152	−0.195

Table 9.7   Robustness analysis on the consumption floor parameter $\bar{c}$: each column reports percentage changes in the aggregate variables in the final steady state with respect to baseline economy

	Sensitivity analysis with respect to $\bar{c}$		
Value of $\bar{c}$ (% of GDP per capita)	5	10	15
Labor tax rate (% points)	0.118	0.127	0.174
Wage rate	0.046	0.024	−0.028
Average hours worked	0.126	0.118	0.077
Aggregate capital	0.182	0.100	−0.080
Aggregate = labor input	0.030	0.026	0.002
Aggregate output	0.078	0.049	−0.026
Aggregate nonmedical consumption	−0.139	−0.152	−0.207
Social assistance recipients			
% workers	0.004	0.013	0.069
% retirees	0.008	0.039	0.171

base for capital taxation, the equilibrium labor income tax τ^w rises from 23 percent to 40.4 percent.

9.5   Conclusions

The model we proposed has important elements of realism, such as the way in which we model Medicare and Medicaid, the uncertain evolution of health status and its effect on productivity, medical costs, and mortality. However, our exercise is not without limitations. We should mention here the most important ones: (a) we do not model the choice of private health insurance, either before or after retirement. In particular, before retirement, we ignore the possibility that individuals that do not have access to an employer-provided insurance could buy private insurance in the market. After retirement, we are ignoring Medigap and other forms of supplemental private insurance not provided by a former employer; (b) we consider households as a monistic unit and do not deal separately with husband and wife, neither in terms of labor supply behavior nor health status; (c) we only compare steady states, rather than computing the transition dynamics toward the final steady state; (d) we treat medical expenditures as exogenously given, while presumably at least some, if not most, of them may be determined endogenously as an optimal choice.

Some of these limitations, and in particular points (a) and (c) could be avoided in more sophisticated versions of our model. Others, such as those in point (b) and (d), would involve a considerable increase in numerical complexity, and the implementation would pose more challenges. In any case, we see the exercise presented in this chapter as a first step in a more ambitious research agenda.

References

Aiyagari, S. R. 1994. Uninsured idiosyncratic risk and aggregate saving. *Quarterly Journal of Economics* 109 (3): 659–84.

Attanasio, O. P. 1999. Consumption. In *Handbook of Macroeconomics*, vol. 1, ed. J. B. Taylor and M. Woodford, 741–812. North Holland: Elsevier.

Attanasio, O. P., S. Kitao, and G. L. Violante. 2006. Quantifying the effects of the demographic transition in developing economies. *Advances in Macroeconomics: The B.E. Journals in Macroeconomics* 6 (1) (online journal).

———. 2007. Global demographics trends and social security reform. *Journal of Monetary Economics* 54 (1): 144–98.

Auerbach, A. J., and L. J. Kotlikoff. 1987. *Dynamic fiscal policy.* Cambridge, UK: Cambridge University Press.

Bell, F. C., and M. L. Miller. 2002. *Life tables for the United States Social Security area 1900–2100.* Actuarial Study no. 116. Washington, DC: Office of the Chief Actuary, Social Security Administration.

Bhattacharya, J., and D. Lakdawalla. 2006. Does Medicare benefit the poor? *Journal of Public Economics* 90 (1–2): 277–92.

Borger, C., T. F. Rutherford, and G. Y. Won. 2008. Projecting long-term medical spending growth. *Journal of Health Economics* 27 (1): 69–88.

Brown, J., N. Coe, and A. Finkelstein. 2007. Medicaid crowd-out of private long-term care insurance demand: Evidence from the Health and Retirement Survey. *Tax Policy and the Economy* 21:1–34.

Brown, J., and A. Finkelstein. 2007. Why is the market for long-term care insurance so small? *Journal of Public Economics* 91 (10): 1967–91.

———. 2008. The interaction of public and private insurance: Medicaid and the long-term care insurance market. *American Economic Review* 98 (3): 1083–1102.

Browning, M., L. P. Hansen, and J. J. Heckman. 1999. Micro data and general equilibrium models. In *Handbook of macroeconomics.* Vol. 1A, ed. J. B. Taylor and M. Woodford, 543–633. Amsterdam: North-Holland.

Buchmueller, T., R. W. Johnson, and A. T. L. Sasso. 2006. Trends in retiree health insurance, 1997–2003. *Health Affairs* 25 (6): 1507–16.

De Nardi, M., E. French, and J. B. Jones. 2009. Why do the elderly save? The role of medical expenses. *Journal of Political Economy* 118 (1): 39–75.

De Nardi, M., S. İmrohoroğlu, and T. J. Sargent. 1999. Projected U.S. demographics and Social Security. *Review of Economic Dynamics* 2 (3): 575–615.

Domeij, D., and M. Floden. 2006. Population aging and international capital flows. *International Economic Review* 47 (3): 1013–32.

Fehr, H., S. Jokisch, and L. Kotlikoff. 2008. Fertility, mortality, and the developed world's demographic transition. *Journal of Policy Modeling* 30 (3): 455–73.

Finkelstein, A. 2004. Minimum standards, insurance regulation and adverse selection: Evidence from the Medigap market. *Journal of Public Economics* 88 (12): 2515–47.

———. 2007. The aggregate effects of health insurance: Evidence from the introduction of Medicare. *Quarterly Journal of Economics* 122 (3): 1–37.

French, E., and J. B. Jones. 2004. On the distribution and dynamics of health costs. *Journal of Applied Econometrics* 19 (6): 705–21.

———. 2007. The effects of health insurance and self-insurance on retirement behavior. FRB Chicago Working Paper no. 2001-19.

Fuster, L., A. İmrohoroğlu, and S. İmrohoroğlu. 2007. Elimination of Social Security in a dynastic framework. *Review of Economic Studies* 74 (1): 113–45.

Huang, H., S. İmrohoroğlu, and T. J. Sargent. 1997. Two computations to fund Social Security. *Macroeconomic Dynamics* 1:7–44.

Huggett, M. 1993. The risk-free rate in heterogeneous-agent incomplete-insurance economies. *Journal of Economic Dynamics and Control* 17 (5–6): 953–69.

Huggett, M., and G. Ventura. 1999. On the distributional effects of Social Security reform. *Review of Economic Dynamics* 2 (3): 498–531.

İmrohoroğlu, A. 1989. Cost of business cycles with indivisibilities and liquidity constraints. *Journal of Political Economy* 97 (6): 1364–83.

Jeske, K., and S. Kitao. 2009. U.S. tax policy and health insurance demand: Can a regressive policy improve welfare? *Journal of Monetary Economics* 56 (2): 210–21.

Kahn, J. G., R. Kronick, M. Kreger, and D. N. Gans. 2005. The cost of health insurance administration in California: Estimates for insurers, physicians, and hospitals. *Health Affairs* 24 (6): 1629–39.

Keehan, S., H. Lazenby, M. Zezza, and A. Catlin. 2004. Age estimates in the National Health Accounts. *Health Care Financing Review* 1 (1): 1–16.

Kotlikoff, L. J., K. A. Smetters, and J. Walliser. 1999. Privatizing Social Security in the United States: Comparing the options. *Review of Economic Dynamics* 2 (3): 532–74.

———. 2007. Mitigating America's demographic dilemma by pre-funding Social Security. *Journal of Monetary Economics* 54 (2): 247–66.

Lyke, B. 2003. Tax benefits for health insurance: Current legislation. Washington, DC: Congressional Research Service, The Library of Congress.

Mendoza, E. G., A. Razin, and L. L. Tesar. 1994. Effective tax rates in macroeconomics: Cross-country estimates of tax rates on factor incomes and consumption. *Journal of Monetary Economics* 34 (3): 297–323.

Palumbo, M. G. 1999. Uncertain medical expenses and precautionary saving near the end of the life cycle. *Review of Economic Studies* 66 (2): 395–421.

Ríos-Rull, J.-V. 1996. Life cycle economies and aggregate fluctuations. *Review of Economic Studies* 63 (3): 465–89.

Selden, T., K. Levit, J. Cohen, S. Zuvekas, J. Moeller, D. McKusick, and R. Arnett. 2001. Reconciling medical expenditure estimates from the MEPS and NHEA, 1996. *Health Care Financing Review* 23 (1): 161–78.

The economic report of the president. 2004. Available at: http://www.gpoaccess
.gov/usbudget/fy05/pdf/2004_erp.pdf.

Comment   Moshe Buchinsky

In this chapter, the authors examine one of the most pressing issues in the
United States, namely the growing medical expenditure. It has been long
documented in the literature that the Social Security Administration (SSA)
spending on Medicaid and Medicare has been increasing over the past two
decades at an unsustainable rate. If we also consider the huge increase in
related spending on the two disability programs that the SSA offers (the
Social Security Disability Insurance [SSDI] and the Supplemental Social
Security Income [SSI]), as well as the old-age program, the SSA is reaching
a catastrophic situation in which it will be unable to sustain itself. While
this is a problem that has been previously recognized in the literature, it has
been studied in a very limited way. In fact, almost all studies resort to partial
equilibrium models that capture very few of a long list of elements that are
interconnected. Examination of a multitude of problems within a unified
general equilibrium model is the main contribution of this chapter. Indeed,
the empirical results suggest that some major policy measures have to be
taken to preserve the Social Security system.

The main features that are modeled are (a) labor supply; (b) health (and,
consequently, mortality); (c) medical expenditures (by institution as well as
out-of-pocket expenses); (d) taxation on income and capital; and (e) budgetary consideration by the government. This is certainly a very comprehensive model that addresses some of the most crucial problems in the
American society and elsewhere. I would even argue that it is the most realistic way of investigating such issues. Furthermore, the current model, in
principle, allows one to carefully study crucial fiscal issues that are endogenously determined.

There are reasons to believe that, if anything, the authors provide a lower
bound for the potential problems to be seen in the near future, maybe even
prior to the year 2080—the end period in the current analysis. This claim is
supported by recent actions taken by the SSA. The SSA has made sincere
efforts to alleviate the situation and created study groups for potential solutions.

There are several alarming results that come out of this study. Obviously,
the results clearly indicate that there needs to be an enormous increase in
taxes to support the increased costs of the SSA due to larger than anticipated

Moshe Buchinsky is a professor of economics at the University of California, Los Angeles,
and a research associate of the National Bureau of Economic Research.

increase in medical expenditure. Moreover, individuals, in general, will be exposed to more idiosyncratic risks that stem from medical disasters. The authors consider two main alternative policy measures that could reduce the required increase in the tax rate, namely (a) a considerable increase in Medicare premiums; and (b) relatively large decrease in Medicare coverage. Neither "solution" is very appealing. Most of the effects that stem from these types of policies amount to some changes in the national accounting but provide no difference from the individuals' point of view. Quite the contrary, these changes simply shift the burden to the subpopulation that is relatively lower-educated, is more likely to be in worse health conditions, and is struggling to make ends meet as it is. The sensitivity analysis provided indicates some changes in the results, particularly in the required tax rate. Nevertheless, the general gleam picture does not change much. However, as I discuss in the following, this is to be expected given that some of the key behavioral variables are assumed to be exogenous, thus not allowing for the possibility of some endogenous behavioral changes.

It is clear that the chapter does a very good job at bringing to the forefront the issues that the United States will undoubtedly be struggling with. Nevertheless, there are some key assumptions that make one a bit nervous taking the quantitative results on their face value. It would be fair admitting that writing a comment on such a chapter is a lot easier than carrying out the analysis incorporating the suggestions and addressing the concerns raised in this comment. As we all know, certain things are simply "easier said than done." The main advantage of the model, namely the imposition of general equilibrium, is, in a way, also what exposes it to some criticism.

With these implied apologies in mind, there are some issues that we should be concerned about:

1. Are the assumptions made realistic enough to substantiate the results?
2. Are there features that should have been endogenously modeled? If so, what effects might these have on the results?
3. Are there "easier" policy measures that can be considered?
4. Are there modeling issues that can be strengthened?

One major drawback of the model, as I see it, is that it relies quite heavily on results obtained in the literature that are based on partial equilibrium models, or sometimes even models that can be categorized as reduced-form models. Generally, it is difficult, if not impossible, to extract the behavioral parameters, such as the ones used here in calibrating the model, from regressions that are not directly suited for estimation of behavioral parameters. While the theoretical model is a general equilibrium overlapping generations model, incorporating parameters in such a fashion, at the very least, raises some questions regarding the validity of the empirical results and their interpretations. An additional fundamental problem that makes it hard to justify the use of parameters from previous studies is the fact that they mostly come from data collected from a nonstationary environment, while the calibrated model is assumed to be in a stationary environment.

This is not to say that a calibration model is not fit to analyze the question at hand, but putting too much emphasis on the quantitative aspect rather than the qualitative results is somewhat misplaced.

Many of the relevant variables are assume to be exogenous. This is the case for the individual types, which are completely characterized by the exogenously drawn education level $e \in \{0, 1\}$. This is also the case with the health transition probabilities. More crucially, the model does not permit endogenous decisions regarding family formation and investment in human capital. Consequently, the demographic structure is, essentially, assumed rather than being the results of sequence of endogenous decisions that are so widely studied in the literature.

I think it is not hard to see that selection can also play a major role in the composition of households in society because of differential decision-making across individuals with varying observed and unobserved characteristics. Changing the household composition may alter the results in ways that we cannot clearly anticipate. Even more important is the fact that the unit of observation in this study is the household rather than the individual. Consequently, there is no room for differential changes and responses between females and males.

Another point for concern is the fact that the demand for health service is formed in a somewhat ad hoc fashion because behavioral responses, such as the ones mentioned in the preceding, can easily lower the demand for health services and may consequently have a large impact on its price level (i.e., q in the authors' formulation may very well be at times lower than 1). This, in turn, can have quite sizable effects on the empirical results. A rough calculation that I performed indicates that the tax increase necessary to keep a balanced budget could be less than half the estimate provided in this chapter.

While it is more than fair to only consider differences between two steady states, there are a number of questions that come to mind regarding the transition period from one steady state to another. One particularly alarming question is whether the system will survive the transition period. What obstacles can we expect to face? Obviously, this question cannot be answered unless individuals' expectations are incorporated. Understanding the formation of individuals' expectations is obviously important but belong more in a micro-type study than the one pursued here. Nevertheless, incorporating these features, that are integral part of human behavior, may shed light on possible reform of the SSA system, providing individuals with incentives to avoid unnecessary use of Medicare, the SSDI, SSI, and so on. For example, the Clinton administration considered a proposal to change the rules that govern the SSDI and SSI programs. This proposal, termed one-for-two benefit offset, essentially reduced the implied marginal tax for individuals who leave the disability role from 100 percent to only 50 percent, giving them more incentive to return to the active labor market.

The health literature show a very clear link between education and investment in health: more highly educated individuals tend to invest more in maintaining and improving their health. In turn, they are generally in better health and are less likely to use medical services of any kind. It would not be difficult to conclude that public investment in education, in general, and health education, in particular, may very well alter people's behavior. It seems that our tendency as economists is often to find the easy way out, that is, to deal with what amounts to an accounting exercise (on the national level), rather than examining more basic questions as to how one might change the fundamentals that govern individuals' behavior, which, in turn, lead to the increasing costs of Medicare (and, for this matter, any other social program).

Finally, I think that it would be wise to reexamine some of the assumptions that are made in this study and, in my mind, could have a significant effect on the results obtained:

1. One must admit that this chapter concentrates on the macro aspects of increased medical use and expenditures. Nevertheless, as is generally found in empirical micro studies, unobserved heterogeneity always plays a major role in explaining human behavior. This element is totally ignored in the current study.

2. The same general idea applies to other aspects of the model. For example, the employer-based health insurance that is exogenously assigned to the individuals is not random. Moreover, decisions about job mobility are tied very closely to employer provided fringe benefits. Some studies find that the choice of health coverage is the single most important aspect of fringe benefits that employees are concerned with.

3. The assumptions that allow one to restrict attention to one-sector economy might be of some concern. In particular, there is strong evidence in the literature of differential adaptation of skilled versus unskilled workers to new environment.

4. In the implementation of the government policies, there is an implicit assumption that all relevant state variables are observed by all parties. This is somewhat questionable. For example, are people that declare themselves to be disabled really disabled? There is substantial evidence that this is not the case. In fact, much of the resources of the SSA operating budget are spent on actions that are aimed at revealing the true status of individuals.

5. Productivity is assumed to be exogenously given and largely constant (up to some very small variation on the assumed parameter). A better approach might be to use regression-based specification of the productivity, whereby productivity is linked directly to observed exogenous and endogenous variables from the model.

6. Throughout the chapter, it is assumed that the government expenditure is fixed at 20 percent of gross domestic product (GDP), while public debt held is fixed at 40 percent of GDP. I think there is room for asking how much government spending should be cut to avoid any cuts in Medicare, social welfare programs, and so on.

7. Measuring welfare improvement: It is important to address issues about welfare gains or losses across different segments of the population. The poor, who are most likely to use social welfare in one way or another, are those who are most likely to lose from any program that will limit their use of Medicare, SSA-old age, SSDI, and SSI.

Italians Are Late
Does It Matter?

Francesco C. Billari and Guido Tabellini

10.1   Introduction

In the discussion of the link between demography and the economy, the main focus of existing research is on population aging and its consequences. The determinants of population aging—below-replacement fertility above all others—are investigated as areas of potential policy concern. For these reasons, societies that age faster, that is, those that experienced particularly low levels of fertility for some decades, are ideal laboratories for studying the demography-economy link. Italy (together with Spain) has been the first country in which fertility reached levels that had not been reached earlier, that is, total fertility rates below 1.3 children per woman. This level, which has been termed "lowest-low fertility" (Kohler, Billari, and Ortega 2002), has appeared during the 1990s and has spread thereafter toward Central and Eastern Europe as well as toward rich countries in East Asia. Italy has become the most aged country in the Organization for Economic Cooperation and Development (OECD), even if the rapid rise in immigration, together with a small increase in fertility, have prevented the total and working-age population from falling during the early 2000s (Billari 2008).

One of the key features of Italy's low fertility is its connection with a late transition to adulthood. In order to get a comparable tertiary degree, young Italians tend to study longer than their counterparts in other nations. They enter the labor market later. They live with their parents longer than their

Francesco C. Billari is professor of demography and vice rector for development at Bocconi University. Guido Tabellini is professor of economics and rector at Bocconi University.

We are grateful to Luigi Pistaferri and the conference participants for helpful comments.

peers elsewhere. They form a partnership via marriage or cohabitation later, and now they also tend to have their first child later. For instance, for Italians born between 1966 and 1970, the median ages at various events were as follows, for men and women, respectively: for completing education: 19.2 and 19.3; for first job: 21.4 and 24.0; for leaving home: 27.2 and 25.1; for first birth: 33.4 and 29.3 (Mazzuco, Mencarini, and Rettaroli 2006). This pattern has been defined as the "latest-late transition to adulthood." In the following, we discuss more in detail how Italy compares to other countries in Europe.

Such late transition to adulthood of Italian youth did not go unnoticed. In October 2007, the Italian Minister of the Economy Tommaso Padoa-Schioppa defined youths who continue to reside in the parental home as *bamboccioni* (big babies); according to the *International Herald Tribune* this is "an Italian word that evokes images of clumsy, overgrown male babies." The Minister also advocated financial incentives to induce youths still living with their parents to abandon their nest.[1]

What are the economic consequences of such late transition to adulthood, besides the immediate implications for fertility? In particular, could this late transition contribute to explain the disappointing performance of the Italian economy over the last decade? These are the general questions motivating this chapter.

Our main contribution is to study how the timing of specific events, such as leaving the parental home, is associated with individual income later in life. Our evidence comes from a survey of Italian men in their 30s, on which we have detailed retrospective information on the (earlier) timing of specific events as well as economic outcomes at the time of the survey. The main finding is that a late transition to adulthood, measured by the date of leaving the parental home, is associated with lower income later in life. Of course, both income and transition to adulthood are jointly determined, and our estimation strategy attempts to infer causality by relying on instrumental variables.

Other recent papers have studied the consequences of the prolonged coresidence between parents and their children. Alessie, Brugiavini, and Weber (2005) focus on the link between coresidence and savings, comparing Italy and the Netherlands. Aassve et al. (2007) study the effect of leaving home on poverty without, however, finding explicit links with coresidence rates (they find that departure from the parental home has a significant short-term impact on poverty in thirteen European countries, with the highest impact in Scandinavia). Finally, Alesina and Giuliano (2007) argue that the strength of family ties (including those between parents and children)

---

1. See, for instance, "Italian Economics Minister Causes Uproar with 'Big Babies' Tax Proposal," *International Herald Tribune*, 5 October 2007, or "Observer: Flowers and Taxes," *Financial Times*, 10 October 2007.

has important consequences for the economy and that the family is a more important economic unit in societies in which family ties are stronger, as in Italy.

The remainder of this chapter is organized as follows. Section 10.2 describes the peculiarity of the Italian case, showing stylized evidence and reviewing studies that have tried to explain this peculiarity mostly with reference to culture or institutional factors. Section 10.3 addresses the link between the delay in the transition to adulthood and the economy through a review of the literature on the demography-economy nexus and cross-country analyses. Section 10.4 is the main contribution of this chapter: it presents a microeconometric evaluation of the effect of delayed home-leaving on individual income in a sample of Italian youths. Conclusions and policy implications are drawn in section 10.5.

10.2   The Italian "Latest-Late" Pattern of Transition to Adulthood

What makes a person an adult? There is no straightforward answer to this question, which has long been studied, especially by historians and sociologists. Certainly, age plays a role: in every society, there are specific ages at which individuals are given specific rights or responsibilities, or under which it is not legal to perform certain behaviors. Examples include lower age limits for working, for drinking, for marrying, and age threshold that entitle individuals to vote or to carry a driving license. During the 1970s, a series of authors in the fields of sociology and social history pointed out explicitly that becoming an adult is a process characterized by a series of events that mark passages from roles that are typical of youth to other roles. In contemporary societies, these events include completing education, entering the labor market, leaving the parental home, marrying (or, having recent trends in mind, cohabiting), or becoming a parent (Elder 1975; Modell, Furstenberg, and Hershberg 1976; Neugarten and Datan 1973). A whole literature on the "transition to adulthood" has flourished since then, exploring the factors that shape the timing of these events and the order in which they appear in life (Hogan and Astone 1986; Settersten, Furstenberg, and Rumbaut 2005; Shanahan 2000). The relevance of these events for the perception of adulthood in the 2000s has also been investigated for the United States, through the General Social Survey (Furstenberg et al. 2004). As we have already noticed in the introduction, research on the consequences of the transition to adulthood has been much more limited.

A general feature of transitions to adulthood in contemporary developed societies is that, overall, its timing has become later (Liefbroer 2005; Settersten, Furstenberg, and Rumbaut 2005). Young adults tend to study longer; enter the labor market later; leave the parental home, cohabit or marry, and become a parent later. Italy, followed closely by Spain, ranks first as far as a late transition to adulthood is concerned. Indeed, Italy and

Spain have been labeled as following a "latest-late" pattern of transition to adulthood (Billari et al. 2002; Billari, Philipov, and Baizán 2001). This pattern is linked to an increasing age at leaving education and entering the labor market, with levels, however, comparable to those of other countries. What is peculiar is the particularly high age at leaving home, union formation, and first birth. Moreover, leaving home is more frequently associated with marriage (and union formation in general) compared to other societies. Table 10.1 documents the latest-late pattern of transition to adulthood using data from standard demographic surveys: Italy has the highest median age at leaving home. It is not a surprise that also the median age at parenthood is the highest for men and the second highest for women; indeed, Italy tops the rankings of late fertility (Billari et al. 2007). Moreover, there is a clear trend toward further postponement, which is confirmed by the most recent research results (Mazzuco, Mencarini, and Rettaroli 2006).

Consistent with the picture on the timing of events, there is clear evidence that young Italians tend to financially depend more on their parents, with respect to their counterparts in other developed countries. Table 10.2 shows comparative data on Europe: in 2001, 74 percent of young Italians aged fifteen to twenty-four declared to be financially dependent on their parents, while this was true for only 19 percent for young Danes and 21 percent of U.K. youth. This trend continues when more recent data are taken into account.

How has this peculiarity of the Italian pattern of transition to adulthood come about? We briefly survey some of the research results concerning the attempt to explain this peculiarity. We roughly distinguish between two lines of explanation: one emphasizes culture or cultural change, the other focuses on economic and, especially, institutional factors that are peculiar to Italy. We mainly consider the age of home leaving, given its key role as a marker of the age at which youth reach a sufficient degree of individual autonomy and responsibility in the transition to adulthood and given that the peculiarity of the latest-late pattern identified in the literature lies on the delayed departure from the parental home.

10.2.1   The Role of Culture

A series of contributions by scholars from different disciplines focus on the role of culture as the key explanation to the peculiarity of the Italian pattern. The late transition to adulthood of young Italians is explained essentially by their preference to coreside with parents, or by their parents' to coreside with children, or both.

In the demographic literature, several authors have emphasized that the Italian (and Southern European) pattern is historically rooted. Coresidential links between parents and children have been strong also in the past, and they pervade all ages. Reher (1998), for instance, distinguishes two basic patterns of family ties and transition to adulthood. The Northern European

Table 10.1   The timing of events in the transition to adulthood: An international comparison

Country	End of education		First job		Leaving home		First union		First birth	
	1950s	1960s	1950s	1960s	1950s	1960s	1950s	1960s	1950s	1960s
A. Males										
Australia	16.6	16.9			20.6	20.0	23.5	24.9		
Austria	18.4	18.6	18.7	18.3	22.9	21.4	24.0	23.6	27.2	28.3
Belgium (Flanders)	18.2	19.0	18.7	19.8	22.7	23.7	24.3	23.2	26.5	28.4
France	18.2	18.2	18.2	18.5	21.7	22.1	23.7	23.8	27.3	29.5
Italy	17.7	18.5	17.5	18.9	24.9	27.2	25.8	28.8	29.2	33.3
The Netherlands		19.2	17.0	18.5	21.3	21.8	23.0	23.0	28.0	28.3
Norway				18.1		22.0		23.7		
Poland	18.2	18.2	19.7	19.6	24.6		24.6			
Spain	14.3	15.7	15.6	17.4	25.1	26.6	25.6	25.1	27.7	
B. Females										
Australia	16.2	17.0			19.6	19.2	21.3	21.9		
Austria	18.0	19.2	18.3	18.2	20.0	19.1	21.0	20.7	22.8	24.0
Belgium (Flanders)			18.4	20.2	21.2	21.7	21.4	22.3	24.2	26.4
Canada	20.7	21.0	20.0	20.4	19.9	20.9	21.5	22.7	25.6	27.8
France	18.2	18.2	19.3	20.2	20.3	20.0	21.4	21.7	24.2	26.4
Italy	16.5	18.5	20.2	21.2	22.2	23.8	22.5	24.2	24.8	27.2
The Netherlands		18.9	16.5	17.5	19.6	19.5	20.0	21.0	25.0	28.0
Norway				18.6		20.2		21.1	23.6	25.7
Poland	19.2	18.9	18.6	18.8	22.4		22.3	22.4	25.3	23.2
Spain	14.0	15.1	17.6	19.5	23.2	22.8	23.2			

Sources: For European countries, Corijn and Klijzing (2001); for Australia, Flatau et al. (2007); for Canada, Ravanera, Rajulton, and Burch (1998).

Table 10.2   **Share of young adults who declare to be financially dependent on their parents or who get most of their money from relatives/partner (%)**

Country	Youth aged 15–24		Youth aged 15–30
	1997 (parents)	2001 (parents)	2007 (relatives and partner)
Austria	41	43	24
Belgium	48	58	32
Denmark	19	19	5
Finland	41	40	17
France	48	61	30
Germany	38	46	26
Greece	51	71	49
Ireland	38	32	19
Italy	68	74	50
Luxembourg	58	66	40
Portugal	51	54	44
Spain	62	67	34
Sweden	34	39	6
The Netherlands	33	43	17
United Kingdom	17	21	14
EU-15 (average)	45	54	29

Sources: Billari (2004) on Eurobarometer data for 1997 and 2001; The Gallup Organization (2007) for 2007.

pattern of *weak family ties* and early transition to adulthood is linked to the medieval habit of leaving the parental home early for agricultural work or to become a servant. On the contrary, in Southern Europe, the *strong family ties* pattern was characterized by extensive periods of coresidence between parents and adult children, in some areas extending to the whole life for at least some of the children; the roots of this Southern European pattern could be found in the meeting between the Roman and the Arab traditions of kinship. Families (and not communities) have historically taken care of vulnerable individuals in the south. Starting from the point of view of historical continuity, nothing is new under the sun concerning the strength of ties between parents and children; nevertheless, increasing economic well-being is allowing to relax constraints, and the delayed transition to adulthood is seen as a results of free choice. Parents from strong family ties societies do not encourage their adult children to leave home. This delay can become a problem from a demographic point of view as the low levels of fertility that arise as a consequence can undermine the survival of the pattern itself (Dalla Zuanna 2001).

Still linked to the specificity of the Italian pattern are the findings of Manacorda and Moretti (2006), who put a key emphasis on the preferences of parents. They see living arrangements as the outcome of a noncooperative game between parents and children. If coresidence is a "good" for parents and a "bad" for children, parents will be willing to trade off some of their consumption in order to "bribe" their children. In other words, children who remain at home are compensated with higher consumption. Therefore, when parents have a preference for coresidence, parental income has a positive effect on coresidence (of course, if children have the same type of preference, there is no need to bargain). They then test this prediction exploiting exogenous changes in parental income induced by a reform in the Italian pension system. As expected, an exogenous rise in parental income increases the likelihood of their children coresiding and reduces the childrens' labor supply.

Manacorda and Moretti (2006) explain the Italian peculiarity of a late departure from the parental home to the extent that Italian parents differ in preferences from other parents. Indeed, U.S. evidence suggests that parents have opposite preferences for coresidence with children, suggesting that for U.S. fathers, privacy is a normal good (Rosenzweig and Wolpin 1993). Manacorda and Moretti also provide descriptive evidence on the positive association between parental happiness and coresidence in Italy. Using data from the World Value Survey (WVS), coresidence with children has a high and positive effect on parental happiness in Italy (with the highest coefficient), followed by Spain and Portugal; in other countries, coresidence with children is negatively associated with parental happiness (the highest negative coefficient being that of the United States, followed by France, Great Britain, and West Germany). Consistent with this, Mazzuco (2006) compares the causal impact of children leaving home on the well-being of parents in France and Italy using data from the European Community Household Panel, where well-being is measured through subjective life satisfaction and health status. He finds that when Italian children leave the parental home, the well-being of parents (their mothers in particular) worsens, while the opposite is true when French children leave the parental home. Finally, according to Manacorda and Moretti, results for the happiness of children go in the opposite direction: they find a positive association between youth happiness and leaving in the parental home in France and the United States, and a negative association in Italy (with the largest coefficient), West Germany, Portugal, the United Kingdom, and Spain.

In table 10.3, we show some results from our own elaboration on the WVS on parents and their relationship with children. Column (1) replicates the findings by Manacorda and Moretti (2006) on earlier waves (although the magnitude of the estimates is different). The association between coresidence with children and parental happiness is higher in Italy than in any other country considered. In column (2) Italy ranks high on values concerning the responsibilities of parents toward children although differences between countries on this item do not seem very relevant.

Table 10.4 documents that, unlike in Manacorda and Moretti (2006), Italian children also score the highest on the association between coresi-

Table 10.3   **Happiness of parents and coresidence with children and values concerning the attitudes of parents toward children**

Country	Parents' happiness and co-residence	Parents' responsibilities are to do the best for their children
Denmark	3.017	0.408
	(1.719)	(0.038)
France	0.446	0.681
	(1.706)	(0.037)
Germany (West)	1.728	0.418
	(1.056)	(0.037)
Italy	5.964	0.645
	(1.714)	(0.037)
Portugal	−3.285	0.763
	(2.940)	(0.037)
Spain	0.159	0.674
	(0.888)	(0.036)
The Netherlands	−1.298	0.563
	(1.949)	(0.038)
UK (Great Britain)	−0.509	0.662
	(1.872)	(0.038)
United States	−0.181	0.644
	(1.628)	(0.036)

Notes: Standard errors in parentheses. Own elaborations on data from the World Value Survey (WVS). First column refers to the 1989 to 1993 wave of the WVS and contains, in a regression on a variable of happiness on a 0 to 1 scale (from not at all happy to very happy), the coefficients (per 100) of a dummy variable that is equal to 1 when parents coreside with children. Regressions are performed separately for each country; controls include gender, age, age squared, health status, marital status (five statuses), employment status (five statuses), family income for men aged forty to seventy-four and women aged thirty-seven to seventy-one who are parents (a similar analysis is in Manacorda and Moretti 2006). Second column refers to all available waves and contains, in a pooled cross-country regression of a dummy variable that is equal to 1 when respondents answer that "Parents' responsibilities are to do the best for their children," the country coefficients. Controls include gender, age, age squared, health status, marital status (five statuses), employment status (five statuses), family income.

dence (with parents) and happiness (column [1]) although here the estimated coefficients are generally not statistically significant.[2] Moreover (column [2]), Italians score the highest on values related to respect toward parents. These data are, therefore, in accordance with a cultural peculiarity of the Italian setting.

Starting from Reher's historical account, Giuliano (2007) explains late home leaving in Italy by focusing on cultural change rather than continuity. She points out that in the early 1970s, the date of home leaving was fairly early in all advanced countries, except that the cultural norm for

---

2. We are not sure why our results differ from those reported by Manacorda and Moretti (2006). One reason could be that we focus only on youth aged eighteen to thirty-four, which we believe is the relevant focus when studying children.

Table 10.4   **Happiness of children and coresidence with parents and values concerning the attitude of children toward parents**

Country	Children's happiness and coresidence	Children should always respect parents
Denmark	2.454	0.357
	(3.242)	(0.039)
France	2.074	0.717
	(2.515)	(0.039)
Germany (West)	1.275	0.472
	(1.618)	(0.039)
Italy	3.926	0.767
	(3.155)	(0.038)
Portugal	–1.352	0.688
	(3.262)	(0.040)
Spain	0.820	0.713
	(1.670)	(0.037)
The Netherlands	1.504	0.387
	(2.732)	(0.039)
UK (Great Britain)	–2.353)	0.600
	(3.048)	(0.039)
United States	0.025	0.688
	(2.231)	(0.038)

Notes: Standard errors in parentheses. Own elaborations on data from the World Value Survey (WVS). First column refers to the 1989 to 1993 wave of the WVS and contains, in a regression on a variable of happiness on a 0 to 1 scale (from not at all happy to very happy), the coefficients (per 100) of a dummy variable that is equal to 1 when children coreside with parents. Regressions are performed separately for each country; controls include gender, age, age squared, health status, marital status (five statuses), employment status (five statuses), family income for individuals aged eighteen to thirty-four. Second column refers to all available waves and contains, in a pooled cross-country regression of a dummy variable that is equal to 1 when respondents answer that "Children should always respect parents," the country coefficients. Controls include gender, age, age squared, health status, marital status (five statuses), employment status (five statuses), family income.

Southern Europeans was to leave parental home at the time of marriage, whereas Northern Europeans had weaker family ties and were not bound by such norm. She then argues that the sexual revolution of the 1960s had a differential impact on Southern versus Northern Europe. Although the sexual revolution occurred in all countries, in Southern Europe, it implied that parents allowed far more freedom within the parental home. As a result, Southern Europeans nowadays stay in the parental home for longer and postpone marriage. In Northern Europe, there was no link between the date of marriage and the date of home leaving, and the sexual revolution did not influence coresidence with parents. This idea is documented using a survey on Italian young adults who coreside with their parents. More specifically, youth living with parents who allow more sexual freedom are more likely to be willing to continue coresiding; this idea is consistent with our children's happiness report in table 10.4. Giuliano also documents the role of culture by looking at second-generation immigrants in the United States, who display similar trends and differences as their peers in the countries of their parents; the postponement of home leaving of young Europeans is correlated with the postponement of home leaving of second-generation individuals of European origins in the United States.

Alesina and Giuliano (2007) further develop the "weak" versus "strong" family ties link with the economy and show that, in societies with strong family ties, the family is a more important economic unit. In these societies, home production is higher, but the labor force participation of young adults and geographical mobility are lower compared to societies with weak family ties.

10.2.2   The Role of Economic and Institutional Factors

Other explanations of the peculiarity of the Italian pattern focus on economic factors. Here the emphasis is on the interaction of economic circumstances with the institutional setting and, especially, welfare.

Becker et al. (2004) point to the peculiarity of the labor market. They explain the late home leaving pattern of Southern Europeans through the central role of *job insecurity*. In their model, children continue coresiding with parents even when working if they see their future income as insecure. The reason is that moving out of the parental home is considered an irreversible choice. Cross-country relationships on coresidence and measures of job insecurity are consistent with their hypothesis. Their microeconometric evidence is on parents: focusing on a pension reform that exogenously affects the income of parents, they show that a higher job insecurity of parents causes a delay in the housing emancipation of young adults. Provincial unemployment rates, on the other hand, do not have an effect on young adult's home leaving rates—according to Becker et al. (2004), this is related to the fact that unemployment rates do not adequately reflect youth's job insecurity.

In an analysis of the European Community Household Panel, Aassve and colleagues (Aassve et al. 2002) show that own income and employment are more linked to the decision to leave the parental home in Italy and other Southern European countries than elsewhere. According to Blossfeld and colleagues (Blossfeld et al. 2005; Blossfeld, Mills, and Bernardi 2006), the increasing job insecurity for young people that is implied by the globalization process is not adequately buffered by familistic welfare regimes like the one prevailing in Italy. For this reason, delayed home leaving is seen as a rational response to job insecurity, especially in societies without adequate welfare for young people.

Giannelli and Monfardini (2003) model the transition to adulthood by considering household membership, human capital accumulation, and work as joint decisions. They focus on Italy. Coresidence with parents is suppose to increase the reservation wage of young adults, They show that, in the presence of poor labor market opportunities (measured via the unemployment rate), youths may opt for investing in the improvement of human capital. Moreover, they emphasize the importance of housing and show that house prices are positively related to the propensity to reside with parents.

Alessie, Brugiavini, and Weber (2005) present a theoretical and empirical model of joint living arrangements and savings decisions in which they argue that coresidence with parents is a rational response of Italian youth to particularly high transaction costs on the housing market. Continuing to coreside with young parents allows young people to save more than they could do otherwise and to be more ready to successfully carry on subsequent housing choices.

10.3   Transition to Adulthood and the Economy: Does Late Matter?

What are the economic consequences of a delayed transition to adulthood? This section addresses this question. We look at three possible channels of influence: on fertility and population aging, on ability, and on labor market outcomes.

10.3.1   Fertility and Population Aging

Individuals typically plan their lives, and especially the transition to adulthood, according to a specific sequence of events, where there is a common "normative" pattern. First, they complete education. Then they become financially independent. Then they enter into a stable cohabiting partnership. Then they have children. This sequencing implies that a delay in achieving any one of these steps also postpones the subsequent ones. In particular, because childbearing comes at the very end, a delay in any of the preceding events entails a likely increase in the age of parenthood. Skirbekk, Kohler, and Prskawetz (2004) have documented this pattern with reference to Swedish women. They exploit the fact that in Sweden, age at entry into school is restricted: children must enter school in the year in which they turn seven. This implies that children born in January tend to complete schooling when they are eleven months older than children born in December. This exogenous variation in the age when completing education can be exploited to study the effect of age on the timing of marriage and fertility. Skirbekk and colleagues estimate that the delay in completing education is transmitted into a delay of marriage and fertility, although not one for one. In particular, the age at first birth for women born in January is higher by almost five months compared to women born in December. This effect of delayed education also persists for the timing of second births, although it becomes smaller. In this Swedish sample, however, completed fertility (i.e., the overall number of children) is not affected by the delay in the age of completed education.

In the case of Italy, an important question is whether the late transition into adulthood can contribute to explain the low fertility rate, which in turn influences the speed of population aging. As discussed in the previous section, Italians now have one of the highest median ages of first birth, relative to other countries or time periods. We suspect that this is an important reason for the low Italian fertility rate. Once age at first birth reaches the mid-30s for men and the late 20s for women, as is the case for Italy, there is not much time left to have a large family.

By using propensity score matching in order to the get causal effects of age at home leaving on fertility and by comparing individuals who leave the parental home before versus after the median age, Billari, Mazzuco, and Ongaro (2006) estimate that by the thirty-third birthday, Italian "early" home leavers have .522 more children (for men) and .700 more children (for women) compared to "late" home leavers. The effect is higher for those who leave home when starting a partnership (+.795 for men, +.817 for women) as compared to those who leave home prior to the start of a union (+.353 for men, +.374 for women).

Through its effect on fertility, the delayed transition to adulthood has key implications on the age structure of the population and of the labor force; on the dependency ratio; and through these channels on aggregate productivity, the government budget, and a host of other variables—see, for instance, Lindh and Malmberg (2007) on how the age structure of the population impacts on macroeconomic variables and can be used in forecasting economic growth.

10.3.2   Productivity

As shown in figure 10.1, the age profile of Italian workers is very different from that observed in other OECD countries. Italian male employment is quite low until about thirty years of age and keeps rising until about forty years of age. In most other OECD countries, instead, the peak employment rate is reached at a much younger age. A similar but less pronounced difference between Italy and other countries can be observed with regard to female employment, except that here the most striking difference is the overall low employment rate at all age groups and, particularly, among older women. This delay in employment is bound to have large effects on labor productivity. Here we discuss why.

Ability and Learning

Fertility is not the only human trait to have a pronounced age profile. A large body of evidence documents that cognitive abilities also decline significantly past a certain age. For instance, Avolio and Waldman (1994) have studied age differences in abilities in the *General Aptitude Test Battery,* exploiting data collected by the U.S. Department of Labor from 1970 to 1984. Although the pattern varies somewhat depending on the specific ability, all abilities decline rapidly once age has reached the mid thirties. By about

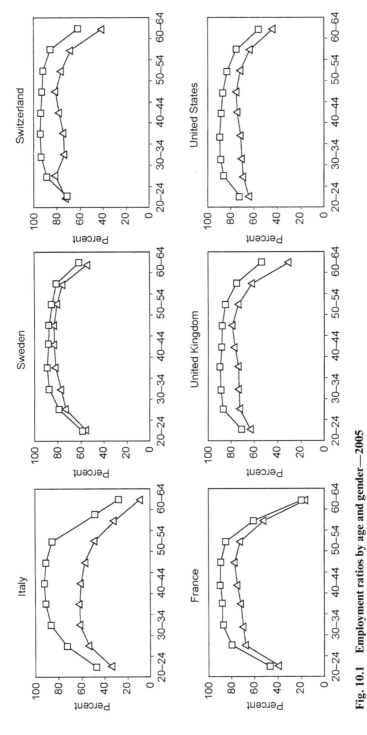

Fig. 10.1 Employment ratios by age and gender—2005
Source: OECD.

fifty years of age, average abilities are about one-half standard deviation below the level reached by the twenty-five to thirty-four-year-old group.

This age-related pattern of ability implies a corresponding pattern in labor productivity. But productivity is also influenced by experience, which rises with age and years spent working. As a result, although the relationship between age and labor productivity is typically hump-shaped, the peak in productivity is reached at a later age than the peak in ability. Skirbekk (2004) surveys the relevant and very large literature. Individual productivity is very difficult to measure because often it is the result of team work. Thus, the specific age where productivity peaks differs across studies, depending on how individual productivity is measured and what the worker's occupation is. Most studies find that productivity is highest for individuals in their thirties and forties, however. Earnings continue to rise even after productivity has peaked, so the peak in earnings is typically reached around fifty years of age.

Although experience rises with age, the ability to learn also declines rapidly as individuals become older. It is well documented that the elderly learn at a slower pace, particularly if what they learn is very different from what they are already familiar with (Rybash, Hoyer, and Roodin 1986) or if learning takes place in complex and rapidly changing environments (Myerson et al. 1990). This is particularly well known for languages: if a language is not learned by a young age, it will never by spoken perfectly.

Exploiting the same method discussed in the previously mentioned study of fertility of Swedish women, Billari and Pellizzari (2008) show that age has a significant negative effect on university performance in subjects requiring mathematical or analytical abilities. In Italy, children must enter school in the year in which they turn six. Like in Sweden, therefore, first-year university students born in January are eleven months older than those born in December, and this age difference is exogenous. Billari and Pellizzari compare the performance of students in economics and management at Bocconi University born in different months. They have a very rich sample, where they can control for a variety of individual features, such as grades in high school, the score in a standardized test at the entrance of university, and family background. University performance is measured by average graduation marks, the probability of ending with full marks, and the average grades in the first and second year of study. Students born in December display significantly better performance than those born in January, that is, they get 0.9 percent higher graduation marks. When focusing on grades in specific courses, they find that older age deteriorates grade performance in analytical and mathematical subjects (December versus January imply 2.1 percent higher marks in quantitative subjects and 1.8 percent higher marks in economic subject) but not in those requiring verbal skills or that are less demanding from a quantitative point of view (such as history, languages, or law).

These findings are remarkable because earlier studies focusing on high school performance, sport performance, or even the probability of completing tertiary education, had found the opposite: younger individuals (i.e., those born in the second half of the year) tend to do worse (e.g. Skirbekk, Kohler, and Prskawetz [2004] and the references cited there). A common interpretation of these earlier results is that they reflect the effect of relative (as opposed to absolute) age: individuals born in the second half of the year have less self-confidence, and this hurts their performance. A unique feature of the Bocconi data set is that it contains information on high school performance and of a general entry test performed by the university. By controlling for the final grade in high school and the performance in the test, differences in self-confidence induced by relative age effects are controlled for. This allows the impact of absolute age to be more correctly estimated.[3]

What does all of this imply for the effect of delayed employment on labor productivity? Figure 10.1 shows that, below the age of fifty, the age profile of Italian workers is delayed by five or even ten years relative to that of other OECD countries. This means that Italian workers are employed for a smaller fraction of their most productive years. Perhaps more important, particularly for male workers, it also implies that they have less time to benefit from experience and that their on-the-job learning is concentrated later in life when their learning ability is impaired. This is bound to have a negative effect on individual productivity although it is hard to quantify.

Matching in the Labor Market

Shimer (2001) points to yet another reason why a delayed first entry into the labor market might have adverse economic effects. Exploiting U.S. states data, he notes that an increase in the share of youth in the working population brings about a sharp reduction in the state unemployment rate as well as an increase in the participation rate. He also shows that turnover in manufacturing also increases sharply when the youth share goes up. A plausible interpretation of this finding is that young workers are more willing to accept job offers and that this creates a positive trading externality (Diamond 1982). As a result, a labor market with a higher youth share attracts more vacancies, boosting job creation and reducing unemployment. Because young workers are more mobile, over time, the matching of workers to jobs also improves, leading to a delayed rise in aggregate productivity.

Of course, delayed entry of young workers into the labor market works in the opposite direction. Entering the labor market at a higher age entails a likely loss of mobility and flexibility. In the presence of trading externalities, the whole economy suffers as a result.

---

3. An alternative explanation is that individuals born in the first quarter have less social skills and, therefore, spend more time studying compared to other more social peers. If this was the primary explanation, however, it would be difficult to explain why younger age is associated with better performance *only* in more mathematical exams.

Effort

Productivity also depends on effort, besides individual ability. A delayed transition into adulthood is also likely to be associated with dampened effort to improve one's economic situation and overall smaller effort on the job. For many individuals, the age between the early twenties and the early thirties is the period in life for investing in one's future. Postponing this phase to older ages is difficult, not just because learning becomes harder, but also because other goals beside work become prominent. It is not just a matter of age, but also of individual attitudes. Being financially dependent, living with one's parents, and staying out of the labor market for long periods of time, are likely to impact on the goals and ambitions of young men and women. Although hard to quantify and assess precisely, these sociological and psychological effects of a late transition into adulthood can be very relevant.

Table 10.5 illustrates how the attitudes toward work vary with age, exploit-

Table 10.5	Values and age		
	Spend time with colleagues (1)	Child quality: hard work (2)	Work will be less important in life (3)
Age below 30 years	−0.23 (0.03)***	0.08 (0.04)**	0.09 (0.03)***
Age above 50 years	0.12 (0.03)***	0.06 (0.04)	0.14 (0.03)***
Male	−0.12 (0.02)***	0.27 (0.03)***	0.02 (0.02)
Part-time worker	0.11 (0.03)***	0.06 (0.04)	−0.08 (0.03)**
Married	0.11 (0.03)***	0.00 (0.03)	−0.01 (0.03)
Has no children	−0.09 (0.03)***	0.06 (0.04)*	−0.10 (0.03)***
Education		−0.04 (0.01)***	−0.05 (0.01)***
Estimation	Ordered probit	Probit	Ordered probit
No. of observations	8,364	10,652	9,999
Pseudo R^2	0.03	0.18	0.04

Notes: Standard errors in parentheses. Sample: employed individuals, from seventeen to fifty-nine years of age, in Austria, Belgium, Canada, Denmark, France, Italy, The Netherlands, Spain, Sweden, United Kingdom, United States, West Germany. Country and wave fixed effects included in all columns. Column (1): Ordered from 1 to 4, higher values mean less time with colleagues. Column (3): Ordered from 1 to 3, higher values mean it is a bad thing.

***Significant at the 1 percent level.

**Significant at the 5 percent level.

*Significant at the 10 percent level.

Source: World Value Surveys, all waves for which data are available.

ing data from the WVS. The sample consists of employed individuals from twelve OECD countries between seventeen and fifty-nine years of age. We control for country and wave fixed effects and other observable features, such as gender, marital and parental status, whether working part time, and (where statistically significant) education level attained. This means that we only exploit within-country variations. The default age group is middle-aged individuals (between thirty and fifty years of age). The table illustrates that individuals below thirty years of age spend more time with their colleagues (column [1]), are more likely to think that hard work is an important quality in children (column [2]), and are more likely to dislike future changes that would place less importance to work in their lives (column [3]).

These attitude differences are bound to have an impact on individual productivity and on career or advancement opportunities. Individuals who enter the labor market when relatively old might end up achieving less compared to others who start their adult and professional life at a younger age.

10.3.3 Aggregate Evidence

The age composition of the workforce varies considerably across countries and time. If the effects of age discussed in the preceding are relevant, they ought to show up in aggregate data as well. The extensive literature on economic growth has not paid much attention to these issues, perhaps because it is difficult to draw inferences from aggregate data.

A recent exception is Feyrer (2007), who studies a panel of OECD countries. Exploiting within-country variations (i.e., always including country fixed effects), he shows that changes in demographic structures are strongly correlated with changes in aggregate total factor productivity. In particular, individuals in their forties appear to be more productive than other age groups. His estimates imply that a 5 percent increase in the size of the cohort in their forties over a ten-year period is associated with faster productivity growth by 1 to 2 percent for each year in the decade. These results are consistent with those mentioned in the preceding and based on analysis of individual data, where the most productive age groups appear to be the thirties and forties.

In a related paper, Lindh and Malmberg (1999) extend the framework of Mankiw, Romer, and Weil (1992) to study the effect of the demographic structure of the population on per capita gross domestic product (GDP) growth in the OECD countries. Contrary to Feyrer, they find that the fifty to sixty-four age group has a positive influence on growth, while the younger groups have ambiguous effects and the older (post-sixty-five) group has a negative effect. This is further developed in a paper in which they use the age structure of population to derive long-term economic forecasts (Lindh and Malmberg 2007).

This type of aggregate analysis provides little information about the effects of a delayed transition into adulthood, however. For this purpose, we would need information on dates of home leaving or similar events. Unfortunately such data are not readily available for a large number of countries or years. Nevertheless, we collected data on the percentage of men aged eighteen to thirty-four who lived with their parents in 2001 for twenty-seven European Union (EU) countries. Figure 10.2 illustrates a residual regression plot between this variable and average GDP growth over 2001 to 2005, after controlling for initial GDP per capita and a dummy variable for the more advanced EU-15 countries. As shown in the figure, the countries with a smaller fraction of young men living with their parents grow faster, and the relationship is significant at the 5 percent level. Of course, this association cannot be interpreted as causal evidence because of possible reverse causation or omitted variables. But it suggests that the hypothesis that a delayed transition into adulthood might hurt a country's economic performance deserves to be taken seriously.[4]

10.4   Analysis of Individual Data

This section studies empirically the effect of the timing of transition into adulthood on individual income levels. Our general hypothesis is that individuals who have a later transition into adulthood earn less income in their adult life, that is, that it matters indeed if Italians are late. Although difficult to estimate, we are interested in a causal effect: we would like to know whether a later transition has a negative impact on lifetime economic opportunities. As discussed in the previous section, this might happen in more than one way: because a late transition reduces previous work duration and previous job experience; because past a certain age, learning on the job becomes more difficult or effort is reduced; or because a late transition changes individual goals and ambitions. Our data do not allow us to investigate the precise mechanism through which this might happen, but they will allow us to assess whether and to what extent this impact is present.

10.4.1   The Data

The Sample

We exploit a longitudinal survey on Italian youth, where we select a representative subsample of about 600 Italian men, on which we have detailed information on key dates marking the transition to adulthood as well as income, education, family background, and so on. Data come from the survey I.D.E.A. (*Inizio Dell'Età Adulta*—Beginning of Adulthood), which was carried out on a nationally representative sample about 3,000 young people

---

4. Data on initial per capita income for Malta and Cyprus were not available, and we thus imputed to these two countries the average initial GDP per capita of the EU countries different from the EU-15.

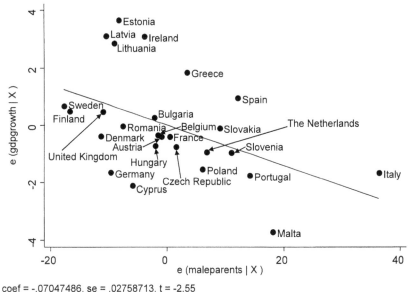

coef = -.07047486. se = .02758713. t = -2.55

Fig. 10.2   GDP growth (2001–2005) and percentage of men aged 18–34 living in parental home in 2001 in the European Union
Note: Residual regression plots after controlling for real GDP per capita in 2000 and a dummy variable for EU-15 countries.

born between 1966 and 1970 (aged about thirty-three to thirty-eight) and 1976 to 1980 (aged about twenty-three to twenty-seven). Interviews were conducted via telephone between December 2003 and March 2004. The sample was stratified by sex, marital status, and residential macro-areas (North, Centre and South of Italy) (Mazzuco, Mencarini, and Rettaroli 2006).

In our analysis, we focus only on men of the second age group (born between 1966 and 1970, therefore aged thirty-three to thirty-eight at the time of the interview), with a sample size of about 600. At that age, most men (even in Italy) have left home and, therefore, the timing of home leaving is known for the vast majority of individuals. In this sample corresponding to the second age group, individuals have left the parental home, on average, eight years before the date of the interview. About 12 percent of the sample has never left the parental home at the time of the interview. We do not focus on women, given the complexity of their labor force attachment in childbearing ages in a place like Italy. Indeed, in Italy, female labor force participation is among the lowest in Europe (13 percent below the EU average) and has not increased during the last decades, especially because of rationing in the child care market (Del Boca and Vuri 2007).

Table 10.6   Monthly income of Italian young adults in the I.D.E.A. survey (ages 33–38, 2003–2004)

	%	N
None	0.3	2
Up to 500 euros	1.6	11
From 500 up to 1,000 euros	15.4	107
From 1,000 up to 1,500 euros	51.2	355
1,500 euros and more	31.6	219
Total	100	694

Note: I.D.E.A. = Inizio Dell'Età Adulta (Beginning of Adulthood).

The Main Variables of Interest

As a *dependent variable,* we focus on *income* at the time of the interview. This variable is reported by the respondent, and in the survey it is measured by five intervals. For respondents who have any type of employment (91.5 percent of our sample, 92 percent of those who have ever left the parental home), a question on monthly income (wage or income from self-employment) is included, with five answer categories: none (could be answered by people who work in a family firm without earning direct income), up to 500 euros; from 500 up to 1,000 euros; from 1,000 up to 1,500 euros; 1,500 euros and more. A frequency distribution of the income variable is reported in table 10.6. The 8.5 percent nonemployed individuals are treated as randomly missing (analyses considering them as zero-income individuals not shown here give similar results).

As we are mostly interested in the direction of effects on income (as the dependent variable), and in the comparison of the effect of late transition to adulthood with other effects, we only show analyses that based on a simple type of coding for income, which we call *income interval* from now onward. We recode the answer obtained by respondents in five categories ("0 euros" = 0; "up to 500 euros" = 1; "from 500 up to 1,000 euros" = 2; "from 1,000 up to 1,500 euros" = 3; "1,500 euros and more" = 4). This variable becomes the dependent one in a series of least squares models (with or without instrumental variables). We also estimated the same series of models using ordered probit, or on log-income intervals (with 0 euro incomes recoded as 1) using interval regression. Results are similar to the ones we show here.

The main indicator of the timing of transition into adulthood is the age at which the respondent left the parental home for the first time for a period longer than six months, for reasons other than the military service (see also appendix A). This variable is called *age of home leaving,* and it is measured in years (it varies almost continuously as the month of home leaving is also known). In our sample, age of home leaving has small but positive correlation with years of education ($\rho = .12$, $p = 0.002$ for the hypothesis $\rho \neq 0$) and with other markers of the transition to adulthood, such as age at first job ($\rho = .11$, $p = 0.0054$) and age at first sexual intercourse ($\rho = .18$, $p = 0.0000$). Table 10.7 contains the descriptive statistics for this variable, together with those of other regressors defined in the next subsection. The main focus of our analysis is whether *age of home leaving* has a causal effect on income later in life. As already mentioned, our analysis cannot shed light on the specific mechanism through which this may happen although we discuss this issue in the following.

We also consider another variable related to the age of transition into adulthood: the quarter of birth. As discussed in the previous section, Italians have to attend compulsory school in the year in which they turn six. This means that when school ends in a "standard" fashion, on average, individuals born in the first quarter are at least six months older than those born in the last quarter of the year and, thus, have had a later transition into

Table 10.7   Descriptive statistics of regressors and instruments in the I.D.E.A. survey (ages 33–38, 2003–2004)

	Mean	Standard deviation	Valid N
Age of home leaving	25.94	4.55	644
Age of mother at own birth	28.12	6.05	732
Education (respondent, no. of years)	12.68	3.35	767
"Too long" education (dummy)	.22		705
Father's education (no. of years)	7.82	4.47	767
Mother's education (no. of years)	7.20	3.80	767
Mother housewife (dummy)	.65		746
Father employed (dummy)	.92		740
Parents divorced or separated (dummy)	.04		767
Number of siblings (excl. respondent)	1.60	1.38	767
Religiosity score (1–5) at age 16	2.43	1.49	759
Lack of self-confidence score (1–4)	2.40	.83	862
Married (dummy)	.69		767
No. of children	.90	.93	767
Age of first job	22.42	6.17	721
Age of first sex	18.20	3.05	693
Northwest (dummy)	.28		767
Northeast (dummy)	.20		767
Center (dummy)	.19		767
South (dummy)	.32		767
Living in main city of the province (dummy)	.56		767
Provincial average income (aggregate, euros in 2005)	24,109.58	6,285.33	753
Youth unemployment rate (aggregate %)	27.52	19.61	733
Empty dwellings (aggregate %)	19.64	8.77	753

Note: I.D.E.A. 5 Inizio Dell'Età Adulta (Beginning of Adulthood).

adulthood.[5] We thus define two dummy variables, called *first quarter* and *fourth quarter,* respectively, that equal one if the individual is born in that quarter (we also experimented with using the month of birth, rather than the quarter, and obtained consistent results). To verify that indeed the quarter of birth influences the timing of significant events, we ran an ordinary least squares (OLS) regression of the age when education was completed against the dummy variables for the first and fourth quarter of birth and the level of education attained, with and without the other regressors defined in the following (the variables for family background and residential location, the variable measuring church attendance, and the dummy variables for the current age group). The results are not shown but are available upon request. Irrespective of the specification, when education is completed, individuals born in the first quarter are younger by about eight months than those born in the fourth quarter, in line with expectations, and the difference is statistically significant. The quarter of birth, on the other hand, has no effect on the level of education attained. This confirms that the quarter of birth influences the timing of transition into adulthood, with individuals born in the first quarter more likely to transition at an older age.

Other Regressors

Throughout our analyses, we control for several observed individual characteristics. For simplicity, we define the name of each variable in italics when the variable is actually reported in the tables. Table 10.7 provides descriptive statistics also on other regressors, while appendix A provides full details on all variables.

Individual Characteristics   *Age* of the individuals is controlled by a set of dummy variables, one for each year of age between thirty-three and thirty-eight. The variable *education* measures educational attainment (defined in years corresponding to the attained school degree). Unfortunately, we do not have information on school or university grades (nor on the subject). We know how many years each respondent actually spent in school or university, however. Thus, to measure differences in school performance, we include a dummy variable that equals one if the time spent to attain the school or university degree exceeded the normally required time by more than two years (alternative definitions such as a more continuously time varying indicator gave similar results). To capture differences in religious upbringing, we also include a variable that measures the reported frequency of church attendance at the age of sixteen (the variable varies from one to five).

5. This legal requirement could be sidestepped by going to private schools as they accept also children who will turn six in the following calendar year (only in the last four years has more flexibility been accepted for public schools). Only 3.6 percent of the students in grade one in private elementary schools were early starters in 2001 to 2002; moreover, in Italy, private schools offer, on average, lower quality with respect to public schools—see Brunello and Checchi (2004).

Family Characteristics. We use several variables related to the family background of the respondent: education attained by the mother and father; the age of the mother at birth; dummy variables for whether, when the individual was sixteen years of age, the father was working and the mother was a housewife; the number of siblings; and a dummy variable for whether parents ever divorced or split.

Contextual Characteristics We also include several variables related to the *location* where the individual lived at the age of sixteen, namely, whether he lived in a city that was also a provincial capital (at the time of the surveys there were 103 provinces in Italy); the rate of youth unemployment in the province in 2001 (i.e., four years earlier than the date in which income is observed, and at about the time when individuals are likely to have considered the decision to leave the parental home); per capita income in the province in 2005 (i.e., the date in which the survey was conducted and income is observed); and three dummy variables, corresponding to the macro regions of residence (north, center, and south).

Finally, in some specification, we also control for some variables that reflect individual attitudes or lifetime choices. Although these variables might be endogenous, like *education,* their inclusion may help to clarify the mechanism through which the variables of interest influence income. Specifically, the dummy variable *married* equals one if the individual has ever been married; the variable *number of children* is self-explanatory; we measure the age when the individual first worked for pay by the variable *age of first job.* And the variable *lack of self-confidence* is a measure of individual attitudes toward one's self and the future, taken from a question that asks whether the respondent agrees with the following statement: "When I think about my future, I see it full of risks and uncertainties." Possible answers range from one to four, with higher values denoting stronger agreement (i.e., more lack of self-confidence).

Variables that are used as instruments are introduced in the following.

10.4.2 Estimation Issues

There are two relevant estimation problems. The first and main issue is unobserved heterogeneity or, more generally, correlation between the variables of interest and the unobserved error term. This problem is most obvious with regard to the variable *age of home leaving.* Relevant unobserved individual features could determine both individual income and the date at which the individual leaves the parental home. The bias in OLS estimates could go either way: on the one hand, more talented and determined individuals could have both higher income and more opportunities to leave home early, which would lead to a downward bias between *age of home leaving* and *income interval.* On the other hand, young men living in disadvantaged areas may be forced to leave home earlier to find a job, or to go to university, which could lead to the opposite bias. We deal with this problem by relying on instrumental variables, described in the following.

The problem of unobserved heterogeneity might also be relevant with regard to *education.* Here, too, the bias in OLS estimates could be positive (if unobserved talent influences both educational attainment and income) or negative (for instance, due to measurement error). As discussed, for instance, by Card (2001), instrumental variable (IV) estimates of the effect of education on earnings are typically above the OLS estimates, which might reflect systematic pitfalls in the IV identification strategies (e.g., heterogeneous effects of education correlated with the instrument) or a negative bias in the OLS estimates. In this chapter, we generally do not attempt to cope with this problem because we lack separate reliable instruments for education (see, however, table 10.10 in the following), and because we are not interested in the effect of *education* per se.

The inclusion of a possibly endogenous variable like *education* or being *married* might bias the coefficient of interest on the variable *age of home leaving.* Appendix B shows that this bias might be positive or negative depending on the assumptions about the relevant unobserved correlations. We discuss this issue in context in the following, and we show that the results are robust to alternative specifications that include or omit these possibly endogenous variables.

The second problem is that the variable *age of home leaving* is only observed if it is lower than current age. About 12 percent of the individuals in our sample have never left the parental home for more than six months, despite their having been at least thirty-three years of age: for them, *age of home leaving* is missing. Thus, we have censoring of an endogenous regressor. We cope with this problem in two ways. First, we ignore it and assume that these observations are randomly missing or, alternatively, we just draw inferences about the sample of individuals who have already left the parental home (rather than all those of thirty-three to thirty-eight years of age). Second, we redefine the variable of interest and measure the timing of the transition to adulthood in alternative ways so as to exploit all observations in the sample, including the individuals that are still living with their parents. Details are discussed in the following.

10.4.3   Results

OLS Estimates

The dependent variable is *income interval* (with the simple coding described in the preceding). We start by assuming that all regressors are exogenous to illustrate the main correlations in the data. Table 10.8 reports the estimated coefficients of the variables of main interest. Standard errors are clustered by province of residence. Column (1) reports the most parsimonious specification; besides the variables reported in the column, we control for all the other

Table 10.8   Ordinary least squares (OLS) estimates—income interval and age of home leaving

	(1)	(2)	(3)
Age of home leaving	−0.028	−0.026	−0.025
	(0.007)***	(0.007)***	(0.007)***
First quarter	−0.185	−0.189	−0.182
	(0.059)***	(0.062)***	(0.061)***
Fourth quarter	0.024	0.013	−0.011
	(0.064)	(0.064)	(0.067)
Education	0.065	0.061	0.068
	(0.010)***	(0.010)***	(0.010)***
Lack of self-confidence		−0.097	−0.100
		(0.037)**	(0.037)***
Married		0.037	0.032
		(0.083)	(0.084)
No. of children		0.055	0.053
		(0.038)	(0.037)
Age of first job			−0.009
			(0.006)
Estimation	OLS	OLS	OLS
No. of observations	497	496	496
Adjusted R^2	0.20	0.21	0.21

Notes: Robust standard errors in parentheses, clustered by province. Other included regressors (all columns): dummy variables for years of age and for macro region of residence; dummy variable for extra time to complete education; frequency of church attendance; number of siblings; mother and father education; dummy variables for mother housewife, working father, divorced parents, living in provincial capital; youth unemployment in 2001 in the province of residence when sixteen years old; average current income in the province of residence. See the appendix for detailed definitions.
***Significant at the 1 percent level.
**Significant at the 5 percent level.

regressors mentioned in the preceding, namely a set of dummy variables for each age group, the variable for church attendance when sixteen years of age, the dummy variable for taking at least two extra years to complete the attained level of education, the full set of variables measuring family background, and the full set of variables relating to residential location.

As can be seen, a later *age of home leaving* has a negative and significant estimated coefficient, while the coefficient of *education* is positive and statistically significant. Both variables are measured in years, so their estimated coefficients are comparable. If these were causal effects, according to the OLS estimates, leaving home one year earlier would increase income by about as much as five additional months of education.

As discussed in the appendix, the inclusion of a possibly endogenous variable like *education* might introduce a negative bias in the estimated coefficient of *age of home leaving*. This would happen if the two variables are positively correlated (as would be the case if for instance the individual does not leave home to move to a university), and if *education* is also positively correlated with the unobserved error term of the income regression. On the other hand, in this case, omitting the variable *education* would introduce an upward bias if *education* has a positive effect on income. To assess the relevance of this problem, we have also reestimated the same equation without controlling for *education*. The results are very similar to those reported in table 10.1: the coefficient of *age of home leaving* estimated by OLS with the specification corresponding to column (1) rises to –0.025 (as opposed to –0.028) and remains significant at the 1 percent level.

Being born in the first quarter of the year also has a negative and highly significant estimated coefficient. This is consistent with the hypothesis that a later age of transition into adulthood reduces income in our sample because as discussed in the preceding, on average, individuals born in the first quarter complete their education when they are eight months older than those born in the fourth quarter. The estimated coefficient is implausibly high, however, both in relation to that of *education* and in absolute value. There is no strong a priori reason why the quarterly pattern of births should be systematically correlated with relevant omitted variables; on the contrary, the variables *first* and *fourth quarter* can plausibly be expected to be exogenous. Thus, this strong negative correlation between income and the first quarter of birth is puzzling.

Of the other regressors, not shown in table 10.8, some of the family background variables are significantly different from zero (income is higher if the mother is more educated and if she is a housewife), older individuals tend to have higher income, and some of the residential location variables are also statistically significant. Overall, the pattern of estimated coefficients is very plausible although there remains much unexplained variation in the data (the adjusted R^2 is 0.20).

To assess the robustness of these results and to gain a better understanding, the remaining columns in the table add other variables that capture individual attitudes or other significant lifetime choices possibly correlated both with *income interval* and with *age of home leaving*. Thus, in column (2), we control for whether the individual is married, how many children he has, and his attitudes toward the future as measured by the variable *lack of self-confidence*. These variables might be correlated with the error term of the income equation; thus, their inclusion might introduce a bias in the estimated coefficient of *age of home leaving*. As discussed in the appendix, the sign of this bias is likely to be positive for all of these additional variables. The estimated coefficients of interest (on *age of home leaving* and *first quarter*) remain stable and highly significant. Of these new variables, only lack of self-confidence has a significant (and, as expected, negative) effect on income. We infer from these results that the correlation between our measure of the timing of transition toward adulthood and income is not due to the events captured by marriage or becoming a parent, and it is robust to controlling for attitudes toward the future.

Finally, in column (3), we also control for the *age of first job*. This is important for two reasons. First, it may provide information on the channels through which a late transition to adulthood impacts on income later in life (a shorter experience on the job versus effects on personality or individual motivation). Second, it is a robustness check for how to date transition into adulthood. Again, this variable might be endogenous, but once more, the results in the appendix suggest that any additional bias on the estimated coefficient of the variable *age of home leaving* is likely to be upward. The results of interest are robust to this inclusion, and the new variable is not correlated with income. This confirms that the timing of transition to adulthood is well captured by the variable *age of home leaving*. It also suggests the estimated coefficient of *age of home leaving* is not just capturing experience on the job. On the other hand, the finding that *age of first job* is not significantly correlated with income ($\rho = 0.01, p = 0.71$) might also be interpreted as evidence that this variable refers to menial or temporary jobs that do not correspond to a milestone event in the transition to adulthood.

Instrumental Variables Estimates

In this subsection, we try to go beyond simple correlations, and we try to estimate a causal effect of the timing of transition into adulthood, as measured by the variable *age of home leaving*. This requires having a theory about why individuals leave the parental home, of the type we reviewed in section 10.2. Our (implicit) theory is that this decision is influenced by two kinds of considerations (besides those having to do with financial independence). One factor is the cost of living alone. If housing is easily available, this cost is lower, and individuals are more likely to leave early. The second factor is the desire to be independent from parental supervision. Our instruments seek to capture these two determinants of the decision to abandon the parental home.

Specifically, we rely on two instruments. The first instrument is an indicator of the excess supply of housing in the area where the individual lived when he was making the decision to leave the parental home (Giannelli and Monfardini 2003). This is measured by the fraction of empty residential dwellings in the province of residence at the age of sixteen, measured in the year 2001. This variable, called *empty dwellings,* captures the first set of determinants described in the preceding. As an alternative variable measuring similar housing market features, we also collected data on the fraction of residential dwellings rented (as opposed to owned) in 2001, also in the province of residence at sixteen years of age. This variable was more weakly correlated with *age of home leaving* compared to *empty dwellings,* however, and for this reason, we did not use it as an instrument.

Note that throughout in the second stage regression we control for the rate of youth unemployment in 2001 and current (i.e., 2005) average income in this same province, as well as for whether the individual currently lives in the provincial capital. Thus, the identifying assumption is that, after taking into account economic conditions as measured by youth unemployment and current income in the province, the supply of housing only matters for the decision to leave the parental home and has no direct effect on current individual income except through the variable *age of first leaving.* This assumption may fail if, for instance, housing conditions influence the kind of jobs that are accepted and this, in turn, impacts on income later in life. In particular, a cheaper housing market might induce young men to accept jobs paying a lower wage, and due to persistence in wages, this induces a positive correlation between housing prices and income later in life (or a negative correlation between *empty dwellings* and the residual of the second stage *income interval* equation). The fact that we control for economic conditions in the province may remove some but perhaps not all of this correlation. Note, however, that we expect *empty dwellings* to be positively correlated with the decision to leave home early (and this is what we find in the following), that is, negatively correlated with *age of home leaving.* Therefore, a negative correlation between this instrument and the unobserved second stage residual would bias the IV estimated coefficient of *age of home leaving* downward in absolute value against our main hypothesis that an early age of transition into adulthood increases income later in life.

The second instrument seeks to capture the individual demand for independence from his parents. We assume that the main reason to seek early independence is early sexual emancipation (see also the central role of sexual emancipation in Giuliano's [2007] arguments). Thus, as a second instrument, we use the reported age in which the individual had his first sexual intercourse (*age of first sex,* measured in years). Recall that here we control for an indicator of school performance (such as the extra time required to complete the attained level of education), for family background, and for religious habits. Thus, the identifying assumption is that, after controlling for these observed individual features, the propensity to early sexual emancipation is uncorrelated with unobserved determinants of individual income at thirty-three to thirty-eight years of age. This assumption may fail if, say, more good looking teenagers are sexually more emancipated and if good looks also help in the labor market. This failure would introduce a negative correlation between the instrument and the error term of the income regression, which would bias the IV estimate upward in absolute value. A downward bias in the absolute value of the IV estimate might also occur, however, if early sexual emancipation is correlated with individual features that are negatively correlated with adult productivity, such as engaging in risky behaviour and reduced interest in academic performance. Some evidence that this might be the case is suggested in the related literature (e.g., Schvaneveldt et al. 2001).

None of our identifying assumptions is foolproof. Nevertheless, the two instruments are uncorrelated, and they capture very different determinants of the individual decision to abandon the parental home ($\rho = .03$, $p =$

0.1717). This allows us to test the exclusion restrictions (under the null hypothesis that at least one of them is valid). Moreover, assessing the robustness of the results to the inclusion of the additional regressors mentioned in the preceding (such as being *married* and the *number of children*) is a further check on the validity of the exclusion restriction concerning the instrument *age of first sex*.

Finally, we also experimented with a third instrument, namely proximity to a big university. Specifically, we constructed an ordinal variable *university*, defined as follows: the variable equals 0 if no university exists in the province of residence at the age of sixteen; it equals 1 if in that province there is a university with up to 20,000 students; and it equals 2 if there is a university with more than 20,000 students. This variable is quite negatively correlated with *empty dwellings* ($\rho = -.36$, $p = 0.0000$), however, so relying on all three instruments deteriorates the fit of the first stage regressions (with no material effect on the IV estimates). The variable *empty dwellings* is also more strongly correlated with *age of home leaving* in the first stage. For this reason, in the end, we rely on the two instruments *empty dwellings* and *age of first sex*.

We now turn to the IV estimates, reported in table 10.9. The three columns report two-stage least squares (2SLS) estimates with robust standard errors clustered by province. The estimated coefficients of *age of home leaving* are always negative and highly significant and very stable across specifications and estimation methods. The remaining pattern of estimated coefficients is otherwise similar to that of the OLS regressions in table 10.8, except that here the variable married has a positive and significant estimated coefficient in some regressions. Relative to the OLS estimates, the estimated effect of *age of home leaving* on income rises significantly in absolute value, and now it even exceeds the effect of education.

One interpretation of this large change is that the OLS estimates were biased downward. As discussed in the preceding, a priori, the bias in the OLS estimates could go either way. In particular, individuals in underdeveloped areas with poor job opportunities may be forced to leave home early and accept jobs that pay lower wages, which would introduce a downward bias in the absolute value of the OLS estimate of interest. Moreover, measurement error in *age of home leaving* is also likely, both because individuals could misreport the true date, but more important, because this variable is really a proxy to a much more difficult to measure transition into adulthood, and it is possible that the projection on the instruments purges some of this measurement error.

An alternative interpretation is that the identifying assumptions are violated. Nevertheless, as shown toward the bottom of the table, the Hansen J test for the validity of the overidentifying restrictions can never reject the null hypothesis at very comfortable p-values (Baum, Schaffer, and Stillman 2003). Appendix C (table 10C.1) also shows the estimation of two just identified models, corresponding to the specifications in columns (1) and (3)

Table 10.9   Two-stage least squares (2SLS) estimates—income interval and age of home leaving

	(1)	(2)	(3)
Age of home leaving	−0.106	−0.105	−0.106
	(0.039)***	(0.039)***	(0.039)***
First quarter	−0.222	−0.225	−0.224
	(0.086)***	(0.091)**	(0.091)**
Fourth quarter	0.039	0.046	0.044
	(0.074)	(0.075)	(0.083)
Education	0.070	0.064	0.065
	(0.011)***	(0.011)***	(0.010)***
Lack of self-confidence		−0.105	−0.105
		(0.044)**	(0.044)**
Married		0.076	0.076
		(0.109)	(0.110)
No. of children		−0.045	−0.046
		(0.062)	(0.062)
Age of first job			−0.001
			(0.008)
Hansen J	0.523	0.631	0.631
Estimation	2SLS	2SLS	2SLS
No. of observations	457	456	456

Notes: Robust standard errors in parentheses, clustered by province. Hansen J refers to the *p*-value of the test of the overidentifying restrictions. Other regressors included in all columns: same as in table 10.8.
***Significant at the 1 percent level.
**Significant at the 5 percent level.

of table 10.9. Thus, in one case, we assume that only *age of first sex* can be validly excluded from the second stage, and, in the opposite case, we only exclude the variable *empty dwellings*. As can be seen in table 10C.1 in appendix C, the included instrument is never statistically significant in the second stage. The estimated coefficient on *age of home leaving* differs somewhat in the two cases, although it generally remains statistically significant, but it turns out to be smaller in absolute value when the excluded instrument is the arguably more suspicious *age of first sex*. Overall, this suggests that the data do not point to obvious violations of our identifying assumptions.

Alternative Measures of Transition to Adulthood

About 12 percent of the individuals in our sample had not yet left the parental home. As a result, the variable *age of home leaving* is missing for these individuals. To include these observations in our sample, here we redefine the measure of the timing of transition into adulthood in a more coarse way.

Our first indicator, *age group of home leaving,* is a discrete variable that varies from one to five, depending on the age group when the parental home was first abandoned. The first group is less than twenty years of age; the last group is past the age of thirty-two; the three intermediate groups correspond to the intervening four-year periods. The distribution of individuals is quite uniform across this partition; in the last age group, about 60 percent of individuals had not yet left the parental home, while the remaining 40 percent did.

The second indicator, *years since home leaving,* is just the number of years since leaving the parental home for the first time (with 0 denoting those that had not yet done so). This variable varies almost continuously, but it does not take into account the interaction between age and number of years out of the parental home.

Tables 10.10 and 10.11 report the estimates using these variables to measure the timing of transition into adulthood, first estimating by OLS under the assumption that they are exogenous (table 10.10) and then estimating

Table 10.10   Ordinary least squares (OLS) estimates—income interval and other measures of the timing of transition into adulthood

	Income					
	(1)	(2)	(3)	(4)	(5)	(6)
Age group of home leaving	−0.145 (0.024)***	−0.114 (0.024)***	−0.110 (0.025)***			
Years since home leaving				0.036 (0.006)***	0.028 (0.006)***	0.027 (0.006)***
First quarter	−0.157 (0.060)**	−0.157 (0.062)**	−0.152 (0.062)**	−0.160 (0.061)**	−0.159 (0.063)**	−0.155 (0.062)**
Fourth quarter	0.026 (0.062)	0.015 (0.061)	−0.006 (0.064)	0.038 (0.061)	0.025 (0.060)	0.004 (0.064)
Education	0.061 (0.009)***	0.056 (0.009)***	0.063 (0.010)***	0.061 (0.009)***	0.056 (0.009)***	0.062 (0.010)***
Lack of self-confidence		−0.113 (0.037)***	−0.114 (0.037)***		−0.112 (0.036)***	−0.113 (0.036)***
Married		0.114 (0.069)	0.112 (0.070)		0.110 (0.068)	0.108 (0.069)
No. of children		0.061 (0.038)	0.061 (0.038)		0.059 (0.038)	0.058 (0.038)
Age of first job			−0.008 (0.006)			−0.008 (0.006)
Estimation	OLS	OLS	OLS	OLS	OLS	OLS
No. of observations	565	564	564	565	564	564
Adjusted R^2	0.20	0.23	0.23	0.20	0.23	0.23

Notes: Robust standard errors in parentheses. Other regressors included in all columns: same as in table 10.8.

***Significant at the 1 percent level.

**Significant at the 5 percent level.

Table 10.11   **First-stage and two-stage least squares estimates, alternative measures of transition to adulthood**

	First stage					
	Age group of first home leaving			Years since home leaving		
	(1)	(2)	(3)	(4)	(5)	(6)
Age of first sex	0.052	0.044	0.041	−0.225	−0.189	−0.173
	(0.019)***	(0.017)**	(0.017)**	(0.075)***	(0.066)***	(0.065)***
Empty dwellings	−0.014	−0.017	−0.017	0.044	0.056	0.059
	(0.006)**	(0.006)***	(0.006)***	(0.027)	(0.026)**	(0.027)**
F test	6.82	7.13	5.82	6.28	6.63	5.97
Adjusted R^2	0.08	0.18	0.20	0.15	0.26	0.27

	Second stage					
	Income interval					
	(1)	(2)	(3)	(4)	(5)	(6)
Age group of home leaving	−0.490	−0.480	−0.486			
	(0.147)***	(0.150)***	(0.156)***			
Years since home leaving				0.120	0.122	0.125
				(0.036)***	(0.039)***	(0.041)***
First quarter	−0.196	−0.209	−0.212	−0.209	−0.225	−0.230
	(0.090)**	(0.093)**	(0.094)**	(0.091)**	(0.095)**	(0.097)**
Fourth quarter	0.039	0.045	0.054	0.082	0.092	0.108
	(0.077)	(0.076)	(0.087)	(0.075)	(0.077)	(0.090)
Education	0.063	0.057	0.054	0.062	0.057	0.052
	(0.010)***	(0.010)***	(0.011)***	(0.011)***	(0.011)***	(0.010)***
Lack of self-confidence		−0.091	−0.091		−0.087	−0.085
		(0.043)**	(0.044)**		(0.044)**	(0.044)*
Married		−0.072	−0.072		−0.094	−0.097
		(0.101)	(0.101)		(0.106)	(0.106)
No. of children		−0.059	−0.059		−0.076	−0.078
		(0.067)	(0.068)		(0.070)	(0.072)
Age of first job			0.003			0.006
			(0.008)			(0.009)
Hansen J	0.758	0.724	0.517	0.55	0.503	0.31
No. of observations	517	516	516	517	516	516

Notes: Robust standard errors in parentheses. *F* test refers to the joint significance of the two instruments. Hansen J refers to the *p*-value of the test of the overidentifying restrictions. Other regressors included in all columns: same as in table 10.8.

***Significant at the 1 percent level.

**Significant at the 5 percent level.

*Significant at the 10 percent level.

by instrumental variables (table 10.11). The specification is as before, and table 10.11 reports both first and second stage estimates. The results are very similar to those reported in the previous subsections. Irrespective of how it is measured, a later transition into adulthood is associated with lower income in the midthirties. Generally, both instruments are strongly significant in the first stage regressions. The second stage coefficients estimated by IV are much larger in absolute value than the corresponding OLS estimates. And the overidentification test fails to reject the exclusion restrictions. Finally, a dummy variable for whether the individual is still living in the parental home (to discriminate more finely between individuals in the last age group) turns out to have a statistically insignificant estimated coefficient (results not shown).

All together, these estimates suggest that the previous results are robust to the issue of censoring for the individuals for which the *age of home leaving* is missing.

10.5 Concluding Remarks

Italians are late. Not just a little, but a lot. They start all adult activities at a much later age than is common in other countries at comparable levels of development, from working, to living alone, to marrying, to having children. The existing literature has sought to explain this pattern and has pointed out that this has relevant implications for fertility and the demographic structure of society.

In this chapter, we have explored a different question. Does a late transition into adulthood reduce the lifetime economic opportunities of individuals? A priori, there are several reasons why this might be the case. On the one hand, a late transition into the activities that are typical of adult age may be associated with more maturity and more clarity in the pursuit of one's goals. Prolonged coresidence with parents might also relax liquidity constraints and encourage the accumulation of more human capital. On the other hand, if the transition is delayed for too long, learning abilities and motivation may be impaired, and the individual may get used to depend on others for his economic well-being and security. More specifically, prolonged coresidence with parents might raise the reservation wage and delay entry into stable jobs. If the earnings profile rises with experience on the job, this, in turn, reduces income later in life, and the effect may be very long lasting if it interacts with learning and motivation. Disparate evidence in the literature on the age profile of abilities and learning capacity and direct evidence on individual motivations suggest that this second hypothesis is not implausible in the case of Italy, given the extent of the delay.

We have studied a survey of Italian men in their midthirties that includes the retrospective reconstruction of the timing of life-course events. We measure the transition into adulthood by the event of leaving the parental home for the first time. The end of coresidence with parents is associated with changes in individual perspectives and in attitudes toward the labor market and lifetime choices in general. This turning point is likely to coincide with greater determination in the pursuit of financial independence and other economic goals. Our main finding is that the age at home leaving matters for subsequent economic outcomes. Individuals who leave the parental home earlier in life earn a higher income when they are in their midthirties. Estimation by instrumental variables suggests that this captures a causal effect, from the age when leaving the parental home to subsequent economic events. Moreover, the age when coresidence is terminated is much more important than the age corresponding to other significant events, such as that of undertaking a first job. Of course, the identification assumptions can be challenged. But the correlations are very robust, and the identification assumptions needed to interpret these correlations as corresponding to a causal effect are not inconsistent with the data.

It is important to stress that in our sample, individual income is measured several years after the first termination of coresidence, on average, more than eight years after the event. Thus, the timing of transition into adulthood appears to have very long-lasting effects. What are the mechanisms through which these effects operate, if indeed there is a causal effect? Unfortunately, the data we study can only shed partial light on this question, and probably several forces are at work. One plausible channel is the date of entry into a career path. We know that earnings keep rising with experience for several decades. Thus, anything that delays the beginning of a career path would have long-lasting effects on individual income. We find that the age when leaving the parental home is much more important than the age of the first job, however. This might be due to the first job being unimportant and uncorrelated with the subsequent main career. But is also suggests that other channels may be relevant, besides the duration of work experience. In particular, prolonged coresidence may impact negatively on individual motivations and ambitions. But in the absence of specific data, this remains a conjecture.

In principle, several policy instruments might be used to affect the timing of the transition into adulthood. An obvious place to start is education policy. The duration of secondary education and even of university education varies across countries. If the returns to education reflect an important signaling component, a shortening of the duration of education might be welfare improving. This recommendation is not as outrageous as it may at first sound. For instance, systematic comparisons of Swiss cantons where secondary education differs in duration have found that students in the cantons with a shorter curricula do not perform worse in standardized tests compared to the cantons with one extra year of schooling (Skirbekk 2005). Even without shortening the school or university curricula, policies may be designed to discourage students from taking too long to complete a university degree (a common problem in Italy).

Housing is a second potentially relevant policy tool. Our data suggest that housing supply is an important determinant of the decision to leave the parental home. Anything that reduces the cost of housing for young men and women might have positive side effects on the economy if our inferences are correct.

The labor market is also an area of key concern. If, indeed, the mechanism behind our results reflects the age at which a stable career is initiated, then a low youth employment rate is very costly for society. This points to the relevance of policies that would facilitate labor market entry for young individuals.

It is far too early to draw specific policy conclusions from these findings, however. It is not just a matter of assessing the robustness of our inferences. Individual well-being depends on more than economic opportunities. It could very well be that Italian young men postpone leaving the parental home while being fully aware that this might reduce their permanent income (for instance, due to a shorter working experience) because they or their parents enjoy coresidence for its own sake. From a social point of view, this behavior would not be suboptimal and would not require any policy intervention, despite the wasted economic opportunities. If, instead, families systematically underestimate the opportunity cost of a late transition into adulthood, or if individual preferences and beliefs change upon leaving the parental home, then a late transition might be suboptimal even if it results from individual choices. Unfortunately, the data at hand cannot discriminate between these alternative hypotheses. Hence, we cannot draw clear-cut policy implications from these findings, even if we could be sure that a late transition into adulthood causes a loss of income later in life.

Appendix A
Variable Definitions in the Individual Analysis

Here we provide the definition of the variables used in the individual analysis. Descriptive statistics are shown in tables 10.6 and 10.7.

Age: This variable is derived by using the date of the questionnaire (day, month, year) and the date of birth of the respondent (day, month, year).

Age of home leaving: This variable is derived by retrospectively asking the year and month of when the respondent first left the parental home for more than six months, excluding military or civil service (which was compulsory for respondents), and subtracting from it the date of birth. This question is also asked to individuals who are currently living with parents and who have left home in the past. In case the month is missing, the middle of the year is imputed. In case respondents do not recall the year, age is asked directly.

Age of first job: This variable is derived using the year and month of beginning the current job (if it is the first one) or by retrospectively asking the year and month of beginning the first job (excluding small jobs during education or jobs that are directed to earn pocket money) and then subtracting from it the date of birth. In case the respondent does not recall the month, this is imputed in the middle of the year. In case the respondent does not recall the year, age at first job is asked directly to the respondent.

Age of first sexual intercourse: For respondents who declare they have already had sexual relationships, age at first sexual intercourse is asked directly. Note that the question is the last one of the questionnaire because it has been considered a sensitive question.

Birth quarter: This variable is derived by using the month of birth.

Education (respondent, father, mother): This variable is derived by recoding the answer on the highest educational level obtained by the respondent (the father, the mother) to obtain the "standard" number of years that are necessary to earn that educational level. If father's or mother's education is missing, 0 is imputed. Levels are coded as follows: elementary school = 5, middle school = 8, lower secondary school = 10, upper secondary school = 13, lower higher education title = 15, upper higher education title = 18, master or higher = 20.

Empty dwellings: This is a variable indicating the share of dwelling that are not occupied by resident persons (%) in the province in which the respondent was grown up (up to age sixteen). Data refer to the 2001 Census. The source is the Italian National Statistical Institute (ISTAT).

Father employed: This is a dummy variable indicating whether, when the respondent was aged sixteen, his or her father was employed.

Income interval: This variable is the answer to the question "How much do you earn with your work, on average, monthly (net income—take into account the average earnings during the last six months)?" This question is posed only to employed respondents. The answer is coded by using five answer categories: none (could be answered by people who work in a family firm without earning direct income) = 0; up to 500 euros = 1; from 500 up to 1,000 euros = 2; from 1,000 up to 1,500 euros = 3; 1,500 euros and more = 4.

Lack of self-confidence score: This variable indicates the agreement of the respondent with the statement "When I think of my future, I see it full of risks and unknowns": completely disagree = 1, disagree = 2, agree = 3, completely agree = 4.

Living in the main city of province: This is a dummy variable indicating whether the municipality of birth of the respondents is the province's main city.

Married: This is a dummy variable indicating whether the respondent has ever been married.

Mother housewife: This is a dummy variable indicating whether, when the respondent was aged sixteen, his or her mother was a housewife.

Northwest, northeast, center, south: These are four dummy variables indicating the geographical area of current residence (northwest is excluded in regressions).

Number of children: This variable indicates the number of children ever had by the respondent.

Number of siblings: This variable indicates the number of sibling of the respondent (excluding him- or herself).

Religiosity score at age sixteen: This score indicate the frequency of going to mass (in Italy, Catholicism is the vastly dominant religion) during the week when the respondent was sixteen. It is coded as follows: at least once a week $= 1$, at least once a month $= 2$, sometimes during the year $= 3$, only on particular occasions $= 4$, never $= 5$.

Parents divorced or separated: This is a dummy variable indicating whether the respondent's parents have divorced or separated.

Provincial average income: This is a variable indicating the average income in 2005 in the province in which the respondent grew up (up to age sixteen). The source is the Istituto Guglielmo Tagliacarne.

"Too long" education: This is a dummy variable indicating whether the reported age at the end of education exceeds by more than the sum of the standard age at entry into the school system of the respondent (in months) and *education.*

Youth unemployment rate: This is a variable indicating the unemployment rate (%) for people aged fifteen to twenty-four in the province in which the respondent grew up (up to age sixteen) in 2001. The source is ISTAT.

Appendix B
Sign of bias from including other endogenous regressors

Here we discuss the possible bias in the coefficient of interest (that of the variable *age of home leaving*) as a result of having other endogenous variables in the regression.

Consider the following equation:

$$Y = a + b\text{Agehl} + cW + u,$$

where Y is income; Agehl is the variable of interest (*age of home leaving*); and W is another possibly endogenous regressor, like *education* or *mar-*

ried. Implicitly we have ignored the other regressors assuming that they are uncorrelated with the error term (i.e., all variables in this equation can be interpreted as the residual component after removing the effect of the other included regressors).

Suppose that Agehl is uncorrelated with the unobserved error term u. Estimating the coefficient b by OLS and denoting by B the resulting estimate, we have (see, for instance, the appendix to Acemoglu et al. 2001)

$$plim\ B = b - \varphi\, cov\ (Agehl,\ W)\, cov\ (W,\ u),$$

where $\varphi > 0$. Suppose the W denotes *education.* It is possible that cov (Agehl, W) > 0 (higher educational attainment implies a delay in getting a job and, hence, might entail a later *age of home leaving*). In this case, if *education* is also positively correlated with the error term of the income regression, both covariances are positive and the coefficient of interest entails a downward bias.

Conversely, suppose that W corresponds to being *married.* Then it is likely that cov (Agehl, W) < 0—to get married, most individuals would leave the parental home. If as plausible *married* is also positively correlated with the unobserved determinants of income, u, then the product of the two covariances is negative, and the inclusion of the endogenous variable *married* introduces an upward bias in the coefficient of *age of home leaving.*

Finally, it is straightforward to see that omitting the variable W from the regression introduces a bias that has the same sign as c cov(Agehl, W). That is an upward bias in the case of $W = education$ (because presumably $c > 0$ and cov (Agehl, W) > 0) and a downward bias in the case of $W = married$ because presumably $c > 0$ and cov (Agehl, W) < 0.

Appendix C
Just Identified Models

Table 10C.1   Just-identified models—income interval and age of home leaving

	Income			
	(1)	(2)	(3)	(4)
Age of home leaving	–0.082	–0.138	–0.083	–0.125
	(0.045)*	(0.078)*	(0.051)	(0.065)*
First quarter	–0.224	–0.223	–0.224	–0.226
	(0.078)***	(0.098)**	(0.083)***	(0.098)**
Fourth quarter	0.032	0.049	0.027	0.059
	(0.070)	(0.085)	(0.087)	(0.093)
Education	0.068	0.070	0.065	0.063
	(0.011)***	(0.012)***	(0.010)***	(0.011)***
Empty dwellings	0.004		0.003	
	(0.005)		(0.006)	
Age of first sex		0.011		0.007
		(0.019)		(0.015)
Lack of self-confidence			–0.103	–0.106
			(0.042)**	(0.046)**
Married			0.054	0.093
			(0.097)	(0.134)
No. of children			–0.018	–0.067
			(0.064)	(0.093)
Age of first job			–0.003	0.001
			(0.010)	(0.009)
Estimation	2SLS	2SLS	2SLS	2SLS
No. of observations	457	457	456	456

Notes: Robust standard errors in parentheses. Columns (1) and (3): excluded instrument is age of first sex. Columns (2) and (4): excluded instrument is empty dwellings. Other regressors included in all columns: same as in table 10.8. 2SLS = two-stage least squares.
***Significant at the 1 percent level.
**Significant at the 5 percent level.
*Significant at the 10 percent level.

References

Aassve, A., F. C. Billari, S. Mazzuco, and F. Ongaro. 2002. Leaving home: A comparative analysis of ECHP data. *Journal of European Social Policy* 12 (4): 259–75.

Aassve, A., M. A. Davia, M. Iacovou, and S. Mazzuco. 2007. Does leaving home make you poor? Evidence from 13 European countries. *European Journal of Population* 23 (3–4): 315–38.

Acemoglu, D., J. Simon, and J. A. Robinson. 2001. The colonial origins of comparative development: An empirical investigation. *The American Economic Review* 91 (5): 1369–1401.

Alesina, A., and P. Giuliano. 2007. The power of the family. NBER Working Paper no. 13051. Cambridge, MA: National Bureau of Economic Research.

Alessie, R., A. Brugiavini, and G. Weber. 2005. Saving and cohabitation: The economic consequences of living with one's parents in Italy and the Netherlands. NBER Working Paper no. 11079. Cambridge, MA: National Bureau of Economic Research.

Avolio, B. J., and D. A. Waldman. 1994. Variations in cognitive, perceptual, and psychomotor abilities across the working life span: Examining the effects of race, sex, experience, education, and occupational type. *Psychology and Aging* 9 (3): 430–42.

Baum, C., M. E. Schaffer, and S. Stillman. 2003. Instrumental variables and GMM: Estimation and testing. *Stata Journal* 3 (1): 1–31.

Becker, S. O., S. Bentolila, A. Fernandes, and A. Ichino. 2004. Job insecurity and children's emancipation. IZA Discussion Paper no. 1046. Bonn, Germany: Institute for the Study of Labor.

Billari, F. C. 2004. Becoming an adult in Europe: A macro(/micro)-demographic perspective. *Demographic Research* SC3 (SC3): 15–44.

———. 2008. Lowest-low fertility in Europe: Exploring the causes and finding some surprises. *Japanese Journal of Population* 6 (1): 2–18.

Billari, F. C., M. Castiglioni, T. Castro Martin, F. Michielin, and F. Ongaro. 2002. Household and union formation in a Mediterranean fashion: Italy and Spain. In *Fertility and partnership in Europe: Findings and lessons from comparative research,* ed. E. Klijzing and M. Corijn, 17–41. New York: United Nations.

Billari, F. C., H.-P. Kohler, G. Andersson, and H. Lundström. 2007. Approaching the limit: Long-term trends in late and very late fertility. *Population and Development Review* 33 (1): 149–70.

Billari, F. C., S. Mazzuco, and F. Ongaro. 2006. Percorsi e tempi di autonomia residenziale: Una valutazione dell'impatto sulla fecondità in Italia [Pathways and timing of residential autonomy: An evaluation on the impact on fertility in Italy]. In *Convegno Famiglie, Nascite e Politiche Sociali [Conference on families, births, and social policies],* ed. Accademia Nazionale dei Lincei, 55–76. Rome: Bardi Editore.

Billari, F. C., and M. Pellizzari. 2008. *Age effects and academic performance: Does month of birth matter?* Milan: Università Bocconi.

Billari, F. C., D. Philipov, and P. Baizán. 2001. Leaving home in Europe: The experience of cohorts born around 1960. *International Journal of Population Geography* 7:339–56.

Blossfeld, H.-P., E. Klijzing, M. Mills, and K. Kurz. 2005. *Globalisation, uncertainty, and youth in society.* London: Routledge.

Blossfeld, H.-P., M. Mills, and F. Bernardi. 2006. Globalization, uncertainty and men's careers. An international comparison. Cheltenam, UK: Edward Elgar.

Brunello, G., and D. Checchi. 2004. School vouchers Italian style. *Giornale degli Economisti e Annali di Economia* 63 (3/4): 357–99.

Card, D. 2001. Estimating the return to schooling: Progress on some persistent econometric problems. *Econometrica* 69 (5): 1127–60.

Corijn, M., and E. Klijzing. 2001. *Transitions to adulthood in Europe.* Dordrecht, the Netherlands: Kluwer.

Dalla Zuanna, G. 2001. The banquet of Aeolus: A familistic interpretation of Italy's lowest low fertility. *Demographic Research* 4 (5): 133–62.

Del Boca, D., and D. Vuri. 2007. The mismatch between employment and child care in Italy: The impact of rationing. *Journal of Population Economics* 20 (4): 805–32.

Diamond, P. 1982. Aggregate demand management in search equilibrium. *Journal of Political Economy* 90 (5): 881–94.

Elder, G. H. J. 1975. Age differentiation and the life course. *Annual Review of Sociology* 1:165–90.

Feyrer, J. 2007. Demographics and productivity. *Review of Economics and Statistics* 89 (1): 100–109.

Flatau, P., I. James, R. Watson, G. Wood, and P. H. Hendershott. 2007. Leaving the parental home in Australia over the generations: Evidence from the Household, Income and Labour Dynamics in Australia (HILDA) Survey. *Journal of Population Research* 24 (1): 51–71.

Furstenberg, F. F., Jr., S. Kennedy, V. C. McLoyd, R. G. Rumbaut, and R. A. Settersten Jr. 2004. Growing up is harder to do. *Contexts* 3 (3): 33–41.

The Gallup Organization. 2007. *Young Europeans. A survey among young people aged between 15–30 in the European Union.* Flash Eurobarometer Series. Brussels, Belgium: European Commission.

Giannelli, G. C., and C. Monfardini. 2003. Joint decisions on household membership and human capital accumulation of youths. The role of expected earnings and local markets. *Journal of Population Economics* 16 (2): 265–85.

Hogan, D. P., and N. M. Astone. 1986. The transition to adulthood. *Annual Review of Sociology* 12:109–30.

Kohler, H.-P., F. C. Billari, and J. A. Ortega. 2002. The emergence of lowest-low fertility in Europe during the 1990s. *Population and Development Review* 28 (4): 641–80.

Liefbroer, A. C. 2005. *Changes in the transition to adulthood in Europe: An empirical analysis of changes among cohorts born between the 1950's and 1960's in Europe and among Dutch cohorts born between 1900 and 1982.* Report for the Robert Bosch Foundation. The Hague, the Netherlands: Netherland Interdisciplinary Demographic Institute.

Lindh, T., and B. Malmberg. 1999. Age structure effects and growth in the OECD, 1950–1990. *Journal of Population Economics* 12 (3): 431–49.

———. 2007. Demographically based global income forecasts up to the year 2050. *International Journal of Forecasting* 23 (4): 553–67.

Manacorda, M., and E. Moretti. 2006. Why do most Italian youths live with their parents? Intergenerational transfers and household structure. *Journal of the European Economic Association* 4 (4): 800–829.

Mankiw, N. G., D. Romer, and D. N. Weil. 1992. A contribution to the empirics of economic growth. *Quarterly Journal of Economics* 107 (2): 407–37.

Mazzuco, S. 2006. The impact of children leaving home on parents' well-being: A comparative analysis of France and Italy. *Genus* 62 (3–4): 35–52.

Mazzuco, S., L. Mencarini, and R. Rettaroli. 2006. Similarities and differences between two cohorts of young adults in Italy: Results of a CATI survey on transition to adulthood. *Demographic Research* 15 (5): 105–46.

Modell, J., F. F. Furstenberg Jr., and T. Hershberg. 1976. Social change and transition to adulthood in historical perspective. *Journal of Family History* 1 (1): 7–32.

Myerson, J., S. Hale, D. Wagstaff, L. Poon, and G. Smith. 1990. The information-loss model: A mathematical theory of age-related cognitive slowing. *Psychological Review* 97 (4): 475–87.

Neugarten, B. L., and N. Datan. 1973. Sociological perspectives on the life cycle. In *Life-span developmental psychology: Personality and socialization,* ed. P. B. Baltes and K. B. Schaie, 53–69. New York: Academic.

Ravanera, Z. R., F. Rajulton, and T. K. Burch. 1998. Early life transitions of Canadian women: A cohort analysis of timing, sequences, and variations. *European Journal of Population* 14 (2): 179–204.

Reher, D. S. 1998. Family ties in Western Europe: Persistent contrasts. *Population and Development Review* 24 (2): 203–34.

Rosenzweig, M., and K. I. Wolpin. 1993. Intergenerational support and the lifecycle incomes of young men and their parents: Human capital investments, coresidence, and intergenerational financial transfers. *Journal of Labor Economics* 11:84–112.

Rybash, J. M., W. J. Hoyer, and P. A. Roodin. 1986. *Adult cognition and aging: Developmental changes in processing, knowing and thinking.* New York: Pergamon.

Schvaneveldt, P. L., B. C. Miller, E. H. Berry, and T. R. Lee. 2001. Academic goals, achievement, and age at first sexual intercourse: Longitudinal, bidirectional influences. *Adolescence* 36 (144): 767–87.

Settersten, R. A., Jr, F. F. Furstenberg Jr., and R. G. Rumbaut. 2005. *On the frontier of adulthood: Theory, research, and public policy.* Chicago: University of Chicago Press.

Shanahan, M. J. 2000. Pathways to adulthood in changing societies: Variability and mechanisms in life course perspective. *Annual Review of Sociology* 26:667–92.

Shimer, R. 2001. The impact of young workers on the aggregate labor market. *Quarterly Journal of Economics* 116 (3): 969–1007.

Skirbekk, V. 2004. Age and individual productivity: A literature survey. *Vienna Yearbook of Population Research* 2:133–53.

Skirbekk, V., H.-P. Kohler, and A. Prskawetz. 2004. Birth month, school graduation, and the timing of births and marriages. *Demography* 41 (3): 547–68.

Comment   Luigi Pistaferri

Introduction

I enjoyed reading this chapter, if for no other reason than because it seems to talk about me and so many of my friends back in Italy! Leaving aside jokes, the topic is actually quite a serious one. Billari and Tabellini show that "lateness" may have important effects on people's economic success (as measured by earnings, for instance) and even on more macro variables (such as growth). The evidence in the latter case is circumstantial, and so I won't spend time discussing it.

The paper is part of a vast research agenda looking at the impact of demographic features on economic outcomes. For various examples, see Alesina and Giuliano (2007). The starting point of the paper is the observation that Italians exhibit "unusual" demographic features: they complete their education later than their counterparts in other industrialized countries,

Luigi Pistaferri is an associate professor of economics at Stanford University, a faculty fellow of the Stanford Institute for Economic Policy Research (SIEPR), a research affiliate of the Center for Economic and Policy Research (CEPR), and a research associate of the National Bureau of Economic Research.

they enter the job market later, they leave the parental home later, and they marry and have children later (if at all). Interestingly, they even die later! Life expectancy at birth for males is seventy-eight in Italy, seventy-seven in the United Kingdom and France, seventy-six in Germany, and seventy-five in the United States.[1] In human capital models, a longer life horizon may change the incentives to invest in education, and this may have important consequences for growth, and so on.

In a nutshell, the paper considers the impact of "late transition into adulthood" on income. It focuses on a sample of Italian males born in 1966 to 1970 surveyed in 2003 to 2004. I should note that the sample is rather small, only about 500 observations. This is partially compensated by the richness of the data set, which includes a five-interval measure of earnings, age of home leaving, age of first sex, exact date of birth, education, parents' education/occupation/marital status, and so on. Billari and Tabellini regress the measure of earnings they have on "age of home leaving" and a number of other covariates and interpret the effect of "age of home leaving" causally— using an instrumental variables (IV) interpretation.

Before commenting on the chapter, it may be of some interest to quantify the extent and dynamics of the phenomenon. I used the 1986 and 2006 Survey of Household Income and Wealth (a representative survey of the Italian population conducted every other year by the Bank of Italy) to compute the proportion of males in various age groups who live with their parents (in the survey, they are classified as "sons" of the head of the household). Figure 10C.1 shows that between 1986 and 2006, the proportion of individuals living with their parents has increased for all ages. For example, in 1986 only 33 percent of thirty-year-olds lived with their parents; in 2006, 61 percent did.

The Story and the Findings

The chapter's main claim is that individuals who become "adult" later suffer a number of disadvantages relative to those who do not. In particular, they have less incentive to work, less motivation, they are less independent-minded, and less able to learn. According to Billari and Tabellini, the economic consequences of such late transition into adulthood could be substantial. The ordinary least squares (OLS) estimates say that leaving home one year earlier would increase income by about as much as five additional months of education. The IV estimate is much larger, suggesting that leaving home one year earlier would increase income by about as much as 1.5 additional years of education. This is quite a large effect. Public policies to push people out of the parental home would be more effective than keep-

1. The country with the longest life expectancy (eighty years) is San Marino, admittedly a de facto Italian colony. More seriously, this reflects some heterogeneity in life expectancy between Northern and Southern Italy.

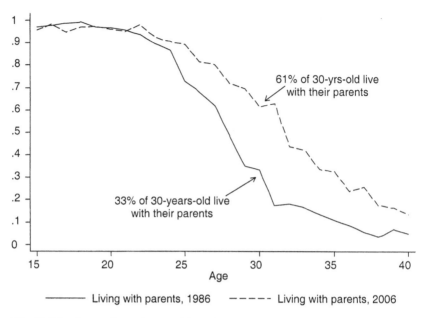

61% of 30-yrs-old live with their parents

33% of 30-years-old live with their parents

——— Living with parents, 1986   ----- Living with parents, 2006

Fig. 10C.1   Proportions of males living with parents

ing the same people in school, as far as measures of economic success are concerned.

As an aside, the chapter finds that people born in the first quarter of the year earn way less than people born in other quarters. To put things in perspective, a three-year university degree has the same return of *not* being born in the first quarter. One possible explanation is that people born in the first quarter are those most likely to be drafted for compulsory military service.[2] Military service involves the loss of one (or more) year of civilian labor market experience, not to mention psychic costs, and so the first quarter of birth variable may be possibly picking up some of these adverse effects.

Validity of Instruments

Billari and Tabellini use two instruments (age of first sex and housing availability at age sixteen) to correct for the endogeneity of the age of home leaving variable. In this section, I play the role of the devil's advocate and discuss reasons why one should doubt the validity of their instruments. Because an exclusion restriction is untestable, a reader will have to weight appropriately defense and criticism of instruments.

The authors correctly argue that age of first sex is a suspicious instrument.

2. Military service in Italy is no longer compulsory, but it was for people born in 1966 to 1970, the cohort used in the chapter.

As suggested (and showed) by Hamermesh and Biddle (1994), beauty can enter the earnings equation; at the same time, beauty may be correlated with age of first sex—beautiful people do it earlier. I can add two further arguments. First, smarter individuals may leave home earlier and may also sexually emancipate earlier (or vice versa, i.e., in the case of "nerds"). Second, there is the possibility of correlated measurement error—especially if leaving home is a "milestone" event.

Speaking of measurement error, I should note at this point that measurement error in age of home leaving seems to be rather large. Take the simple model in which age of home leaving, measured with error, is the only covariate:

$$y_i = \beta_0 + \beta_1 x_i^* + (a_i - \beta_1 e_i + v_i)$$

Here y is earnings, x is "true" age of home leaving, x^* is its measured counterpart, e the measurement error (so that $x^* = x + e$), a is unobserved ability, and v a random disturbance. It's easy to prove that the OLS bias is partly measurement error bias and partly ability bias, that is,

$$p \lim \hat{\beta}_1 = \beta_1 + \frac{\sigma_{x^*a}}{\sigma_{x^*}^2} - \beta_1 \frac{\sigma_e^2}{\sigma_{x^*}^2}.$$

Using the OLS and IV estimates, it's easy to show that (after some manipulation) that

$$\frac{\sigma_x^2}{\sigma_{x^*}^2} \leq 0.27$$

and, hence, the noise-to-signal ratio must be quite high (73 percent or more) to be consistent with the estimates reported in the chapter. This casts some doubts on the extent of accuracy of the data (which are primarily of the "recall" type).

Billari and Tabellini seem to put more faith in their second instrument (housing supply). But could this also be an invalid instrument? A possible argument is as follows. Assume that people leave the parental home only when they find an acceptable job and suitable housing. This means that there is a trade-off between the offered wage and the cost of housing (individuals may accept a low-paid job if they find cheap housing or may be willing to pay more for housing if they are offered a high wage). Hence, marginal individuals who face lower cost of housing accept lower offered wages. But in the data, wages are very persistent; hence, the housing market conditions when entering the labor market (and leaving the parental home) may still be correlated with wages today, which invalidates the instruments.

As a parallel argument, I should note that housing market reforms have not reduced the stock of stay-at-home children, which would suggest that the instrument has little power. Consider the case of the *Equo canone* (rent control) legislation. Introduced in 1978, it regulated criteria for establishing rent levels, yearly increases, the duration of contracts, and repossession procedures. It ended up protecting the "insider" and restricted severely the supply of rental units. Rent controls were finally abolished in 1992. Yet, as figure 10C.1 shows, the proportion of youth living with their parents has increased, not declined. The chapter uses cross-sectional variability rather than the time series variability I am describing here, which may have more to do with provincial differences in wages rather than heterogeneity in the supply of housing.

Are there any remedies to possible failure of instrument validity? The ideal way to get at the "causal" effect would be to neutralize the effect of (permanent) unobserved ability. Here panel data is of little help because leaving the parental home is an irreversible decision. One could think, however, of using within-family variability, that is, twins or siblings' experience. While there are no data of this kind for Italy (as far as I know), in the United States, the Panel Study of Income Dynamics (PSID) tracks individuals after they have left home and formed their own household. This could allow identifying siblings leaving home at different ages.

Causality and All That

Perhaps a more fundamental issue is to establish whether age of home leaving is truly causally (rather than spuriously) affecting earnings. Billari and Tabellini cite three different reasons why a true causal effect may be expected. First, youths who don't live with parents are pushed to work more, and this affects their career profile. Second, they are younger and, hence, have a higher ability to learn on the job. Third, they are more independent-minded, and this may affect their productivity (a "taste heterogeneity" explanation).

Note that the first two reasons cited point to an "indirect" mechanism (through labor market experience) rather than a direct one. This means that if one had a reliable measure of full-time labor market experience, age of home leaving would be redundant (and, hence, *not* causal). Puzzlingly enough, the variable that is best associated with labor market experience (age of first job) explains nothing, perhaps because, as Billari and Tabellini note, "this variable refers to menial or temporary jobs that do not correspond to a milestone event in the transition to adulthood."

What the chapter leaves a bit hanging is a convincing discussion of the mechanism(s) that is behind the effect of age of home leaving on earnings. A possible story is as follows. Take two equally smart individuals (so that ability differences are neutralized)—and assume that for exogenous reasons one is living at home with his parents, and the other on his own. Why would these two individuals be differently productive on the job? For individuals living with their parents, the cost of consumed goods is lower (they get public goods for free—rent, electricity, etc.). They also spend less time in nonwork, nonleisure activities (laundry, ironing, cooking, etc.). Hence, (most of) their consumption of goods and time is effectively insured, and a moral hazard problem arises—they may put less effort on their job and, hence, get lower wages. Individuals who have left the parental home cannot afford this, particularly if the decision to leave the parental home is irreversible.

Conclusions

I want to conclude with two observations, one on the possible benefits of "lateness" and another on the policy implications of the analysis.

The chapter is all focused on stressing the costs of being late. But what about the benefits? A broader welfare analysis would consider also the benefits of leaving home later, such as increased leisure, economies of scale, and so on. Staying with the parents may signal that children care about their parents. Parents could reciprocate later in life (after kids have left) by supplying a variety of goods and services: insurance (i.e., help if income shocks strike and insurance markets are absent), liquidity (i.e., informal credit if financial markets are imperfect), and time (i.e., child care that would be too expensive to buy on the market). This means that the income loss due to a late transition into adulthood could be partially balanced by informal insurance, liquidity, and time. In other words, the extra years spent with parents may be a form of investment. Young Italians may well be utility maximizers given the constraints faced.

The chapter provides a number of policy recommendations, such as shortening the duration of college degree, discouraging students from overstaying in college, reducing the cost of housing, increasing its supply, and introducing policies aimed at easing young people's entry in the labor market. But knowing the mechanism behind the "causal" effect of "leaving home later" on earnings is key for any policy recommendation to be effective. Suppose individuals stay with their parents because that's the only way to get help to buy a house or because they need to save in anticipation of that event (Loan-to-value ratios in Italy were around 50 percent before recent financial market liberalization). Then what would change the incentives to leave are credit market reforms rather than housing (or labor) market reforms.

To sum up, I applaud Billari and Tabellini for writing this extremely interesting chapter on "lateness" and measures of economic success. Future research should try to come up with a convincing story regarding the mechanism behind the causal effect that is being uncovered.

References

Alesina, A., and P. Giuliano. 2007. The power of the family. NBER Working Paper no. 13051. Cambridge, MA: National Bureau of Economic Research.

Hamermesh, D., and J. Biddle. 1994. Beauty and the labor market. *American Economic Review* 84 (5): 1174–94.

Contributors

Orazio Attanasio
Department of Economics
University College London
Gower Street
London WC1E 6BT, England

Alan J. Auerbach
Department of Economics
508-1 Evans Hall, #3880
University of California, Berkeley
Berkeley, CA 94720-3880

Francesco C. Billari
Department of Decision Sciences and
    DONDENA-Centre for Research on
    Social Dynamics
Bocconi University
via Roentgen 1
20136 Milan, Italy

Axel Börsch-Supan
Mannheim Research Institute for the
    Economics of Aging (MEA)
Building L13, 17
MEA, University of Mannheim
D-68131 Mannheim, Germany

Moshe Buchinsky
Department of Economics
9357 Bunche Hall
Box 851477
University of California, Los Angeles
Los Angeles, CA 90095-1477

Thomas Davidoff
Sauder School of Business
University of British Columbia
Vancouver, BC V7R 3J9, Canada

Victor R. Fuchs
Freeman Spogli Institute for
    International Studies
616 Serra Street
Stanford, CA 94305-6055

Gopi Shah Goda
Stanford Institute for Economic Policy
    Research
Stanford University
579 Serra Mall
Stanford, CA 94305-6015

Caroline Sten Hartnett
Department of Sociology
University of Pennsylvania
3718 Locust Walk, McNeil Building
Philadelphia, PA 19104-6299

Adam Isen
The Wharton School
University of Pennsylvania
3620 Locust Walk
Philadelphia, PA 19103

Larry E. Jones
Department of Economics
University of Minnesota
1925 Fourth Street South
Minneapolis, MN 55455

Sagiri Kitao
Federal Reserve Bank of New York
33 Liberty Street
New York, NY 10045

Alexander Ludwig
University of Cologne
CMR-Center for Macroeconomic
   Research
Albertus-Magnus-Platz
50923 Köln, Germany

Amalia R. Miller
Department of Economics
Monroe Hall
University of Virginia
PO Box 400182
Charlottesville, VA 22904-4182

Enrico Moretti
Department of Economics
549 Evans Hall
University of California, Berkeley
Berkeley, CA 94720-3880

Luigi Pistaferri
Department of Economics
Stanford University
579 Serra Mall
Stanford, CA 94305-6072

James M. Poterba
National Bureau of Economic
   Research
1050 Massachusetts Avenue
Cambridge, MA 02138

Samuel H. Preston
School of Arts and Sciences
289 McNeil Building
University of Pennsylvania
Philadelphia, PA 19104-6298

Warren C. Sanderson
Economics Department
Stony Brook University
Stony Brook, NY 11794-4384

Sylvester J. Schieber
Watson Wyatt Worldwide
901 North Glebe Road
Arlington, VA 22203

Alice Schoonbroodt
Economics Division
School of Social Sciences
University of Southampton
Southampton SO17 1BJ, England

John B. Shoven
Department of Economics, Room 132
Stanford University
579 Serra Mall at Galvez Street
Stanford, CA 94305-6015

Betsey Stevenson
The Wharton School
1454 Steinberg-Dietrich Hall
University of Pennsylvania
3620 Locust Walk
Philadelphia, PA 19104

Guido Tabellini
Department of Economics
Bocconi University
via Roentgen 1
20136 Milan, Italy

Michèle Tertilt
Department of Economics
Stanford University
579 Serra Mall
Stanford, CA 94305-6072

Shripad Tuljapurkar
Department of Biological Sciences
Herrin Labs 454
Stanford University
Stanford, CA 94305-5020

Steven F. Venti
Department of Economics
Dartmouth College
6106 Rockefeller Center
Hanover, NH 03755

Giovanni L. Violante
Department of Economics
New York University
19 West 4th Street
New York, NY 10012-1119

David A. Wise
Harvard University and NBER
1050 Massachusetts Avenue
Cambridge, MA 02138-5398

Author Index

Subject Index

Milton Keynes UK
Ingram Content Group UK Ltd.
UKHW011830300923
429712UK00002B/19

9 780226 754727